THE OMNI INTERVIEWS

THE

OMNI

INTERVIEWS

EDITED BY PAMELA WEINTRAUB

AN OMNI PRESS BOOK

TICKNOR & FIELDS · NEW YORK · 1984

Some of these interviews first appeared in *Omni* magazine in altered form.

Copyright © 1984 by OMNI Publications International, Ltd.

Library of Congress Cataloging in Publication Data
Main entry under title:

The Omni interviews.

A collection of interviews previously published in
Omni magazine.
1. Biology—Addresses, essays, lectures. 2. Science—
Addresses, essays, lectures. 3. Biologists—Interviews.
4. Scientists—Interviews. I. Weintraub, Pamela.
QH311.046 1984   500   83-26501
ISBN 0-89919-215-7
ISBN 0-89919-269-6 (pbk.)

Printed in the United States of America

V   10   9   8   7   6   5   4   3   2   1

ACKNOWLEDGMENTS

This book is a collaboration of many — interviewers, interviewees, and countless people at both *Omni* and Ticknor & Fields. Those who deserve particular note are Robert Weil, *Omni*'s book editor, for his unwavering critical eye and invaluable advice; *Omni* interview editors Dick Teresi (now the magazine's editor), Kathleen Stein, Judith Hooper, and Monte Davis; and Regina Dombrowski, who designed the cover. Other people who helped with this volume include Frances Apt, Murray Cox, George Goldey, Babette Lefrak, Nancy Lucas, Francesca Lunzer, Gene Mooney, Beverly Nerenberg, Gwen Norman, Marcia Potash, and Peter Tyson.

Special thanks also go to Bob Guccione and Kathy Keeton, whose vision of *Omni* provided the energy and impetus for this book; to Helen E. Fisher and Carol A. Johmann for expanding their interviews with no compensation except the satisfaction of a job well done; to the scientists who spent extra time on this volume, including Hans Bethe, Brian Josephson, Richard Leakey, Ernst Mayr, Gerard K. O'Neill, Cyril Ponnamperuma, and Jonas Salk; and to Katrina Kenison, Chester Kerr, and James Raimes of Ticknor & Fields for their insights and encouragement.

Finally, I would like to thank my husband, Mark Teich, for the enormous support he provided during my work on this volume.

— Pamela Weintraub

CONTENTS

LIST OF CONTRIBUTORS

Yvonne Baskin is the author of *The Gene Doctors: Medical Genetics at the Frontier* (William Morrow). A free-lance science writer living in California, Baskin interviewed Roger Sperry.

Monte Davis, *Omni*'s first interview editor, is now a consulting editor at *Psychology Today*. He is presently producing a video documentary on high energy physics. Davis interviewed Freeman Dyson and Gerard K. O'Neill.

Helen E. Fisher is a research associate in the anthropology department at the New School for Social Research in New York City. She is currently collaborating on a textbook called *Introduction to Physical Anthropology* (W. H. Freeman), and her anthropological study, *The Sex Contract* (William Morrow, 1983), has been translated into five languages. Fisher interviewed Richard Leakey.

John Gliedman is writing a book that explores the philosophical implications of modern-day physics. He teaches psychology at the State University of New York's Empire State College and writes articles on psychology, physics, biology, and evolution. He spoke with Brian Josephson.

T. A. Heppenheimer, author of the best-selling *Colonies in Space*, will publish *The Man-Made Sun: The Race to Develop Fusion*, as an Omni Press Book with Little, Brown in 1984. He is a frequent contributor to *Omni* magazine and lives in California. Heppenheimer spoke with Hans Bethe.

Philip J. Hilts is a science correspondent on the national staff of The *Washington Post*. His book, *Scientific Temperaments*, was published by Simon & Schuster in 1983, and he is now working on a book about the future of human reproduction. He interviewed John McCarthy.

Michael Hollingshead is executive editor of Marvel Comics' new Titan Science Series and is working on a book about the origins of life with Harvard biologist Stephen Jay Gould. Head of the video section at the University of Hollywood, Hollingshead interviewed B. F. Skinner.

Judith Hooper is writing a book on the brain/mind relationship with *Omni* editor Dick Teresi for Macmillan Publishing Company. She is a regular contributor to *Omni* and lives in New York City. Hooper interviewed John Lilly, Candace Pert, and Karl Pribram.

Carol A. Johmann is a cell biologist turned magazine journalist and lives in Connecticut. She is now working on a major revision and update of the classic high school textbook *Modern Biology*. She interviewed Ernst Mayr.

David Monagan, a regular contributor to *Omni* and other national magazines, is a free-lance writer living in New York City. He interviewed Albert Hofmann.

Tabitha M. Powledge is a senior editor at *Bio-Technology* magazine. She is a regular contributor to the magazine as well as the editor of its news and features section. She interviewed E. O. Wilson.

David Rorvik, a free-lance writer living in California, recently published *The Rites of Life*, a book on prenatal development. He is now at work on a book about aging, and his revision of *Choose Your Baby's Sex* (Dodd, 1977), with coauthor Dr. Landrum B. Shettles, will be published by Doubleday in March, 1984. Rorvik interviewed Francis Crick.

Albert Rosenfeld is a consultant on future programs for the March of Dimes Birth Defects Foundation and is presently updating his book *Prolongevity* (Knopf, 1976). He is also adjunct professor in the division of human genetics at the University of Texas Medical Branch in Galveston. Rosenfeld interviewed W. Donner Denckla.

John Stein, an international banker at Commerce Union Bank in Nashville, Tennessee, interviewed George Schaller.

Robert B. Tucker, a magazine journalist specializing in political issues and social trends, currently teaches in the Writers Program at UCLA. He interviewed Ilya Prigogine.

Eileen Zalisk has won several awards as a radio and TV journalist. She has also worked with the American Institute of Physics and is now project programmer for the Aerospace Museum/California Museum of Science and Industry in Los Angeles. Zalisk spoke with Cyril Ponnamperuma.

INTRODUCTION

"The human mind," Albert Einstein once said, "is not capable of grasping the universe. We are like a little child entering a huge library. The walls are covered to the ceiling with books in many different tongues. The child knows that someone must have written these books. It does not know who or how. It does not understand the languages in which they are written. But the child notes a definite plan in the arrangement of the books — a mysterious order which it does not comprehend but only dimly suspects."

When *Omni* magazine got off the ground in 1978, its goal was to absorb whatever it could of that library, distilling its variety and magnitude for readers around the world. From the beginning, monthly question-and-answer interviews with scientists were a keystone of *Omni*'s attempt to understand the universe. While others believed only writers could explain science to the public, *Omni*'s editors felt that scientists themselves might be best at conveying the complexity and wonder of their work.

To the public of the 1970s, most scientists were hardly saints: the archetypal researcher, popular notion had it, was a hard-nosed ego-maniac with concern only for the nitty-gritty details that would ensure successful results — and the next round of grant money. He lacked social grace and social conscience, was reluctant to speculate, and *hated* communicating with the layperson. But as *Omni* interviewers went about their task, they found that nothing could be further from the truth. Whether it was Dr. Jonas Salk discussing the origins of the universe, or physicist Freeman Dyson contemplating its end, the scientists we interviewed were delighted to ponder, pontificate, and project.

It is difficult to generalize about the researchers in this collection. They are, of course, among the pioneers of twentieth-century science. They are the people who found the cures, developed the theories, built the computers, the robots, and the bombs. Each, however,.

harbors his or her own vision — a context and perspective out of which a unique creativity evolved.

If there is a single characteristic shared by those in this book, it is a willingness to question beliefs we've inherited from the decades and centuries before. Those who study evolution — including Richard Leakey, Ernst Mayr, and E. O. Wilson — discuss the mythology of religion and the shift in values created by Darwinian thought. Neuroscientist Candace Pert grapples with questions about the nature of reality and the nature of God. Roger Sperry, father of the bicameral mind, rejects the idea that we can fathom the brain by understanding all of its parts. Nobel Prize–winning physicist Ilya Prigogine suggests that his radical concept of time would alter our notion of life. And scientists like John Lilly and Brian Josephson (who won a Nobel Prize at the age of thirty-three for discoveries in the field of superconductivity) here explain why they gave up conventional scientific work in search of such intangibles as human salvation and the soul. After investigating the most provocative questions of our time, in fact, these interviewees have universally agreed on at least one thing: like Einstein's child, we're at the *threshold* of scientific understanding; in terms of gleaning the truth, we humans have barely begun.

Capturing even a glimmer of this understanding for our readers has meant many hours of work by interviewers and interviewees alike. Our reporters, in fact, tend to leave their subjects exhausted. Judith Hooper, for instance, finally wound up her talk with a bleary-eyed, pregnant Candace Pert at four in the morning; Yvonne Baskin visited Roger Sperry on three occasions, and spoke to him a dozen more times over the phone, before she felt her interview was complete; and Ilya Prigogine was interviewed three separate times over a period of years before we had a conversation that we felt truly reflected his ideas.

The monthly interview has gained in depth and perspective over the years. During *Omni*'s six years of existence there have been four gifted interview editors: Monte Davis, Dick Teresi, Judith Hooper, and Kathleen Stein. Each has learned from the one before, going on to refine the form and make an invaluable contribution of his or her own. This book, in a sense, is the culmination of that learning process. Thus, with those years of trial and error in mind, we have revised and expanded one third of these interviews from the original magazine versions.

If the short story is life raised to art, then the Q & A interview is conversation raised to art. To achieve such conversation, we sought out the great scientific thinkers — those who could shed some light on the magnificent mystery of Einstein's library — and talked and talked and then talked to them some more. Then, by editing — deleting redundancies and hesitations, but never the idiosyncrasies of spoken language — we honed each interview until its meaning shone crystal clear.

Omni has published some seventy interviews over the years. This book contains twenty of the best.

— Pamela Weintraub

Origins

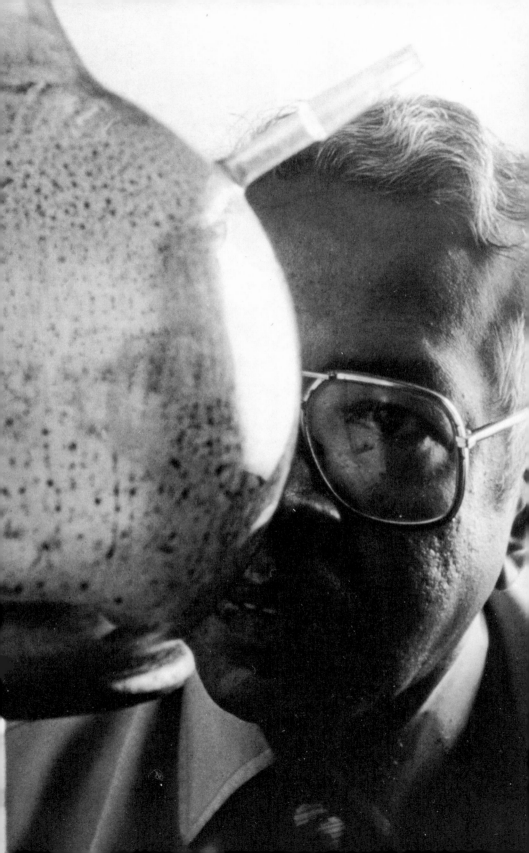

Seeds of Life
Cyril Ponnamperuma

Physicists might eventually be able to come up with a grand unification theory that encompasses not just subatomic particles and the basic elements, but the code of life as well. Who knows? Life elsewhere in the universe may even be five feet tall and standing on two legs.

The shelf behind Cyril Ponnamperuma's desk is lined with colored sticks and balls — models of the molecules that gave rise to life. A can of Campbell's Soup placed in front of the molecules is relabeled to read Primordial Soup. And on the wall is a picture of Julia Child stirring one of Dr. Ponnamperuma's reeking organic concoctions. The room, needless to say, reflects the preoccupation of its occupant, for this intense and lively man has spent his career trying to answer one encompassing question: How did life begin?

"All life has a common chemical beginning," said Ponnamperuma. "If we examine the smallest microbe or the most intelligent human being, the molecules are the same. We can trace a continuum from the formation of the elements at the beginning of the universe to the appearance of replicating systems. We can draw a line from eighteen billion years ago to the time when the first man walked on Earth."

Ponnamperuma was born in Sri Lanka, then Ceylon, and received a bachelor's degree in chemistry from Birkbeck College of the University of London in 1959 and his Ph.D. from the University of California at Berkeley in 1962. The following year he joined NASA's Exobiology Division and became chief of the chemical evolution branch. Since 1971 he has been professor of chemistry and director of the Laboratory of Chemical Evolution at the University of Maryland. He is also

Photograph: John White

chairman of the board of Sri Lanka's Dambala Institute, an organi-
zation whose goal is to turn the dambala plant — otherwise known
as the winged bean — into a major source of protein for the third
world.

When Ponnamperuma isn't traveling around the world speaking for
the institute, he spends much of the day creating organic compounds
that might have been formed in the primordial sea. To validate his
theory that these very molecules gave rise to life, he studies the
chemistry of ancient terrestrial rock, meteorites, the neighboring plan-
ets, and interstellar space. The chemist talks about his work with all
the pleasure of a poet reciting favorite lines. Clearly he sees himself
as one in a long line of scientists and philosophers who have sought
answers only to the biggest questions.

Today Ponnamperuma suspects that, although organic matter is
common in the universe, life is not. He does believe that there is life
in other star systems, however — perhaps even intelligent life.

Eileen Zalisk interviewed Dr. Ponnamperuma for Omni *in 1980. I*
spoke to him in 1982 and again in 1983. The three discussions form
the interview that follows.

OMNI: How do you define life?

PONNAMPERUMA: We think of something that has four legs and
wags its tail as being alive. We look at a rock and say it's not living.
There's a difference between these two. Yet when we get down to
the no man's land of virus particles and replicating molecules, we
are hard put to define what is living and what is nonliving.

We can come up with a working definition of life, which is what
we did for the Viking mission to Mars. We said we could think in
terms of a large molecule made up of carbon compounds that can
replicate, or make copies of itself, and metabolize food and energy.
So that's the thought: macromolecule, metabolism, replication.

But I think that as a result of our observations we are beginning
to think of life as a property that is more and more common in the
universe. In everything there is a certain measure of life.

OMNI: Has your own definition of life changed over the years?

PONNAMPERUMA: Well, I suppose I see more in it now. The
definition I just gave you was only a practical definition to use in
going to another planet, such as Mars. If you were to ask me about

our laboratory experiments, "When do you get to the point when something is living?" I would answer, "When we see replication." If we had replication of a molecule alone in some of our vessels, I believe we would have the beginnings of life there.

OMNI: The questions you ask about how life began have been asked by philosophers and theologians and some chemists before you. Can you put the work you are doing into historical context?

PONNAMPERUMA: For centuries the idea of spontaneous generation was regarded as an explanation of the origin of life. Aristotle put his idea forward in his *Metaphysics*, where he gave us the example of fireflies rising from the morning dew. The Flemish physician and chemist Jan Baptista van Helmont gave us a very interesting recipe, titled "How to Make Mice." It instructed: "Dirty undergarments encrusted in wheat; twenty-one days is the critical period. The mice that jump out are neither weanlings nor sucklings, but fully formed."

It was the work of Louis Pasteur, who proved that living creatures did not appear in sterilized food unless they were introduced from the outside, which dealt the deathblow to the whole idea. In 1864 he told the French Academy, "Never will the idea of spontaneous generation recover from this mortal blow."

But today we are coming back to the idea of spontaneous generation. We are not talking about frogs from the primordial ooze or mice from old linen. Rather, we are looking at an orderly sequence, from atoms to small molecules to large molecules to replicating systems — to a continuum in the universe from its beginnings eighteen billion to twenty billion years ago to the time when the first man walked on Earth.

OMNI: Some of the first scientific speculations on the origins of life were made by Charles Darwin. You frequently quote the letter he wrote to his friend William Hooker, in 1871, in which he says, "If we could conceive in some warm little pond, with all sorts of ammonium and phosphoric salts, light, heat, electricity, etc., present, that a protein compound was chemically formed ready to undergo still more complex changes . . ." How does your work connect with what Darwin theorized?

PONNAMPERUMA: Well, Darwin's warm little pond has in it the germ of the entire concept of chemical evolution. What we try to do in the laboratory is to re-create Darwin's warm little pond.

When Darwin wrote to Hooker, he was trying to extend his own ideas. There's no doubt that if we accept Darwinian, or biological, evolution, we must postulate a form of evolution before it, and that would be chemical evolution. Chemical evolution is the process that started with the beginning of the universe and that led to the appearance of life on Earth. Darwin's ideas along those lines were rather ignored for a long time.

Then, in 1924, the Russian biochemist Alexander Ivanovich Oparin argued that there was no fundamental difference between living organisms and lifeless matter, and that life must have arisen in the process of the evolution of matter. In 1926 the British scientist J. B. S. Haldane wrote a paper suggesting the formation of primordial broth by the action of ultraviolet light on the earth's primitive atmosphere. Haldane gave us the idea of the primordial soup.

OMNI: Those who study chemical evolution have been creating their *own* primordial soup in the lab for decades. Can you explain the whys and wherefores of those efforts?

PONNAMPERUMA: Chemical evolution is based on the idea that the building blocks of life were made before life began. Start by examining the history of the earth — the earth is about 4.5 billion years old, and we believe the oldest life on Earth appeared before 3.8 billion years ago. We have reached that conclusion because of the fossils of living molecules found in 3.8-million-year-old sedimentary rocks at Isua, in Greenland, which are among the oldest known rocks on Earth. So, our goal in the lab is to learn what happened between 4.5 and 3.8 million years ago. The idea is that during this early period there was a primordial soup that underwent chemical reactions, giving rise to life.

Our early efforts were aimed primarily at proving this scenario. The first one to try was Melvin Calvin, with whom I studied at Berkeley in the early sixties. Calvin believed that the atmosphere of the early earth was primarily carbon dioxide, so he filled a flask with carbon dioxide. Then, to simulate radiation on the primitive earth, he used alpha particles, synthesizing some simple compounds, such as formaldehyde and formic acid. The next people to try their luck were Harold Urey and Stanley Miller. Miller and Urey calculated that the early atmosphere was rich in hydrogen, so they mixed hydrogen with methane and ammonia in a flask, simulating the early atmosphere and oceans. Then they applied lightning — the electric spark — and when they examined the water, they found basic organic chemicals, including amino acids, the building blocks of protein. The suggestion was that this flask contained the primordial soup of organic molecules from which we evolved.

OMNI: How does that classic experiment hold up today?

PONNAMPERUMA: As it turns out, today we believe that the hydrogen in the primordial atmosphere was lost very rapidly. In fact, the early atmosphere was mostly carbon dioxide, much as Calvin envisioned. Calvin simply forgot to add nitrogen to his flask. If he had, he would have gotten amino acids. And we would be talking about the Calvin experiment, not the Urey-Miller experiment.

OMNI: You've done Calvin's experiment, but *with* the nitrogen, I take it.

PONNAMPERUMA: Our experiments go through all the stages of the changing primordial atmosphere. But we're no longer striving to show what Calvin, Miller, and Urey tried to show — that a primordial soup stocked with organic molecules must have existed on the ancient earth. That's been proven. We're trying to show that these basic organic molecules — the primordial molecules — combined to form larger, replicating molecules made of protein and nucleic acids [the building blocks of genes]. If we can create such molecules, we will, in effect, have created the genetic code. [The genetic code is the specific pattern of DNA molecules that instructs our bodies to produce the proteins of which we're made.] If we can create the genetic code, we will have created life itself.

OMNI: In other words, you're trying to create life in the lab out of inanimate matter. Do you really believe you'll succeed?

PONNAMPERUMA: Once we understand the chemistry more fully, yes. We have to find out why these very basic molecules of protein and nucleic acid interact. Using various physical and chemical techniques, we'll find out how they fit together. At the moment, for instance, we're using a technology called nuclear magnetic resonance to analyze the way protons move as some of these molecules come together. If we understand the forces that drive these molecules, we can combine them. Though we've just begun our studies, we've already come to realize that the genetic code is not a random formula: there is a fundamental relationship between all the molecules of which life is composed.

OMNI: Is the relationship so fundamental that these same molecules might come together and form the same code, and the same type of life, throughout the universe?

PONNAMPERUMA: We're gradually reaching that conclusion. If you look at the specific amino acids and proteins that make up life on Earth, you'll find they're ideally suited to their function. I think we'll eventually prove that the genetic code is universal.

OMNI: Are we perhaps being too narrow in our definition of life? Is it possible that in other places there is life based on something other than the DNA–RNA–amino acid apparatus we've been talking about?

PONNAMPERUMA: It's certainly a valid question. It is possible, but most unlikely. And the reasons are simple.

The periodic table of elements that exist here on Earth is the same elsewhere. The elements are the same. The chemistry of the compounds is the same. The movement of electrons around the nucleus of the atom will be the same, whether it is here or on Alpha Centauri. And as far as life is concerned, carbon is the center of everything. The nearest chemical to it from a structural point of view is silicon. But I think the similarity is merely superficial.

Take the difference between carbon dioxide and silicon dioxide. One is a gas; the other is quartz. In spite of four and a half billion years of evolution and the abundance of silicon available, you don't see silicon in functional, living molecules, only in nonliving molecules.

I would conclude that it is highly unlikely that the chemistry anywhere in the universe will be any different. It will be a nucleic acid–protein life. As a matter of fact, physicists might eventually be able to come up with a grand unification theory that encompasses not just subatomic particles and the basic elements, but the code of life as well. Who knows? Life elsewhere in the universe may even be five feet tall and standing on two legs.

OMNI: Then you think that Darwinian evolution — including mutation and natural selection — controls the form of life on other planets, too?

PONNAMPERUMA: The process of natural selection, of course, has to come in to improve the original form and create biological variety. But evolution at the molecular level is not precisely Darwinian. Instead, we're talking about a process of change. It's much more of a straightforward process.

OMNI: You mean a chemical reaction?

PONNAMPERUMA: A chemical reaction. Which things react better with what.

OMNI: You say that the genetic code is essentially the same throughout the universe. But what evidence is there besides the laboratory simulations?

PONNAMPERUMA: We also study meteorites. Meteorites are small pieces of rock from the asteroid belt that get trapped in the earth's gravitational field and fall to the ground. They are believed to have been formed, like the planets, from the solar nebula some four billion six hundred million years ago. Among the meteorites are some that are classified as carbonaceous chondrites, which contain organic matter. These meteorites give us an unusual opportunity to study organic compounds of extraterrestrial origin.

Under the glass there is the Murchison meteorite, which fell in Australia on September 24, 1974. That is the meteorite in which, for the first time, we were able to establish very clearly the presence of extraterrestrial amino acids.

Since that time we have looked at other meteorites — the Mighei, which fell in the Soviet Union in 1966, and the Murray, which fell in Kentucky in 1952. In each case we were able to establish the indigenous nature of the amino acids.

Incidentally, we had a tremendous bonanza of meteorites in 1980. An expedition to Antarctica during December and January of that year brought back three thousand new fragments of meteorites. Twenty-eight are carbonaceous chondrites. These meteorites are a great resource, since they appear to be uncontaminated by terrestrial organic material. They give us evidence of amino acid formation that may have been occurring even before the planets were born. So, short of going to the asteroid belt and bringing back a meteorite, we have some of the cleanest evidence available.

OMNI: Any other evidence?

PONNAMPERUMA: Since about 1968, radioastronomers have been directing their telescopes at the interstellar medium. At first they didn't expect to find anything except hydrogen and maybe some silicates. But they were astounded to discover hydrogen cyanide, formaldehyde, and fifty-three other organic molecules — the very stuff from which proteins and nucleic acids can be made. As a matter of fact, even ethyl alcohol has been observed. A colleague here at

Maryland, who discovered ethyl alcohol, called me up soon after that
and said, "Cyril, I made a calculation on the back of my envelope,
and I've learned that in the constellation of Orion there are 10^{19}
fifths of alcohol." Orion is laden with alcohol; the universe is reeking
with organic matter. You could say that the universe is in the business
of making life — or that God is an organic chemist. It was a
staggering discovery.

OMNI: You have also looked for life or prelife on both the lunar
surface and on Mars. What were the results?

PONNAMPERUMA: Well, we examined fractions of every lunar
sample that was brought back from *Apollo 11* through *Apollo 17*. We
made an extensive search for traces of organic material that might
be indicative of chemical evolution. We found about two hundred
parts per million of organic matter, but no evidence of amino acids,
no evidence of any molecules of organic significance. This showed
us that if there was any organic matter on the surface of the moon
that dated from the very early stages of the solar nebula, it has been
destroyed.

When we went to Mars, it was a different story. Our task on Mars
was to play the part of the devil's advocate. What happened on the
surface of Mars was that the mass spectrometer told us there was
less than ten parts per billion of organic matter. It was surprising —
less than on the moon. So, in the absence of organic matter, the
chances of any life seem to be very small. Hardly likely, in fact.

OMNI: What are the implications of the fact that you are able to
create these biological molecules in the laboratory and to find them
in the meteorites, yet when you actually look at other worlds, you're
not able to find any indication of them?

PONNAMPERUMA: That's a very good question. All that we know
about the surfaces is that this organic material has disappeared. We
don't expect to find any on Venus. The temperatures there are too
high. Mars is too oxidized. However, when you move away from the
sun and look at Jupiter and Saturn, especially Jupiter, the whole
planet is just laden with organic material. It's a boiling cauldron of
organic molecules. So the synthesis of organic molecules under the
right conditions is certainly no problem.

But once having formed, they disappear if the conditions change.
So there are certain narrow limits within which these molecules, once

formed, will survive — at least to the point where life would originate.

OMNI: If life didn't originate elsewhere in our own solar system, what is the likelihood that it originated somewhere else in the universe?

PONNAMPERUMA: Well, as I told you earlier, I do think it is likely. There are 10^{23} stars in the universe. If that is the case, there are 10^{23} possibilities for life. But not all stars have conditions around them that are suitable for life. Optimistic calculations, such as those of Al Cameron, at Harvard, say that 50 percent of all stars may have around them conditions suitable for life. More conservative estimates say 5 percent. Whether 5 percent or 50 percent — or even 1 percent — of 10^{23}, it is still a very big number.

Put this together with what I've said about our laboratory studies of chemical evolution in the universe, and the chances for life seem very great.

OMNI: What about the possibilities of intelligent life that can communicate with us?

PONNAMPERUMA: Once again, if we push our arguments to their logical conclusion, we can say there must be intelligent life elsewhere.

In the one example where we know it has happened, here on Earth, one draws the conclusion that biological evolution is an inevitable result of chemical evolution. And intelligence may be an inevitable concomitant of biological evolution.

OMNI: There seems to be another point of view emerging. In terms of intelligent life, perhaps we are alone in the universe.

PONNAMPERUMA: I beg to differ. I think we've barely begun to scratch the surface. Give us time. Right now only a few searches are being made.

OMNI: What searches are going on?

PONNAMPERUMA: Well, the newest effort, conducted under NASA sponsorship, is directed at continuously monitoring deep space with large radio telescopes for unusual signals, presumably from an extraterrestrial civilization. There's not much money being poured into the effort, but when something unusual is found, other, more powerful radio telescopes could concentrate on the spot from which the signal came. The current effort is at most a screening.

OMNI: How does this search differ from past searches?

PONNAMPERUMA: We're listening in on many more radio channels now, and, as I said, we're listening constantly. We've never done that before.

OMNI: Is the current effort likely to detect an extraterrestrial communication?

PONNAMPERUMA: No, this alone won't do it, but it's a beginning. In order to detect a signal, you probably have to look for at least thirty years. You need a process of detection and, just as important, a method of interpretation.

OMNI: But how can you be so sure there are messages out there for us to intercept?

PONNAMPERUMA: If there are civilizations as advanced as we are, there must be messages, even if they weren't left for us. *We've* sent a message, giving an account of what our life here is like. There must be others. There must be books, even libraries, out there to read.

OMNI: Even if messages do exist, though, why are you so sure they've been sent in the form of radio waves? Couldn't they have been coded in an infinite number of ways?

PONNAMPERUMA: Well, electromagnetic radiation — including light rays, x rays, and radio waves — is the fundamental energy of the universe. Any civilization would use electromagnetic radiation to communicate — it's the natural thing. Now, why radio waves? Well, there's a particular radio wave length — twenty-one centimeters, to be exact — where background radio noise is least. If you wanted to get a clear signal out, you might send it at that frequency. And there's another twist to this. Twenty-one centimeters turns out to be the length of waves emitted by hydrogen, the most common element in the universe. And even more fortunate, the other radio wave length subject to little interference is eighteen centimeters. That turns out to be the wavelength of the hydroxyl molecule, made up of one oxygen atom and one hydrogen atom. Hydroxyl [OH] combined with hydrogen [H] yields water, or H_2O. It makes most sense to send signals at any point at or between those two frequencies. As chemists, we are delighted to greet our extraterrestrial neighbors at this cosmic waterhole, which is at once convenient and symbolic.

OMNI: What do you think will happen to us when we finally make contact?

PONNAMPERUMA: We'll see a whole shift in consciousness. Such a discovery would have the same kind of impact as the Copernican revolution or Darwin's theory of evolution.

OMNI: For one thing, it might make us feel less important.

PONNAMPERUMA: Well, we're not unique. But I don't think our importance would be diminished. On the contrary, we'd feel less freakish, part of a magnificent cosmic plan.

OMNI: Speaking of magnificent plans, what do you think of Francis Crick's theory of panspermia — the idea that life was sent to Earth eons ago by an intelligent, extraterrestrial civilization?

PONNAMPERUMA: There's no way of disproving Crick's idea, but I feel uncomfortable with it. Panspermia, actually, is an old idea first put forward by Lord Kelvin, who suggested that life came to earth on the back of a meteorite. This was revived by Arrhenius at the turn of the century, and now we get it in a different form from Crick. Crick postulates the existence of a civilization somewhere watching the earth. According to his theory, that civilization knew *exactly* when the primordial soup was ripe for injection with a germ that could live and develop. He puts forward this idea because he feels that the chance of life evolving through a natural sequence of events is rather slim. So what does he go and do? Suggest an even more improbable thing: that an alien civilization has seeded the earth at precisely the right instant of geologic time. Sometimes I wonder whether he really believes what he wrote. I reviewed *Life Itself*, Crick's book on the theory, and I quoted his wife, who said the whole idea was science fiction.

OMNI: What do you think of the astronomer Fred Hoyle's theory that diseases come from space?

PONNAMPERUMA: The suggestion is bizarre. Hoyle contends that each time you have a cold, it's because a virus has fallen down from a comet in heaven. So when Halley's Comet comes around in 1985, the human race might get wiped out. I'm willing to buy the idea that organic molecules are there in comets; maybe even under special conditions you might get to the point where cometary life evolves. But to get a virus, specific to a human, evolved completely away from the earth is very, very hard to accept. You've got to throw away all of modern biology. The other difficulty I have with Hoyle is his theory that interstellar molecules are really bacteria. As a matter of fact, we had a meeting here on comets and the origin of life, and Hoyle's collaborator showed a slide that said, "Interstellar Grains = Bacteria." One of his arguments was that the infrared spectrum of the interstellar grains resembled the infrared spectrum of cellulose. If there's cellulose in space, he said, there must be a bug that produces it. They've recently concluded that if you take bacteria and crush them, you get the same kind of spectrum. So they argue that in 3 degrees Kelvin, in the deep cold of space, these bacteria are alive. And that, to me, is very hard to accept. First of all, how did the bacteria ever evolve to that point? Second, how do they survive? And third, I can produce a hundred different things that will yield the same kind of spectral pattern.

OMNI: Hoyle and Crick are brilliant scientists. Why have they come up with such flaky theories?

PONNAMPERUMA: Everybody has his blind spot or his Achilles heel, and scientists are no exception. Many of them believe they are impartial in their thinking and uninfluenced by their surroundings. Some are very egoistic, and put forward ideas they feel the whole human race has got to bow down and accept. Others might be excellent in one area of science — astronomy, for instance — yet believe they have insight into all fields, without an awareness of the pitfalls. Scientists are human — they're as biased as any other group. But they do have one great advantage in that science is a self-correcting process.

OMNI: A collective venture.

PONNAMPERUMA: That's right. If Hoyle's recommendations had been followed, for instance, we would never have landed on the moon, because he told us it was all covered with dust, and that everything would just sink right in. If we had believed Carl Sagan, we would have found the surface of the moon covered with organic matter. People like Hoyle are bold thinkers. But you've got to be bold and, at the same time, have a solid foundation in science.

OMNI: Is it possible that life might be starting up on earth again, right now?

PONNAMPERUMA: Up until recently, we believed that was impossible. As a matter of fact, the whole basis of our work was the idea that the conditions that gave rise to life disappeared, so we had to re-create them in the laboratory. But recently we've been considering the concept of *neoabiogenesis*, the theory that terrestrial life is arising again. The idea gains support primarily because of the information we've got from the Galápagos vents, the hydrothermal vents deep under the sea. These vents are actually regions where the earth's crustal plates are pulling apart, spewing sulfur and volcanic heat. Here you have conditions that seem ideally suited for life to begin — you have gases coming out of the crust of the earth, you have the right kind of soil, you have the energy. It's an incredible thought, but what happened four billion years ago might be happening again right now. How can one test this hypothesis? Only by going down to the vents themselves.

OMNI: Are you planning a trip?

PONNAMPERUMA: We were talking about it at a meeting here not too long ago. We invited a geophysicist, some microbiologists, and so on, and they all said it seemed like a reasonable scientific undertaking — if we could get the money. It would cost about $5 million to take a submarine down there, bring some material back up, and test the hypothesis. So, scientifically, it is not an unreasonable suggestion. But our difficulty would be to separate very primitive, recently evolved microbial life from microbial life that has been part of the ocean for eons.

OMNI: How would you do that?

PONNAMPERUMA: The evolution of any species can be studied at the molecular level. Species that are related on the evolutionary tree will always have gene sequences in common. A bacterium newly evolved at the vents would be vastly different, in the genetic sense, from one that had ancestors in the original primordial ooze. But I must emphasize: even if the sequence of genes differs, we expect the genetic code itself — the individual molecules making up the genes — to be the same as ours.

OMNI: If you did go down there and find newly evolving life based on the same genetic code we have up here, wouldn't that be evidence for your hypothesis that the genetic code is universal?

PONNAMPERUMA: Yes, it would be just as dramatic as finding our genetic code on Venus or Mars.

OMNI: Could neoabiogenesis be occurring on land in our realm as well?

PONNAMPERUMA: Probably not. You need sterile conditions for

the genesis of life. Up here, microbes would gobble up the prebiotic molecules as soon as they were formed. If one managed to escape a microbe, it would be oxidized by oxygen.

OMNI: How did you happen to get interested in the field of chemical evolution?

PONNAMPERUMA: I had a very strange odyssey. Both my parents were academically oriented. My father was the principal of a school. I had an uncle who was a chemist, and my earliest memories are of him doing all kinds of experimental work in the kitchen. So there was a scientific interest, but at that time I didn't think it would come to anything. Then I had the fortune to meet a remarkable man named J. D. Bernal. He taught us physics, and once, instead of giving us a lecture on electricity and magnetism, he spoke about the origins of life. And that's the first time I learned that one could do experimental work on the origins of life. After that I had the experience of going from one excitement to another, from one university to another, from meeting people to getting involved in the NASA space program at just the right time. I stayed there until 1971, then I came here to the University of Maryland.

OMNI: Despite your immersion in chemical evolution, I take it you've also kept up with the issues of the third world.

PONNAMPERUMA: My whole family is very internationally oriented. One brother is at the International Rice Research Institute in Manila, the other was head of a UNESCO program for Asia. I've become an American citizen, but I feel more a citizen of the world with an American passport. And this naturally draws you into activities that can help others on the international scene.

OMNI: What are you involved in now?

PONNAMPERUMA: For one thing, I'm involved in the Dambala Institute. Dambala, otherwise called the winged bean, is an underutilized plant we hope will become a major source of protein for the third world.

OMNI: Why dambala?

PONNAMPERUMA: It's a remarkable plant. You can eat the leaf, like spinach; you can eat the bean, like the green bean; you can eat the tuber. When it's dried, it is like soya. It has a large amino acid content. But no one had taken much interest in it.

OMNI: Why is that?

PONNAMPERUMA: It's an enigma, really. It's hard to believe that this plant grew in my backyard when I was a kid.

OMNI: Did you eat it?

PONNAMPERUMA: Oh yes, it was the poor man's vegetable. We ate it as a vegetable, but never thought of it as a source of protein. It became of potential value to scientists when the U.S. National Academy did a study of underutilized plants. They highlighted the winged bean as one example of something that could be studied. As a result of these recommendations, *Time* magazine had a little paragraph about dambala in an article. Soon after that, I was having lunch with the president of Sri Lanka, and he pulled out a folder and showed me this clipping and asked me, "Do you know this plant?" And I said, "Of course I do," and then he said, "I'd like to make Sri Lanka the dambala capital of the world. Help me do something about it." So this is how I got involved. I arranged a meeting in Sri Lanka of the people I knew were interested in the dambala; this led to an international meeting one year later, at which we had about 150 people from around the world. There's a lot of interest in dambala in Indonesia, in Thailand, in Nigeria. The scientists at the meeting made a spontaneous motion to go ahead with an institute. Right now I'm chairman of the board of directors, but we're looking for someone else to raise money, to get programs going.

OMNI: Do you think plants like dambala will solve world food shortages?

PONNAMPERUMA: Such plants offer a temporary, short-range solution. In the long run, they constitute only one of many ways of dealing with the problem. The other solution I'm interested in working on is related to what I've been doing in the laboratory — making amino acids, making carbohydrates, and making protein. Today I'm making protein in order to show how life originated. But suppose you could make carbohydrates and protein in the lab, directly from the atmosphere, without plants or animals as intermediaries . . .

OMNI: The way we make polyester?

PONNAMPERUMA: That's right, we could take carbon, nitrogen, and hydrogen from the atmosphere and convert them directly into food. I'm not suggesting we give up plants and animals altogether, but the potential is there. I'll give you an example: I'm working with

NASA to develop food for astronauts from carbon dioxide in the atmosphere of the space vehicle.

OMNI: How long do you think it will be before we use such a system to make food for the world at large?

PONNAMPERUMA: I think if an attempt is made, it may not be long. We could make as much as 20 percent of our food that way. Right now the limiting factor is the energy: we would currently have to power such a system with electrical energy or ionizing radiation, and that would be too costly. But suppose we came up with a way of using light from the sun? That would make the system economically feasible. And food made this way would be available completely independent of climate.

OMNI: How do you have time to participate in such a variety of projects all around the world?

PONNAMPERUMA: I have to work twice as hard. The day never ends. I try to do all my reading at night. And then, I have some very good people working for me — I can't do every experiment myself. I spend a lot of time discussing the research with them. What I miss most is the time for writing. I often have three or four papers that should have gone out to the press, but they keep getting delayed. That's the situation now. I was in India recently for a series of lectures, and during that time I thought, As soon as I come back, I'll get those papers written. Now it's time for me to go again, and I haven't gotten to them. But they'll get done somehow.

OMNI: Dr. Ponnamperuma, you've spent most of your life tracing our evolutionary path back to that original primordial soup. But do you have any thoughts about humankind's future?

PONNAMPERUMA: The Laws of natural selection and survival of fittest normally dictate the direction of evolution. But humans can now break that pattern because they *understand* what's happening. The moment you evolve a human level of intelligence, you can control the process. And that's what's going on now — I call it *directed* evolution. I don't believe we'll ever evolve wheels on our feet, though some people feel that's an alternative to automobiles. I do believe, however, that we'll use technologies such as genetic engineering to improve our capacities and eradicate disease. We'll see better muscular regulation, as well as cures for cancer, viral infections, and all kinds of enzyme deficiencies. Once we better understand what's going on at the molecular level, we'll be able to do in tens or hundreds of years what would take nature billions. Right now human genes come together when people get married — it is a chance mixing of the gene pool. But once we've grasped the whole genetic process, we'll be able to arrange our lives so that we know what children we'll give birth to. Of course, some people say how terrible, to take all the surprise and fun out of it. But on the other hand, we might get to the point where we begin to understand the value of such knowledge. If you know that certain genes coming together are going to result in mental illness, for example, you might want to prevent that from happening. Or you might want to control human breeding so that you get to the point where people are more intelligent. It's obvious to me that intelligence is a genetic thing, and whatever one may say, genes for brilliance seem to run through certain families. Look at the Huxleys. We don't want to have everybody looking the same way, but on the other hand, I think if there is a measured discreet use of this knowledge, life could improve.

OMNI: Aren't you afraid of creating a *Brave New World* sort of situation?

PONNAMPERUMA: That danger exists. Take the situation we're in today with atomic energy. Understanding the atom is a tremendous boon, but we've also used our knowledge for destruction. So that danger is always there, but it shouldn't prevent us from the pursuit of the knowledge or its application.

OMNI: How would you institute the genetic control you're talking about?

PONNAMPERUMA: Someday, I hope, we'll have a library of genes to help us.

OMNI: Once we've completed our own evolutionary journey, do you think we'll send terrestrial life to other worlds, engaging in directed panspermia of our own?

PONNAMPERUMA: Who knows? We'll certainly have the potential. There are always people who want to explore, who want to go and look at things, whether it's the North Pole or Antarctica. So from that point of view, we'll always have terrestrial life leaving the solar system and inhabiting other worlds. That would be a natural consequence of progress.

Sperm from Deep Space
Francis Crick

I came to realize that sufficient time had elapsed for life to have evolved twice — that is, a civilization capable of sending out rockets could already have come into existence at the time the solar system and the earth got going.

Francis Crick began his scientific career as a physicist and then, in his thirties, daringly switched to the emerging field of molecular biology, which led him to a Nobel Prize. Today, decades later, still driven by the same eclectic curiosity, he is doing brain research. Given the remarkable versatility that serves his protean pursuits, it is not surprising that Dr. Crick grapples as imaginatively with the challenges of outer space as he does with those of inner space. Indeed, in his most recent book, Life Itself, *he deals with both themes simultaneously, boldly theorizing that the seeds of life on Earth did not spring unbidden from the prebiotic soup — the spontaneous product of chance biochemical events — but, instead, were* sent *here in a rocket designed on some distant sphere by "creatures like ourselves." Crick admits that the idea of "directed panspermia" — this seeding of life — is imbued with "the stink of science fiction"; nonetheless, he argues that the theory has about it a "tissue of plausibility" perhaps more compelling than any attached to more "orthodox" explanations of the origins of life on this small planet.*

Crick was born in England in 1916. He earned his doctorate relatively late in life, at Caius College, Cambridge University, in 1953, the same year he and James Watson launched a biological revolution with their discovery of the structure of DNA, the master molecule that contains the genetic code. In prose that was uncharacteristically restrained for both of them, Watson and Crick announced their breakthrough to the world in the April 25, 1953, issue of Nature, *in an article that began, "We wish to suggest a structure for the salt of deoxyribonucleic acid (DNA). This structure has novel features which are of considerable biological interest." Behind the scenes, they exhibited less modesty. Within hours of completing their model of the "double helix," which represented in detail the structure of the double-stranded DNA molecule, Crick, according to Watson, was telling "everyone within hearing distance that we had found the secret of life." The upstart duo — until then virtual unknowns in the world of biochemistry — beat out Nobel laureate Linus Pauling in the race to solve the DNA puzzle. Suddenly, they saw themselves in league with the immortals; they persuaded Watson's sister, for example, to spend a Saturday afternoon typing up their* Nature *report by telling her that she would thus be "participating in perhaps the most famous event in biology since Darwin's book."*

Though he is seldom seen by the public, Crick has acquired, in large part because of Watson's characterization of him in his 1968 book The Double Helix, *a reputation as a brash, brilliant eccentric given to manic bursts of energy, peals of raucous laughter, loud and rapid speech, and an honesty of expression that some find abrasive and others tactless. In fact, Watson recalled, there were those at Cambridge who feared Crick: "The quick manner in which he seized their facts and tried to reduce them to coherent patterns frequently made his friends' stomachs sink with the apprehension that all too often in the near future he would succeed and expose to the world the fuzziness of minds hidden from direct view by the considerate, well-spoken manners of the Cambridge colleges."*

For their DNA work, Crick and Watson, together with the physicist Maurice Wilkins, shared the 1962 Nobel Prize in physiology and medicine. Since then, Crick has lectured and taught at numerous institutions, including Harvard University and the Rockefeller Institute. In 1966 Crick, who readily acknowledges his atheism, published Of Molecules and Men, *an attack on "vitalism," which he has described as the belief that "there is some special force directing the growth or the behavior of living systems which cannot be understood by our ordinary notions of physics and chemistry."*

Today — modest, soft-spoken, decidedly tactful, and, by his own admission, somewhat "mellowed" — Crick apologizes for the weightiness of his present title, Distinguished Research Professor at the Salk

*Institute for Biological Studies, in La Jolla, California. It was there,
in Crick's office, overlooking a bluff from which hang-gliders try the
air above the Pacific Ocean, that David Rorvik conducted this interview
in 1981.*

OMNI: Few events in science have so captured the public imagination as the drama that attended your DNA work. The immunologist
Sir Peter Medawar, himself a Nobel Prize–winner, called your DNA
work "the greatest achievement of science in the twentieth century."
Do you agree with him?

CRICK: I've often told Peter I didn't think that was true, because
I think there have been breakthroughs in physics that have been
equally important, if not more important. If he had said "in biology,"
there are people who would agree with him.

OMNI: You were reported to be unhappy with James Watson's
book *The Double Helix*, which begins with the famous line, "I have
never seen Francis Crick in a modest mood." In fact I understand
you once wrote him, telling him that his "view of history is found in
the lower class of women's magazines." Do you still feel that way
about the book, and how well do you get along with Watson these
days?

CRICK: We get along fine. I wasn't very keen on the book, mainly
because I don't like personal publicity. I think one has to look at
the book not really as history but as a fragment of Jim's autobiography. When you look at it that way, it takes on a different complexion.
As for my being immodest, I think he meant exuberant. And if I've
changed my mind about the book, it's because it did a better job
than I expected of showing nonscientific people how a certain type
of scientific research was done.

OMNI: According to Maurice Wilkins, you were in what he called
a very difficult position at the time you did the DNA work. You were
already thirty-five, you had no secure job, and you were still working
for your doctorate. Did those seem like particularly desperate times?

CRICK: Curiously, no. Science, in those days, was expanding
rapidly, and there was always the feeling that if you couldn't get a
job here, you'd get one there. If I were now in the sort of position I
was in then, I would be much more anxious about my future. But in
plain fact we were enjoying our work so much back then that we
didn't worry in that way, and the prize came by itself very much

later. Now, Jim implies in his book that he was thinking about the prize, but if he was, he kept it to himself.

OMNI: The Columbia University biochemist Erwin Chargaff, who was the first to discern the regular pattern of the bases making up the DNA molecule — an observation you and Watson built upon — once said of the two of you, "In our day that such pygmies throw such giant shadows only shows how late in the day it has become." Chargaff has over the years made a number of wittily denigrating remarks about you and Watson. Did he feel ripped off?

CRICK: Well, it's absolutely true that every time Erwin was at a meeting, there was a new joke at our expense. He did discover the pattern, but he didn't go on to see what it implied. I think that he feels a little bitter that he missed it. He occasionally writes as if he did see it, but it's quite clear that he didn't.

OMNI: In other words, he saw that certain bases were present in direct proportion to other bases, but he didn't understand how that fact might help reveal the structure of DNA.

CRICK: That's right.

OMNI: What about the chemist Linus Pauling? Were you surprised that you beat him?

CRICK: It was a surprise to us when he produced a structure that was obviously wrong. He made an elementary mistake in chemistry and put a hydrogen on a phosphate group. I distinctly remember taking the textbook off the shelf to see what the phosphate group was really like, because I don't know a lot of chemistry. And, of course, the irony of it was that the text was by Linus Pauling. He also had bad luck in that he didn't have good x-ray data.

OMNI: Might Pauling have beaten you if he had applied himself to the DNA puzzle as vigorously as he had to some others?

CRICK: I think that is very possible. I mean, Pauling was very good at this sort of thing. After all, what we did in tackling the structure of DNA was simply to copy the methods that Pauling had used in determining the alpha helix structure of proteins.

OMNI: You've said that from Pauling you learned "boldness" in scientific research. What did you mean?

CRICK: When you start in science, you are brainwashed into believing how careful you must be, and how difficult it is to discover things. There's something that might be called the "graduate student syndrome"; graduate students hardly believe they can make a discovery. People like Pauling see things in a broader way. They are prepared to make assumptions and describe bits of the evidence and go ahead to solve the problem without having to have everything already in place.

OMNI: Do you follow the new gene-splicing work and genetic engineering?

CRICK: Not so much. Since I came to the Salk Institute five years ago, I've spent more and more of my time on neurobiology, learning about the brain, and much less of my time on molecular biology. I'm now particularly interested in the brain in relation to the mammalian visual system.

OMNI: Why the visual system?

CRICK: The brain is a challenge, and I guess I wanted to start somewhere. I'm interested both from the theoretical point of view — trying to work out, for example, what we do to analyze depth and just how it is that we see color — and also in terms of the neuro-anatomy, the neurophysiology of vision. Some of this has been worked out in part in other animals: I'd like to see whether those data can be related at all to human vision. Since I don't have a lab of my own, I look at the work of others. My task is, in part, one of synthesizing things.

OMNI: Have you published in this area?

CRICK: So far only one paper with two colleagues — about the problem of how one can see in such fine detail, in finer detail than one would imagine possible, because, even though the receptors in the eye are placed close together, they are not as close as one would imagine they would have to be for some of the detailed vision that is possible. The idea we offered was that the message gets sampled and then reconstructed in the cortex; we suggested a process whereby that could take place.

OMNI: In a sense, brain research is at that embryonic stage where there are still many exciting possibilities for discovery, just as there were in molecular biology thirty years ago.

CRICK: Yes, it's rather like looking at an organism and knowing there must be some instructions in there, yet not knowing how to unravel them. Back in the early fifties, we didn't quite understand what a gene was. Yet today's work, based on the discoveries of 1966, represents a second revolution in molecular biology.

OMNI: Some people say the new molecular biology is so potent, it might inadvertently hurt us. Do you believe, for instance, that we might accidentally create an Andromeda Strain with the new recombinant techniques?

CRICK: I think everybody agrees now that the dangers were exaggerated. And I think the scientists ought to have good marks for considering that the experiments might be dangerous. But what they didn't realize is that if they, the scientists, thought the work might be dangerous, the lay public would think it was much more dangerous. That's one lesson we have learned.

As far as we can see from attempts to make organisms under highly contained conditions, the dangers are extremely slight. I think you have to say, however, that any new technology introduced on a big scale is going to have consequences — medical, social, or economic — and recombinant DNA techniques will certainly have an impact, just as computers or television has had.

OMNI: In the past you've been supportive to some extent of the ideas of the late Dr. Hermann Müller, the Nobel Prize–winning geneticist who advocated "germinal choice," a program that would encourage the combination of only the "best" human ovum and sperm cells. This idea was embraced not long ago by a group that claims to have among its sperm donors some Nobel laureates. What is your opinion of that project?

CRICK: Well, I personally have not contributed, although the gentleman who runs the sperm bank to which you refer lives only a few miles away from here. I'm not so sure I have such a high opinion of Nobel laureates that I want to see them as the fathers of the population. I do think, however, that some thought should be given to the question of who the parents of the next generation should be. I believe that this particular program, though I think it's not going to do any special harm, is only scratching the surface.

OMNI: In the past you've in effect said that no newborn infant should be declared human before it has passed certain genetic tests; if it fails those tests, it should forfeit its right to live. Is that your position?

CRICK: That's a slight exaggeration, the way you phrased it. It isn't that I strongly advocate that argument. I put it forward as something that people might think about, because it has certain advantages in eliminating babies that are grossly unfit. And, as you know, the medical profession, in a quiet way, does exactly that. I've come to realize that this is an issue about which people have very strong feelings. There would have to be a lot of change in public opinion in order for what I call "legal birth" to catch on. But it's the sort of idea that, in the long run, should be given attention. I think you have to take into consideration the feelings of the parents. The feelings of the baby at that stage don't really amount to anything.

OMNI: Viewpoints like those have earned you the enmity of many religious people, some of whom clearly regard you as being on a par with the Antichrist. Even your new book, *Life Itself*, has been characterized as an attack on religion. Niles Eldredge, of the American Museum of Natural History, in New York City, accuses you of being "insensitive" in your treatment of religion. He claims that you are as dogmatic in your way as Jerry Falwell is in his, and that you want to make a religion or a god out of science. Do you care to comment?

CRICK: I think what Eldredge means by *insensitive* is that I say what I think about religion. I don't think I really regard science as a religion. I wouldn't want to see it form an established church, with bishops, and have heresy hunts and do all the other things religions are apt to do. I feel that faith should be based on science. Frankly, I'm not very happy having large numbers of people holding beliefs that I feel don't correspond to the facts. I think that's bound sooner or later to lead to conflicts of the sort we have seen erupt so often between people of differing religious views. Nor do I look with favor upon people who are trying to distort the teaching of biology, for example, in order to accommodate their religious beliefs.

OMNI: Has the resurgence of the "religious right" alarmed you? And how do you feel about the politicization of religion?

CRICK: I've been surprised and disappointed. It is getting to the stage where it might be considered alarming.

OMNI: You've written that "a modern scientist, if he is perceptive enough, often has the strange feeling that he must be living in another culture." What did you mean?

CRICK: I was referring to antiscientific views, religious views, irrational views — the fact that even among some educated people there is hostility toward science. All of this in a sense makes one feel as if one were living in another culture. It can be as simple as going out to dinner, being exposed to a random selection of people, and finding that they do not look at the universe as you do. This is not to say that I insist that everyone agree with me on everything. I'm talking about utilizing the facts we have at hand in formulating a view, as opposed to basing that view on faith, superstition, the supernatural, and so on.

OMNI: Do you find this cultural discontinuity frustrating?

CRICK: I used to find it extremely irritating. I'm afraid I'm becoming more tolerant as I get older — unless people thrust their views down my throat. When I was younger and more brash, I would just tell people they were talking nonsense. Yes, I suppose I would prefer to be — I wouldn't say in a homogeneous culture; that's too strong — in a culture in which the point of view of people like me was more or less held by the great majority of people.

OMNI: Let's talk more about your book *Life Itself*. What prompted you to take up the idea that life was *sent* here by the inhabitants of another planet?

CRICK: Well, the idea first arose at a meeting in Soviet Armenia in 1971, organized by the Russian and American academies of science, on the fascinating topic of communicating with extraterrestrial intelligences. At that meeting, we discussed the idea that the uniformity of the genetic code makes it look as if life went through a rather narrow bottleneck. In addition, I came to realize that sufficient time had elapsed for life to have evolved twice — that is, a civilization capable of sending out rockets could already have come into existence at the time the solar system and the earth got going. Leslie Orgel, a biochemist at the Salk Institute, and I, in collaboration, came up with the idea of directed panspermia.

OMNI: Didn't your real interest in writing this book lie not so much in trying to sell people on the idea of directed panspermia as in demonstrating the mental exercises required to explore the circumstances that might make the theory both attractive and plausible — that is, to explore the fundamentals most of us gloss over that relate to time and space, the general nature of life, the conditions that existed on the primitive earth, the physics of space travel, and so on and so forth?

CRICK: Yes, that certainly is what I was trying to put over. I wanted to show how you went about judging this idea against the background of other knowledge we possess.

OMNI: On the other hand, the theory is not at all preposterous, as you seek to demonstrate. What are some of the things that make it attractive?

CRICK: The easiest way to see that it's attractive is to realize that we might find ourselves doing the same thing a thousand or two thousand years from now, seeding life in the same way.

OMNI: So, as you explain in the book, the apparent arbitrariness and astonishing uniformity of the genetic code and the various conditions that must have existed on the primitive earth — all of these things make it difficult to understand how life could have got started on its own. But aren't there alternatives other than directed panspermia? What about Fred Hoyle's idea that life was generated, and perhaps still is being generated, throughout the cosmos by prestellar molecular clouds that become biologically active?

CRICK: I know of the idea, and I must say I regard it as very fanciful. It seems to me that such circumstances would make it even more difficult to get life going. And, then, the experimental data put forward to support the idea are extremely flimsy.

OMNI: At one point in your book you sum up by writing, "An honest man, armed with all the knowledge available to us now, could only state that, in some sense, the origin of life appears to be almost a miracle, so many are the conditions which would have had to be satisfied to get it going" by itself. Many religious people would certainly agree with you.

CRICK: Yes. Well, I rather regret having used the word *miracle*. I had my pencil poised to scratch out that word, but I thought, "What the hell!" Let's just say that all of these factors present us with a real problem.

OMNI: Unless we imagine that life had been sent here by extraterrestrials, in which case the problems are of another order. How would galactic farmers go about getting their seeds to the target planets intact and still viable?

CRICK: Generally, in deference to the basic laws of physics, I rule out the possibility of space travel at, or exceeding, the speed of light. The journeys I talk about take thousands of years and employ rockets that travel at about one one-hundredth the speed of light. Speeds of that order appear feasible and would put thousands of stars that might have planets capable of supporting life within ten thousand years' reach of us. Either you have the rocket manned with people who can somehow survive all that time through successive generations — not my idea of the good life, by the way — or you need unmanned rockets carrying some other form of life, rockets sufficiently reliable that all the components will still work upon arrival. There are technical problems, but none, I should think, that couldn't be solved by us, for example, within a few hundred years.

OMNI: What form of life would these galactic Johnny Appleseeds send?

CRICK: Before they'd even think of sending anything, they'd first have to believe that there were lots of places in the galaxy where life could flourish, but that *starting* life was so rare and difficult an event that, in fact, it hadn't started in most of those places. Then we have to assume that they had some sort of missionary zeal, that they wanted to get life started in these otherwise sterile places. When you look at all of the options, it turns out that perhaps the most attractive one would be to send bacteria. They are small and can be frozen for long periods of time and can survive upon arrival under many adverse conditions that would kill more advanced life forms. And, of course, the senders may have used gene-splicing techniques and the like to create bacterial forms best suited for the prebiotic conditions of the target planets.

OMNI: What would they have sent if it were Earth they had in mind?

CRICK: Well, they would then likely have sent bacteria or possibly yeast. Yeast would have been tempting; it's a eukaryote — a cell with chromosomes, a true nucleus, and so on. Yeast would have had the potential of greater mobility, would have started things out at a more advanced stage of evolution, and so on. And yeast, like bacteria, can survive without oxygen. The trouble is, the fossil records show no sign of eukaryotes until later. But perhaps it was sent and then discarded some of its fancier attributes in order to survive in the beginning.

OMNI: You've also suggested some reasons that advanced civilizations might decide *not* to seed the galactic boondocks. What are some of those reasons?

CRICK: Well, technology, launching a major space program — all that sort of thing can become very costly and very tedious. People might simply get bored with technology after a while; they might turn completely inward, even become hedonistic.

OMNI: Exploring inner space, perhaps with the use of new drugs, rather than outer space?

CRICK: Yes. Of course they might also destroy themselves through war or accident before they could get around to such an ambitious program.

OMNI: Do you tend to be pessimistic about our own future?

CRICK: I have mixed feelings. In the long term, I'm optimistic; in the short term, pessimistic. I think the next, say, one hundred years will be risky, but I doubt that even nuclear war would completely extinguish the human race.

OMNI: There was a point you made in your book to which I think a lot of people would take exception. You suggested that meat-eaters are more likely than vegetarians to pursue an aggressive space program.

CRICK: I presume you are a vegetarian.

OMNI: An imperfect one. But, in fact, most people who avoid meat do so for health- and science-related reasons, not for religious or mystical reasons. I have a hunch space exploration has far more enthusiasts among science-minded vegetarians than among meat-eaters.

CRICK: I think I have to say that my remarks on this were a little dated, yes.

OMNI: You took some risks in writing a book that even your wife says stinks of UFOs and *Chariots of the Gods*. Were you worried at all about being misinterpreted or misunderstood?

CRICK: Yes. I was mildly apprehensive in the beginning, when I first started lecturing on the subject. But then I saw that most people understood that I wasn't being fanatical about it — that it was, in many ways, an exercise, as we discussed earlier.

OMNI: You have a few things to say about UFOs. You say even the unexplained sightings are probably without significance. Why do you feel that way?

CRICK: Because when there is publicity about sightings that turn out to be explainable, the percentage of unexplained sightings goes up, suggesting that these, too, are caused by something in people's psychology rather than by something that is actually out there. The

UFO evidence forms no coherent residue; it never gets better.

OMNI: On the subject of extraterrestrial visitations, is it possible that directed panspermia might have been used for something less than purely altruistic reasons? For example, might it have been used to create oxygen environments on planets for later exploitation?

CRICK: People have wondered whether you could do that — seed the planet with bacteria of the sort that could make the environment such that, at a subsequent stage, higher organisms could come here. It's one version of directed panspermia.

OMNI: Then there's the idea that life may have spread all over the universe but, for various reasons, is not apparent to us — that we may even be part of a cosmic wildlife park under constant surveillance by ecologically minded galactic game wardens.

CRICK: Yes. That wasn't my idea, but it is also possible.

OMNI: You have written that it may be dangerous for us not to know whether or not we are alone in the universe. Why dangerous?

CRICK: There's always the possibility that we will be invaded. We'd like to know for scientific reasons, but there might also be reasons of defense.

OMNI: So much science fiction assumes that any such visitation would be for our illumination and benefit.

CRICK: I would be surprised if it were totally beneficial or benign, whatever its nature.

OMNI: You have pointed out that, whereas carbon compounds floating in water appear the most likely system for getting life started here, things might be quite different elsewhere in the universe. Silicon might replace carbon, for example, and liquid ammonia might replace water. What sort of life, based on a silicon-ammonia system, could we expect to see emerge on another planet?

CRICK: People have made these suggestions, but no one has made what I would call detailed suggestions. Others have said that these things are not ideal — that ammonia, for example, is not as good a solvent as water, and that silicates don't merge with other elements to form the right kind of molecules as easily as carbon does, and so on. So I think all one can say is that those are possibilities, but they seem rather remote to me.

OMNI: But would life from those other systems resemble us?

CRICK: It wouldn't look like us, no. But I'm not so sure that if it evolved from the present system somewhere else, it would look like us, either. The assumption is that if life is going to evolve, it has to evolve by natural selection, because that is the only way you can get a complicated system started from simple chemistry and physics. What molecules might be utilized by life elsewhere in the universe is open to question. Certainly, even if it were based on carbon, it doesn't have to be exactly the same type of proteins we have here.

OMNI: You suggested indirectly that if the dinosaurs had been left undisturbed, they might eventually have developed science and technology. Is it safe to assume then that scientists do not necessarily have to be mammals?

CRICK: No. I don't think they have to be mammals, but I have the funny feeling that the dinosaurs didn't look terribly promising. I was rather trying to suggest the opposite — that the dinosaurs might not have invented science and technology. But, you know, that's really guesswork until we know more about just how evolution works, because, even though we understand the principle of natural selection, we still don't have a complete understanding of it. We hope to have all that within another generation. It's a little bit curious to have arguments about how something evolved when we don't know in complete detail yet how evolution works. It's more logical to find out how evolution works, and then discuss how an organism evolved. Nobody is going to be as logical as that, however, because the discussion is such fun.

Evolutionary Spiral

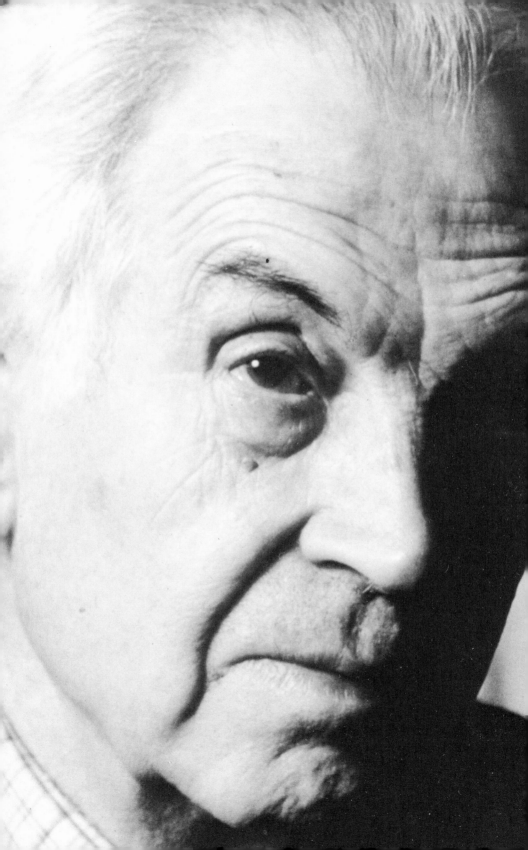

Darwinian Flights
Ernst Mayr

Discussion of evolution has been completely eliminated from most textbooks, because otherwise the books wouldn't sell in the Bible Belt. The poor kids in school are being brainwashed. They aren't exposed to the facts.

It took a rare bird to change the course of evolutionary biology — a red-crested pochard, to be exact. One morning in 1923, Ernst Mayr, on the verge of entering medical school (he came from a family of physicians), spotted a pair of red-crested pochards on a lake near his hometown in Bavaria, Germany. Since that particular bird had not been seen in Central Europe for seventy-seven years, no one at first believed his tale of having sighted one. Eventually, Mayr found a believer in the person of Erwin Stresemann, Germany's leading ornithologist. Although Mayr's family had groomed him for a medical career, Stresemann persuaded young Ernst to work at the University of Berlin's Zoological Museum during the summers. In no time Mayr became "so enchanted with the work and with the idea of following in the footsteps of Darwin and other great explorers of the wonders of the tropics" that he forsook the M.D. for a Ph.D. in ornithology. It was a course he has pursued for six decades, bringing him to his present position, that of professor emeritus of zoology at Harvard. (It should be noted that another nature lover, Darwin himself, also gave up medical school to pursue evolutionary biology.)

Mayr's desire to explore the tropics was quickly fulfilled, thanks to a chance meeting in 1927 with the Englishman Lord Rothschild of Tring, at a zoological conference in Budapest. Birds of paradise had gained renown at the turn of the century for their exotic plumes, which adorned the bonnets of every fashionable lady, and Lord Rothschild

Photograph: Tony Guccione

wanted to add certain rare specimens to his own famous collection. So, under His Lordship's sponsorship, Mayr soon found himself bird-watching and -collecting in the mountains of western New Guinea. But Mayr never found the rare birds; in fact, in what he calls his "favorite left-handed discovery," he disproved they existed as a separate species.

What Mayr did find in New Guinea, and subsequently in the Solomon Islands, was that he had an abiding interest in the diversity of species and in the role played by population size and geographic isolation in establishing new species. These evolutionary concerns were central to Mayr's career for the next twenty-five years.

In 1931 Mayr came to the United States to work at the American Museum of Natural History, and soon became curator of the newly combined Whitney-Rothschild bird collection. During his years there he wrote Systematics and the Origin of Species, *the book that changed biology's concept of what a species is. According to the old notion, organisms belonged to different species because they looked different. Wrong, said Mayr, and he showed that the earmark of a true species was reproductive distinctiveness: one species cannot breed with another species.*

This revision of the definition of species has had far-ranging implications. It has helped sort out the confusing array of hominid fossils that show the path of our own evolution. It also laid the cornerstone for what Mayr considers his most important work, a 1954 theory on how new species become established. Having been ignored or rejected for more than a decade, the theory's acceptance has been one of Mayr's "joys of research."

In an enormously creative collaboration, Mayr worked with the great biologists Theodosius Dobzhansky, Julian Huxley, and George Gaylord Simpson in formulating the modern synthesis of evolution — an attempt to integrate, within the framework of Darwin's theory, the findings of geneticists and of naturalists.

In 1953 Mayr went to Harvard's Museum of Comparative Zoology, which he later directed. Increasingly he focused on the development of concepts and the history of ideas in biology. These interests culminated in the publication, in 1982, of The Growth of Biological Thought, *volume I. The book, a 974-page tome of broad themes and vast scope, explores the origins and implications of evolutionary theory. Reviewers have called it Mayr's "crowning work."*

To Mayr, now seventy-nine, his ultimate achievement is that he is "finally making an impact with respect to the philosophy of biology and in proclaiming biology's emancipation from the physical sciences." That impact is sure to grow with his latest projects: Volume II of Growth, which will explore the issues of physiology and molecular biology, and another book dealing with the philosophy of biology.

In 1982, Carol A. Johmann, a science writer and former cell biologist, met with Mayr in his museum office, where, peering around piles of papers on his desk, he spoke with passion about his favorite subjects. Johmann talked to Mayr again in 1983 and combined the two conversations in the interview that follows.

OMNI: It is clear from your books and articles that you think evolution is the most revolutionary biological concept ever unveiled and that Darwin is the greatest of all biological thinkers. Why?

MAYR: Because he changed man's thinking. Before Charles Darwin, everyone thought that there was a limited number of kinds of things, that they were not variable, and that they were sharply separated from one another by distinct gaps. For instance, it was thought that species did not change at all. They had a certain amount of variability, but could never go beyond it. Darwin replaced this thinking with what we now call population thinking — the idea that all living things exist as populations of unique individuals. These populations may form separate species, but each is so variable that it can change in the course of time through the process of natural selection.

Another of Darwin's ideas was that all organisms are descended from common ancestors — all the way back to the one-celled organisms. We now have abundant evidence that all life is descended from one single source.

OMNI: How did that change our view of ourselves?

MAYR: It made us realize that man is part of this complete stream of life, that man is an animal, and that man and the primates — particularly man and the anthropoid apes — have a common ancestor. It completely destroyed the old idea that man is an entirely distinct creature that has nothing to do with the animals. Since Darwin, every *knowing* person agrees that man is descended from the apes.

OMNI: Does it surprise you that, a hundred years after Darwin's death, the general public is still fascinated by evolution?

MAYR: No. Evolution has an impact on every aspect of man's thinking: his philosophy, his metaphysics, his ethics.

OMNI: Do you think Darwin would have been surprised by the continuing resistance to the theory of evolution?

MAYR: Probably not. He found a good deal of resistance even among his closest friends. He admired no one more than he did his contemporary, the British geologist Charles Lyell. Lyell accepted evolution very reluctantly about ten years after the publication of *Origin of Species*. He never accepted the theory of natural selection. Even the naturalist Alfred Russel Wallace, who, with Darwin, proposed natural selection as a theory, always had reservations as to whether it explained the evolution of man. In fact, Wallace distinctly said no, man was indeed separately created.

The really surprising thing is that Darwin published his book in 1859, and by 1874 there was no serious opponent among scientists to the theories of evolution and common descent. Natural selection was still being argued about, but evolution, as such, was not. Today, of course, there is no such thing as the theory of evolution; it is the fact of evolution. After all, we have geological strata that date back three and a half billion years and we find in them the remains of a steady succession of life that can be dated very accurately. This is a fact. We know that genetic recombination makes every generation new as compared to the previous one and provides for change. This, too, is a fact. The only arguments now are over technical problems, but the basic fact of evolution is so clearly established that no scientist worries about it anymore.

OMNI: Do you think, as some scientists have claimed, that evolutionary theory is heading into its most exciting decade since Darwin published *Origin of Species?*

MAYR: No, I don't think so. Whatever has been done in recent years is only an elaboration of the original Darwinian framework, not a drastic change in any way. The idea of evolution has not been touched; the idea of common descent has not been touched; the idea that species change has not been touched; the idea that new species originate when populations separate has not been touched; and the idea that natural selection is the major mechanism by which all these changes are made has also not been touched.

OMNI: Yet there are still misconceptions about some of those ideas. Perhaps we should review what evolution involves.

MAYR: All right. Let's begin with chance. In the period immediately after 1859 and the publication of *Origin*, five chief mechanisms were suggested as being responsible for evolution, three of which were opposed to Darwinian thought. The first was that there is a built-in drive that inevitably and inexorably pushes evolutionary lines to ever-greater perfection. This teleological concept of evolution has been so totally refuted that no one pays any attention to it any longer.

The second was that evolution consists of the sudden production of new individuals, or, as Richard Goldschmidt [a geneticist] called them forty years ago, "hopeful monsters," which represented new types of animals and plants. Well, that, too, has been thoroughly refuted.

The third, usually referred to as Lamarckism, was the idea that the environment can directly influence the genetic material and that a species adapts to the environment by inheriting from its parents their learned or acquired characteristics. Molecular biology has shown that that is impossible. In an elemental test disproving Lamarckism, biologists cut the tails off mice for about a dozen generations. The offspring of those mice continued to be born with tails.

So these three are eliminated, which leaves only two more: natural selection and chance. In the Darwinian, and the modern, interpretation of evolution, both occur. Evolution consists of two stages. The first is the production of new individuals. That involves producing eggs and sperm — each of them genetically unique — and then the fertilizing of an egg by a sperm. This stage involves a great deal of chance, but no selection. Then begins a second stage, which is the development of the newly formed fertilized egg into a viable organism. From that point on, natural selection very much enters the picture. In effect, organisms with traits best suited to the natural environment reproduce and pass genes on to the next generation more frequently than their less fit brethren. Over generations, therefore, the offspring of those best equipped to handle the environment will prevail. They will, in essence, have been *selected*. This is what we mean by natural selection. So in each generation you have a combination of the chance phenomenon and the selection phenomenon.

OMNI: You have said, as others have, that the role of natural selection is creative — that its function is more than simply to ensure the "survival of the fittest." You have even compared the role played by selection to that of a sculptor.

MAYR: The reason I use the metaphor of the sculptor is that the production of new individuals is a process of constantly making entirely new genetic combinations and exposing them to competition, to the elements — in short, to selection. Every generation starts new. As the geneticists put it, all the genes of the previous generation are poured back into the gene pool of the species, or the population. Out of this gene pool are lifted new individuals, totally new combinations of genes that are again exposed to selection. And that, in my eyes, is quite a creative process.

OMNI: This process leads not only to new individuals but also to the formation of new species — a subject that has occupied much of your career. What did you see on your expeditions to New Guinea and the Solomon Islands that got you interested in species?

MAYR: The first thing that really brought the idea of species home to me was the experience in the mountains of New Guinea when I was still working for Lord Rothschild. At the time, the nominalist school of philosophy was popular. It said that objects are just arbitrary, linguistic categories. For example, there are chairs and tables that we call furniture, but furniture itself does not exist. The nominalists applied the same thinking to biological species. They said species don't exist. They are just names.

But I discovered that the very same aggregations or groupings of individuals that the trained zoologist called separate species were called species by the New Guinea natives. I collected 137 species of birds. The natives had 136 names for these birds — they confused only two of them. The coincidence of what Western scientists called species and what the natives called species was so total that I realized the species was a very real thing in nature. This was something very different from the nominalist philosophy.

Then I asked myself by what mechanism these groups can maintain their integrity, their discreteness, and not get mixed up with each other. The answer led automatically to the biological species definition.

OMNI: How exactly *do* you define the biological species?

MAYR: The modern concept of biological species was made widely known through my writings [in the early 1940s], but it wasn't originated or invented by me. As much as eighty years earlier, people had very similar ideas. Before that, the species concept was very much what is called the morphological or typological or essentialistic concept. Something was called a different species if it looked different from other species. My predecessors and I called attention to the fact that this was a very sloppy way of defining species. We have many kinds of creatures that look identical, and yet we know they are different species. For instance, up to the thirties, nobody could understand the occurrence and spread of malaria in Europe. It turned out that what was considered to be a single species of mosquito was actually six different species, morphologically identical, but having different chromosomes. Moreover, only some transmitted the disease. The opposite problem is that there are individuals that are strikingly different in appearance, yet they belong to the same species. In the northern United States, for example, the blue goose and the snow goose couldn't look more different, and so they were once considered to be different species. Then biologists discovered that the geese represent color variations within the same population. They were freely breeding with one another.

Now we say that two populations are different species if, when in contact, they do not interbreed. The reason they don't interbreed is that they have certain biological properties, referrred to as isolating mechanisms, that have a genetic basis. The process of speciation, then, is the acquisition of such isolating mechanisms. And that can happen, according to the majority of biologists — and I have been pushing this very hard — only when populations are geographically isolated. In geographic isolation, populations genetically reorganize. Later, if they can no longer interbreed after the extrinsic isolating factor breaks down — say, a mountain range is eroded away, or a land bridge forms over a body of water — and the populations are together again, then they have become different species.

OMNI: You are now talking about the theory of speciation that you developed in the forties and fifties.

MAYR: There are two theories of geographic speciation. The classical one is that a single species would be split in two by a new geographical barrier. In the course of looking at many examples of speciation, I came to the conclusion that this was not the common way of speciation. Instead, I proposed that what really happens is that a small group of individuals, sometimes a single fertilized female, goes beyond the periphery of the species range and establishes a new colony. This founder population is subjected to a great deal of inbreeding, which sets up certain genetic pressures. Also, the environment is different. There are different fauna and flora, and the climate differs somewhat. All these selective pressures lead to a much more rapid and drastic genetic reorganization.

I encountered this situation in the Solomon Islands. When I went from island to island, I discovered that each was inhabited by one representative of a group of related species. These birds — flycatchers, owls, pigeons — were either in the process of speciating or else had already completed that process of genetic reorganization. Each island's representative was clearly derived from the others and, moreover, derived during a period of isolation on the island.

OMNI: But there is still controversy over how species arise. We have the Darwinian idea, which says that species form gradually. We also have the idea of punctuated equilibrium, proposed by Niles Eldredge and [Harvard paleontologist] Stephen Jay Gould, which says that the reason fossil records are incomplete is that species arise suddenly, persist unchanged, and then disappear. Isn't their theory based on your concept of founder populations?

MAYR: Their 1972 paper is indeed based on my so-called peripatric speciation theory [published in 1954], which simply says that speciation can occur in an isolated founder population. And I agree that the fossil record will not ordinarily show any transitional forms between species, because the changes happened very rapidly in small, isolated populations. But where I radically disagree with Gould — or at least with some of Gould's earlier papers, since he has lately retracted most of this theory — is that such speciation is instantaneous. The rate of evolution can be very rapid and yet still be gradual.

OMNI: How can that be?

MAYR: Any population change is gradual, by definition.

OMNI: So it is a conflict between perspectives of geological time versus populational time?

MAYR: As Gould said in one of his papers, to a geologist, fifty thousand years are like one moment. Well, in fifty thousand years a new genus can arise by gradual evolution! Of course the paleontologist will say, "This is an outright jump, because, for me, that is a moment." In his latest papers Gould seems to distance himself from that position. If somebody were to say, as Goldschmidt did, that in this founder population a new individual is produced, which, by itself, is a new species, that would be real punctuation. I reject that. I say it is all gradual, but very rapid.

OMNI: In other words, paleontologists cannot find transitional fossils — the proverbial missing links — because they aren't obviously different species. Is that what you mean?

MAYR: Let's put it more bluntly. Paleontologists are totally unqualified — because of their time scale, methods, and materials — to discuss this particular process. It has to be studied by population biologists. Such scientists have demonstrated many cases in which a peripherally isolated population has changed rapidly and drastically, in terms of geologic time, but still changed through generations as a population.

OMNI: How does population size affect the rate of evolution?

MAYR: The size is crucial. In a large population, the probability that any deviating genetic change, or mutation, will become established and spread is close to nil. Each genetic change would occur only in one individual. It would be diluted within the large population. Thus, most changes are discriminated against and lost. On the other hand, in a founder population there are only the offspring of one mother, or at most, a few. This results in a very high chance that if something new is produced in the genes, it will, if superior, replace the old.

OMNI: Why does it matter what species are and how they diversify?

MAYR: For one thing, it has a bearing on explaining hominid evolution. You've heard of the fossils of *Australopithecus africanus*, *afarensis*, and *robustus* and of *Homo habilis* and *erectus*. Up to the 1940s, the way in which all these varieties may or may not have led to the evolution of modern man was totally confusing. It wasn't until the adoption of these new ideas on what species are, and how they evolve and originate, that this mess of anthropological findings could be straightened out. Now it is reasonably clear that there was a time when the hominid line consisted of partly isolated populations, some of them perhaps undergoing peripatric speciation. Out of that came *Australopithecus robustus* and *Homo habilis*. *Robustus* eventually became extinct when it met with competition from *Homo erectus*, which had evolved from *habilis* and which led directly to man. So, by having this concept of biological species and speciation, we can now explain human evolution far better than we could before.

OMNI: Since the fossil record is unable to show how species develop, would you agree with Harvard microbiologist Bernard Davis's statement that molecular biology will supplant paleontology as a tool for understanding evolution?

MAYR: I think this is a somewhat nasty way of putting it. I would say that molecular biology in the near future will undoubtedly make the greatest contribution, but that doesn't exclude other branches from continuing to make contributions.

OMNI: Molecular biologists provide a window on the past by examining the diversity of life and the relatedness of species at the molecular level — at the level of DNA itself. How do their findings bear on the mechanisms of speciation and natural selection?

MAYR: I recently participated in a conference at which the molecular biologist Walter Fitch was asked this very question. He concluded that whatever molecular biology has found, none of it is in conflict with the Darwinian interpretation of evolution. If major changes in our thinking do come about, I think they will concern the roles that different kinds of DNA play in evolution. We now know that the classical idea of a gene — paraphrasing Gertrude Stein, a gene, is a gene, is a gene — is all wrong. There are many different kinds of DNA and they have various functions. In most cases, we still don't really know what their functions are. Even if the functions were known, it would still be rather unclear what their roles in evolution are. That is the big frontier in current evolutionary research. Now the techniques of molecular biology will help us solve this mystery. We can compare the genetic content of founder populations with that of their parental populations. We can study all these kinds of DNA and their effect on evolution in very small populations and in big populations. But questions about evolution will never be answered by molecular biologists alone.

OMNI: You have long been involved in getting people in different disciplines of biology to collaborate. You were one of the architects of the so-called modern synthesis of evolution back in the 1930s and 1940s. What was that about?

MAYR: We had two main branches of evolutionary biology — the laboratory geneticist and the field naturalist — and each was highly ignorant of what the other knew. As a result, they were both one-sided in their explanations. The geneticists had always concentrated on a single gene pool. They very much neglected what I call horizontal evolution; that is, species formation and geographic variation among groups separated by space and time. By contrast, the naturalist knew what happened to the organism in the real world. Bringing the two branches together led to a broader, more sophisticated, more mature interpretation of evolution, though it was still within the Darwinian framework.

OMNI: This new interpretation was formulated by the writings of Theodosius Dobzhansky, Julian Huxley, George Gaylord Simpson, and yourself, among others. Was it an independent undertaking or a concerted effort on all your parts to forge a synthesis?

MAYR: We didn't sit down together and forge a synthesis. We all knew each other's writings; all spoke with each other. We all had the same goal, which was simply to understand fully the evolutionary process. Since we all worked in somewhat different areas of the field — Dobzhansky in genetics, I in systemics, Simpson in paleontology, and Huxley in various areas of zoology — we approached it from somewhat different directions and therefore made the contributions that our particular specialized knowledge permitted.

Prior to the synthesis the people in various fields had specialized views that were often in conflict with those of others. By combining our knowledge, we managed to straighten out all the conflicts and disagreements so that finally a united picture of evolution emerged.

OMNI: For a long while, however, wasn't the significance of evolution rather neglected?

MAYR: Yes. When I came to Harvard in 1953, there hadn't been a course offered on evolution in something like twenty to thirty years. Evolution was considered old-fashioned. "Oh, yes, we know that man descended from the apes, that common descent explains everything, that species are not static. What else is there to know?" In the mid-forties I applied to the grant committee of the American Philosophical Society for money to start a journal to be entitled *Evolution*. All the members of that committee — historians, physicists, chemists, astronomers — favored giving me the $5000 I requested. The only dissenting voice was that of embryologist Edward Conklin, the only biologist on the committee. He said precisely what I just told you: "Evolution is a well-established fact; what else is there to know?" Now, of course, *Evolution* cannot handle all the manuscripts it gets, and there are several other journals devoted to evolutionary biology. To paraphrase Dobzhansky, nothing in nature makes sense except in the light of evolution.

OMNI: Do you think young biologists are being taught not to be so narrow?

MAYR: I would hope so, but I don't know. My own courses have always been very broad, but some of my colleagues' courses are not equally so.

OMNI: Isn't such breadth almost mandatory for an understanding of biology as a whole?

MAYR: Yes, but it's very hard to achieve. Even in one's own specialized field, so much is being accomplished nowadays that it is difficult to keep up. If you were to tell scientists they had to know about their neighboring fields and a little bit about philosophy and history and so forth, they would throw up their hands in despair.

OMNI: A communication gap also exists between biologists and other scientists. What makes that gap so difficult to bridge?

MAYR: Ever since the great success of the Scientific Revolution — the revolution of the physical sciences, of Copernicus, Galileo, and Newton — people in the physical sciences have thought that physics *alone* was science. For a long time they thought they could ignore anything that was not physics. Some well-known physicists have even referred to biology as postage stamp–collecting or as dirty science.

People in physical sciences were also reductionists. They thought that everything could be explained in terms of atoms and elementary particles. We have had a great intellectual revolution in this area. We all realize now that such flagrant reductionism is very bad. Many things, even in physics, cannot be explained that way.

Physical scientists also thought that anything that cannot be measured and expressed in numbers is not science. We now find that with certain biological phenomena, including man, qualities are just as important — in fact, more important. Eventually, younger physical scientists realized that what the older generations had told them was a lot of nonsense, and they became less intolerant of other branches of science. This has helped a great deal to eliminate the gap between biology and the physical sciences.

OMNI: In your book *The Growth of Biological Thought,* you suggest that that intolerant attitude was responsible for holding back biology.

MAYR: Oh, it certainly was. It has fostered discrimination in the awarding of grants and scholarships, in the creation of new positions — all that sort of thing. Part of the message of my book is that this narrow-minded attitude has done damage to science as a whole, and to biology in particular. The philosophers all thought the physical scientists were right, so they, too, ignored biology. It's only in the last twenty-five years or so that the philosophy of biology has begun to be developed. I must have six or eight books on my shelves called *The Philosophy of Science*. You look inside them and find not a word about biology. Yes, they have held biology back very badly.

OMNI: A 1982 Gallup poll indicated that 44 percent of the American population prefers the statement "God created man pretty much in his present form at one time within the last ten thousand years" over other statements that included the concept of evolution, with or without God's help. I was astonished that this figure was so large. Are you surprised?

MAYR: No. I think our American elementary education is really absolutely horrible. Discussion of evolution has been completely eliminated from most textbooks, because otherwise the books wouldn't sell in the Bible Belt. The poor kids in school are being brainwashed. They aren't exposed to facts.

This same 44 percent of the population is probably equally ignorant of world history, of the basic reasons for conflict in the Middle East, of the causes of the two World Wars. The majority of people are incredibly ignorant. I have lived in New York City suburbs, where, in most of my neighbors' houses, not a single book was to be found. It's shocking, but there is nothing that can be done except to try to improve our schools.

OMNI: In your recent book, you lay the blame on Christianity for the "intellectual stagnation" of the Dark Ages and for the fundamentalist mentality of today.

MAYR: I blame Christianity as a whole only for that attitude during the Dark Ages. It is the branches of Christianity in the Bible Belt which want to introduce the teachings of the Bible on an ﹍ footing with established scientific fact, that are responsible for new nonsense.

OMNI: Do you think Christians who do accept evolution as fact can resolve their dilemma by regarding the Bible's story of creation as a myth?

MAYR: A metaphor, a myth. You know, even the most atheistic scientist doesn't know how the world got started, nor does anyone know what was there before the Big Bang. Just look at the incredible qualities of our molecules: nucleic acid molecules that replicate so beautifully; phosphates that can transfer energy; proteins, enzymes that facilitate all sorts of metabolic processes. Once, after giving a lecture on evolution to a church group, I was asked whether I believed in miracles. Much to their surprise, I said yes. They asked, "What do you mean by miracles?" I answered, "It's a miracle that molecules have these qualities." There is much that scientists cannot explain, but to say that molecules have these qualities because God made them that way doesn't add anything to our understanding.

OMNI: Is this what you meant when you wrote that "virtually all biologists are religious"?

MAYR: Yes. You see, *religious* is a very broad term. Just think of Julian Huxley's book *Religion Without Revelation*. We all feel a tremendous awe of nature, but that doesn't preclude our wanting to know the facts.

OMNI: You recently lectured on the Continent and in England. What is the attitude there with respect to creationism?

MAYR: This sort of ridiculous scientific creationism, or whatever it is called, was unknown in England. I participated in a television debate that was to include a creation scientist, and they couldn't find one. They had to import an American. I don't know whether this is something we should be proud of or not.

OMNI: There is no creationist movement over there?

MAYR: They are afraid they might get it. I received a letter from someone in Germany the other day that said that all the bad things that America produces always get to Europe sooner or later, and now creationism is beginning to rear its ugly head.

OMNI: Do you think there is an unusual amount of antiscience sentiment now in the United States?

MAYR: There is more antiscience sentiment now than there was, say, forty or fifty years ago, and it's stronger in Europe. It's based partly on ignorance and partly on equating science with technology: science is responsible for pollution; science is responsible for the atom bomb. What is rarely mentioned is that science is responsible for eliminating smallpox, for giving us antibiotics, for stretching the human lifespan — for virtually all the good things we enjoy.

OMNI: How can people's fear of science be reduced?

MAYR: As somebody once said, the only way is to stop doing science, to do nothing anymore, because doing science is a Catch-22 situation. Scientists can always stumble on something bad while working toward something good.

The basic reason I do science, and that most scientists I know do science, is simply that we want to understand our world. Some people say the principal purpose of science is to better the lot of mankind. And, of course, when scientists go to Congress to lobby for funding, they always use this argument. It's the only one Congress understands. But if we all wanted to understand the world better — a feeling that was so strong in Jefferson's day — then we would all be for science. And if we found that there were certain drawbacks to science, why, then, we would fight those drawbacks, but not science as a whole.

OMNI: Perhaps the most remarkable development in human evolution was the rapid increase in the size of the brain, which allows us to control our environment. Can you guess why primitive humans needed to develop such a large brain in such a hurry?

MAYR: I feel that the development of speech was the most important reason for the increase in the size of the human brain. The social structure of the hominid groups required the development of a more efficient system of communication. That caused a tremendous selective pressure for increased brain size. But other things were going on simultaneously. The latest research indicates that the early remains of *Australopithecus africanus*, found in South African caves, were mostly those of victims of leopards. Later remains were not. So, some time in there, the hominids learned how to defend themselves. That also created a selective pressure for brain development in terms of the design and use of weapons. Even the primitive forerunners of religion and ritual would have contributed to selective pressure for increased brain size. The development and performance of rituals require more brain, and a larger brain facilitates the further development of the rituals.

OMNI: Our brains guide our behavior, but there is some controversy over whether the brain is programmed more by our genes — by our evolutionary heritage — or by culture.

MAYR: There is no such question. Some of our brain cells are programmed; others are not. I've written a paper in which I show that, in the evolution of man, more and more of the brain's closed programming, which dominates and controls behavior that cannot be changed, was replaced by open programs in which learning can fit something into the brain. It's only the "nurture" people who say behavior is determined by nurture to the exclusion of "nature." The nature people have always said it's both. They realize that believing in a genetic component of behavior does not mean believing in genetic determination.

OMNI: In other words, the genetic component merely gives us a potential?

MAYR: That's right. Of course, that potential may very often be loaded in one direction or another. For instance, say little boys have an aggressive loading in their behavior. Then you have to teach them not to hit at everything that annoys them.

OMNI: It sounds as if you believe there are sexual differences in the genetic component of behavior.

MAYR: I've never met a psychologist who has made a close study of these things who has denied this.

OMNI: Darwin suggested something called sexual selection as an additional mechanism for evolution. What is that?

MAYR: Natural selection normally concerns such things as a better adaptation to climate, a greater ability to find or utilize food, a greater ability to escape enemies or to resist sickness. If one individual acquires any one of these traits and leaves it to his or her descendants, it benefits the whole species. There is another category of traits that merely add to the reproductive success of an individual and do not benefit the species. For example, male birds of paradise have gorgeous plumes. If one has plumes more gorgeous than his brother's, he may attract more females and leave more offspring. The gorgeous plumes, however, don't do anything for his species. That's what Darwin saw more clearly than the geneticists did between 1900 and 1970, and what he called sexual selection.

OMNI: Do you think it has affected human evolution?

MAYR: It must have. Probably not now, but certainly in the past. I don't necessarily agree with Darwin that sexual selection was responsible for the development of differences between the races, but it may have contributed to those differences. There may have been, say, a group of females in some isolated human population who considered curly hair preferable to straight hair and who therefore favored males that had curly hair. Soon all the offspring in that population would have had curly hair.

OMNI: Sexual selection implies that females have an esthetic sense.

MAYR: That is an inescapable conclusion.

OMNI: Has it some purpose?

MAYR: There doesn't have to be a purpose. One notion is that the female has to come into readiness to have sex with a male. If there is something pleasing about that male, it may facilitate the female's getting into that condition, and so it might increase the reproductive success of both the female and the male.

OMNI: You have written that "adaptive superiority and reproductive success no longer coincide in man." What did you mean?

MAYR: I was addressing myself strictly to the number of offspring individuals produce. One study of the birth rate of blacks found that blacks with doctoral degrees have an average of 1.6 children, while blacks in the ghetto have five or six children. It is a matter of simple mathematics that this is not natural selection in the good old-fashioned sense.

OMNI: Are we still evolving?

MAYR: Well, we are changing. It depends entirely on how you define evolution. Most people mean evolving to a higher level. Every modern evolutionist absolutely vetoes that. Even Darwin wrote, in the margin of one of his books, "Never use the words *higher* and *lower*."

OMNI: How can we prevent the dilution of our gene pool?

MAYR: It's the old Catch-22 problem again. You would have to dictate who could reproduce. You would have to invent methods of testing the quality of people and then decide, "Well, you scored below six thousand. Therefore, you can't have any children. This guy scored above ten thousand. We'll use his sperm to inseminate twenty-five women." That sort of thing is totally intolerable. So all we can do is concentrate on education.

OMNI: Do you think cultural evolution is most important right now?

MAYR: Cultural evolution is now infinitely more important than genetic evolution.

OMNI: Has mankind greatly reduced the general gene pool by accelerating the extinction of so many animals and plants?

MAYR: Very much so. Right now we are witnessing absolutely shocking destruction of tropical forests. Every day probably ten to twenty-five species are being exterminated by man. And of course we're also disrupting founder populations, so that new species cannot develop. All the pollution in this country is nothing compared with the destruction of the tropical forests.

OMNI: In *Evolution and the Diversity of Life*, you wrote, "The very survival of man on this globe may depend on a correct understanding of the evolutionary forces and their application to man."

MAYR: Man must realize that he is part of the ecosystem and that his own survival depends on not destroying that ecosystem. Man, to me, is a very marvelous creature. If we lose all those qualities by which man differs from the other animals, what's left is a creature that is just another animal. If we don't place a higher premium on the truly human characteristics, then I don't see any particular hope for the future.

The worst problem is the population explosion. A stable global population would be the first step in the salvation of mankind. But as long as we have church authorities, especially the popes, who proclaim, "Go out and breed as much as you can," there is no hope for mankind.

OMNI: You're unexpectedly pessimistic about the future of life on Earth. What do you think the chances are of the existence of extraterrestrial life?

MAYR: None. The origin of life is such an improbable event. It requires such a precise combination of conditions that the chance that it will occur is infinitesimal. I know of only two reputable biologists who believe in life in outer space. [Mayr declined to name them.]

OMNI: One of the latest theories on the origin of life was proposed by Francis Crick . . .

MAYR: Ah, Francis Crick is a physicist and thinks like a physicist. He knows next to nothing about the biology of higher organisms. Forget about it!

OMNI: You don't agree that the seeding of Earth from outer space is even possible?

MAYR: Oh, come on. It's always some physicist who comes up with these totally nonsensical theories about biology. Life originated on Earth because, at some particular moment, conditions were just right. Anything is possible, but why bother with outer-space theories? Why shouldn't life have originated here on Earth?

OMNI: How do you approach doing science?

MAYR: As I discuss in my new book, there are two ways of looking at science. One says science consists of making discoveries. The other says, science consists of developing or refining concepts. The second, in my opinion, is far more sophisticated, and that has been my concern for the past thirty years or so.

OMNI: Does that concern have its roots in the kind of education you received?

MAYR: It may well have. I had a broad education, including nine years of Latin and seven years of Greek. I had to take a minor in philosophy to get my Ph.D. Moreover, I come from a family whose interests are wide-ranging.

OMNI: What is the philosophy of life that keeps you so vigorous and involved at age seventy-nine?

MAYR: I was very careful in the selection of my ancestors.

Sapiens Rising
Richard Leakey

We will grow bigger because of better food, but there are not going to be any new physical adaptations. Parts of the anatomy that are no longer used at all may disappear. But if we survive, we will survive unchanged.

In 1972, Richard Erskine Leakey, middle son of the paleontologists Louis and Mary Leakey, announced a new discovery: he and his team had unearthed a two-million-year-old hominid skull. The fossil, dubbed number 1470, laid to rest one of science's most controversial issues: when, exactly, the genus Homo *had evolved. Leakey's find showed that our earliest human ancestor,* Homo habilis, *had been born at least two million years ago, much earlier than most people were prepared to accept. This was not Richard Leakey's first stroke of luck nor his last. Starting with his conception, he seems to have been in the right place at the right time. Like his father, Richard was born in Kenya, with Kenya in his blood.*

Louis Leakey was born of English missionaries in a mud-and-thatch hut in Kabete. As a boy he learned the bushcraft of the Kenyan grasslands from local Kikuyu playmates and was initiated into the Kikuyu tribe, among whom he earned the respected name White African. In 1935 Louis married Mary, an archeologist, and for the next thirty-eight years this remarkable team unearthed hundreds of East African fossil treasures and toppled existing theories of human evolution.

No less was expected of Richard. As soon as he could walk, he trailed behind his parents through the badlands of Olduvai Gorge, in neighboring Tanzania (then Tanganyika), sometimes crawling over desolate rock escarpments to search for early signs of man. Louis and

Photograph: Anthony Wolff

Mary encouraged him to track wild animals, build his own traps, and sit quietly to study the activity at a termite mound, a bird's nest, or a waterhole. At night Richard played beneath the camp lantern as his parents fingered their newest finds, talking fervently of bones, stones, and human origins.

By the time he was a teen-ager Richard was a competent naturalist, fluent in Swahili, skilled at bushcraft, and an ardent Kenyan patriot. But he was no student. He preferred the out-of-doors and dropped out of high school to spend his days escorting visiting scientists around his parents' dig at Olduvai. Then, to become independent of his heritage, he entered the safari business. But that didn't last. Shortly after his twentieth birthday he set off to investigate some deposits in northern Tanzania and a member of his party found a hominid fossil bone. He returned home determined to become an anthropologist.

Over the following months, Leakey completed his last two years of high school and passed the entrance exams to a university in England. As restless as his father, however, he again skipped school to join one of Louis's research teams. But this wasn't satisfactory, either. As he recalled, "I wanted my own show."

In 1968 Richard's break came. He had accompanied his father to Washington, D.C., where Louis was presenting his plans to his sponsors, the Research Committee of the National Geographic Society. When the business was over, Richard astonished everyone by mapping out his own plans for a new dig in an unknown area of Kenya — around Lake Turkana. Then he asked his father's sponsors to foot the bill. Agog, they did, but with this warning: "If you find nothing, you are never to come begging at our door again."

If Richard Leakey is endowed with his father's perspicacity, he also seems blessed with what has become widely known as Leakey's Luck. Lake Turkana soon became a motherlode of fossil bones. And the same may be true of a new site in the Samburu Hills, a fossil-loaded area north of Nairobi, Kenya. There, some of Leakey's teammates have found hominid fossils that could be as much as eight million years old. The importance of such a find would be immense. Between eight million and four million years ago there is a blank, a void in the fossil record. And there are fossils from the period directly after this void, proving that our ancestors walked fully erect. Thus, the myste-rious period between four million and eight million years ago may contain the day when our hominid lineage branched off from the ape stock and started down the road toward modern man.

Leakey told Omni *it was still too soon to discuss the finds at Samburu. But he readily discussed a bitter controversy over what may have happened after the fossil void. As Leakey related it, it all began in 1976, when Don Johanson, a paleoanthropologist and director of the Institute of Human Origins, looked for fossils along the Hadar River, in the Afar Triangle area of Ethiopia. There he unearthed about 40 percent of the ancient skeleton that became known as Lucy. Some months later Johanson found the "First Family," remains of thirteen individuals who, he claimed, had died together in some swift disaster. While Johanson believes both sets of fossils belong to a heretofore unknown species* (Australopithecus afarensis) *ancestral to modern man, Leakey suggests that the bones may represent an evolutionary dead end that never leads to* Homo *at all.*

When Leakey is not out finding or analyzing bones, he is serving as director of the National Museums of Kenya, Africa's largest natural history museum. He has also set up a United States–based research foundation, FROM (Foundation for Research into the Origins of Man). It was in 1982 and 1983, while visiting the FROM offices, in New York City, that Leakey was interviewed by Helen E. Fisher, an anthropologist.

OMNI: It strikes me that we may be on the verge of establishing when man and the ancestors of the apes diverged, and in what respect human beings have evolved. Do you think that's so?

LEAKEY: I think both mysteries will be solved during this century. I'm sure of it. The only thing I would ask is whether, in fact, man and the apes ever really did diverge. We have a much more complicated technology, of course. But it's perfectly obvious from the genetic story and the molecular story, as well as the evolutionary story — documented by fossils — that the only things that really distinguish us from the chimpanzee and the gorilla are that we walk upright and that the present-day species of human has an expanded brain.

OMNI: Can you trace your theory of the evolution of bipedalism [two-legged walking] and brain reorganization, starting with the environment of twelve million to fourteen million years ago?

LEAKEY: Much of Africa — and particularly East Africa, which is now characterized by desert, scrub, a few forests, mountains, and rivers — was probably much wetter then. It probably had much more vegetation, and, although there were probably areas of marsh grass and swampland in the lowlands, the habitat was really better suited to forest animals than to open-country animals. But during this stage there apparently were some significant changes in weather. These were perhaps brought about by global changes — partly by the uplifting of East Africa, which created major mountain zones.

Whatever the cause, the effect was to make a number of new econiches in a period of just less than twelve million years. So some twelve million to nine million years ago, the open savannas were appearing. Into this niche moves one of the large apes. Presumably, it will evolve and change form. And I think the first adaptation would be bipedalism. I think we have to look somewhere between five million and seven million years ago for the development of bipedalism, because it is well established as having existed by four million years ago.

OMNI: Can you describe the evidence for that?

LEAKEY: Yes. In the early seventies my mother returned to Laetoli, a site in Tanzania that my parents had discovered in the thirties. In 1976, she discovered footprints of ancient hominids. These three-and-a-half-million-year-old footprints provide unequivocal evidence of bipedality. The suggestion is that whoever, whatever, made these footprints walked as we do, with feet rather like ours.

OMNI: What was the environment at Laetoli like at the time the footprints were made?

LEAKEY: Grassland, open country, plains.

OMNI: Why do you suppose these ancient hominids adopted bipedalism?

LEAKEY: It wasn't for any one reason. I think it was an intricate complex of evolutionary behaviors. First of all, those early hominids were probably preadapted to it. Their ancestors had lived in the trees, where they spent most of their time upright, manipulating objects with their hands. On the ground they may have stood on their hind legs to hurl projectiles or to brandish branches at predators. Surveillance would be another antipredator behavior that would tend to favor an upright stance. If they stood up on their hind legs, they would of course have had a wider view of their surroundings. A third element was an improved ability to carry objects. Walking upright, they had free hands. The same stick waved at predators also could have been used as a tool to dig up roots. And gradually, as they became more bipedal — for several interacting reasons — the very changes in the feet and pelvis would have forced them to evolve even more in that direction.

OMNI: Noel Boaz, a paleoanthropologist, recently suggested that an increase in relative cranial capacity occurred among hominids about five million years ago. This would coincide with your dates for the beginning of bipedalism. Do you think encephalization [increasing brain size] started that early?

LEAKEY: There could have been a general increase in relative brain size to go with bipedalism. But I'm not sure that bipedalism necessarily calls for being smart. So if there was initial encephalization around five million years ago, as Boaz suggests, it certainly wouldn't have done any harm. But I think that encephalization — the speciation event that I think led to the development of Homo — came later, perhaps about three million to four million years ago.

OMNI: What gives you that idea?

LEAKEY: According to the fossil evidence, about two or two and a half million years ago, there was already more than one hominid species, all bipedal. Of those, one was on the line leading to a large-brained creature with intelligence. Another probably retained its unspecialized features, including small brains and small teeth. Yet another had small brains and large teeth. These last two groups probably didn't really evolve into anything beyond what they were three million years ago.

OMNI: You're basically referring to two types of creatures in the genus *Australopithecus* and one creature on the line leading to the genus *Homo?*

LEAKEY: Exactly.

OMNI: In your book *Origins*, you say that these different hominids lived together around Lake Turkana. What do you suppose life may have been like for these creatures? How, for instance, did they manage to live without conflict?

LEAKEY: Well, more than one species of similar animals live at Lake Turkana, even today. Different species, by definition, are ecologically separated. They occupy different niches, eat different things, and they would not be in competition except in times of great abundance. In my own garden in Nairobi, for instance, we have three separate species of monkey. In times of plenty, when the trees are fruiting and there's no shortage of food, they all feed in the same fig tree, with no threat to one another. But when food is scarce, they use their specialization, their specific adaptation, and they separate out.

OMNI: So how does that apply to the three hominid species at Lake Turkana?

LEAKEY: All primates feed on the same general food; it's just that a particular species may take more of one kind and less of another. We don't really know exactly how things were divided; all we can say is that by the time you get to two million years ago, there's evidence of the beginnings of technology, the first tools. Obviously one species was using those tools to take more meat from large carcasses than the others.

OMNI: That species would be *Homo*, large brain and all?

LEAKEY: That's right. The species with intelligence was omnivorous but consumed a lot of meat. The species with large teeth probably ate food that was particularly coarse, some kind of vegetable matter. And the third species probably ate small fruits and berries, rodents, birds' eggs, a lot of different things.

OMNI: Do you think meat-eating had anything to do with the evolution of the human brain?

LEAKEY: Absolutely. It has been suggested that brain growth was stimulated by increased meat-eating after an initial period spent in scavenging the carcasses of dead animals. Why? Because you can't eat sufficient amounts of meat to survive unless you've got sharp implements to cut with; otherwise you couldn't get through the thick carcasses. I think the regular use of stone tools — in fact, the origin of technology and culture in a human sense — began when hominids started to depend on hunting meat. And the end result was that increased technology stimulated the evolution of the brain.

OMNI: What do you think made those hominids turn from scavenging to hunting?

LEAKEY: The unreliability of the animals they depended on for the meat they then scavenged, and the fact that these animals sometimes contracted feline flu or other feline diseases and then died off.

Suddenly our ancestors were left without any source of meat. So they had to start supplying it for themselves.

OMNI: Yet, when the zoologist George Schaller walked through the Serengeti plain in Tanzania for a week some time ago, he found half a ton of edible dead meat. If he can find so much meat, even now, after all the overkilling of animals, don't you think those early hominids might have flourished just by scavenging, without any need for hunting at all?

LEAKEY: The hominids weren't able to move the distances that large cats could. If George Schaller had made the same trip a month later, he wouldn't have found half a pound of edible meat. Game moves; game isn't always in the same place. To get their meat, hominids had to hunt and kill. Hunting, technology, culture, language, large brains, meat-eating, all relate to each other. They all stimulate each other. The feedback loop created by all these things got civilization truly underway.

OMNI: You yourself found a large, two-million-year-old hominid skull called number 1470, for which you received a great deal of acclaim. How does that fit into the picture?

LEAKEY: First of all, I didn't find it; it was found by one of my colleagues, Bernard Ngeneo, who was simply out looking for fossils, as we did in those days on a daily basis. He found some scraps of bone, mostly very small, belonging to a human skeleton.

OMNI: Where was that?

LEAKEY: At Koobi Fora, the fossil-hunting camp on the eastern shore of Lake Turkana. He reported the find to me, and I was there a few days later. We screened an area of about forty yards by twenty yards on the side of a hill over a period of about three weeks, and it was not until about three weeks had elapsed that we had enough fragments collected to begin actually to piece the bits together. And it was only once we started piecing bits together that we realized we had a skull that had had a largish brain. It was different from the small-brained forms that we had thus far found at Koobi Fora.

OMNI: How large was the cranium?

LEAKEY: It turned out to be 770 cubic centimeters.

OMNI: How large were the others you found?

LEAKEY: Five hundred and thirty cubic centimeters.

OMNI: And our own craniums?

LEAKEY: Thirteen hundred to fifteen hundred cubic centimeters.

Anyway, contrary to the popular caricature, in which we stumbled across this great skull, shouted "Eureka!" and leaped up and down, it took weeks of boring, dusty work before the penny dropped and we realized that we had actually found something rather important. Okay? It was a very unexciting, nonevent.

OMNI: What did your colleagues think of it?

LEAKEY: Once it had been pieced together, people were very excited. But they were excited because it gave physical evidence of something that had long been suspected.

OMNI: Which was?

LEAKEY: That, just as my father had suspected, a large-brained hominid called *Homo habilis* lived two million years ago. And that this hominid called *habilis* had lived right alongside a multiplicity of other small-brained hominids that were on the road to extinction.

OMNI: Your father's colleagues had always disliked that theory.

LEAKEY: Not all. But even as late as 1973, there were people who still opposed the multiple-hominid scenario. Number 1470, however, really settled that.

OMNI: Did your father feel vindicated after you found skull number 1470?

LEAKEY: "Vindicated" would suggest that he never really had much faith in his own prediction. But my father is like me. Once he decided that he was right, he didn't need any further vindication. If the others couldn't see it, it was they who needed vindication. The number 1470 skull made others realize that he'd been right; he himself knew it all along.

OMNI: Does number 1470 confirm the theory that our ancestors were using tools two million years ago? In other words, did you find any implements buried with the skull?

LEAKEY: Number 1470 was not found with any tools. But it was found in strata that elsewhere produced tools. At Olduvai Gorge and at Lake Turkana we've found tools that are close to two million years old. These tools are very simple. They're basically flakes of stone that were struck from small pebbles and cobbles. The flakes have been utilized, as you can see from the abrasion along the sharp edges. They're often found associated with the broken remains of the animals on which they were presumably used.

OMNI: Does that indicate anything about the way *Homo habilis* may have lived?

LEAKEY: Well, these tools are often found amid the remains of a wide variety of animal species [each, presumably, from a separate hunt], so the assumption is that people were camping at these sites for periods of time, in excess of a single occupation. In other words, people were probably coming back to one place at the end of the day. Thus, the model of the food-sharing hunter-gatherer seems particularly appropriate to human evolution at this early stage.

OMNI: Do modern hunters and gatherers like the Kung people of the Kalahari Desert in Africa tell us anything about our ancestors?

LEAKEY: They do give us insight into another pattern of human behavior, a pattern, by the way, that's going to disappear very soon. But they're not our ancestors, and we cannot say that our ancestors lived just as they do. First of all, our ancestors almost certainly were living in much better circumstances than the hunter-gatherers of today, who are impoverished because of the encroachment of different human-settlement patterns.

OMNI: So ancient hunters and gatherers had a prosperous existence?

LEAKEY: Probably. Back then, the best areas were free for them to utilize.

OMNI: Okay, so it's perhaps two million years ago in the lush wilderness of Africa, and we've charted the emergence of *Homo habilis* — tools, incipient language, and all. What happens next?

LEAKEY: The person you need to ask is God, you know, not me!

OMNI: But he isn't around. Or at least he isn't talking. Why don't you give it a shot?

LEAKEY: Well, after this point there was no evolutionary jump. What you find is that from two million years ago until about a half a million years ago, brain size and complexity just seem to keep growing. That trend is just there; it doesn't seem to accelerate or happen very suddenly. Eventually, large-brained hominids spread all over the world.

OMNI: But how did that happen?

LEAKEY: All you can say is that *Homo habilis* is more primitive than his descendant *Homo erectus*, or what we call *Homo erectus*. The transition between the two, if such a transition exists, is simply one in which the same character gets further developed. The brain gets slightly larger, and if you enlarge the brain, other things change: the cranium must grow larger to accommodate that brain, and once you enlarge the cranium, you've got to reduce the lower face, or your head gets out of proportion.

OMNI: So *Homo habilis* evolved into *Homo erectus*, and *Homo erectus* evolved into modern man. Was it one particular line of *Homo habilis* that led to us, or did modern man evolve in many places at many different times?

LEAKEY: The human species was born when one isolated group of bipedal apes got itself stuck and then speciated to get better survival value out of eating meat. That speciation event created *Homo habilis* in Africa in one place, at one time, some two million years ago. Once that speciation event had occurred, the new species flooded back into the areas occupied by ancestral populations, expanding the habitat and expanding the range, and, through the gradual process of mutation and natural selection, acquired larger brains, increased intelligence, culture, technology, and language. This second, gradual process of evolution occurred wherever humans lived.

OMNI: How do you account for that? It sounds as if you're suggesting a theory of parallel evolution.

LEAKEY: No, I am not. Since the beginning of culture, two million years ago, man has been doing things that are not natural in the normal animal kingdom. He arranged partnerships, arranged cross-cultural links. There was theft of women, theft of men, raids, and so on. You had a gene flow throughout the whole of the *Homo* range, throughout time, which caused the same evolutionary stages to occur almost simultaneously everywhere. Let's put it this way: if *Homo habilis* is a really different species from *Homo erectus*, and if *Homo erectus* is a different species from *Homo sapiens*, then we've got a very complicated story. If *habilis* and *erectus* are simply figments of our imagination, or artifacts of our incomplete comprehension of evolution, then we can view the same question very differently. I would argue that once you had the large-brained creature *Homo habilis*, you basically had the species *sapiens*; the earliest stage of *Homo sapiens* may well be number 1470 and his brethren, recorded as two million years old.

OMNI: You're saying that the species called *Homo habilis* by your colleagues was really *Homo sapiens*, just as we are?

LEAKEY: Yes, or rather, a prototype, if you like. You divide what we call *habilis, erectus, neanderthal,* and modern *sapiens* into stages or grades — not species. Then you don't have to account for parallel evolution, which really seems unfeasible.

OMNI: This is obviously a new theory. Have you had any reaction from your colleagues?

LEAKEY: Mixed reaction.

OMNI: What bothers the people who don't like it?

LEAKEY: Perhaps that they didn't think of it themselves.

OMNI: I guess they agree, at least, that ten thousand years ago, with the advent of the agricultural revolution, mankind made the last crucial jump to modern times?

LEAKEY: Agricultural revolution, neolithic revolution — these are exaggerated concepts. Migration out of Africa began one and a half million years ago with the *Homo erectus* stage. Soon people were wandering all over the world. By thirty thousand years ago, *Homo sapiens* were in the Americas, Northern Europe, Asia, and Australia. That's when you began to get a strange change in the way people lived.

OMNI: Can you explain?

LEAKEY: In some places, specifically Central America and the Middle East, people began to settle down in caves and permanent hunting camps, as opposed to being nomadic. The consequence of settlement seems to have been the domestication of plants and animals. Selective domestication resulted in what we now call agriculture and the agricultural revolution. By ten thousand years ago, some populations around the world were planting crops, domesticating animals, and staying in one place, as it were, forever.

OMNI: *Homo sapiens* apparently emerged more than fifty thousand years ago, yet agriculture didn't begin until about ten thousand years ago. Why did it take so long for that final step? And why did it happen everywhere pretty much at once?

LEAKEY: Nobody knows the answer. It's one of the great remaining puzzles. But one reason may have been climate.

OMNI: How so?

LEAKEY: Environmental change usually causes living species to do different things. But what the change may have been, I simply don't know.

OMNI: You've written that the hominid line diverged from the ancestors of the apes about six million years ago. Yet, as you know, Vincent Sarich and Allan Wilson, of Berkeley, have developed a method of isolating blood proteins of related species, counting the look-alike qualities, and establishing when similar species separated. Using this technique, they have established that man and ape diverged four million years ago. They've been in the lab, looking at DNA, while you've been in the field, looking at bones. What do you think of their method of tracing what's called the molecular, or biological, time clock? And do you feel their findings cast any serious doubts on your theories?

LEAKEY: I think the technique is intriguing. As scientists start looking at some of the microstructures — the DNA molecules — we are going to understand early man better. Moreover, their calibration point is very far back. Apparently the clock started ticking at about the time the prosimians [a major group of small furry primates] diverged from the rest of the primate stock. That's forty million to fifty million years ago. So the fudge element of one or two million years doesn't worry me. We are not in disagreement. Perhaps when the technique was first put forth there was a little more dogma attached to it to make it a little more dramatic. Sarich is a very strong personality, and I respect him.

OMNI: Do you think those in the field of evolution are unusual for being so dramatic?

LEAKEY: I think some are.

OMNI: What do you think there is about this field that attracts dramatic personalities?

LEAKEY: People on the front edge are often quite dramatic. In any field, people who are leaders became leaders because they are unusual. Maybe they are bold, or maybe they do strange things. I think if you examine physics, medicine, or any other science, you will find the same holds true. It is just that, because fields like anthropology are smaller, one is more aware of these personalities. There seem to be proportionately more in this profession.

OMNI: Speaking of dramatic personalities, what about Jon Kalb, the geologist who discovered that the Awash Valley area of Ethiopia was rich in fossils? Kalb accuses colleagues of falsely portraying him to Ethiopian security agents as a CIA spy. He has been absolved, but his career is on the rocks. He hasn't mentioned any names, but his long-standing disagreement with Don Johanson is known to anyone who's read Johanson's recent book, *Lucy*. And it was Johanson who took over Kalb's sites after Kalb was ousted. Moreover, in this same article, Kalb claims that when Johanson found the famous three-million-year-old knee joint — which proved that, by that time, some hominid was walking totally erect at Hadar — he concealed it from his teammates, then announced it at his own press conference in Addis Ababa [the capital of Ethiopia]. What is your reaction to this Kalb-Johanson incident?

LEAKEY: I think it is tragic to have to fight about this issue in the popular press. And if one is criticizing another person for being unethical, it doesn't help to be unethical oneself. To attack Don in the press won't help scientific research in Ethiopia.

OMNI: You and Don have had your own conflicts. I remember one moment on Walter Cronkite's television program "Universe" when you reacted to Johanson's theory. Johanson had just diagrammed his model of human evolution. He claimed that the fossils he'd found at Hadar — the skeleton of the hominid Lucy as well as a group of individuals called the "First Family" — were three to four million years old and part of a new species he'd named *Australopithecus afarensis*. *Afarensis*, according to his diagram, had split into two groups, with one evolving into *Homo* and the other into a more advanced species of *Australopithecus*. You drew an X through the whole chart. Did you do so because you felt that *afarensis* was a sideline that never led to man?

LEAKEY: That's not exactly what I was saying. My concern is simply that Johanson's sample is large. There are many individuals, and there is a lot of variation among those individuals. He also claims that the fossils belong to the same species as the creatures that made the footprints at Laetoli, a thousand miles away. But there is so much variation within the collection that it is difficult to accept all these bones from such distant places as a single species. Furthermore, we are told that all these fossils represent a single species because the reputed First Family assemblage all died together in some catastrophic event. How does Johanson know this? These fossils could have been deposited at different times, over a period of months or even years, by a carnivore that was selecting this particular species, or this particular group of a species, to feed on. Certainly this assemblage doesn't speak to me of a single family that all died in one place simultaneously.

OMNI: In other words, *Australopithecus afarensis* could be . . .

LEAKEY: Two species instead of one.

OMNI: Which two?

LEAKEY: I don't know, but if you've got two species later on, maybe these are the antecedents of both later species. All I've said is it's too soon to be dogmatic. Moreover, I have never, not for one moment, suggested that what we are calling *Australopithecus* wasn't ancestral to *Homo*. What I've said is, we seem to have one australopithecine contemporary with *Homo* at Lake Turkana, from around three million years ago. This one clearly cannot be the same one that is the ancestor of both man and *Australopithecus*. You have to go further back to find the earlier australopithecine type that will be common ancestor of man and later *Australopithecus*. Don claims that he has found it. I say, as do others, maybe and maybe not.

OMNI: That is certainly a point of view your father would have supported. He believed that *Australopithecus africanus* could not be ancestral to *Homo*.

Tell me, what did you think of your parents' profession when you were a child?

LEAKEY: Well, I enjoyed the out-of-doors, but I never really thought I would go into anthropology, because I wanted to be independent. I wanted my own career and my own identity.

OMNI: Did you get along with them?

LEAKEY: I don't know whether one would say that I got along very well or very badly. It was a good relationship, but one based on a great deal of independence.

OMNI: The story is that you had conflicts with your father and then reconciled with him before he died.

LEAKEY: Well, it makes good copy. We did fight on numerous occasions. There were intellectual battles. There were parental conflicts with the errant son. And there were administrative problems.

OMNI: Were you the errant son?

LEAKEY: Sometimes one is errant. One doesn't always follow straight. I was involved in administering the museum my father had started. I was doing things differently from the way he had done them. And, as he was working in the museum that I was running, I think at times he wanted things done differently. I simply said that I'm running it and we are doing it this way. That's the sort of problem that led to the story of our conflict. It was never as serious as it was made out to be, and, indeed, during the last nine months of his life we got on extremely well.

OMNI: What do you consider to be your father's greatest achievement?

LEAKEY: He will be most remembered for his pioneering work in drawing attention to Africa — particularly to East Africa — as the place where fossils of human ancestors would be found in great number. He also pioneered in demonstrating that you could observe primates in the wild and that they would become habituated to behaving naturally in the presence of observers.

OMNI: Speaking of behavior, what do you think of the field of sociobiology? As you well know, sociobiologists hypothesize that there is a biological component to behavior, that behaviors like altruism and belligerence evolved just the way our teeth did, by differential selection. They believe that some human behavioral patterns are genetically determined. What are your perceptions of sociobiology?

LEAKEY: It is a very big question. The story of social insects, such as bees and ants, is quite fascinating, and I think much has been said that is quite close to the mark. But you run into problems when you then apply the same ideas and principles across the board to humans and other mammals. I think it is better to think of human behavior as developing rather than as evolving. The processes are different. For example, the development of culture isn't evolution in the sense of an organism's evolution, with genetic changes and genetic drift. The development of culture relates to things that can be passed from one generation to another through learning.

How this relates to genes, I don't know. But the most important thing to remember is that our culture gives us the ability to override genetic messages, as bees and ants cannot. And I think there is very little of human behavior that can't be overridden. Perhaps there is a genetic base for the instinctive smile of an infant. The human laugh may have a genetic base, too, but laughter is prompted by different situations in different cultures.

It is a very complicated issue, and I think it is being grossly oversimplified. There is always the worry that if you start saying behavior has a genetic base, then you have to say that people are never going to be able to do anything but what they are doing. Just as misleading, I feel, is the debate you get into about inferior and superior races and social classes. I do think there are differences among groups, but I think all human beings have the same innate ability to override those differences, given proper education.

OMNI: Yet as a white man living in Africa, and as an expert in the field of evolution, you must find that people use your theories to try to prove that one race is inferior to another. How do you deal with that?

LEAKEY: Well, I think it's less and less common to hear anybody assert superiority of race, except in the tragic situation of South Africa. I think people are increasingly aware that race is a quite different issue from intelligence, competence, and culture. Perhaps the most important conclusion to be drawn from evolutionary biology, or studies of evolution, is that we all share a common heritage, or common evolutionary background. I would argue that if you're going to use the evolutionary studies the way they have to be used, on the basis of the evidence they've produced, they would go against the racist position. And I would design my own response, if confronted, on that basis.

OMNI: Can you explain?

LEAKEY: Well, all the present races probably originated at about the same time. The longest you can take any group back — undifferentiated in terms of skeletal anatomy — is probably about thirty thousand years. Before that, they were *Homo sapiens*, but different from the present population of *Homo sapiens sapiens*. If people live in one particular part of the world, they begin to develop characteristics that suit that particular part of the world. And this doesn't only apply to continents. For instance, you can't say Africa's dark and Europe's light. Go to Sicily — people are very dark. Go to Ethiopia, and people are very light, and they're both indigenous populations. Color and shades of color relate specifically to degrees of latitude, nothing else. Moreover, color is probably a very superficial trait that takes no more than fifteen, twenty, or thirty generations to evolve. And it's not permanent. If you move people away from heavy sunlight, they tend to get lighter. If you lead people into areas of heavy sunlight, they tend to get darker. It's simply a bodily defense against ultraviolet light. Dark skin protects against the overproduction of vitamin D.

OMNI: Another issue arises from new evidence that chimpanzees scout the border of their territory for so-called enemies, then raid neighboring areas, kill the resident chimpanzees, and usurp their territory. This isn't too different from twentieth-century world affairs. Do you think that this behavior in chimps is learned; in other words, cultural?

LEAKEY: It might be. You've got to remember that very few animals left in the world are living in their original habitats. A lot of this behavior may ultimately be learned because of the environment we've created — an environment that confines them within certain boundaries.

OMNI: What do you think of some of the language studies with so-called talking chimps, such as Washoe and Koko? Washoe looks in the mirror and says, "Me Washoe." Koko can say, "Fine animal gorilla" in sign language.

LEAKEY: I think those studies show not so much the great wisdom of the chimpanzee, but, rather, the great stupidity of man. We should have realized long ago that we weren't so special. I mean, it doesn't take a scientist to realize that a chimpanzee or a dog is an intelligent animal. Instead, it takes a bigoted human to suggest that it's not.

OMNI: Why are such beliefs so prevalent?

LEAKEY: Well, it's all related to the idea that we have a soul, and that only we are allowed to have souls, because we are in God's own image. It's dangerous ground to suggest that other creatures have a soul or even half a soul.

OMNI: Do you think they have souls?

LEAKEY: I think they do, yes.

OMNI: Has your knowledge of Swahili and of Africa contributed to your understanding of ancestral cultures?

LEAKEY: Yes. I think that growing up in Africa and being a naturalist have enhanced my ability to perceive and interpret some of the evidence we have found.

OMNI: It seems to me that you are counterbalancing a trend toward specialization with your own, more general, approach.

LEAKEY: Well, it was not a deliberate effort, but I think that a natural history museum is an important place to do research. The tendency in America has been to put these studies into the rarefied intellectual atmosphere of university departments. In a museum such as the Smithsonian, the American Museum of Natural History, the British Museum, or our own institution, the National Museums of Kenya, one gets a number of specialists in the natural sciences who have a better feel for the reality of life. Our museums in Nairobi have research departments in all the natural sciences, including botany, ornithology, entomology, primatology, ichthyology, and mammalogy, to name a few. Naturalists usually are more reliable in understanding the biological sciences.

OMNI: What do you read?

LEAKEY: I read scientific papers pertaining to subjects that interest me, but I do not read any novels, nor do I read classics or history. Most of my waking day is taken up either with administration or with travel.

OMNI: What do you think about being a public figure?

LEAKEY: I think being a public figure is fun. But it seems like more fun before you are a public figure and while you are becoming one than when you are one. Being surrounded by admirers is initially very good for one's ego. But after a while the public expects you to be somehow different and do special things. And I don't do special things. I am a perfectly ordinary, normal person who does normal, ordinary things. The other problem is that when one says something, no matter how innocent it is intended to be, it can quickly be misconstrued or sensationalized. Comments made at lectures take on meaning that is weighted, which makes one very cautious about what one says. I have no doubt that, as a result of the level of public attention I've received in the last decade, I have become a much more private person. I value the intimacy of family life. While I'm at work, I'm a public figure. I work in a public office and I'm available to anyone for anything. But once I leave my office, I am extremely difficult to reach.

OMNI: What do you do in your spare time?

LEAKEY: I work a lot. But cooking is my greatest love. I don't cook from recipes. I use my imagination. My dishes tend to be very French and usually quite rich.

OMNI: Can you give me a Leakey recipe?

LEAKEY: No. They are far too complicated, but I will try to give you an impression. The other night there were two of us for dinner, and I cooked a sauce. I used shallots, garlic, butter, and three quarters of a bottle of very good red wine that reduced, through simmering, to less than half a cup. I also included fresh Devon cream from England, which I prepared gently with the juices of chicken and marrow beef that I had simmered the day before. This I poured on a small piece of steak, very quickly pan-fried so that it was very well cooked on the edge but very rare in the middle. Then I served it with French bread that I had also made.

OMNI: Who does the shopping?

LEAKEY: I do.

OMNI: Does your wife enjoy cooking?

LEAKEY: She enjoys eating.

OMNI: Since you travel the world on business, what do you do for a vacation?

LEAKEY: I pursue my other hobby, sailing. I've got a thirty-six-foot sloop, and I like distance sailing — blue-water ocean sailing. No telephone, no contact, and once I'm gone, I'm gone.

OMNI: Could you use your imagination and tell me what you think man will look like a few million years from now, provided we solve our global problems of war and pollution?

LEAKEY: I don't think it requires any imagination at all. If we are correct in understanding how evolution actually works, and provided we can survive the complications of war, environmental degradation, and possible contact with interstellar planetary travelers, we will look exactly the same as we do now. We won't change at all. The species is now so widely dispersed that it is not going to evolve, except by gradualism. And gradualism is going to be ruled out by medical science. We will grow bigger because of better food, but there are not going to be any new physical adaptations. Parts of the anatomy that are no longer used at all may disappear. But if we survive, we will survive unchanged.

OMNI: What about the brain?

LEAKEY: The brain is continuing to be used to a greater extent than it was in previous generations. We have more technology, more culture, more complex societies, because of our intellect. But I don't think the size of the brain will change.

OMNI: You are still a young man and you have already made a tremendous contribution to anthropology, to other sciences, and to the education of the general public. What do you hope will be your greatest achievement in life?

LEAKEY: To continue enjoying it. I'd like to die happy. I think I will.

Battling Extinction
George Schaller

If we don't have oil anymore, I think our technology will find
some alternative. But the things we can never replace — not in
a million years — are the species we are wiping out. There will
be no opportunity to correct mistakes.

Exit, pursued by a bear. *This famous Shakespearean stage direction
has at times been a reality in the life of field zoologist George
Schaller. In Schaller's case the pursuers have also included a gorilla,
a lion, a tiger, and many other wild beasts. It's all in a day's work
for the director of the Animal Research and Conservation Center (ARC)
at the New York Zoological Society — the Bronx Zoo — in New York
City. An award-winning writer on wildlife, Schaller has studied birds
in Alaska, gorillas in Zaire, tigers in Nepal, jaguars in Brazil, and
most recently giant pandas in China.* A National Geographic *television
special earlier this year documented his study of the endangered
panda. Schaller's research has gained him great respect in the scientific
community, but his ultimate goal is to protect the animals he studies
from the droning roll call to extinction.*

*To his role as a scientist, therefore, Schaller must add the respon-
sibility of being an educator and lobbyist for conservation. Dollars for
conservation are not easily won. But if the complex demands of his
chosen course discourage him, his quiet confidence coolly masks whatever pressures he feels. For his conservation efforts he has received
many national and international awards, including the 1980 World
Wildlife Fund's Gold Medal, that group's highest recognition for strides
in conservation. Schaller shrugs off the acclaim, preferring to talk
about endangered animals and the people who inspire and encourage
his work, like his wife, Kay.*

Photograph: John Muth

Although Schaller's work as a field zoologist is confined to strict scientific methodologies, his writing reveals a dimension of deeper understanding, a feeling of kinship with the animals he observes. His Serengeti Lion *received the National Book Award in 1973, and* Stones of Silence *(1980), about wildlife in the Himalayas, attests to his skills as a writer as well as a naturalist.*

Physically, Schaller is an unassuming figure — a modestly built, trim, well-toned fifty-year-old, who likes to wear sneakers in the field. "But his eyes hold the power to snare you," says John Stein, who interviewed Schaller in 1983. They are eyes that have caught and held fleeting visions of nature few other people have had the patience and determination to wait for.

Because of his urgent wish to communicate the serious consequences of species annihilation, Schaller granted this rare interview. But during the course of the long conversation, the storyteller emerged, and his meticulous attention to detail and vivid recollection of events allowed the listener to feel as if he too were sitting side by side with a cheetah, or had glimpsed a young male panda, partially obscured by fog, high in a spruce tree.

Perhaps it is the sense of identity that comes from sharing space with animals during the long, solitary months in the field that inspires Schaller's dedication to conservation. After talking with him in his rural Connecticut home, Stein could not help feeling that Schaller's dedication was something almost visceral; that after too many months away from the open terrain Schaller himself may experience a sense of being caged. And that his obsession comes from having seen his own reflection in the eyes of so many animals endangered by man.

OMNI: How did you originally become interested in the work you do?

SCHALLER: I find this a difficult question to answer, for the simple reason that, as far as I know, it's the only thing I've ever been interested in. I started out in wildlife management. But wildlife management consists mainly of raising more animals for hunters to shoot. That did not appeal to me. But then the whole field of behavioral ecology — studying the relationships between animals' behavior and the environment — became prominent, and that is basically what I've been doing. My activities include a very strong conservation component — that is essential these days. Many animals are disappearing so fast that if you don't conserve them, you soon won't have any left to study. At best, you'll have some fine obituaries.

Explaining why you are doing something involves your whole psychological basis, your whole being. If you really like observing things alone for hours and days and months and years, your personality has to be such that you basically enjoy being alone. You have to be fairly self-contained.

OMNI: If you could ignore economic factors and could say, "X percent of the year I would like to be alone in the field," what would that percentage be?

SCHALLER: I don't know how long I could be satisfied being alone to indulge my private passions. I'm very fortunate in having a wife who is willing to come along with me; so there's a focal point, a base to which I can return at frequent intervals. But I like the feeling that I can go off when I want.

OMNI: If you had to pick one favorite spot in the world, where would that be?

SCHALLER: For living conditions, range of wildlife, and beautiful climate, it's difficult to find a place better than the Serengeti National Park, in Tanzania. You have endless space, millions of animals. If you're looking for another kind of beauty, you can go to the Virunga volcanoes, where I studied mountain gorillas. That's on the border of Zaire, Rwanda, and Uganda. The scenery is spectacular; there are forests, plains, active volcanoes — and you have the gorillas, which are among our closest living relatives. But the weather in the mountains may be rather grim.

It's very difficult to say "This is the place I'm going to stay." Obviously I haven't found it, because I keep searching all over the world. For just what, I do not know.

Any remote area will tend to give you a feeling of peace. You may have a lot of problems, but you live from day to day, an existence very different from our modern hassle here, where you are tense from things that happened in the past, that are happening now, and that you are worried about in the future. When you are in the field, when you go camping, it takes you a while to shed some of the tension.

OMNI: What value does the natural world hold for us?

SCHALLER: If you exterminate all or most animals and plants, humankind will automatically die, too. Most of our food comes from animals and plants. Approximately 40 percent of all the drugs we use are based on animal or plant products. Preventing the extermination of species is one of the most basic, and probably the most urgent, issues facing us today. Species disappear constantly, quietly, slowly, with seldom anyone to note their passing.

OMNI: How many species are there in the world?

SCHALLER: Nobody knows. Certainly five million to ten million. Most have never been scientifically described. The ones that are described are often the big ones that you can see. But there are millions of others — insects, worms, microbes — small ones that are still unknown. The same applies to plants. Yet, they're disappearing at a tremendous rate, because their habitats are being destroyed by human population growth.

OMNI: How fast is this extinction process?

SCHALLER: Many species will be gone by the end of the century at this rate. It is estimated that thirty-five to fifty acres of rain forest are chopped down every minute. People will still say, "So what? We don't need them." But if you took all the major environmental issues that we have today — overpopulation; depletion of minerals, particularly depletion of oil; soil erosion; turning pastures into desert — these are really, in the end, all secondary, because we can solve them. If we don't have oil anymore, I think our technology will find some alternative. But the things we can never replace — not in a million years — are the species we are wiping out. There will be no opportunity to correct mistakes.

OMNI: That is quite a finality.

SCHALLER: Exactly. If we wipe out a species, then we're simply wiping out all our options for the future. Among those plants we're wiping out, there are going to be species that could well be critical food sources. Hundreds and hundreds of drugs yet to be discovered can be derived from plants and animals. Take, for example, hibernating black bears. Their bile juice contains a substance that, if injected into humans, dissolves gallstones. Also, when a bear hibernates, he lives off his fat. His cholesterol levels are tremendously high, but he doesn't have heart attacks. Why not? So from a hibernating black bear you've got two medical phenomena with direct applications to humans. Then there's the capybara — an oversized guinea pig — which has an antileukemia factor in its blood. Sharks are remarkably resistant to cancer. Just about any creature may ultimately benefit humankind.

OMNI: How can this concept be presented to the public?

SCHALLER: People who are against conservationists often say, "You put animals over people." But I don't think any thoughtful person does that. You've got to let the public know that life operates by biological rules. You can preserve wildlife, but it takes some forethought, an adjustment of values and priorities, and it takes some trade-offs.

A good current example is the California sea otter. There are approximately eleven hundred sea otters left in California. Because they happen to eat abalone, the shell fishermen shoot them. But sea otters also eat sea urchins, which in turn eat kelp. In areas where there are no sea otters, sea urchins have eaten so much kelp that the kelp beds are virtually gone. This is ruining the kelp industry. Additionally, the kelp provides protection for fish. Consequently, sport fishing has gone into decline. The knowledge needed to solve the dilemma is available. It only needs to be applied in an ecological and social context.

Look at Japan's international image because of whaling, as another example. The behavior of the Japanese as well as the Russians and Norwegians in this matter is disgusting. For what are the whales being killed? For a few hundred jobs and products that are not needed, since there are cheap substitutes. If this continues, it will be the end of living and the beginning of survival. The world is being totaled. Only internal pressure by the people, by everyone, can change such an attitude.

OMNI: What effectively generates this kind of pressure in the United States?

SCHALLER: One thing that makes conservation at all successful in this country is the work of all the private conservation organizations — Sierra Club, Wilderness Society, Audubon Society, Defenders of Wildlife, and others — that put pressure on the government. And God knows this government needs all the pressure that can get put on it, because it has the worst attitude toward the environment of any administration in this century.

I read a frightening statistic the other day: 40 percent of Americans don't see the relationship between poverty and environmental degradation. Obviously, many Americans remain ecological illiterates. Look at Saudi Arabia. Superwealthy people at play in the world's largest sandbox. But based on what? On a nonrenewable resource. Once the oil is gone, there is little but sand.

It's the same here. Once our resources are depleted and the environment is degraded, there's no way we'll be able to maintain the American life style. The wealth of nations lies in their soil, and countries are beginning to realize that. They are learning that they can greatly modify their environment only at the risk of their own survival.

Still, they permit multinational corporations to operate with few restrictions — converting forests, stripping minerals, depriving their people of a future — because of sheer avarice. The multinational companies have a moral obligation to establish conservation programs in the countries whose resources they take. They operate on a principle of short-term gain, however, even if this ultimately will cause their demise. For their own long-term survival, corporations must help preserve the resources of developing countries. In their own jargon, they are using the capital of finite resources rather than the interest.

OMNI: What will the United States look like in the future?

SCHALLER: The future is here. Just look around and see what has happened in other countries. Areas in Pakistan that are now utter deserts had forests with lots of wildlife some two thousand years ago. But people chopped down the forests. They put little, ephemeral fields into areas where wind blew the soil away. Now there is nothing. In a hundred and fifty years the United States has lost one third of its topsoil. And I think about two hundred fifty million acres are turning into desert because of overgrazing and other mismanagement. In the West the water table is dropping so fast that by the end of the century the big worry for survival will be water. The facts are known. What we need now are administrative visionaries who see beyond today's crises, who work with a broad perspective, drawing lessons from the past and applying them to the future.

OMNI: What are your views on the triage system, which proposes that we should help only those animals with the best chance of survival?

SCHALLER: I think the idea of triage is utterly ridiculous. The fact that you ask the question indicates the downward trajectory of our thoughts regarding our ecological future. Who is to judge what to save and what not to save? And on what basis are we going to make those judgments? What we consider inconsequential now may be critically important when that animal is analyzed in terms of its role in environment or the drugs it produces. Therefore, we must fight for everything.

OMNI: If by some divine decree you were allowed to save one particular species forever, which one would you choose?

SCHALLER: Well, for selfish reasons, I'd say man. But this automatically dooms many other species.

OMNI: Are there any specific consumer goods threatening various animals' existence?

SCHALLER: The biggest consumer problem in the United States is the pet trade — importation of wild animals as pets. Tropical fish, turtles, butterflies, songbirds — it sounds trivial, but you are dealing with millions of animals. For example, at least a hundred million tropical fish are imported every year, most of them from certain coastal areas. Parrots, brought in by the thousands, are popular because they live a long time and are colorful. Some of these parrots may cost more than $5000 apiece. At such extreme market values you can be sure local people out in the bush are going to catch and sell as many as possible.

OMNI: The smuggling of exotic birds has become like the drug trade, with boats, drop-off points, and the escalation of prices.

SCHALLER: As far as I'm concerned, the import of all exotic animals and plants should be banned, except for those needed by educational and scientific institutions. If the dealers want to breed their own for the pet trade, great. As it is, the suffering of most pets is tragic. Turtles and lizards and snakes usually die a slow death: they're maintained at improper temperatures and often die of starvation. Large mammals — where do they end up? People desperately try to give them to zoos which can't keep them at all.

OMNI: How have zoos fared in trying to preserve various species?

SCHALLER: For years many species in zoos have simply died out for no obvious reason. The fact is that inbreeding — constantly mating father to daughter, and so forth — decreases the viability of the young. Many of them are born dead or die soon after birth. This can be resolved to some extent by keeping larger herds, but it's better accomplished by exchanging animals to increase genetic variability. We just shipped three Siberian tigers to China to add some new blood to their tigers there.

Zoos now also keep stud books for their rare species. Each mating and each offspring is recorded so that you can take care as much as possible not to mate relatives. One aim of keeping large herds of endangered species in captivity is that the animals can perhaps be returned to the wild some day. For some of the hoofed animals it's certainly possible. The New York Zoological Society did that with the buffalo early in this century, and it has recently been attempted with the Arabian oryx.

Reintroductions of big cats, however, are unlikely. People fear them. They may agree that a tiger has a right to exist, but they will object to its practicing that right in their neighborhood. And if the population has been inbred too much over the years, it may have lost some of its genetic variability. This may not hurt the survival of the young directly, but it may prevent their successful adaptation to the wild.

OMNI: The bigger the herd, the better the chance of preserving genetic variability. Is the same true with managing preserves in the wild?

SCHALLER: Yes. Let's say you have a relatively small reserve that has only ten tigers. Well, the chances are that those will ultimately die out on their own, anyway. The population is simply too small. Islands, whether real ones or islands of habitat, have a smaller variety of animals than expected. That is very important to remember when establishing parks, which must be as large and as ecologically varied as possible. But at this stage one is glad for any new national park, no matter how small, to serve as a genetic reservoir for at least some species.

OMNI: What about genetic engineering with regard to protection from extinction?

SCHALLER: Zoos are now taking the first step to freeze semen. The Bronx Zoo did an interesting experiment two years ago, and other zoos are now following. They took the fertilized egg from one species, in this case a gaur [a species of wild cattle from India], transferred it into a domestic cow, and let her carry it to term. By such a method you can raise more animals in a year than you could normally. But that's not really genetic engineering as such.

OMNI: It's embryo transfer.

SCHALLER: Yes. That has a future. But then, on the other hand, you have to worry about what future most species have in captivity. Zoos can only keep a very, very small number, and the costs are tremendous. There are about 750 Siberian tigers in captivity. That's far more than there are in the wild. Now, let's just say conservatively that it costs $5.00 a day to take care of one tiger. Multiply that and see how much it costs to feed those 750 per year — over a million dollars. Then you can see the kind of investment zoos have in endangered species. One can preserve a few species in captivity, but for the great majority, there's no hope.

OMNI: Is it possible to take a piece of genetic code and store it so that if a species dies out in the wild, it can be re-created and bred anew?

SCHALLER: To accomplish that we would have to learn how to preserve the material so that we could use it if it was needed again. That is still very difficult. We don't even know how to freeze the sperm of some species and maintain its viability. The ovum is even more difficult. Ultimately there will be better ways, but those are of secondary importance at present. The effort should be made to keep animals in the wild. If you have a tiger only in captivity, is that really a tiger, or is it just a reminder of a better past?

OMNI: It's amazing that India, for example, has been able to keep its tigers.

SCHALLER: Indeed. Tigers wander through some villages at night, and they'll kill a cow or buffalo. One has to admire such tolerance. Can you imagine even the harmless mountain lion showing up in the suburbs here? People would have the militia out. There'd be panic. For a lot of these species, there's no real future unless you fight to save them in the wild.

OMNI: Your main area of study right now is the panda. Would you give us some background?

SCHALLER: The pandas are, of course, completely Chinese animals. They have always existed only in China, except during the Pleistocene Age, when a few of them were in Burma. The panda depends almost completely on bamboo. Bamboo has a peculiar life cycle, in that it usually sends up vegetative shoots, and then these grow into a stem. But at long intervals — and the interval can be 15 to 60 or even 120 years — the bamboo, instead of sending up shoots, sends forth flowers and seeds. Then that plant dies. Later the seeds send up a second generation. So virtually all the bamboo on one whole mountain range will bloom and die at the same time. If your main food is bamboo, you've got it tough indeed. Suddenly all your food is gone.

In the past, most areas have had a couple species of bamboo, but people moved into many of the valleys and cut down all the bamboo at the lower altitudes, leaving only one species high up. So now, in some large areas, if the bamboo blooms and dies there is no alternative food source for the panda. They starve, as happened in the mid-seventies. Nobody knows how many pandas starved then, but 138 bodies were found. That's an animal of which there are only about a thousand left.

The Chinese were very concerned, and they invited the World Wildlife Fund to collaborate on a panda study and prepare a management plan for the conservation of the pandas.

OMNI: And the World Wildlife Fund asked the New York Zoological Society to do scientific research?

SCHALLER: Yes. The program is really in three parts. One is to improve breeding in captivity. Pandas just do not do well in captivity, as far as breeding is concerned. So William Conway, director of the Zoological Society, went to China and worked with the Chinese to design a captive-breeding facility. We have two veterinarians, Emil Dolensek and Janet Stover, who twice went to China to work with the Chinese on artificial-insemination procedures and so forth.

That's one part of the program — captive management. The second part will establish an emergency plan in case the bamboo dies again. And the third part will study the ecology and behavior of pandas so that a solid conservation-management program in the wild can be initiated.

OMNI: A panda has a friendly appearance, yet in one encounter you were chased up a tree. Are they generally aggressive?

SCHALLER: They are generally very nonaggressive and self-contained. It's very difficult to know what a panda is thinking. If you have a cat or dog at home, you usually know what the animal is feeling by its facial expressions and its ear and lip positions. The panda has very little facial expression. Most of the time it has a very placid demeanor. But if something triggers attack, a panda can be rather dangerous. There have been two serious injuries in the Chicago and London zoos. In China people think a panda is so cuddly that they can just go into a cage and give it a big hug.

OMNI: You mentioned facial expression. Do you think an animal's facial expressions accurately depict its emotions or thoughts?

SCHALLER: They certainly depict emotions.

OMNI: When you see an animal that looks as if it's smiling, do you think it's happy?

SCHALLER: You have to learn each species' expressions. Its expressions are not necessarily similar to our expressions. The smile of an animal can mean any number of things, depending on the kind of smile. The inward smile of an alligator is fixed, meaningless as an expression. Baring of teeth can mean aggression in baboons. Or an animal can draw its lips back, which in cats and dogs indicates fearfulness. For example, you usually see stuffed tigers with a big snarl. Basically, that's a fearful response. When a tiger is attacking seriously you don't see the teeth; the lips are way forward. So hunters who have their trophy skins mounted with mouths in a big, fearful grimace — I don't think that's what they intended to convey. Certainly an animal like a gorilla conveys a tremendous amount of information through its eyes. They are subtle and silent mirrors of the mind, reflecting a changing pattern of emotion.

One time I watched a male lion die after a fight with another male, and I saw the amber fires fade from his eyes. It was sad and deeply moving. It's hard to know, however, whether what you actually perceive is happening or if you are merely projecting your emotions and knowledge into the scene. That has come to be recognized as a very basic problem in our so-called objective science. You've no doubt read about a similar problem in physics. The very fact that you are looking at something and are interpreting it changes the incident in line with your preconceptions. A person from a different culture may perceive something very different, yet it may be just as true. A person raised in the aggressive West, with its Judeo-Christian culture, where dominance and struggle is a sanctioned concept, may see or watch a society of animals in terms of dominance — and I do. Whereas a person who is raised in an environment based on cooperation and altruism is going to perceive a very different society, because the focus is different.

OMNI: In working with the Chinese in the panda study, have you found concepts or techniques in their scientific methodology and research that differ from yours?

SCHALLER: The basic approach is the same. The one advantage I have is that China has had so much political turmoil in the past thirty to forty years that the scientists have had difficulty gaining access to literature and just getting together with others and chatting about their work. They have excellent biologists in China, and I depend on them for many things, from botanical identification to complete collaboration in gathering panda data.

OMNI: Is the Chinese concern for the panda emblematic of a slightly better defined national political policy on endangered species than we have in the West?

SCHALLER: Well, until liberation, when the Communists took over in 1949, there was really no policy. Then China was just beginning to get things in order when the Cultural Revolution came. The Cultural Revolution set everything back ten years. But since the mid-seventies, the Chinese have focused on environmental problems. They realize the mistakes they made in their agricultural practices — the denuding of watersheds and so forth. They are now setting up more reserves per year than any country in the world; more than seventy exist so far. So conservation is a great force right now, but it's still in its developmental phase. Of course, the Chinese are extremely proud of the panda. It's a national treasure.

OMNI: Speaking of Asia, there was a tiger known as the son of Chuchuchi. In Nepal he killed a couple of people. The researchers were very concerned that this young tiger, having once tasted human flesh, might turn into a man-eater. Is there any validity to that?

SCHALLER: It's not the kind of subject for which one has valid statistics. Animals in general are rather conservative in the foods they eat. If a mother raises her cubs on human flesh, I think the chances are very good that they will also take to man-eating.

OMNI: A large cat is an amazingly effective hunter.

SCHALLER: You could walk from my office to the house and you would never see the tiger lying underneath that spruce tree, they hide so well. He would make one leap, and he'd be down on you. So there's no way you could escape. But the fact is, you can walk with perfect impunity in the densest tiger forest, and you don't have to worry, unless there's an animal that is known to be a man-eater.

OMNI: What other reasons cause some animals to become man-eaters?

SCHALLER: Sometimes they've been injured and can't hunt effectively. They've become desperate. But in Tanzania we traced the development of a man-eater, a young male lion that I watched grow up from a cub. He apparently saw drunks walking home at night down the village road, and he started picking them off. The unsteady walk of the drunks perhaps triggered the attacks. When a lion hunts he will pinpoint a sick animal stumbling, and he'll go after it. There's no easier prey in the world than man, if he doesn't have a gun. He's so easy to catch and has absolutely no defense. Therefore, it's amazing that so few big cats take to eating humans.

OMNI: Describe your best days.

SCHALLER: The best kind of days for me, I think, are those when an animal seems to accept my presence. We have expelled ourselves from the Garden of Eden — humankind has become an outsider. Nearly all animals are afraid of us, and that needn't be, because it is well known that if animals are not disturbed in an area, they don't have much fear. The lions in the Gir forest of India, for example, hang around the villages, where they catch cows. You can walk to within ten feet of some of those lions if you care to. They don't run away; they just look at you.

Near one national park in Canada, bighorn sheep come into town and wander around the streets, because they're not bothered by people. This can be the case with virtually all animals, if they are not hunted. So when I get into a situation where an animal accepts me, I get a tremendous pleasure.

OMNI: What are some instances where you've felt welcome in the animal kingdom?

SCHALLER: I was studying mountain gorillas, which for years were thought to be rather ferocious. One day not too long after I started, I was sitting on a low branch of a tree. The gorillas were curious about me, and one of them climbed up into the tree and sat on the same branch with me to look me over. Well, I had a great feeling of elation that an animal was willing to give me that much of a chance, to reach out for me.

Another similar instance happened in the Serengeti Park. I was walking across the plain in the middle of nowhere, and I saw a cheetah. I just quietly walked toward it. I got down on my hands and knees to lower my silhouette and crawled closer, and it just kept looking at me. I then sat down quietly within six feet — the distance between you and me. And we stayed there side by side. Certainly that cheetah had never had a person on foot that close.

Such encounters are exhilarating. At another level there are meetings with rare and secretive animals in the wild, whether it's sleeping on a mountainside close by a snow leopard that stays near a kill or seeing a panda for the first time.

OMNI: How long did it take for you to see your first panda in the wild?

SCHALLER: I was in the forest every day — cold, wet. Finally, after two months, I saw my first panda, a youngster who'd been chased up a tree by an adult who still waited below.

After you work very hard for something, you are obviously very pleased when your efforts are finally rewarded. That's especially true when something is rare and beautiful like a panda, which no Westerners had seen in the wild since the thirties. At that time Westerners were there not to admire and learn, but to kill and capture, which, to our modern sensibilities, sounds revolting. The young panda high up in the spruce that day sent long, drawn hoots of distress across the silent and snowbound hills. Fog sometimes obscured him. Although no detail seemed to escape me, it was hard to believe that the creature really existed.

OMNI: Have you ever had a close call with an animal in the field?

SCHALLER: Oh, I've been in difficult situations, but only because of carelessness. One time in India I was walking through the forest and stopped at a big rock. And I had this very strong feeling that something was wrong — I'm not talking about extrasensory perception. It may be that I smelled something or heard something subliminally. Then I looked around, and just at that moment, a tiger looked over the top of the rock. Our faces were about two to three feet apart. The animal had been asleep on the sloping rock facing away.

But animals can sense your lack of aggression. So I quickly backed off and went up a tree. The tiger just came out and sat underneath the tree, sort of looking at me out of curiosity. After a few minutes I clapped my hands and said, "Go away tiger, go away," and the tiger got up like a big Saint Bernard and walked off.

The same with the gorilla. I remember one rainy evening I was hurrying home. Before I knew it, I was right in the middle of a gorilla group. They all were sitting quietly underneath the trees in the rain, and there I was among them. They just looked up. I backed off the way I came, and not a gorilla moved or made a sound. Again, they seemed to know that I was not dangerous. If you carried a gun, it would be a very different matter. Carrying a gun gives you a cocky demeanor that animals certainly can sense.

OMNI: Is there any animal that you're afraid of? One that has such a disposition that you'd rather avoid an encounter with it?

SCHALLER: Any large animal is potentially dangerous if approached too closely or carelessly. If an elephant doesn't like my presence, I get worried, because the elephant is one animal you can't climb a tree to escape very easily. Most animals tend to give you the benefit of the doubt, but you can always meet an oddball who once had a bad encounter with man or is in a bad mood. I remember once I met a lion while driving in my Land-Rover. It must have been 100 to 150 feet away. I stopped to see which one it was — if I could recognize the individual, since many were ear-tagged. It was a young male, a stranger to me. Suddenly he charged the car and bit a big hole in the fender. There was no direct provocation. Well, he probably had been beaten up by some other lion and was disgruntled.

OMNI: Can you think of the instance when you were the most uncomfortable?

SCHALLER: Not really. I've never been in any situation where I felt critically worried about survival. Comfort, or the lack of it, seems to be a constant presence when you're in extreme environments, hot or cold. A truly serious situation usually means that you've made an error along the way.

OMNI: Is there an explorer of the past or a naturalist or someone else that you hold up as a hero or model?

SCHALLER: Many have now written eloquently on behalf of conservation and wildlife, but two have influenced me most, directly or indirectly. One is Aldo Leopold, whose book *Sand Country Almanac* has become the bible of the modern conservation movement. Unfortunately, I never met him, since he died in the late forties.

In 1956, however, I was an assistant to Olaus Murie during an expedition to northeastern Alaska. That area, which is now the Arctic Wildlife Range, was established as a result of his efforts. In his late sixties he was a renowned naturalist, a fine artist and writer, and president of the Wilderness Society. Yet, in spite of a lifetime in the wilderness, he still approached each day full of curiosity and with an undimmed capacity for wonder — recording and attempting to understand, looking and listening to everything with a responsive heart. He had a tremendous generosity of spirit that I greatly admired and still try to emulate.

OMNI: What is the craziest or wildest thing you have ever done?

SCHALLER: If you were to ask me what is the best thing I've ever done, I would say it is marrying my wife, Kay. She has followed me all over the world and has been an indispensable helper. In fact, she has been the one stable thing around which everything has revolved.

But the craziest thing? I should have her here to remind me of the crazy things I've done. My life may sound romantic to some people, but basically it's very mundane, except that it's led me to exotic places with exotic animals. I get letters from people saying, "I think it's just wonderful for you to go out and study animals, and I want to do that, too." But anyone soon finds out that most of the work is rather prosaic and uncomfortable. You're usually in a country where you're not really wanted — a foreigner, always the outsider. You can never become a part of the local culture. For that matter, if you are studying animals, you are usually as far from people as possible. And what does an animal do most of the day? It eats or sleeps, and more often than not it does so where you can't observe it. Still, I would not trade this free and lonely life for any other. It obviously does not suit everyone, however.

OMNI: But I can imagine that somewhere along the line you must have departed from a well-thought-out, conservative approach and put yourself in jeopardy for purposes of better observation. I can just see you doing that. The lions are feeding. They've killed a bunch of animals, and maybe you've gotten too close.

SCHALLER: Oh, well, we are interpreting that differently, which is an indication of my personality. When I work, I don't think, "This is exciting." I work. Sure, I've been in situations that in retrospect I should perhaps not have been in. But at the time, I needed certain information and took calculated risks to get it.

Take an example: you have some high grass, some bushes, and some jungle crows sitting silently in the bushes, waiting. The chances are good that a tiger has killed something there. Now, you want to know what species the tiger has killed, and you want to determine the age and sex of the kill; you want to collect droppings of the tiger, and you want to identify the tiger itself if possible. What should you do? Should you come back in a couple of days when the hyenas may have carried off the remains, or do you check on the site now? The crows in the bushes may mean that the tiger is still there.

You sit there for an hour, quietly listening, hoping you'll hear something. Nothing happens. So you very carefully go in. Sometimes the tiger is gone. Sometimes it isn't. Usually the tiger has heard you and crouches down and waits, judging your actions. You don't even know the animal is there, until it suddenly rises, some fifteen feet away, and walks off. It is a rather tense situation, but it's part of the job. You can magnify such an incident to any level you want, especially if the tiger growls, as it may do. The glimpse of the tiger moving away on silent paws through golden grass is, to me, the vision that lingers. To someone else such an encounter may become the highpoint of a book, an illustration of life among dangerous beasts. It's all a matter of perception.

The New Epoch
Jonas Salk

The human mind may be seen as a form of matter that has become conscious of itself, conscious of evolution, and conscious of its capacity to participate in evolution. We are a product of evolution, and the embodiment of the process as well.

When the success of Jonas Salk's polio vaccine was announced in 1955, there was a national celebration. Salk's research, funded by the March of Dimes, promised to obliterate one of the most treacherous diseases known to man. True to expectation, the incidence of polio in the United States fell by 92 percent within five years. And Salk himself, one of the first to use the vaccine, received a citation from President Eisenhower, as well as a Congressional medal for "great achievement in the field of medicine."

But Salk's grand achievement touched off a bit of controversy within the medical community. Some doctors seemed jealous of the attention heaped on one of their brethren, and, as Salk now explains, "the whole experience gave me much food for thought about people. . . . I realized that something was needed to help people understand each other, and I knew that the problems of man were not all going to be solved only in the laboratory. I saw a wide gap between human knowledge and its use for improving the human condition, for aiding what I call human evolution."

Salk's desire to advance human evolution resulted, in 1963, in the founding of the Salk Institute for Biological Studies in La Jolla, California. The institute, a center for research on cancer, brain science, and genetics, is also concerned with the social consequences of science and technology. And it is this last field in which Jonas Salk has been particularly involved. "The threat that we are to ourselves," he says,

Photograph: Christopher Springman

"manifests itself in the form of nuclear weapons, the economic crisis, problems associated with development of the third world, problems associated with resources, with the pollution of the planet."

Jonas Salk believes we must use foresight to correct the problems we've created. Doing just that, he has, over the last two decades, produced four books: Man Unfolding, The Survival of the Wisest, World Population and Human Values *(written with his son Jonathan), and* Anatomy of Reality *(part of the "Convergence" series started by editor/philosopher Ruth Nanda Anshen).*

The writings discuss his latest brainchild, a theory of "metabiological evolution" — cultural evolution that takes place as a result of human consciousness and creativity. His dream is to understand cultural evolution as well as we now comprehend biological evolution. "In a sense," says Salk, "the nature of evolution itself has evolved. In order to survive the dangers created by the evolution of the human brain, we've got to understand evolution in the metabiological realm."

I first met Jonas Salk in 1982 in his spacious La Jolla office, decorated with paintings by his wife, Françoise Gilot. We met on four subsequent occasions in their Manhattan apartment. Our goal: to let our discussion roam wide and evolve.

OMNI: In *Anatomy of Reality,* your latest book, you say that very early in life you started imagining that you actually were those objects you wanted to study. Later, as a scientist, you used this same technique, imagining yourself to be a virus and even the human immune system attacking the virus. Can you explain how you discovered this method, and how it helped you understand science?

SALK: It seems to be a way of thinking that comes naturally to me. I wasn't always aware of my mind working that way. It's only now, as I look back over my life, that I realize what was happening. This helped me understand how things work in nature. For instance, when I was developing the influenza and then the polio vaccines, I had to understand how the immune system worked. How was it that immunity resulted when an individual came into contact with an infectious agent like a virus? I tried to imagine what might be taking place, then design an experiment to test that notion. You might say that I was having a dialogue with nature, a way of bringing together intuitive feelings with reasoned thought.

OMNI: How did this mode of thinking contribute to your biological research?

SALK: To see that in perspective, we should go back to my early orientation as a physician. I was trained as a generalist in medicine, but not as a biologist per se. I wasn't trained academically in any of the fields in which I ultimately worked: immunology, virology, oncology, neurology, and evolution. I've always entered as an outsider and was self-taught, in a way, in order to contribute in the ways I had chosen.

Basically, I entered each of these fields because of the questions and answers that arose as I thought about these areas more and more deeply. It seemed to begin when I decided to study medicine. I wanted to bring the science of chemistry into medicine, which, in those days, was not quite as scientific as medicine is today. As luck would have it, at the end of my first year in medical school, I was given the opportunity to work as a research fellow in chemistry; I could have left medicine at that point to get a Ph.D. in chemistry, but I elected to remain in medicine to get an M.D. degree. I even did a two-year internship in internal medicine. I worked in surgery, pediatrics, and in all the specialties. And it was at the end of this period that I entered the field of research as a career. But my research has had a clinical orientation. I continue to think and function as a physician: if there is something wrong, I must fix it.

OMNI: How did all this lead to your work in immunology?

SALK: My early interest was captured by a paradox in two medical school lectures, each of which presented a different point of view. In one lecture, we were told that it was *not* possible to immunize against a virus disease with viral particles that had been chemically treated so that they did not cause infection. Instead, we were told that immunization against virus disease could be accomplished only by using *live* viral particles. There was a danger to this technique, however, since the administration of live viral particles might still induce the disease. In another lecture, we were told that we *could* immunize against diseases like tetanus and diphtheria with vaccines made of chemically treated toxins that were no longer toxic.

The bell rang and the lights went on! It seemed to me that what was possible for tetanus and diphtheria should similarly be true for virus-caused diseases.

I perceived the situation this way: since successful killed-virus vaccines had not yet been developed, it was simply assumed that it couldn't be done. As we now know, it can be done, but in order to determine why it had not yet been done, it was necessary to think about it first, to construct hypotheses and theories that then guided the experimental research. I didn't begin to pursue this question seriously until three years later, when, quite by chance, I had an opportunity to work in a laboratory that was involved in influenza research. And that was when I learned the skills basic to the development of killed-virus vaccines.

When I worked on the polio vaccine, I had a theory. Experiments were done to determine what might or might not occur. I guided each one by imagining myself in the phenomenon in which I was interested. The intuitive realm is constantly active — the realm of imagination guides my thinking.

OMNI: It was this line of thought, I take it, that led to your current interest in evolution and the human mind.

SALK: Yes. After the effectiveness of the polio vaccine was announced in 1955, I received a lot of public attention — positive from the general population and negative from some colleagues, perhaps due in part to envy for all the public attention. The whole experience gave me much food for thought about people — what we think and why we don't all see things in the same way. I realized that something was needed to help people understand each other, and that the problems of man were not all going to be solved only in the laboratory. I saw a wide gap between human knowledge and its use in advancing the human condition, for aiding what I call human evolution. I had been reflecting on evolution, and a broader concept of the word emerged in the course of my experiences.

OMNI: Can you explain that a bit more?

SALK: I like to compare my experience of evolution to the experience of this interview. We talk about many things at random. This leads to discoveries that would not have been made if we had decided precisely what to say ahead of time. In a sense, that's also how I've come to experience evolution in science, for example. When I think about or conduct experiments, I don't set out to prove anything. I simply pose questions. I accept whatever answer emerges, and, depending on the answer, I then ask another question. If something perplexing invades my mind, then my mind seems to work by itself on whatever attracts its attention, selecting and discarding in the process. The circumstances of my life helped me to be reflective and meditative — qualities that I see as adaptive and evolutionarily advantageous. I sometimes wonder if the particular kinds of questions to which we are attracted may not be genetically determined! For instance, I was attracted to study medicine and biology for a profession, but not physics. I was not drawn to become a nuclear physicist, nor am I an Oriental scholar.

Over time, I've discovered that I'm not really in control of my own mind. Often, I merely observe it and its machinations. The analytic part of my mind — the observer — and the analogic part of my mind — the accumulator of experience — are in constant dialogue, challenging and testing the fit of concepts and formulations.

In this inner dialogue, I frequently find myself more interesting company than others. And after meetings or activities or events or travel, I need time to be alone to talk to myself about what happened, what it all means. The best time for me to discover what is going on in my life and in my mind is when I awaken. And then, without disturbing anything, I simply watch what's happening, writing down whatever seems to crystallize.

I became interested in the mind as an instrument of evolution when I realized the way in which the content of my own mind was evolving. As a result of that process, the substance of my thoughts is different from what it was one or two or three or four decades ago. My mind seems to be continuous with the process of evolution from the beginning of time.

OMNI: How so?

SALK: For example, we see that during the nine months of human gestation, ontogeny [the development of a single organism] recapitulates phylogeny [the evolutionary development of a species through time]. As the human fetus develops, its changing form seems to retrace the whole of human evolution from the time we were cosmic dust to the time we were single-celled organisms in the primordial sea to the time we were four-legged, land-dwelling reptiles and beyond, to our current status as large-brained, bipedal mammals. Thus, humans seem to be the sum total of experience since the beginning of the cosmos. As I grew older and my consciousness expanded, I developed the capacity to sense and to recognize what had gone before. The human mind may be seen as a form of matter that has become conscious of itself, conscious of evolution, and conscious of its capacity to participate in evolution. We are a product of evolution, and the embodiment of the process as well.

OMNI: You apparently see the human mind as the pinnacle of the evolutionary spiral. Can you explain how you think the mind might have emerged, and how it relates to other elements of the evolutionary process? You might start by explaining how it all began.

SALK: When I try to imagine how the universe may have started, I envision a shimmering web of energy. Out of this web a few specks of matter coalesced in an orderly arrangement. The quantity of matter increased. Then gravitational forces and the pressures they generated resulted in an explosion — the so-called Big Bang. In time, matter from that explosion formed stars and planets as well as macromolecules, and under the conditions that existed on our own planet, the precursors of life finally emerged. All that happened up to this point I call *prebiological* evolution.

As the organic precursors of life interacted, they formed self-reproducing macromolecules and cell membranes. I think of the cell as the unit of life, just as I think the atom is the unit of matter. The beginning of life marked the beginning of *biological* evolution, sometimes referred to as Darwinian evolution. Increasingly complex organisms evolved until human forms appeared — and with them, the development of the human mind. With the advent of man came the capacity to create new forms that would not otherwise exist.

OMNI: And those forms include?

SALK: Buildings, ideas, computers, radio, television, airplanes, nuclear weapons, physics, chemistry, biology, philosophy. The mind is like a volcanic eruption, and the force behind it exists in that extra layer of the cerebral cortex. The human mind has altered the rate of evolution in a staggering way. If time since the birth of the cosmos were compressed into a single day, the enormous changes brought about by the human mind would have happened in part of a second. I refer to the evolution of human consciousness and creativity as *metabiological* evolution. I'm not trying to coin new words just for the sake of doing so. Rather, I'm trying to unify, to tie it all together. I could call the three phases chemical evolution, biological evolution, and cultural evolution. But then the connection between them may not be clear. When I refer to prebiological, biological, and metabiological evolution, then the unifying connection is implicit. The three phases are part of what I call universal evolution — in which we see revealed the evolution of evolution itself. And in all three realms of evolution, I recognize the existence of a fundamental relationship, which I call a binary relationship.

OMNI: Can you explain?

SALK: I see everything in nature, everything in the universe, as composed of networks of two elements, or two parts. This became apparent to me when I realized there were also two parts of my mind — an observer on the one hand, and a thought process on the other. This discovery was hardly new, but somehow it set my imagination free. I began to associate seemingly unrelated observations and events, and patterns began to emerge. I observed that like my mind, a living cell could be divided into two parts: a DNA-packed nucleus and a surrounding cell body, or soma. The DNA forms the genes, which, when decoded, direct the making of proteins for the soma, as well as proteins that catalyze the production of more DNA. The soma, meanwhile, protects, serves, and ensures the survival of the DNA. Now, this is an interesting relationship; without *both* components, life would not exist. I began to see a similar binary relationship at the level of the atom, between the nucleus and the electron, and I recognized that the same thing was evident for species and individuals. You cannot have species without individuals, nor individuals without species. The same relationship can be seen between the environment and the organism. In all of the phenomena of nature, I saw two kinds of functions: the breaking down and the building up, the destructive and the constructive. Also, a part of the mind deals with totality and puts things together, and another part takes things apart. The physiologist sees things in their wholeness, and the anatomist dissects them; both approaches are needed and useful. Finally, I postulated the existence of corresponding mental attributes that I first called being and ego, then intuition and reason. These attributes seem related to brain structure as suggested by Roger Sperry's theory, which talks about intuition seated in the right hemisphere, and the equivalent of reason seated in the left.

OMNI: But is this relationship between the hemispheres of the brain and the qualities of intuition and reason really solid? I can understand, in a tangible way, how the nucleus and electrons are binary components of the atom, and how gene and soma are binary components of the cell. But when it comes to the brain, I find the analogy troublesome. Every time I pick up a new book or article, I see another explanation of how the brain really works. Part of my problem is understanding the brain as a physiological entity.

SALK: Well, it is my problem, too. We have no difficulty with the cell, because of its material nature. We have no trouble with the atom, because we see the mechanics of this relationship. But when we come to mind, we're dealing with something that Roger Sperry calls mentalism — he sees the mind as an emerging property of the brain. According to his definition, the emergent whole is different from and greater than the sum of its parts. The brain has now become so complex as to evidence the emergent qualities of intuition and reason. These qualities can be experienced subjectively, and we can see their impact objectively in the world.

OMNI: It's all very easy to go from an indecipherable brain to the emergent properties of intuition and reason. But between those two things, don't you think there must be something to explain the connection, a mechanism that's not yet understood? Mentalism just seems a little easy to me.

SALK: It doesn't go as far as we want to go. I would like to go beyond that, by dissecting and understanding these two different properties of mind, if you like, on the assumption that there are two physiological, and therefore structural, elements equivalent to gene and soma. For the moment, I'm calling these elements intuition and reason, merely as a convention.

OMNI: And so you would say that these things, these two properties have a physiological base, though neither you nor anyone else could say what it is, because we simply don't understand the workings of the brain sufficiently.

SALK: That's right. And the concepts of intuition and reason suggest that physiological structures must exist by virtue of the effect they produce, in the same way as, for example, the physical existence of a virus was suspected before a virus was ever seen. I'm simply proposing the existence of two connected sets of phenomena, two related elements that make up the mind. This view provides me with a basis upon which I can think about the mind and its relationship to the human brain.

This is illustrated by the way in which experiences have an effect upon the nervous system, the brain, the endocrine system, and the immune system. An example is seen in the bereavement syndrome, where, in the year following the death of a spouse or a child, there's a higher frequency of serious illness and mortality amongst grieving spouses and parents. Can we minimize the bereavement effect by putting and maintaining the human mind in a better state of balance? If we could, we might not understand precisely what we were doing at first. But eventually we'd understand the correlates. They would be measurable or detectable in terms of peptides, in terms of endorphins, in terms of brain waves, in terms of other tangible factors. These could be regarded as elements of the mind and its components — intuition and reason. When we deal with the mind, we're dealing with emergence and integration at higher and higher levels of complexity.

OMNI: Then you do believe we must understand biology, at least as it relates to the brain, in order to understand ourselves and control evolution in the metabiological realm.

SALK: Yes and No. During the course of evolution, higher levels of complexity resulted from the synthesis and integration of elements. Most scientists tend to go in the reductionist direction. They dissect things, and as they dissect, they remove the properties of the whole. It's like taking a squirrel apart, separating all its enzymes, proteins, and nucleic acids, then asking how it doesn't climb a tree. Therefore, in order to understand mind we have to study cellular units of the brain that *all together* are responsible for mind phenomena.

OMNI: Then we can understand what's happening in the metabiological realm, even if we don't understand its parts, well enough to alter events on that level — to deal with nuclear bombs, overpopulation, oppression of the poor.

SALK: That's how I see it. And we can influence these things by altering our attitudes, our values, our perceptions. We tend to behave and respond according to how we see things.

Before too long we are going to realize that war, and certainly nuclear war, is not to anyone's advantage. We've reached the limit, and we're beginning to recognize that we need to evolve in order to survive. I see signs that human beings are starting to react to the new reality, to the new context into which they've been born.

OMNI: But the dangers we're discussing may be imminent. How can we evolve that fast?

SALK: Because the mechanism involved in metabiological evolution is different from that of biological, or Darwinian, evolution. In Darwinian evolution, the basic mechanism is genetic mutation, followed by selection of the organisms most likely to survive. After many mutations and over many generations, radically different creatures with divergent behaviors evolve. In metabiological evolution, on the other hand, I see the basic mechanism as the mutation and selection of ideas. As in Lamarckian evolution, metabiological evolution proceeds as individuals pass on traits that already exist.

OMNI: Then genes play no role here?

SALK: I'm not talking about genes. I'm talking about behavior patterns that may or may not be related to particular genes. I see it this way: people have the genetic potential to be either constructive or destructive, cooperative or competitive. Those who are essentially constructive will tend to join forces to perform constructive acts. Those who are destructive will tend to band together for destruction. My hope is that the constructive group will self-select and self-organize and reinforce its behavior through education and training until it grows in size, transmitting its behavior from one generation to the next.

OMNI: In *Anatomy of Reality* you envision small groups of pro-evolutionary people forming "sociometabiological islands of sanity" to fend off destructive forces; eventually, the constructive forces would survive. That sounds rather frightening, almost as if you imagine warring bands of good and evil that may clash. Do you mean it that way?

SALK: No, I don't think in terms of clashing. I'm simply suggesting that people form such islands to protect each other from being destroyed. Those who form such islands would act in a positive, constructive way — their behavior would enhance their chances for survival, and they would try to transmit their ideas and strategies to all others.

OMNI: Until eventually the whole world was one large island of metabiological sanity?

SALK: If we're going to make it, ideally that's what needs to happen. I'm simply suggesting the mechanism whereby this can come to pass. If we understand this, we can help it to happen.

OMNI: But if we can in fact alter the course of metabiological evolution so that we arrive at this sanity, aren't we faced with the problem of eradicating certain traits from the human population? If, as you suggest, some of these traits have a genetic basis, we're faced with a lot of sticky questions. Some people may refer to such evolution as an insidious form of genocide.

SALK: There's always danger that ideas of this kind will be misunderstood, so I speak about them with some trepidation. But the fact of the matter is that human beings have been exterminating each other for a long time; we must recognize that. It has happened before, and it's happening in the world today; I needn't recount examples with which everyone is familiar. The hope is that this destructive, devolutionary behavior might be contained, ameliorated, reduced, so that evolution will proceed in the most advantageous way possible.

OMNI: But the traits you talk of eradicating are those very characteristics which may have helped us evolve in the first place: aggression, and the competitive spirit, have honed *Homo sapiens* through the millennia.

SALK: I'm not for eradicating such traits. I'm for transformation through *self*-regulation. I'll tell you what I imagine. I imagine that people who are greedy may recognize that it will be to their advantage to be less greedy, or not greedy at all; they may learn to restrain their greed for some other, greater advantage.

OMNI: Do you really believe such cooperation — such control — is possible, given what we do know about the human brain? We not only have a cortex, the seat of thought, but, beneath it, our mammalian and reptilian brains — the centers for all those drives you're hoping to quell. How can we suppress drives rooted in our physiology?

SALK: It may well be that we're still not evolved enough to overcome such drives. But if that's so, then metabiological processes can help us take the next evolutionary step. If there's a need, then the brain may be sufficiently plastic to respond. In the course of evolution, the cortex has developed the capacity to restrain the more primitive brains that are also part of us. More recent additions to the brain may be seen as modulators of those responses which cease to be advantageous. In the course of life's experiences, the brain evolves functionally, but it probably also evolves structurally. It's very likely that the cortex, when stimulated, develops in the same way that muscles get larger when exercised. Eventually, we'll realize that if we destroy the ecosystem, we destroy ourselves.

OMNI: And possibly give rise to another metabiological realm. The biosphere could give rise to one experiment in metabiological evolution after the next.

SALK: Precisely. I think you've got it now.

OMNI: If the experiment doesn't work this time, it may work next time. In all of the vast cosmos, it's bound to work somewhere.

SALK: Don't worry about the cosmos out there; I'm interested in *this* piece of the cosmos right here.

OMNI: Suppose we succeed at metabiological evolution. What's the next evolutionary step?

SALK: The challenge before us is to use the capacities that we possess, to take responsibility for our own evolution. We're all in it together, and if we let others destroy us, we've become the co-authors of our own destruction. Therefore, we may have to change the way we relate to each other and enter into a kind of relationship which I call mutualism, or mutual cooperation.

What I'm thinking of is an ecosystem dominated by mutually advantageous relationships rather than mutually destructive relationships. That's what I mean by managing our competitive instinct — seeing if we can learn to compete to find who could be the most cooperative.

Now, this may evoke the response "That's not what human nature is like." I know that. That's obvious. What is not obvious is that we may have, in our future, another evolutionary phase that may be of this nature. I can project a scenario in which we avoid the catastrophe by having our peace talks *before* rather than after the war. I too know what's going on in the world; I see the same thing that everybody else sees. My imagination, however, suggests that a better solution can be found. By a series of evolutionary approximations, we have our remarkable eyes, an incredible hearing mechanism, and our unbelievable mind. If evolution is an error-making and error-correcting process that we're in the midst of right now, then we need a few more error-correctors to emerge.

OMNI: Dr. Salk, in writing about metabiological evolution you often invoke a powerful symbol called the sigmoid curve. Can you explain the meaning of the curve and its relationship to your work?

SALK: I'll start by explaining the origin of the concept itself. During the sixties I had the sense that the world was coming apart or was, at least, changing rapidly. It was apparent in the rate of population growth, in the exploitation of natural resources, and in the widespread occurrence of social and political disturbances. And I attributed what was happening to what I analogized would happen in, let us say, a colony of fruit flies. At first the colony is a self-replicating system in which the environment is ideal. All necessary resources are present, and procreation occurs at a rapid rate. But then, as the fruit flies multiply, resources are consumed.

In the case of the fruit fly colony, we see evidence of a feedback effect. Somehow, it seems that the fruit flies would receive a signal to reduce their rate of replication. If we draw a graph, plotting the number of flies in the colony against time, the curve that results is s-shaped, or what's known as sigmoid. In the first half of the curve, population increases slowly and then dramatically. In the second half of the curve, population growth decelerates and then levels off as the food supply diminishes. If the reproduction rate didn't level off, the flies would exhaust the system and self-destruct.

OMNI: And these organisms have a mechanism that is not a conscious mechanism; it's a built-in genetic, biological mechanism that tells them to lower their reproduction rate.

SALK: They don't have to hold a town hall meeting. The behavior is built into the system; it's emerged in the course of evolutionary time. Those organisms which behave in this intelligent or wise fashion are the ones that were rewarded by survival and/or evolution. Their behavior, and the sigmoid curve, illustrate a fundamental law of nature.

OMNI: How do you relate what you saw during the sixties to the sigmoid curve?

SALK: The turbulence and population explosion of the sixties convinced me that we were nearing the end of the first phase of the sigmoid curve, in which population increases, and approaching the second part of the curve, in which population growth levels out — what I call the point of inflection. I theorized that the conditions and circumstances prevailing in phase A and phase B must of necessity be different. Thus, population growth is just one parameter measured by the sigmoid curve. The curve reflects changing values as well. During phase A, society values individual power, competition, and independence. During phase B, we will value individual *and* group consensus, collaboration, and interdependence.

Over the past several centuries human population growth and

values have corresponded to what is expected in the first phase of the sigmoid curve. But world population growth is now beginning to decelerate. We're experiencing the turbulent effect of rapidly changing values, and in the future we may see both population growth and values change in accordance with what may be expected in the second half of the curve. We're approaching the point of inflection. But in order to survive, we must learn to facilitate this transformation ourselves. We're in the midst of a crisis, but the fact that population growth has already begun to level off even in the less-developed countries suggests that we are at the point of inflection. A hundred years from now, we will recognize that in the late twentieth century we were going through an enormous evolutionary change. This change seems very much like the punctuated equilibrium referred to by some evolutionary biologists.

OMNI: *Some* biologists, as you say, believe in punctuated, or rapid and sudden, evolution, while others believe that evolution is gradual, taking place at a snail's pace over geologic time. Can you reconcile these two points of view?

SALK: Evolution has been going on in a progressive way ever since the emergence of the cosmos, yet there have been some major events that are clearly punctuational: the emergence of life from matter, and the emergence of consciousness from life. I see punctuation in human population growth, particularly as reflected in the sigmoid curve when population mounts dramatically, then suddenly plateaus. And I see punctuation in the emergence of concepts, scientific discovery, and technology.

It is as if universal evolution, which includes the three phases of evolution, reflects perpetual creation, as when order emerges out of disorder, or cosmos emerged out of chaos. The mathematical language of creation and emergence will come from the relatively new field of nonlinear dynamics [the study of sudden, nonlinear changes], which physicists, chemists, and biologists are using to explain the order that emerges from random, or chaotic, systems.

OMNI: Those who are using nonlinear dynamics to explain the brain say that in some ways the workings of the mind may be compared to a stream going past a rock. When the stream is moving very slowly, it slides smoothly past the rock. If it moves more quickly, it forms vortices; those vortices may seem chaotic, but they actually take on an organization of their own. Then, if the stream moves even more quickly, the vortices form vortices. Each time the stream reorganizes, you have a punctuation point, also called a phase transition. Do you think this analogy applies to your concept of evolution?

SALK: Yes, it does. It is as if evolution is a process in which matter interacts with itself over the flow of time, resulting in self-organization. For example, I met you as you were moving about in your professional work as a science journalist, and we have now formed a relationship in the dialogue we are having. Something is emerging out of this dialogue, this relationship, that would not have occurred if we had not encountered each other. We, as a result of that something, will have an effect on others, who will encounter the product of our interaction and will be drawn into vortices resulting from that encounter in the stream of time. The interacting entities can be physical, biological, or intellectual. As a result of the interaction the properties change, and they continue to change, because this is an endless process, giving rise to higher and higher orders of complexity.

OMNI: You say that we need to evolve in order to survive. And evolution, your theory goes, is propelled forward by a punctuation — by dynamic interactions resulting in phase transitions. Yet according to nonlinear dynamics, that phase transition will occur only if some powerful force jolts the system. What force will jolt *us* into the awareness required for the next phase in metabiological evolution? How will we overcome the anti-evolutionary forces that seem to be leading us toward extinction?

SALK: The jolt is going to arise internally, causing a reorganization similar to that of the swirling stream. An inner force is generated in much the same way that the internal pressure produced by gravity generated the Big Bang. I see the whole of humankind becoming a single, integrated organism. It's the organism of humankind that will go through a phase change, by virtue of the threat we are to ourselves.

OMNI: Can you be more specific?

SALK: The threat that we are to ourselves manifests itself in the form of nuclear weapons, the economic crisis, problems associated with development of the third world, problems associated with resources, with the pollution of the planet — with all of those things which are threatening to the life of the organism of humankind and therefore to the individual members of the organism. The threat will affect our perception of ourselves as well as one another, and we will soon recognize that we are *both* the victim *and* perpetrator of the critical state of the world. Now, this state of affairs will be more evident to some than to others; some individuals will have more insight and foresight than others. Some will have greater sensitivity. I look upon each of us as I would an individual cell in the organism, each of us playing his or her respective role.

OMNI: It seems to me that most people, even if they're aware of these problems, have other things on their minds. Don't you think there's going to have to be more of a squeeze before a large enough number of people take action?

SALK: I hope not, but I'm afraid I agree with you. There is a time frame, a dynamic, and it would be useful to understand it. I think a great deal about this. I'm reasonably sure that fifty years from now, we will not be making nuclear weapons. It may be a hundred years from now, it may be a thousand years from now, but it doesn't matter. I try to imagine how the making of nuclear weapons will come to an end, and I ask what we can do to hasten it.

OMNI: What do you come up with?

SALK: In facing such a question, I project myself into the future and look back at myself and my fellow human beings in the present, and I say to myself, What is it that needs to be done now in order to bring about change much sooner? That's what I mean when I talk about conscious metabiological evolution. It means adding consciousness and choice, not allowing things to occur by chance. It means using foresight; it means not only feedback but also feed-forward, defined as a projection of our imagination.

OMNI: Yet if I look back from the future, as you've just suggested, I see a relatively powerless group protesting nuclear armament, and a powerful group building bombs, committing genocide, and deploying the MX, the Pershing, and a spate of other missiles. If I follow the process that you're talking about, I can't really imagine all of this coming to a halt without the insanity of it in some way being emphasized. And that sort of emphasis has to be a horrible thing.

SALK: You can see now why religions were based on implicit threats — the wrath of God, the consequences in this life, or the afterlife, of actions contrary to what was considered ethically and morally correct. The threat of nuclear war is, in a sense, equivalent to the holy wrath. In order for it to deter us, there needs to be a critical event, a critical mass, a moment of punctuation. Evolution proceeds gradually; then all of a sudden, a critical event of some sort occurs, for whatever the reason. Such an event has occurred.

As science and technology emerged out of the past, they gave rise to our capacity to develop more and more powerful weapons of destruction to gain some advantage over our enemies. What can we do with this weapon in order to gain some advantage? We ask that question in a moment of clarity, and we recognize that this weapon is useless, because its use would also be to our disadvantage.

OMNI: Well, some people realize that; other people say we can win a nuclear war, that we can gain an advantage. And those are the people who control the government now.

SALK: That's correct. Therefore, the rest of us must speak out. What I see manifest here are the pro- and the anti-evolutionary forces in metabiological evolution. I've come to the conclusion that the forces of evolution, both for and against, are poised and locked in this struggle, and the only way to survive is to evolve beyond the point at which we are now.

OMNI: How do we define the members of the two opposing groups, though? In biological evolution, there's a struggle between two species fighting for a niche in an ecosystem. Is there an analogy in the metabiological realm?

SALK: In the biological realm, two sets of genes — two separate species — are struggling to survive in a single ecosystem. In the metabiological realm we have struggling ideologies. One ideology is analogous to one set of genes; another ideology is analogous to another set of genes. And the two ideologies then attempt to dominate each other, to replace each other, to survive, to establish, to spread. Now, I say, Let's take the conflicts that exist and use them constructively to see if we can invent a way to convert the opposition to apposition. Perhaps we can resolve our differences. After all, we have reached a point at which it is to our mutual disadvantage to continue to proceed as we're proceeding. It is to our mutual disadvantage to spend huge sums of money on weapons to destroy ourselves, when that same money could be used constructively to improve the human condition.

OMNI: Yet when you start talking about one ideology being superior, and needing to engulf another in order for the species as a
whole to survive, you get into a kind of political problem. How far
can you go to perpetuate your ideology? Should you become an
evangelist? Should you form a Soviet utilitarian-type state? Should
you go to war? What are you paying to spread your ideology? Will
everyone perish if you don't spread it?

SALK: I'm convinced that we are impelled by an innate evolutionary force. We have an evolutionary instinct — not merely a survival
instinct — to improve the human condition. It's for this reason that
we are engaged in biomedical research; this is why we are trying to
understand how to manage our lives with the resources available.
We have come face to face with competing ways of improving the
conditions of life on the planet. We're competing for the minds of
people in the developing countries, for resources, and for economic
advantage. So this is a continuation of the process of biological
evolution in the metabiological realm, using metabiological tools,
which are those of the mind.

OMNI: There are two basic ideologies now warring for control of
the world: the communist ideology and the capitalist ideology. Yet
both groups promote nuclear weapons, and a lot of other anti-evolutionary things. The point may be to evolve totally new ideologies.

SALK: New strategies and new ideologies. We must recognize that
we are the victims, and that the process of evolution has pitted us
against each other. With our superior knowledge and intellect over
and above those of other species, we need to recognize that we are
going to have to do something about it. We are coming up against a
wall that we're going to have to get over or around, which means a
phase change. And we ourselves must influence the outcome. If we
don't, then we will go the way of the dinosaurs. But we should try
to do otherwise. That makes a more interesting game. Of course the
sun will become extinct three to five billion years from now. Of
course the cosmos is itself evolving, and this planet is going through
a life cycle.

Given all this, we may feel that conscious evolution is futile —
it's all going to end for us eventually, anyway. But we're not so
constituted; by our very nature we're not allowed to give up. And it's
for this reason that I invoke the idea of the evolutionary force acting
upon us, in us, through us.

I see more and more people concerned with conflict resolution, more and more people speaking out. I think that we're evolving rapidly in the metabiological realm; being in it, in the process of evolution itself, it's sometimes difficult for us to see. But inasmuch as I have the capacity to get outside myself into what I call outer time and outer space, and take a look down at where we are, I can recognize the existence of these movements and these trends. I'm simply trying to call attention to what I see, saying that these have evolutionary significance, and that the process of metabiological evolution is occurring at an accelerating rate. And I also say that the determinant in natural selection is human choice.

OMNI: Dr. Salk, when we've finally emerged, do you think we'll have the same physical form we do today? For instance, some scientists say that gene-splicing technology, a product of metabiological evolution, will be used to change the species *biologically.* Some researchers even believe recombinant DNA technology will help us increase life span, brain size, and intelligence.

SALK: I believe that if we wish to contribute to human evolution, we can do so more rapidly, more effectively, and more efficiently metabiologically than biologically. Even if a gene could be altered and then transferred to a number of individuals, you would still have to rely on the slow process of biological evolution to transform the species. For instance, scientists at the Salk Institute, in collaboration with others, created a giant mouse by transfer of genes for growth hormone. While this trait is transmissible to succeeding generations, it will be a slow process. We can induce metabiological evolution much more rapidly and efficiently because we can transmit changes via education and early experience. By training infants at birth and soon after, we can evoke different sets of characteristics — ones that are positive, constructive, and creative, rather than their opposites. It's not too different from agriculture, and that's why I use the term homoculture.

OMNI: Yet metabiological evolution does feed back into the biological realm.

SALK: Of course. The discovery of insulin has changed the gene pool with respect to the number of diabetics that survive. Control of malaria has increased the amount of sickle cell anemia in the world. There are many people alive today who would not have lived under conditions that prevailed when infection was rampant and physical prowess important. Now it's the mind that's important. This is why I talk about the survival of the wisest as distinct from survival of the fittest in the traditional tooth-and-claw sense.

OMNI: Many evolutionary scientists would view this new trend in a negative way. They'd say we're weakening the gene pool, and that the forces of metabiological evolution, which maintain all the defective physical forms, are actually *devolutionary*.

SALK: It's true that all this may be seen as the beginning of the end. But I see it as the beginning of a new beginning. Some individuals with physical impairments have fantastic minds. Take Stephen Hawking, the British physicist with amyotrophic lateral sclerosis. The longer he can be kept alive, the more he'll contribute to the metabiological gene pool, which is the pool of ideas.

I often think that if my own life had been curtailed after my earlier work was done, I would not now be synthesizing my experiences. We still have a great harvest to reap from individuals who will have lived over a longer life span, whose wisdom and experience can still be drawn upon. We have not yet recognized the great potential of the aging superstars. Some people look only at the negative, rather than the positive. The so-called weakening of the gene pool may be a price we are paying for a far greater advantage.

OMNI: You've essentially spawned a new philosophy that needs to be spread if it's to have an impact. Do you have any hope for your writings in this regard?

SALK: I hope they'll provide people with a way of seeing themselves in relation to others and the cosmos. It is in the nature of man to be curious about the so-called eternal questions. Since I've confronted these questions, I'm offering what has become apparent to me. My questions are similar to those that mystics and philosophers have always asked. But I think we may do a better job of answering them in the twentieth century, by merging the epistemology of human experience with the epistemology of science.

I do believe that my ideas will filter out. These things have a way of permeating the atmosphere. An idea gets into space, in one form or another, and reaches the eyes and the ears and eventually the mind. As I now write, my ideas are in a more abstract form, perhaps, than is useful to most people at the moment. I wish I could immediately transpose them from the abstract to the concrete. You're helping me to do this by teasing out examples of what I see in the abstract.

OMNI: The more we talk, the less abstract it all seems.

SALK: That's what I find happening when I talk to people this way. I've been asked many times how I'm going to communicate my ideas, and I say, through dialogue. They can be best understood when we're in the presence of each other, when we're close enough to make contact in all modalities — eye contact, ear contact, feeling, expression. It's like music or dancing. I *want* to communicate to you; you *want* to receive. And I want to receive from you what it is that you understand or don't understand, because I desire very much to communicate this understanding — not only to you, but to others. It's interesting for me to observe those who respond to my writings with great enthusiasm, those capable of comprehending them on a particular level. They are the ones who have evolved the receptors to recognize and react.

OMNI: What about less educated people around the world? How will you reach them?

SALK: I think it's most necessary to reach those who are active determinants of the evolutionary process — the thinkers, the writers, the artists, the scientists, the intellectuals, the teachers. We need to reach the leaders of the various belief systems, those who can influence others. We need to find an ecumenical way, a common way, of seeing the world. For me, the critical determinant of human evolution is the realm of human values — and that is a matter of education and choice.

Quest for Consciousness

Charting Joy and Sorrow
Candace Pert

Just as a person may totally understand a television set — can take it apart and put it back together again — but understand nothing about electromagnetic radiation, we may be able to study the brain as input-output: sensory input, behavior output. We make maps, but we should never confuse the map with the territory.

Visitors wander through a labyrinth of olive-drab corridors until they find the office with the name CANDACE PERT *and a child's drawing signed* VANESSA *posted on the door. Next door, rats slumber or scratch in their cages, dreaming of the day they can escape electrodes, syringes, and imperious gloved hands. Here at the Biological Psychiatry Branch of the National Institute of Mental Health (NIMH), in Bethesda, Maryland, the business is the mind: slices of cortex aglow with chemicals that, if you heed Candace Pert, contain all our joys and sorrows.*

In 1973, when Pert was a twenty-six-year-old pharmacology graduate student, working under Dr. Solomon Snyder at Johns Hopkins University, in Baltimore, she startled the neuroscience community with her discovery of the opiate receptor. A receptor is a site in the brain where molecules of a drug or naturally produced chemical fit like keys in a lock. The fact that the brain possesses receptors for morphine and heroin, Pert said, suggested that it must also produce its own version of these substances. And two years later the Scottish scientists John Hughes and Hans Kosterlitz discovered our body's natural opiates — the endorphins. A new era in neuroscience was born.

Photograph: Anthony Wolff

The discovery of the opiate receptor heaped instant renown on Pert and Snyder. Then, in 1978, Snyder, Hughes, and Kosterlitz received the Lasker Award, commonly considered to be a steppingstone to the Nobel Prize. Candace Pert did not. But she did soon find herself unwittingly famous, as the controversy over her exclusion from the award seeped out of the hushed chambers of dispassionate research into the streets of public opinion. The young graduate student's name began reverberating even in the sacred editorial pages of Science. The opinion of many informed researchers was that Dr. Pert had been denied her due.

Today, still reluctant to talk about the Lasker Award controversy, Pert has only cordial words for her former mentor. The opiate receptor may have been a cause célèbre, but she'd rather discuss her current work on the Valium receptor — which she flippantly refers to as the Hoffman–La Roche receptor — or the mysterious target sites in the brain where angel dust works its black magic. Her photographs of intricate brain-receptor patterns, illumined like so many inner galaxies, remind us of how little is known about the workings of the human mind. From where do our thoughts arise? How does the brain regulate behavior? Do our neurochemicals, like seasonings in a biological soup, make us sad or happy, psychotic or sane? Pert intends to find out. "I'm tinkering around inside the human computer," she has said. "People are just very complicated electronic mechanisms, and our emotions of love, hate, anger, and fear are wired into our brains."

A graduate of Bryn Mawr College, with a Ph.D. from Johns Hopkins, Pert now works at the NIMH right next door to her husband, Agu Pert, a behavioral psychologist. "I'm his biochemistry consultant, and he's my psychology consultant," she said. The couple live with their three children on one of Bethesda's tree-lined streets.

Judith Hooper interviewed Candace Pert in her lab and at home in 1981.

OMNI: Some people have compared the present explosion in neuroscience to the splitting of the atom. Do you think we're on the verge of a neuroscience revolution?

PERT: Yes. There used to be two systems of knowledge: hard science — chemistry, physics, biophysics — on the one hand, and, on the other, a system of knowledge that included ethology, psychology, and psychiatry. And now it's as if a lightning bolt had connected the two. It's all one system — neuroscience.

Behavior isn't such a mysterious thing. I think it emanates from microcircuits of electrons flowing from one neuron to another. What we're working on now is connecting up neurochemical facts — the brain's "juices" — with circuit diagrams of the brain. Circuit diagrams are what people called neuroanatomists have been concerned with for years — the actual connections between the neurons, the wiring of the brain. What's happening now is that we're learning which neural pathways secrete endorphins and which secrete other neurojuices.

There's no doubt in my mind that one day — and I don't think that day is all that far away — we'll be able to make a color-coded map of the brain. A color-coded wiring diagram, with blue for one neurochemical, red for another, and so on — that's the neuroscientist's ambition. We'll be able to describe the brain in mathematical, physical, neurochemical, and electrical terms, with all the rigor of a differential equation.

OMNI: Will such a diagram account for consciousness?

PERT: No, it won't. Just as a person may totally understand a television set — can take it apart and put it back together again — but understand nothing about electromagnetic radiation, we may be able to study the brain as input-output: sensory input, behavior output. We make maps, but we should never confuse the map with the territory. I've stopped seeing the brain as the end of the line. It's a receiver, an amplifier, a little, wet minireceiver for collective reality.

OMNI: In *The Doors of Perception*, the book Aldous Huxley wrote about his mescaline experiences, he theorized that the brain and the nervous system function as a "reducing valve," or filter, that enables us to experience only a fraction of "reality." Is brain research validating Huxley's theories?

PERT: Yes. Huxley's mind would be blown by neurochemistry. Our brain defines how much reality is let in. Reality is like a rainbow or like the electromagnetic spectrum. Each organism has evolved so as to be able to detect the electromagnetic energy that will be most useful for its survival. Each has its own window on reality. Humans can perceive the part of the color spectrum between infrared and ultraviolet. Bees can't see red at all. They can see up through several shades of purple. We cannot. In fact, our team at NIMH has proposed that the endorphins, our natural opiates, are a filtering mechanism in the brain. The opiate system selectively filters incoming information from every sense — sight, hearing, smell, taste, and touch — and blocks some of it from percolating up to higher levels of consciousness. Nobody really knows what the world looks like, as philosophers like Bishop Berkeley and David Hume observed. Everybody's version of the world is significantly different.

OMNI: While we're on the subject of the natural opiates, let me ask you about the discovery of the opiate receptor in 1973. You were a graduate student, but yours was the first name on the paper you published with Solomon Snyder. So I assume you did the actual lab work.

PERT: Yes. I was a graduate student in Dr. Snyder's laboratory at Hopkins. He was my mentor, and I have nothing but the fondest feelings for him. He's a brilliant and wonderful teacher. The importance of our work is that the opiate receptor was the first receptor ever found in the brain. But the opiate receptor turns out to be one of thirty or forty different receptors in the brain that can be detected by using the technique I developed. My method was to use radioactive compounds to bind to a drug. We just ground up the brain tissue and measured how much of various radioactive drugs "stuck" to various brain tissues. We found the sites to which the radioactive opiates attached. And that led to the discovery, in 1975, by Hughes and Kosterlitz, of our naturally produced opiates.

OMNI: Then Snyder, Hughes, and Kosterlitz were awarded the Lasker Award. Why were you excluded when you obviously did the seminal work?

PERT: That was a long time ago, and, to tell you the truth, I'm sick of being asked about the Lasker Award, as if I were a grumbling lady scientist who had done nothing else since then. I think there is other research for which I'm known. The politics of science is far less important, to my mind, than the core of scientific inquiry, which is the search for truth. That's the awe-inspiring part of it.

OMNI: Still, didn't you write to Mary Lasker, declining your invitation to the award ceremony? And isn't it true that you did not entirely "hold your tongue," as is expected of women, graduate students, and others low down in the scientific hierarchy?

PERT: Yes. I wrote to Mary Lasker at the time because I was not about to sit through a luncheon and be patted on the head. But I don't care to perpetuate an image of Candace Pert, Scarlet Lady of Neuroscience. I have no feud with Sol, whom I respect very much, and the discovery of the opiate receptor itself is, in a sense, ancient history. I'm now working on the angel dust receptor and the Valium receptor. Our brains probably have natural counterparts for just about any drug you can name. No one has yet actually found the brain's own marijuana, but I think that's because marijuana doesn't interact with the brain as THC [tetrahydrocannabinol], but as another breakdown product.

As far as women in science go, people have been analyzing the critical point at which women get stuck, and basically the problem is that they don't get those faculty positions which you must have to get grants. The female position is "postdoc for life" or research associate. Eighty-five percent of the American scientists who have been stuck at the level of research associate for twenty-five years or more are women. Research associates are Ph.D.s with a lot of responsibility who are never really the boss, calling the tune. On paper, you work for this excellent person who received grant money, but you're not good enough to be on the faculty yourself.

OMNI: It has been said that women hold themselves back by trying to please. Is that a stumbling block for women scientists?

PERT: Women scientists are women. Studies show that there's some hardwiring in that department; for example, women smile more than men do. I've observed it myself at meetings. In tense situations when important theoretical issues are being discussed, women smile a lot when they make their statements.

OMNI: Do you believe that all our behavior — even loftier emotions, such as altruism or romantic love — can be traced to biological phenomena? E. O. Wilson and other sociobiologists propose, for example, that thousands of years of natural selection have shaped our brains into highly refined survival instruments and that, at bottom, even the noblest sentiment is only survival instinct.

PERT: Well, many psychologists believe that there are only a few basic drives: sex, hunger, thirst, and escape from pain. They theorize that something more complex, say, the desire to discover a cure for cancer, can be traced back to a series of reinforcing events. Its source might be a very primitive feeling of well-being when your mother stroked your head and talked to you about medicine.

OMNI: How does brain chemistry work into the scheme?

PERT: Well, if you were designing a robot vehicle to walk into the future and survive, as God was when he was designing human beings, you'd wire it up so that the kinds of behavior that would ensure the survival of that species — sex and eating, for instance — are naturally reinforcing. Behavior is modifiable, and it is controlled by the anticipation of pain or pleasure, punishment or reward. And the anticipation of pain or pleasure has to be coded in the brain.

We're starting to understand that emotions have biochemical correlates. The brain is just a little box with emotions packed into it, primarily in the limbic system below the cortex — the old mammalian brain. Remember the experiments conducted in the 1950s, in which rats were given the chance to self-stimulate different parts of the limbic system by pushing a lever? They stimulated the pleasure center in the brain until they fell from exhaustion. Well, it turned out that the electrical stimulation caused the release of brain chemicals associated with pain or pleasure. The endorphins, for instance, are very pleasurable. Larry Stein, at the University of California at Irvine, has suggested that the natural opiates are the brain's own internal reward system. It seems that when humans engage in various activities, neurojuices associated either with pleasure or with pain are released.

OMNI: Do all animals have these reward and punishment chemicals?

PERT: Yes. Endorphins are being studied in the leech. Insects have endorphins and many of the other neurochemicals that regulate our own emotional circuitry. There's evidence that even unicellular organisms have these chemicals. I've always understood, theoretically, about the unity of life — that we're all composed of DNA molecules and protein. But I've never experienced that understanding as directly as I have in the last few years. I've been looking through the microscope at the brains of different mammals, and when you've seen one brain, you've seen them all: a cat brain, a dog brain, a monkey brain. We're all made up of the same building blocks, the same structures. A lot of the key work in neuroscience has been done on invertebrates like clams, spiders, crabs, octopuses, and leeches — creatures that are very primitive.

OMNI: Would we be anthropomorphizing to suppose that, say, cockroaches feel some sort of emotion?

PERT: No. They have to, because they have chemicals that put them in the mood to mate, and chemicals that make them run away when they're about to be killed. That's what emotions are often about — sex and violence. We humans are stuck with some sex-and-violence circuitry, but we have the intellectual ability to transcend our programming.

OMNI: Is there a schism these days between biologically oriented brain researchers like yourself and analytical psychiatrists who think free association and dream interpretation are the ultimate tools for understanding human behavior?

PERT: Yes. The present era in neuroscience is comparable to the time when Louis Pasteur first found that germs cause disease. Before that, disease had been attributed to demons, bad air, or an imbalance of the bodily humors. But do you think every doctor said, "Oh, it's bacteria; let me find out how to give those vaccinations that Louis Pasteur discovered"? It didn't happen that way. They were still bleeding people to cure infections. The old guard had to die out.

There are people who theorize that autism is caused by something like a father's not paying enough attention to a child and a mother's being a little too pushy. Yet there's scientific evidence that it may be associated with something as physical as the mother's bleeding during a certain month of pregnancy.

OMNI: With the advent of psychiatric drugs, our understanding and treatment of mental illness have become increasingly "biological," haven't they?

PERT: That's right.

Incredible shame is associated with mental illness. People will confide the most intimate details of their love life before they'll mention a relative who has had a serious mental breakdown. But the brain is just another organ. It's just a machine, and a machine can go wrong. One neurochemically coded system may have a kink in it. In the last twenty years psychiatry has come out of the Dark Ages. We know that many forms of mental illness are associated with an imbalance in brain chemicals, and we have drugs that are closely related to those chemicals to treat that imbalance. All psychiatric drugs work at the vulnerable part of the brain — the synapse [the point at which a nerve impulse passes from one nerve cell to another]

— where they mimic or block the brain's natural chemicals. But our drugs are still very crude. In fact, there are only three basic psychiatric drugs: neuroleptics like Thorazine for schizophrenia, antidepressants for depression, and lithium for manic-depressive illness. Similarly, when antibiotics were first being used, we had only sulfa drugs given for everything. Later, we had penicillin and other very specific drugs.

OMNI: In the year 2000 will we have recourse to the ampicillins and the tetracyclines of the mind?

PERT: Two thousand? Much sooner, I think. I had envisioned the impact our discovery of the opiate receptor would have on biochemistry and pharmacology, but I had no idea of its impact on psychology. The future of psychiatry will be totally changed. Our future treatment of mental illness will probably deal with receptors, which we now know are constantly fluctuating. With some receptors, the actual number of receptors decreases; with others, the actual number may not change, but the way the receptor is coupled to the neuron's membrane does.

Dr. William Bunney, here at NIMH, thinks that the waxing and waning of receptors is the key to understanding mental illness. He has found that some manic-depressives cycle between depression and mania every twenty-four hours. Every afternoon at four o'clock, say, they'll click sharply from depression to mania. It's called the switch. And there's only one cure: lithium. My husband, Agu, demonstrated that lithium stops the sharp oscillations and stabilizes the receptor for the neurochemical dopamine. There's evidence that the insulin receptors fluctuate in diabetes. Manic-depressive psychosis is like diabetes of the dopamine receptor.

OMNI: How will this knowledge transform psychiatry? What will a psychiatric consultation be like ten or fifteen years from now?

PERT: We'll do a "total receptor work-up" with a PET [Positron Emission Tomography] scan, which measures metabolic activity in various parts of the brain. We'll drop in a very selective drug with a radioactive isotope, which will "light up" the brain, and then we'll be able to get a three-dimensional look at the receptors — which areas are okay, which need tuning. We're going to have computerized maps of the brain — of all the different substances we know of and some we haven't yet discovered. One day we'll have each neurotransmitter on a separate floppy disc. We'll know the different distributions in the brain, and we'll find out a lot about what goes wrong. Then maybe the patient will be given a highly specific dose of, say, ten drugs that will straighten things out.

On the other hand, it's all in the mind anyway. Perhaps what this is telling us is that drugs can never be as subtle as our own neurochemicals, which can be released in one spot and not another. Drugs assault the whole brain at once. Who knows? The future psychiatric treatment may consist of autohypnosis, meditation, exercise, diet modification, and so on.

OMNI: Is it true that researchers are already looking into schizophrenics' brains with PET scans?

PERT: Yes. The technique is still in its infancy, but they're already finding startling differences between normal brains and those of schizophrenics. Parts of the front of schizophrenics' brains are dark on the scans, as if they were turned off.

OMNI: Do such drugs as heroin affect the sensitivity or the number of receptors?

PERT: Absolutely. Heroin bludgeons the opiate receptors into submission, functionally shrinking them. And there's evidence that the younger the brain, the more vulnerable its receptors are. If you give a pregnant rat one shot of Valium, for example, its babies will have half as many Valium receptors when they grow up. This raises frightening questions about current obstetrical practices. Babies whose mothers were given Demerol during pregnancy are affected by the drugs. For example, they fail to habituate to background noise as readily as normal babies do. There is hard evidence that this condition lasts at least two weeks. Whether it extends into adolescence is not known. And of course drugs are just analogs of our own internal chemicals anyway, and there's evidence that life events prompt the release of neurochemicals. So our experiences probably affect the distributions of receptors.

OMNI: What would Sigmund Freud say? Are his theories concerning the Oedipus complex, wish fulfillment, and repression now as antiquated as the concept of the geocentric universe?

PERT: There's nothing that Freud ever said that I can't relate to. Not only was he an incredible genius, but he was also the first psychopharmacologist. His treatise on cocaine, which he wrote before the turn of the century, was a masterly psychopharmacological paper. And of course he experimented with cocaine himself. He was interested in the underlying neuromechanisms of mental disorders. If he were alive today, he'd be a neuroscientist. Also, he was right about the unconscious. In studying the way the brain processes information, we've learned that much information never reaches the conscious mind. As incoming information travels from the senses up through higher and higher levels of the nervous system, it gets processed at each stage. Some is discarded; some is passed on to the higher regions of the brain. There's a filtering — a selection — based on emotional meaning, past experience, and so on. We think repression occurs at the synapse, where the message is either blocked or transmitted.

OMNI: Once we come up with highly refined maps of the brain, would you expect to find differences between the brains of men and those of women?

PERT: Well, at a certain level of consciousness it's very upsetting for a woman to think she's any different from a man. I went through that phase in the late sixties. I wore a lumberman's jacket and boots and really denied any differences between men and women except for the most obvious difference in sex organs. But of course you need a whole different brain circuitry to operate those different sex organs. So I think that in a few years we'll be able to look into the brains of a man and a woman and see differences. At Stanford, recently, researchers found an area in the rat brain that was bigger — it contained more neurons — in males. And wherever you have different neurons, those neurons are secreting different neurochemicals. So, yes, I think we'll be able to figure out the chemical coding for the differences between the sexes.

OMNI: But why should there be sex differences in the brain? Is it because evolution favored different characteristics in males and females?

PERT: Yes. Of course men and women have entirely different attitudes toward sex, and those attitudes are due to physiological differences in the brain. Men derive an evolutionary advantage from spreading their seed as much as possible. Women, on the other hand, need to choose a mate who will stay around and take care of them and their offspring. So I'd expect to find a part of the female brain that is devoted to making that kind of choice. Women are programmed to fall in love with whomever they make love with, no matter how ludicrous the person. As soon as they look into the eyes of their partner, they've had it. Men can act as if they're really in love, but it's a case of out of sight, out of mind. The brain doesn't know the Pill was invented. Women have been programmed since time immemorial to get that guy back to take care of any offspring that might ensue. After all, our mothers had babies, our grandmothers had babies; women alive today are the result of a long line of women who reproduced. When a woman chooses not to have children, it's a momentous decision, at odds with her programming.

OMNI: Would you expect to find a kind of mothering or nurturing circuitry in the female brain?

PERT: Definitely. The female brain was designed to enable a woman to teach another organism to survive. I think the reason that the X chromosome is bigger than the Y chromosome is that it takes much more information to produce a brain that can raise a baby to the point where it can survive than a brain that merely impregnates and runs. Evolutionary theories have made too much of the bands of cavemen working together to hunt down a bull, and they've forgotten the women back at the cave, who have chosen which men to mate with — and I do think it's a choice. Maybe when we look for the origins of language, we should look to the cavewomen communicating with their offspring and with one another.

OMNI: What about violence? Are men innately more aggressive than women?

PERT: Each sex has to grapple with its own programming, and I think the female program is easier to deal with. Women don't realize how much men have to struggle to control themselves. In their early teens, when testosterone starts to surge, young men feel angry. There is now a proven connection between violent behavior and elevated testosterone levels. A Y chromosome is a real cross to bear. It's a predisposition toward angry, violent, competitive, macho behavior.

OMNI: But is the male program evolving, in your opinion, now that communication and peaceful coexistence are more important survival skills than physical prowess?

PERT: Yes. There was an article in *Newsweek* about men like the late John Lennon staying home to take care of their children. We've come a long way. Men have gradually developed paternal feelings, and bit by bit the concept of monogamy has grown. So men are becoming more civilized. Someday they may be as civilized as women. The women's movement is also a sign that the female element is becoming respected by our society. It's a sign of the civilizing process of the evolution toward peace.

It's interesting that the main reason that many people oppose the Equal Rights Amendment is that they are threatened by the idea of women going into combat. Well, I think once you have women in the trenches, you'll have no more war. My feeling is that if there had been women in every trench during World War One, the women on both sides would have communicated with one another, and they all would have celebrated Christmas Eve together. Women are natural peacemakers. The Christian mythology is just a very elegant and complex metaphor about mother love. Mary stands for mother love, forgiveness, and compassion. Jesus understood that love was the key. "Love thy neighbor." "Blessed are the peacemakers." I always say it was great for God to send his only son, but I'm waiting for him to send his only daughter. Then things will really be great.

OMNI: You and your husband are both neuroscientists. Has your perspective on the brain influenced the way you raise your own children?

PERT: Well, people have said that any neuroscientist who is not a parent is at a serious disadvantage, because you're missing the opportunity to watch a little machine being programmed right before your eyes. When we were first married, my husband was a graduate student in learning theory, and we believed in John Watson. We believed that a child was a tabula rasa, that learning was everything. I can remember our son crying and my husband saying, "Is he diapered? Is he fed? Then everything is fine. Don't go in." We waited outside the door, and he fell asleep. We did it, we thought — brilliant, rational parents of the twentieth century, using behavioral principles. Then nine years later we had our little girl, and we couldn't do anything with her. She slept with us until she was five years old. So we've come to believe that the brain unfolds as a flower unfolds. Of course it's nice if the flower grows in a supportive environment, with rain, good soil, and sun.

OMNI: The size and structure of the human brain have remained unchanged for thousands of years. What do you think is the next step in evolution, if there is one?

PERT: Well, evolution has no purpose except to enable a species to reproduce and survive. Each creature is a finely evolved machine for that. Richard Dawkins, who wrote *The Selfish Gene*, says that a duck is basically a robot vehicle for the propagation of duck genes; a human being is a robot vehicle for the propagation of human genes. Yet somehow it seems to be requiring greater and greater intelligence for human genes to propagate. We're evolving toward perfect knowledge. Remember, all human beings alive today are the offspring of a long chain of ancestors, each of whom was smart enough to survive.

OMNI: Can the brain ever really understand the brain?

PERT: Yes, absolutely, in terms of matter — in Newtonian terms, if you like. Until recently I've visualized the brain in Newtonian terms. I've pictured the neurochemicals and their receptors as hard little locks, keys, and balls, like the drawings in textbooks. But now I've come to see the brain in terms of quantum mechanics — as a vibrating energy field, with all these balls, locks, and keys just being ways to perturb the field.

As I've said, the receptors aren't static locks; they're constantly oscillating and moving. It's like the difference between Newtonian and Einsteinian physics. I remember studying physics at Bryn Mawr and getting a glimmer of what "reality" is. I was just vibrating on the brink of experiencing everything as matter and energy. But you quickly return to your everyday consciousness. You can write equations about "Reality," with a capital R, but you think in Newtonian mechanical terms. Consciousness is before the brain, I think. A lot of people believe in life after death, and the brain may not be necessary to consciousness. Consciousness may be projected to different places. It's like trying to describe what happens when three people have an incredible conversation together. It's almost as if there were a fourth or fifth person there: the whole is greater than the sum of its parts.

OMNI: Einstein and other physicists have described experiencing an almost religious awe when contemplating the laws of the universe. Do you ever feel that way about the brain?

PERT: No. I don't feel an awe for the brain. I feel an awe for God. I see in the brain all the beauty of the universe and its order — constant signs of God's presence. I'm learning that the brain obeys all the physical laws of the universe. It's not anything special. And yet it's the most special thing in the universe. That's the paradox.

Holographic Brain
Karl Pribram

For the first time in three hundred years science is admitting
spiritual values into its explorations.

---

*Computers and monkeys seem to pervade Dr. Karl Pribram's office,
as they do his working life. While Stanford University undergraduates
cycle through the green-and-gold afternoon, Karl Pribram, the father
of the holographic brain, hunches over a computer terminal in his
office. A pensive, sad-eyed monkey gazes down from a framed portrait
on the wall, and a huge stuffed baboon — "my newest graduate
student" — squats in an armchair. Suddenly, his program disentan-
gled, Pribram leaps up, grinning, his expression evidence that the
uncharted vistas of the brain must be thrilling beyond compare.*

*When, in 1941, the Austrian-born Pribram — a twenty-two-year-
old Wunderkind on the brink of a neurosurgery residency — earned
his M.D. from the University of Chicago, the brain was still a shadowy,
mysterious organ. The young doctor's goal: to bridge the gap between
the minuscule firings of single brain cells and the enigma of
consciousness.*

*The chance came in 1946, when Pribram went to the Yerkes Lab-
oratories of Primate Biology, then in Orange Park, Florida, to work
under the tutelage of Karl Lashley, a physiological psychologist. (Pribram briefly became acting director of Yerkes after Lashley retired in
1956.) Lashley was cutting slices out of rats' brains to see whether he
could trace particular memories — memory traces, or engrams — to
particular parts of the cortex. But when his trained rats still performed
learned tasks with large amounts of their brain tissue removed, Lashley
put forth the unorthodox notion that memory is somehow distributed*

throughout the brain. Pribram, who joined Lashley in his quest for the engram in chimpanzee brains, would mull over the idea for more than twenty years before launching his own revolutionary theory.

Meanwhile, during a decade of pioneering laboratory research at Yale, Pribram's scalpel was probing the workings of a thousand monkey brains. Operating on living animals, he invented new surgical techniques to reach the deep core brain, a vast, silent terra incognita then ignorantly called the rhinecephalon, or primitive "smell brain." After he had made expeditions to such unfamiliar topographies as the amygdala and the hippocampus, the smell brain stood revealed as the nexus of emotion — the seat of love and hate now called the limbic system. By the time he moved to Stanford's Center for Advanced Studies, in 1958, Pribram had charted other neuroscientific New-foundlands as well. He had associated the inferior temporal cortex with vision, and the superior temporal cortex with hearing. In the heyday of lobotomies, his lab work proved that the frontal lobes, with their intimate links to limbic centers, were not some vestigal appendix to be cut as a routine psychiatric panacea. ("I nearly got kicked out of Yale for saying things like that," Pribram recalled, happy to have the last laugh.)

Not merely a virtuoso surgeon, Pribram was also formulating theories on the puzzles of perception and memory: how we recognize a familiar face; how a lifetime of memory is packed into an organ the size of a melon; how light waves travel from an object to the eye to the retina to the brain's visual cortex, thereby conjuring up an image. In 1960 came Plans and the Structure of Behavior, *coauthored by Pribram, George A. Miller, and Eugene Galanter. The book was a "Marseillaise" to psychology's coming cognitive revolution and a death knell of doom to behaviorism. Still later, Pribram began pondering classical puzzles: Where is such a thing as consciousness encoded in the brain? And is the "mind" contained within the physical organ, or is it something separate and soullike?*

By the late 1960s, the philosophical and the pragmatic had coalesced for Pribram into one of brain science's grandest and most controversial theories: Pribram's holographic model of the brain. What Pribram proposed, simply, is that the brain stores information in mathematical codes similar to those used in holography, the lensless photographic process invented by Dennis Gabor in 1947.

Unlike an ordinary photograph, which is a two-dimensional image of an object, a hologram is an eerily lifelike three-dimensional image formed by light. Its code, stored on film, doesn't look anything like the visual image, but is, instead, a record of the light-wave patterns scattered by the photographed object. Imagine dropping two pebbles into a pond and freezing the surface so that the overlapping ripples record the pebble's passage through a moment of time. So it is with a hologram. A beam of light energy — a laser, in most cases — is split in two, one part traveling directly to the holographic film as a reference beam while the other is first bounced off the object to be photographed. The two beams then collide on film, and it's the pattern of this collision that the hologram records. On the actual film all one can see is an apparently meaningless pattern of dark and light swirls. But when the film is illuminated by a reconstruction beam — that is, a laser beam identical with the original reference beam — a three-dimensional image of the photographed object results. It's as if the light waves formed by the object had been frozen in time on the holographic plate.

It is in much the same way, says Pribram, that memories and images may be stored in our brains. And just as many different holograms can be superimposed upon one another, so infinite images can be stacked inside our brains. Perhaps when we recall something particular, Pribram suggests, we're using a specific "reconstruction beam" to zoom in on a particular encoded memory.

Pribram also fixes on another quality of the hologram: it stores the same wave pattern across its entire surface, repeating it over and over. Should you drop and shatter a hologram and salvage only a fragment of the plate, you will have enough to reconstruct the entire image. Pribram feels that the brain's scattered code similarly allows memories to survive sometimes awesome brain damage. What we call "mind," he theorizes, may be stored in the physical brain as a sort of ghostly hologram — located everywhere and nowhere at the same time.

While some of Pribram's fellow brain researchers frankly regard his theory as wild, few would deny the grandeur and brilliance of the model. No less would be expected from this wiry, gentle-voiced, sixty-two-year-old renaissance man, author of masterly books and articles on such diverse subjects as philosophy, Freudian theory, neurophysiology, and language.

Pribram has also made an unusual sacrifice for his science. In

1980, as the neuroscientist was examining the exploits of Washoe, the "talking chimp" at the University of Oklahoma, a trainer placed her meal nearby. The chimp, perhaps suspecting Pribram of threatening her food supply, suddenly raked the scientist's hand against the sharp bars of her cage, and he lost two thirds of a finger. But that has not stopped Dr. Pribram from performing delicate neurosurgery.

Karl Pribram was interviewed at his Stanford office by Judith Hooper.

OMNI: You're an interdisciplinary man in what is, of necessity, an interdisciplinary field: brain science. Here at Stanford, don't English and history majors sit cheek by jowel with the regular science jocks in your undergraduate neuropsychology course? That seems quite unusual.

PRIBRAM: Yes, I don't have any prerequisites, though it helps to have had some biology and perhaps a psychology course. I think we ought not to keep the science all to ourselves. We really should be teaching brain science in high school. When I've given lectures to high school students, they have no more trouble than my medical students across the way here.

I also had several business school students in my graduate course in cognitive neuropsychology this past year. Because they are studying the marketplace, they're interested in understanding the brain to find out why people have certain motivations. I found their viewpoints fascinating, because, back in the 1950s, I tried to apply economic theory to brain theory. The students' input refreshed an old interest of mine, culminating in the concept of a "cognitive commodity."

OMNI: What is a cognitive commodity?

PRIBRAM: It is something conceived by the brain of man, then actually constructed in the real world. For instance, when I look at my desk, my immediate perception is of a desk, not of pieces of wood or metal of certain colors and shapes. But our brains could not have been built to recognize desks, chairs, books, rugs, and other constructions of our culture. So all sorts of qualities like color, intensity, movement, shape, and so on must be processed and re-processed simultaneously. How can this be? We must be constructing our perceptions on the basis of our experiences.

But, in addition, we go out and construct "perceptions" in the world. We make tables and bicycles and musical instruments because we can perceive them in our mind's eye; we can conceive of them.

OMNI: In other words, just as the human brain constructs images out of sensory messages, it also projects its own thoughts as objects in the natural world.

PRIBRAM: Exactly. And that means we always have the mind available to us as a frontier. The brain operates in such a way that we can always construct new commodities. People are starving. There is a lot of grain growing, but not in the right places. So scientists at the University of California at Davis develop new kinds of grains that can grow in India. We don't have to paint ourselves in a corner and say, "Well, we've had it."

OMNI: You've referred to the brain as an organ that mediates between an organism and its environment. It's as if you can't conceive of mind existing in a vacuum, is that right?

PRIBRAM: Right. We can use the analogy of gravity. You can't dig into a mass and discover gravity, because it's not a thing. Just as gravity describes the relationship between masses, so, too, mind, consciousness and such terms refer to relationships between organisms and their environment. We won't find mind either by digging into the brain, as many neurophysiologists hope, or by searching its environment, as behaviorists attempt to do. That's a bit different from the way Sir John Eccles [1963 Nobel laureate in physiology and medicine] looks at the mind. He does seem to think of consciousness as everywhere, surrounding us.

OMNI: What is it about the human brain that gives it the enormous flexibility you've described?

PRIBRAM: A short answer is, I don't know. But there are some leads. In human brains, the ratio of cortex [gray matter] to basal ganglia [the very front end of the brain stem] has increased, accounting for consciousness and so on. And the computing power is greater than in other species, of course.

OMNI: Do you think of "consciousness" as something that animals possess, or is there a distinct consciousness that you and I have and that chimpanzees, for example, lack?

PRIBRAM: There are at least three different ways in which the word *consciousness* is used. First, we have states of consciousness, such as sleep or waking or coma, that can pertain to animals as well as humans. Then we use the term to speak of conscious or unconscious processes. If John is in a grouchy mood, you might refer to his "unconscious problems." But when a cat hisses, you don't say the cat's unconscious conflicts have determined its behavior. When we talk about conscious or unconscious processes in human beings, we're talking about degrees of self-awareness. Finally, in addition to the state and process definitions of consciousness, we've got the contents of consciousness — what we pay attention to.

OMNI: To what extent are nonhuman primates and other higher mammals capable of "self-consciousness," with an awareness of self as distinct from the outside world?

PRIBRAM: We've tried to test this. The usual test is the mirror test, in which you paint the animal's forehead and place it in front of a mirror. If it tries to rub the paint off, you know it's aware that the image is of itself. The major apes — gorillas, chimpanzees, and orangutans — do this, but the minor apes, such as gibbons, don't. It's an interesting cutoff. But I'm worried about the mirror test, because gibbons, which are very socially aware, fail it.

OMNI: Washoe has learned about 150 signs in American Sign Language, and, here at Stanford, Penny Patterson has trained a gorilla named Koko to communicate with such hand signals. Do you consider that language?

PRIBRAM: Koko can put together strings of three words. It is certainly communication, which is what Penny and Washoe's trainers, Allen and Beatrice Gardner, are interested in. Loads of communications pass, even between my dog and me. He wags his tail, and I know he's happy. What Koko and Washoe do isn't our kind of language, however; it lacks the rich syntax of human natural utterances. But it's marvelous communication. They can communicate more richly than monkeys and not as well as human beings. That's what evolution is all about.

OMNI: Reading of your experiments with primates, one is struck by what seems to be their very complex intelligence. For example, chimps that learned to trade poker chips for food developed a primitive economic system, hoarding chips and exchanging them among themselves. Yet you say there's a huge difference between chimpanzee and human intelligence. Is our intelligence unique?

PRIBRAM: Of course it is. How many chimpanzees are sitting

across from each other, interviewing each other, recording the interview on tape, transcribing it into a manuscript? I'm tempted to say that humans are as different from nonhuman primates as mammals are from other vertebrates. We're not unique in possessing intelligence, but our kind of intelligence is very, very different.

OMNI: I take it you wouldn't agree with John Lilly's ideas that porpoises may be as intelligent as we?

PRIBRAM: How does one measure "intelligence" across species? I was down in Florida, working with porpoises and whales, and our team was trying to get electrical recordings from porpoise brains. We ran into some problems in anesthetizing dolphins for surgery, and because I heard Lilly had been thinking about these problems, I invited him to come down. He joined us on the third or fourth expedition and got the brilliant idea of tape-recording porpoise vocalizations and then playing them back at half-speed. He found this fantastic richness of communication, most of it at frequencies above our hearing range.

In one sense, porpoises are smarter than we. They don't make wars. They swim around in a temperature-controlled environment. By the way, I did some testing a long time ago and showed that porpoises distinguish between Strauss's "Vienna Woods" waltz and all other Strauss waltzes. They had been fed to it. When I played other waltzes, they ignored me, but when I played "Vienna Woods," they started jumping around the platform.

OMNI: It was number one on the porpoise Top Forty?

PRIBRAM: Yes. Their auditory nerves are as big as my wrist, you know. And they have no olfactory sense at all — no smell. They live in a world very different from ours.

OMNI: You've often stated that language is a key aspect of our uniquely human intelligence.

PRIBRAM: Language is very important, especially if in our definition of language we include music, mathematics, and other languagelike systems. On the other hand, natural language has a special place. I remember reading about how Helen Keller learned her first word, the sign for water. She had sensations of cold running wetness on her hand, and suddenly she realized that this feeling was connected with the word *water*. For the first time she could distinguish between herself and the world. Immediately afterward she ran home and found a broken doll, and she realized she had broken it. She could separate subject from object — "I-broke-doll" — and take responsibility for her actions.

OMNI: Before language, Helen Keller seemed to live in a continuous, undifferentiated present. Don't you need language to store experience, to have what John Eccles calls "continuity memory" — the sense of a continuous self?

PRIBRAM: Whatever produces language also produces that kind of memory. They seem to arise together, but continuity of self may not be a consequence of language. Language and feeling of self may both stem from some underlying source.

OMNI: Is the human being specialized to produce language, or was language an accidental by-product that, once developed, structured the brain in certain ways?

PRIBRAM: I think it goes both ways. You know, if you're born without a limb, there's no representation of that limb in the part of the cortex that ordinarily controls the limb. Other areas of the body take over. If that part of the brain is electrically stimulated, you activate the feeling not of a phantom limb, but of some other part of the body.

OMNI: You've devoted much of your career in neurophysiology to figuring out precisely how our brains construct what you call a "World Out There" and a "World Within." That is, our sense receptors distinguish between a Cuisinart that is over there in space and a remembered or imagined Cuisinart. How do we distinguish between the two?

PRIBRAM: Well, this question calls to mind the psychologist William James's ideas about self-consciousness. By selectively attending to our bodies' distant senses, we make a distinction between ourselves and the outside world. When we don't make these distinctions, as in an oceanic experience, we are back to Keller's initial state. There seems to be a stage in an infant's development before he clearly differentiates between "Mommy" and "me."

I once participated in a series of experiments performed by George von Bekesy, of Harvard University, to show how we locate an object out in space. If two small vibrators are placed symmetrically on two of your fingers, you will experience the sensation caused by the vibrators as jumping back and forth for a while, then as existing between the fingers. In the case where I was involved, von Bekesy strapped one set of vibrators on my right arm and another on my left. I felt a spot over there, and it would jump back and forth. Suddenly, after about half an hour, I said, "What did you do?" He said, "I haven't done anything. What did you feel?" And he had this odd grin on his face. I said, "It's out there." I could feel a solid object in front of me, between my arms!

OMNI: Then it's no accident that we have two symmetrically placed ears, eyes, and so on with which to perceive the outer world?

PRIBRAM: Right. Now, I'm not saying the world out there is an illusion. I am confident that this table and this chair exist. But the kind of mathematical process that von Bekesy simulated with his vibrators is basic to how our brains construct our image of a world out there. I say "construct," because the perception of so-called hard reality isn't really as immediate and direct as it seems, but rather, the end result of a complex coding operation.

OMNI: How does the brain represent the World Within, the subjective realm?

PRIBRAM: Whenever you're experiencing an emotion — when you're scared or ecstatically in love or whatever — all kinds of visceral-autonomic changes take place in your body. All these metabolic and endocrine happenings in your body become represented in the brain's core by receptors for sex hormones, blood-sugar levels, temperature, and other functions. Just as your perceptual systems enable the brain to make maps of the outer world, input from within your body allows your brain to construct an inner world.

We react emotionally whenever there is a discrepancy between the "map" we've established over a long time and what our body chemistry and autonomic nervous system — heart rate, blood pressure, and so forth — are telling us now. We have an alerting mechanism, an autonomic charge, when we notice something novel. But of course it can't be novel unless there is something familiar with which to compare it. Patrick Bateson, of the zoology department at Cambridge University, has shown that animals build familiarities in an environment, and when something different happens, imprinting occurs. He had chicks in a cage in which they were exposed only to vertical stripes. As a result, the chicks ceased to respond to vertical stimuli. He showed them horizontal stripes, and wow! They followed anything with horizontal stripes.

OMNI: Presumably, we humans are vulnerable to imprinting, too?

PRIBRAM: We are. We fall in love. The autonomic charge comes with novelty within the framework of the familiar — the young lady who resembles, and yet is so different from, our mother, for example.

OMNI: Don't we habituate to novelty? Doesn't the response fade?

PRIBRAM: Oh, yes, it works only for so long. That's the problem with marriage. You just get more jaded in all your tastes; you've got to have more refinement. Less and less is novel. Or, let's say, the novelty is more and more subtle, because you've got a larger and larger store of familiarity against which to match incoming impressions.

OMNI: You've written about certain kinds of epilepsy and other brain disturbances that in some respects mimic transcendent experiences. What happens then to the World Out There and the World Within?

PRIBRAM: Abnormalities in the limbic system, the brain's center of emotion, can produce alternate states of consciousness. Patients with lesions in that area have feelings of *déjà vu* and *jamais vu*, when the unfamiliar seems familiar and the familiar, strange.

In transcendent states the distinction between what is most familiar, the self, and the unfamiliar "other" disappears. As we saw in the case of Helen Keller, the distinction isn't there originally. Once the distinction is made, it's there. Then, in states of consciousness best described in Eastern mystical philosophy, self and other merge once more. This is consciousness without content, oceanic consciousness. It could be that the techniques of yoga and Zen have manipulated the neurochemistry of systems related to the limbic brain.

OMNI: Presumably you've witnessed such cases during the course of your career?

PRIBRAM: Yes. I once knew a very nice and intelligent lady who worked as a psychologist at Napa State Hospital, here in California. I was lecturing there. One day she mentioned that she was going to a party that night. When I saw her a week later, I asked her about the party, and she said, "Oh, I never got there. I was tired and fell asleep." Later in the day someone else happened to mention the party and asked her whether she had enjoyed it. She said, "I didn't go." The other person replied, "But you were there. You seemed to be having a good time, even though you seemed a little phased out. I thought maybe you'd had a little too much to drink."

The lady had a type of epilepsy. She remembered going to her room and nothing after that. So she assumed she'd dropped off to sleep. Actually, she'd gotten dressed, gone to the party, had a good time, and returned home. But all that never became part of her familiar-continuous self.

OMNI: That's fascinating. The question is, who was experiencing the party?

PRIBRAM: I don't know. Perhaps the "self" is a particular code. Unless our experience is translated into that code, it stays outside of what we recall as our experience.

OMNI: And you get what is known as "automatism," when someone acts as if on automatic pilot.

PRIBRAM: Yes. No doubt you know the famous case of H.M., who had severe epilepsy and whose temporal lobes were operated upon in 1953. I happened to see him after his operation. He was, I think, about twenty-eight years old. I asked him about his life, his marriage, and so forth. He said everything was essentially the same. Then we started talking about a trip to Africa that he had planned. He got all excited, because I knew the areas he planned to visit. Then I gave him some learning tasks, simple things to recall, such as telephone numbers, and he did very well. I was called out of the room to answer the phone. When I came back, I asked, "Where were we? Do you recall the numbers I gave you?" Neither of us remembered. I was about to ask more questions when he suddenly asked, "Have you been in here before?" I'd been gone about five minutes, but the interruption had diverted the stream of familiarity.

OMNI: I think that would interfere with one's normal emotional life. What if you were in love with someone one moment and forgot the person's existence the next?

PRIBRAM: I've known some people like that. Actually, H.M. functioned, more or less, although not too well. He pinned lists to himself — grocery lists, places he was supposed to go, and so on. But he couldn't plan anything.

The problem is one of coding. British researchers have found that if you give such a patient a list of words to remember, then imbed that list in another list and ask him which words he has seen before, he'll say, "I don't remember." But when you get him to memorize additional lists, he'll make intrusion errors: some of the words he's been shown in the first list will show up as wrong answers. That means the traces of the words have been stored in the brain somewhere, but they are not accessible to retrieval.

Yet retrieval per se isn't the problem, because the patient can retrieve everything that happened before surgery. Thus, it seems that current input isn't coded appropriately so that it can be retrieved. I think we haven't paid enough attention to the fact that the brain must code and recode everything over and over again. We change. You aren't the same person you were five years ago.

OMNI: The subject of coding brings us to some crucial paradoxes about memory that eventually led you to propose your holographic model of the brain. Did these ideas begin to take shape while you worked with Karl Lashley?

PRIBRAM: Yes. I worked with Lashley at Yerkes back in the 1940s. He'd been making lesions in rat brains, looking for the engram, or memory trace. Since he could destroy a good deal of cortex without disturbing the rats' behavior very much, it looked as if there wasn't a good one-to-one correspondence between a particular memory and a particular part of the cortex. And of course people who have a stroke or who suffer other brain damage don't lose part of their memory stores. So we know the memory store must be a distributed store. But we must make a crucial distinction. The memory store — the storage system — is distributed, but the retrieval mechanisms are not; they are highly localized. I can retrieve something by rereading it, hearing it again, talking about it, or writing about it, and all these mechanisms can be separately damaged by brain injury. They are all separate mechanisms.

OMNI: Did you join Lashley in his search for the elusive engram in rats' brains?

PRIBRAM: No. Based on his work on rats, Lashley was saying that there is no difference between different parts of the brain, at least when it comes to such higher functions as memory. Coming from human neurosurgery, I said to him, "We dropped the idea that these functions are all over the brain a century ago." But he showed me persuasive evidence that even in humans the situation was not as simple as I had believed. So we started a program on intermediate organisms — chimpanzees and monkeys.

Lashley had a genius for skepticism, for poking holes in all the myths that had grown up about how the brain works. His strength was that he was antitheory, or, as he said when I once confronted him with that thought, "No, I am not antitheory, only anti other people's theories." He felt that not only memory but perception also resulted from mechanisms we completely failed to understand. How is it, for instance, that when I view your face from different distances or different angles, I still perceive the same face?

OMNI: Does that mean memory and perception can't work like an ordinary photographic image, with a point-to-point correspondence between object and image?

PRIBRAM: Right. There can't be a single brain cell that says, "Bzzz-Judy's face" or "Bzzz-Judy's nose." Perception must be a very flexible sort of thing, not a pattern that's wired in.

In the mid-sixties, by which time Lashley was dead, I got interested in possible explanations of perception. The one thing that everyone believed in at the time was that feature detectors were its basis. That's the idea that each neuron responds to a particular feature of the sensory input — such as redness, greenness, verticality, and so on — and that these features are later combined to put together a whole image.

OMNI: The trouble is, that doesn't allow for a richness of perception, does it? And it raises the problem of how we can recognize new inventions, like tables, toasters, and so forth.

PRIBRAM: Correct. It would also mean that a new feature detector has to be used every time I get closer to, or farther away from, something, or when I look at it from another angle. But it's still the prevailing theory. Torsten Wiesel and David Hubel, of Harvard, were awarded the 1981 Nobel Prize in physiology and medicine for pioneering work that led to it, though, of course, they're not as naïve as some of the interpreters of their work.

Brain cells do selectively respond to features, but not uniquely so. The same cell responds to a color, a movement in a certain direction, the velocity of the movement, luminosity, and so on. Each cell is something like a person with many traits. So when you abstract blueness, you must address all the cells in the network that detect blue.

OMNI: When did you propose an alternative theory of perception?

PRIBRAM: I came up with an alternative in the mid-sixties to suggest that maybe Lashley was right, and the simple one feature–one cell notion was wrong. Sensory input addresses neuron networks, and patterns within that network constitute features. But one of the problems both Lashley and I had always had was, what constitutes these patterns? Then Nico Spinelli, working with me here at Stanford, found an old article in *Scientific American* that Eccles had written before he got the Nobel Prize. In it, Eccles said, "I've been looking at synapses all my life, and I've been able to look at them only one at a time. But synaptic events always occur together; many synapses are activated simultaneously in a pattern."

Of course I kicked myself. We'd been puzzling about this for a decade, and Eccles just sort of dropped it as an aside.

OMNI: Could you explain exactly what it is that makes up these patterns in the brain?

PRIBRAM: The changes in electrical potential at the fine branches of nerve endings. If you look at a whole series of these synaptic events together, they constitute a wavefront. Each wavefront sort of lines up [like the water molecules that make up a wave traveling the ocean]. One comes in this way, another that way, and they interact.

OMNI: This realization led you to propose that the brain, like the hologram, stored information in the form of interference patterns, patterns of interacting waves similar to those formed when light beams, or ripples in a lake, collide. This sort of model seems to solve several perplexing problems: the fact that memory is distributed; the fact that I can recognize a face regardless of angle and distance; the fact that a whole universe of memories and perceptions can be housed in the same group of cells.

PRIBRAM: Correct. Radio and television programs are carried by waves and are then transformed into complex auditory and visual images. If you took a cross-section of the airwaves at any moment in time, the cross-section would resemble a hologram. To decode it, you need a radio or TV receiver. Our senses feed information into such receivers.

Now you might ask, why doesn't the brain simply print an image, as in photography? A holographlike code automatically takes care of imaging from different distances and angles. The problem of grain is solved; you can have very fine-grained textures. And perhaps most important, if you're looking at, say, a table, you'll know the table's color, texture, dimensions, luminosity, distance, and that table's relation to all other tables you've seen.

OMNI: Therefore, if I used an imaginary instrument to peer into your brain and see your neurons firing and so on, I couldn't see what you saw or felt, because that exists in code, doesn't it?

PRIBRAM: A holographlike code. I use the word *hologram* here not to designate optical engineering devices, but rather the mathematical formulas on which they are based.

OMNI: I'm a little puzzled by one thing. When I first read about the holographic brain, I thought of it as a metaphor. Then I began to think you meant it as an actual model. Which is correct?

PRIBRAM: Both. First it was a metaphor. Then, starting with my book *Language of the Brain* [1971], a model developed, because the mathematics fitted the data gathered in several laboratories around the world. There are no laser beams in the brain. I'm simply saying that the brain performs certain operations, coding and decoding sensory input, that can be described by the same mathematics that define the hologram.

OMNI: Haven't you proposed the idea that spiritual reality lies in the holographic domain, and that there may be ways to gain access to it in the brain?

PRIBRAM: Yes, it would be a matter of abrogating our retrieval systems; that is, getting rid of our senses so that we could experience only the interference patterns themselves. What would that look like? Ask the mystics, though they have trouble describing it. But the purpose of science is to make sense of the world, and mystical experience makes sense when one can provide the mathematical formulas that take one back and forth between the ordinary world, or "image-object" domain, and the "frequency" [or interference-pattern] domain. The frequency domain is "mystical" in that there is no space and no time. Our brains apparently can jump back and forth between space-time reality and the frequency reality, or perhaps they always keep track of both worlds at once.

OMNI: The holographic brain theory is attractive to parapsychologists, as well as to psychologists of the Gestalt school, because it could account for psychic phenomena. Do you believe that extrasensory perception may occur in the frequency domain, beyond the senses?

PRIBRAM: Well, people have invoked the idea for ESP, and to some extent I would go along with it. I don't know whether psychic phenomena occur or not, but at least there's a basis for understanding them if they do.

OMNI: I was interested in your comment that the world may be a hologram, and that perhaps the individual brain is a part that contains the whole. Of course the idea that the *atman,* or soul, in all creatures is a record of the universal atman is basic to Oriental mysticism.

PRIBRAM: The world is not a hologram. It can, however, be described or modeled by a hologram. But the hologram principle is working everywhere, and descriptions of spiritual experiences sound holographic. The holographic domain is holistic in a different sense from the Gestalt use of the word. In Gestalt, the whole is greater than, and different from, the sum of its parts, whereas in a hologram, every part is distributed in the whole, and the whole is enfolded in its parts. David Bohm [professor of theoretical physics at Birkbeck College of the University of London, and author of *Wholeness and the Implicate Order*] has derived the same idea from quantum physics, and it leads to a scientific understanding of the spiritual aspects of man's experience. For the first time in three hundred years science is admitting spiritual values into its explorations. That's terribly important. If you deny the spiritual part of man's nature, you end up with atom bombs, a technocracy devoid of humanity.

OMNI: Do your colleagues in neuroscience consider your holographic brain theory to be soft, or heretical?

PRIBRAM: The hard-nosed scientists don't understand, I think, and they feel I've overgeneralized, which I haven't. The exceptions are physicists, engineers, radar scientists, and crystallographers, who are trained to make mathematical models of what they observe. My ideas aren't so foreign, either, to the people who invented the CAT scan (a computerized, three-dimensional, x ray of the body) and image-makers in general.

OMNI: What has the holographic model suggested to you about the ancient riddle of the mind-brain relationship? It seems to me you're suggesting that just as you can't physically locate the image anywhere on the holographic film, you can't really locate the mind in the brain. Can you express that better than I just have?

PRIBRAM: I think you've expressed it very well. Mind isn't located in a place. What we have is holographlike machinery that turns out images, which we perceive as existing somewhere outside the machine that produces them. We know our eyes are involved, but I don't image you on the surface of my retina. Even though the codes are in my brain somewhere, I perceive you over there on the chair.

OMNI: One problem that has beset mind-brain theorists is the precise liaison between mind and brain; that is, where exactly does a nonphysical mind, or soul, connect with the physical organ?

PRIBRAM: That is true. The problem for all of us has been one of downward causation. How mental properties emerge from the brain organization is easy to see. But then, as Roger Sperry [the California Institute of Technology neuroscientist whose split-brain research earned him a Nobel Prize in 1981] says, mind has to turn around and operate on the brain. But Sperry hasn't specified how this happens. Eccles proposed the same idea and once suggested that mind operates as a "cognitive caress" on the brain's association areas, the parts of the brain not devoted to sensorimotor systems.

Eccles wrote a book with the philosopher Sir Karl Popper, entitled *The Self and Its Brain*, in 1977. If you read the book carefully, you see that Popper and Eccles had some very different ideas about that dualism [the idea that the mind is separate from the brain]. What Popper says is that we create artifacts in our environment — books and so on — which he calls "World Three." Then we read these books, and this programs our brain and forms memory traces, which in turn form new behaviors that result in new books and other artifacts, and so on. I have no basic quarrel with Popper, though I prefer the term "cognitive commodity" to World Three.

OMNI: How exactly do you think the mind acts on a physical system?

PRIBRAM: Think of water, composed of molecules of gas, hydrogen, and oxygen. You put these molecules together in a certain way, and you get water. The emergent properties of water are wetness and the fact that it floats when it freezes and vaporizes when it boils. The wetness of water and the fact that it floats when it freezes have allowed it to accumulate on the earth in oceans, glaciers, and polar icecaps. The emergent properties of water have moved the molecules from being evenly distributed in the air and on the earth's surface to being concentrated in pits called oceans; the emergent properties have changed the distribution of hydrogen and oxygen on our planet.

Now let's apply this analogy to the mind problem. As mental beings, we have the feeling of freedom under certain conditions. That feeling of freedom, that mental property, has emerged from our particular brain, from the organization of its molecules, cells, and so on. And it changes the distribution of human beings on the earth.

People want to leave Communist countries and come to the "free world." People strive toward frontiers or into outer space. The point is, a mental property, the feeling of freedom, changes the distribution of people throughout the world.

OMNI: To extend that idea, hasn't neuroscience shown that mental experiences actually affect our brain's chemical and physical structure?

PRIBRAM: It's tricky, but one can say that you redistribute the flow of nerve impulses on the basis of ideas as well as sensory input. When you look at something over and over again, you begin to recognize it; it becomes differentiated, detailed. Though there's no direct evidence yet, I'm quite sure the same is true of thoughts. If I think and rethink something, I must be changing the patterns of neural processing.

OMNI: Maybe this is the neurophysiological basis for the way mental habits become lodged in us. Maybe something like psychoanalysis, which is a mental activity, influences the brain's physical structure by reprogramming one's thoughts.

PRIBRAM: Freud not only suggested that, but he drew a diagram that resembles what we now recognize as a nerve net. It looks like a little, hierarchically organized nerve network, and it appears in his *Project for a Scientific Psychology,* in a section on thinking. Instead of making new connections in an overriding way, as we would by behaving in a certain manner, Freud wrote, thinking makes miniconnections. It's like what happens when I go out in the world and build a table: if I make a mistake, I must take the table apart and do it over completely. However, if I plan it out in my mind or draw a diagram, I see my errors before they're irrevocably embodied, and I gain flexibility. By the way, it's possible to see Freud's metapsychology as an early neuropsychology, but that part of Freud's theorizing is not well known to experimental psychologists and neuroscientists.

I delivered the Freud Memorial Lectures at the University of London last year on the one-hundredth anniversary of Freud's receiving his medical degree from the University of Vienna. And I said that at least Freud had in mind the problems we're still worrying about in current neuropsychology. He had his solutions and his model. In some places his model is correct; in others it's dead wrong. But at least it's a model. It isn't a bunch of abstractions, which is what metapsychology has become. If we go back to its roots, we can straighten things out.

OMNI: That suggests that the current gap between analytical psychiatrists and neuropsychologists such as yourself is built on a false premise. It didn't have to exist.

PRIBRAM: Yes. And, you know, everyone came to my London lectures except the older, dyed-in-the-wool analysts, even though they had invited me to speak. They boycotted the talk because the subject was biology; they couldn't relate to it.

OMNI: Though you were trained in the methods of behaviorist, stimulus-response psychology, you speak quite a different tongue. And you once predicted that the "soft sciences" of today may form the core of the hard sciences fifteen years from now. Can you explain that?

PRIBRAM: Back in the 1940s and 1950s, the behaviorists thought they were the hard scientists. They dominated psychology, basing their work on good, hard science, with an impressive technology.

The problem with behaviorism was that words like *awareness* and *consciousness*, even *perception*, were taboo. Let me give you an example of why psychologists can't neglect awareness. Lawrence Weiskrantz, of Oxford, and Elizabeth Warrington, of the National Hospital, in London, have described patients with blind sight: an operation on one side of the brain's visual cortex has made them blind in the opposite visual field. It turns out they'll be 80 or 90 percent accurate in pointing to, and describing, shapes in the blind visual field. But when you ask them what they saw, they say, "Nothing." They were "guessing." So some of the parts of the brain are working, but the parts that generate reflective awareness have been removed surgically. When a blind-sight patient sees something and tells me he can't see, that makes me think there are two levels of seeing: one that consists of instrumental behavioral responses to optical information, and another that refers to subjective awareness.

It is extremely awkward to try to account for everything by looking at inputs and outputs alone, and eventually the attempt to build a psychology without talking about states and processes like awareness fell apart. You can't even sell books without using subjective terms. If B. F. Skinner had called his book *Conditioned-Operant FIs* [Fixed Intervals] *and VIs* [Variable Intervals], how many books would he have sold? But *Beyond Freedom and Dignity* — wow!

Through the Looking Glass

Albert Hofmann

I think the insight that many people got from LSD is that the Creator exists. If you see the wonder of creation, it seems impossible that it was produced by accident. There must be something spiritual behind it, something we name God.

On a gentle spring day in 1943 Dr. Albert Hofmann, an eminent research scientist working in his laboratory at the Swiss pharmaceutical firm Sandoz, Ltd., was stunned by the unimaginable: a passage to another world. But the terra nova that Dr. Hofmann discovered was within himself. And the route to it was a fickle, obscure-sounding compound called lysergic acid diethylamide, which neither he nor anyone else suspected as a trap door to the self's secret chambers.

It was the hope of lifesaving medicines, not artificial paradise, that prompted Hofmann to turn to the study of the alkaloids of ergot, a parasitic grain fungus, or rust, in the early 1930s. The common nucleus of these substances had been baptized "lysergic acid." By isolating and synthesizing lysergic acid derivatives, Hofmann had developed the basis of crucial drugs for controlling the bleeding that follows birth, as well as for aiding in cerebral and circulatory disorders. But in 1938, one compound remained perplexing: LSD-25. Something about the drug drew the chemist back to it five years later.

As it happened, he accidentally absorbed some of it through his skin, and the peculiar genie of LSD-25 stepped forth, unbidden, in a daydream Hofmann knew he shouldn't be having. This was man's first acid trip. Subsequent experiments by Hofmann and his Sandoz colleagues confirmed that the substance had the awesome power to shift the perceptions of the mind.

Photograph: Henner Prefi

But nothing Hofmann learned from his experimental illuminations with LSD, psilocybin, and other hallucinogens could have prepared him for what happened next. In 1963 he received a request from a Harvard lecturer named Timothy Leary for three and a half million doses of LSD and psilocybin. Though the request was denied, news of the chemist's discovery had by this time spilled into the streets. The result was a decade of chemical heavens and hells.

How did the psychedelics he fathered forty years ago affect his own life — and Western culture? Hofmann tried to answer that question when he spoke with David Monagan in 1981, soon after the publication of his book LSD: My Problem Child.

OMNI: Many people may be puzzled that you would write a book about LSD now, almost forty years after you discovered it and a decade after its use, and presumably interest in it, peaked.

HOFMANN: As a scientist, I was trained to make experiments first and describe the results afterward. The 1960s were really a cultural experiment with LSD. I waited to watch how it would all turn out, how it would end, how attitudes would evolve. My book is a discussion of that experiment.

OMNI: Looking back, many people see Timothy Leary as the personification of the LSD culture. You corresponded with him in the sixties and met him in Switzerland in 1971 and 1973. As the "Father of LSD," did you consider him your most charismatic disciple, or were you wary of him?

HOFMANN: I never could make out what he really intended. I had the feeling he was naïve: he was so enthusiastic about LSD that he wanted to give it to everyone, even to very young people. I told him, "No, give it only to people who are prepared for it, who have strong, stable psychic structures. Don't give it to young people." He said that American teen-agers are so experienced that they are like grownups in Europe.

We did not agree about this at all. I had the same argument with my friend Rudolf Gelpke, the Islamic scholar and drug researcher. He told all his friends, "You must take LSD." I never said that everyone should take it. If someone asked me, I told him exactly what LSD does, and I left it up to him to judge whether to take it. And I think that's the point of my writing this book.

OMNI: Could you tell us what the first moment was like, when you discovered the psychotropic effects of LSD-25?

HOFMANN: While working on ergot alkaloids in 1938, I first synthesized lysergic acid diethylamide, but it didn't seem to produce any psychic effects when it was tested on lower animals. Only in working with the substance again, one day in 1943, when I somehow began to have this daydreamlike but not disagreeable experience, did I discover it in my own body. Because I knew I hadn't ingested anything [it had been absorbed through his skin], I realized that the substance involved must be very, very active. I was determined to get to the bottom of it, and three days later I arranged to take what I believed to be a very weak dose — 0.25 milligram.

After about half an hour the effects started. I tried to take notes in my laboratory journal, but after a few pages I realized I couldn't write anymore. Everything started to change, so I said to my assistant, "Let's go home. This won't be so easy after all." Automobile use was restricted during the war, so we started home on our bicycles.

OMNI: Thus the story about the drug-crazed Dr. Hofmann pedaling madly through the streets of Basel.

HOFMANN: Yes. I kept pedaling harder and harder, and I thought I was locked in one spot. Finally, I got home, and everything had changed, had become terrifying. My neighbor came in and looked like a horrible witch; my assistant's features grew twisted. I became very anxious, because I didn't know whether I would be able to come back from this strange world. Because it was the first time . . . .

OMNI: Did you feel that you had left this world altogether? Or did you know anything that would help you explain it; did you have any knowledge of mescaline or of crazed visions suffered by people in the Middle Ages who happened to eat ergot fungus on their bread?

HOFMANN: I knew nothing about mescaline then, and, though I had heard about hallucinations and nervous disorders associated with ergot, nothing I had read could have prepared me for what I began seeing. The symptoms increased terribly, until I lost all sensations of my body. I had the feeling that I was already dead, that my heartbeat had stopped, that I was completely out of my body.

It was a terrifying experience, because there were my children and my wife to consider. But even while that was happening, I realized I had just made a very important discovery, because no known toxic substance in the world would have had any effect at all in such a small dosage. I was still able to think about that.

OMNI: Yours sounds more like a terrifying experience than an uplifting one.

HOFMANN: Yes, at first. But by the time the doctor got there, the horror had softened somewhat, and I was already starting to come back from the feeling that I had died. I started to see an endless variety of colors and even to enjoy them. I thought, *Yes, now you have come back to life*. It was beautiful to feel at home again, to feel that I could come back to our everyday world from the strange world where I had been.

I had the feeling that things had changed their meaning, and I watched with great happiness, a kind of rapture, as every sound — a car door closing or the doctor talking — was accompanied by a stream of corresponding colored images, abstract pictures. That night I had a good sleep and awoke the next day without any hangover.

OMNI: When you first reported such an unearthly experience, did any of your colleagues at Sandoz doubt the truth of what you were saying?

HOFMANN: Only with regard to the amount of the drug, because nothing then existed in pharmacology with effects at a fraction of a milligram. But then Professor Rothlin, the head of the pharmacological department, and two of his assistants decided to check it out by taking only about a fourth of what I had taken — 0.06 milligram. They too underwent impressive experiences.

OMNI: Then you and others at Sandoz followed with a series of controlled laboratory tests of LSD — tests you have said weren't very satisfactory. Why not?

HOFMANN: We used low doses — 0.05 milligram — in a controlled setting with interviewers, Rorschach tests, written explanations of what we were going through. These weren't especially meaningful experiences, personally. I thought it would be more interesting to see how it would work in artistic surroundings.

OMNI: Did you feel that you not only had discovered a new area of scientific research but had also — through your personal experiments — opened a door into another world of individual experience?

HOFMANN: The whole thing started within my normal work as a chemist. Then I became interested in the matter of how reality, the existing world or one's experience of it, could be changed and broadened so completely.

I arranged to explore these things in a nonlaboratory setting in 1951 with the pharmacologist Herbert Knozett and the German novelist Ernst Jünger. I would say it was the first truly psychedelic experience, though what we took was a low dose and didn't go very deep. But it was beautiful. I believed I was in North Africa among the Berber tribes. I saw all these beautiful, exotic landscapes, oases, while a Mozart record played like music from above. However, it was not a religious experience.

OMNI: When did you have your first religious experience with LSD?

HOFMANN: Well, the very first time I had the feeling that I had left the world forever. It was frightening, but nonetheless a profound experience, because I was confronted with death and came back.

OMNI: Did your LSD experiences with Jünger advance your friendship to a higher plane?

HOFMANN: I think that our friendship over the last thirty years would have been deep even without LSD. We should have two lives — one in which we take LSD and one in which we don't — to prove what its effects really are. One will never know, but I think taking LSD was a very deep experience to have had together.

OMNI: In those early years did you think that you were playing with fire, or did you feel you had found something marvelous?

HOFMANN: My hopes for LSD were absolutely concentrated on the psychiatric field. From my own experience, I realized that LSD could be a useful agent in psychoanalysis and psychotherapy, that patients could leave their everyday, ordinary reality with it by getting out of their problems and into another sphere of consciousness. I also thought it could be important for brain research.

But my own LSD experiences had a touch of danger to them, and I never thought LSD would be used as a pleasure drug, as it was when it hit the drug scene in the United States in the 1950s. Apart from psychiatric use, I thought of LSD as being appropriate for an elite, you might say, for artists and writers and philosophers.

OMNI: But you were impressed by Aldous Huxley, who, while not advertising the drugs to the masses, remained very evangelistic about psychedelics?

HOFMANN: Yes, I felt closer to Huxley's point of view than to Leary's, but even Huxley believed in LSD's potential for a much broader public than I did. I had no contact with Huxley until 1961, when we had a beautiful meeting at the Sonnenberg Hotel, outside Zürich. We were together again a great deal at the World Academy of Arts and Sciences, in Stockholm, in 1963, but he was already suffering from cancer.

OMNI: Regardless of your own intentions, LSD use spread among perhaps millions of people in North America and Europe in the sixties, and more than a few of these people had intensely disruptive experiences. In your book you describe the many sadly confused and unstable hippies who made pilgrimages to your house in Switzerland. Did you ever regret your discovery and feel that you, like Einstein with the atom, had unwittingly created a monster?

HOFMANN: No. I can honestly say that I haven't, because I've always pointed out the dangers. The unstable people would have used something else, perhaps something worse, like heroin, if there had been no LSD. And the main point is that LSD was developed in the course of an investigation whose aim was to produce new medicines; it wasn't to produce a psychedelic. But I think the production of this psychedelic was very important.

OMNI: You say that you used LSD yourself, along with other hallucinogens, such as psilocybin and morning-glory seeds, about twenty times. Yet, like many others, you've stopped using them. Why?

HOFMANN: The last time I took LSD was in 1972 with Jünger. I think I got out of LSD all that it could do for me, and probably the same was true for many other people. It's really not LSD that produces deep effects. It can only stimulate what's in the person already. If there is nothing inside, nothing comes out.

OMNI: What about all the bad reactions?

HOFMANN: The surroundings, the setting, are very important. Much of the sixties' drug scene involved mindless, indiscriminate use in the wrong kinds of places, like bars, that led to all these bad accidents. Even in its medical and psychiatric use, the surroundings should be special, artistic, not just a laboratory or office setting.

OMNI: Do you think there was overuse, as well as misuse, of the drug in the sixties? The late John Lennon, for instance, was reported to have done LSD more than a thousand times.

HOFMANN: I don't see the reason for such repeated use. It's even destructive, because such a powerful experience should be respected — and worked out. When you use something habitually, its value is decreased.

OMNI: Leary and Richard Alpert, or Baba Ram Das, made pilgrimages to the East after taking LSD. Did "tasting of the lotus" tempt people to abandon this reality for an ever greater escape?

HOFMANN: I've never been able to understand these people. What I got out of LSD, I carry about inside me. I have to stay in my own daily life. To see the flowers in my own garden is to see all the mystical wonder of existence, of creation. You don't have to go to India to see it.

I think the insight that many people got from LSD is that the Creator exists. If you see the wonder of creation, it seems impossible that it was produced by accident. There must be something spiritual behind it, something we name God.

It is true that some people had negative experiences, too. You see, we always have this ambivalence, the experience of the good and the bad together. They are always connected and never separated.

OMNI: Someone once said that one thing LSD did was to give us back a sense of danger that had been effectively removed from our sanitized, middle-class life. Is there any truth to that?

HOFMANN: Yes. Everyday consciousness is a balancing on a very narrow line — a line that falls on either side into the abyss. It is a balance we need in order to exist. Otherwise the danger is that we become crazy. The LSD experience is schizophrenic to the extent that you simultaneously remember your ordinary reality and also see another reality, another world.

OMNI: What about the rumors of long-term physical damage from LSD?

HOFMANN: There's no evidence of lasting physical damage of any kind. The things that were said about chromosome damage, for example, were all based on isolated observations that later studies proved untrue.

OMNI: Did the LSD experience change enough people to affect society; that is, to become a social force? Do you think there is less passion for the unknown now than during the sixties?

HOFMANN: I believe that the revolution of consciousness some people experienced during the sixties will have an influence on them for the rest of their lives, whether they took LSD or didn't.

It is a crazier time now, but in a different way. In the sixties, there was a psychological revolution, a search for another reality. Now there is anxiety about the terrible things that could happen, fear of war and the destruction of nature, energy problems. These are more practical questions; the sixties had a more mystical component.

OMNI: Were you yourself changed? Did the chemicals you examined alter the chemist who created and synthesized them?

HOFMANN: As head of the department for natural-products research, I remained the experimental chemist in the laboratory, working on isolating the active principles of different plants for medicine. But through LSD I also became interested in mysticism and all the substances that affect the mind. Personally I have been changed, of course, especially in my conception of reality.

I realized that we have the choice to see things in different ways, that there is no such thing as an objective reality. We have the opportunity to choose a philosophical attitude corresponding to our personality. People may look at a grim aspect of reality and believe that it is the only true one, not knowing that they have the potential to alter their lives by looking at another aspect.

OMNI: But given the more rational state of mind that prevails in the eighties, what possibility is there that people will again seek to delve into their unconscious in order to explore these inner alternatives and potentials?

HOFMANN: I'm not sure how things will or should compare with the sixties, but interest in meditation, in getting behind this rational side to a deeper truth of things, has now become increasingly important. LSD can be used to help one make a breakthrough in meditation.

OMNI: How do you envision the future of LSD? Can a person still use it to leap through to another level of experience?

HOFMANN: Yes. I see it having an important role as an adjunct to meditation, and in psychoanalysis, brain research, and treatment of the terminally ill. The final goal of meditation is a visionary experience of reality, and some people who have meditated extensively may feel prepared to go a step further.

OMNI: Do you practice any particular type of meditation or espouse any technique?

HOFMANN: Everybody should do it in his own way. I begin with the knowledge that our human organism is made up of the same things, the same compounds, that are found in animals, plants, and all living matter around us. When I meditate, I feel united with nature and protected in it. The knowledge that we've gotten of reality from all our research in the natural sciences is really the myth of our time. We have to meditate on this knowledge in order to give it deeper meaning.

OMNI: What kind of meaning?

HOFMANN: We should experience the wonder of creation in our lives. I think that no one should be so deeply impressed by this as should a natural scientist, because if, as a chemist, I see a flower, I know all that is involved in synthesizing a flower's elements. And I know that even the fact that it exists is not something that is natural. It is a miracle.

How can a plant synthesize these elements all by itself? How can it create these unique colors and forms? These are the questions we always have to ask ourselves, and we will see that the existence of every single flower is a mystical happening. We now have such a wonderful scientific picture of the universe — we know about the stars and nebulae and all these fantastic things — and we should meditate on just these things.

OMNI: Do you believe in God?

HOFMANN: Of course. I believe in the Creator, and the Creator is God.

OMNI: Do you believe in an afterlife?

HOFMANN: Yes. I don't know in which form, but I believe that, as Goethe said, "Things cannot disappear; they can only change." Science has also established this, that nothing disappears completely. Matter is simply changed into new forms of energy. I believe this is true for the spirit, too.

OMNI: Isn't it extremely difficult for people living in cities, which you characterize as "dead," to have this religious experience?

HOFMANN: Yes, it's an immense problem that people living in cities are surrounded by dead things. One is not part of pavement or concrete. People become sick when they have to live in a second-hand, man-made reality and no longer have contact with living nature, with creation.

OMNI: In your book, you discuss a strange level of relations between man and nature. When you first took the Mexican mushroom *Psilocybe mexicana*, in Switzerland in the mid-fifties, you were overwhelmed by Mexican imagery, despite your attempts to focus on other things. And you say that Gordon Wasson, the author of *The Wondrous Mushroom*, had this experience repeatedly. Are you suggesting that different plant hallucinogens carry their own images or archetypes?

HOFMANN: I think that's very possible. Not only did Wasson and I have that experience with psilocybin, but so did Rudolf Gelpke's wife — in a very interesting way. She was a graphic designer, and after taking the mushroom, she started drawing. She had never been to Mexico or even seen Mexican art, but she drew these startlingly Mexican designs. She didn't even realize this until she took a look at some Mexican art a few months later and was amazed by the similarities.

OMNI: Is this where you got your ideas about a crack in the rational concept of reality, about hallucinogens working at a borderline where mind and matter merge?

HOFMANN: No. I got those ideas from my experiences with LSD, from the fact that a trace of this substance can transform one's consciousness, even transform twenty thousand people. There is a poem by Goethe that says, "How could our eyes see the sun, unless they are sunlike themselves?" I have changed that to say, "If there were not something of mind in matter, how could matter change the mind?" This does not mean that we are simply made up of matter, but that the material world has a spiritual element.

OMNI: Are there any natural substances in the brain with the same active principles as LSD or other hallucinogens?

HOFMANN: None are identical, of course, but the active principle of the magic mushroom psilocybin, for example, is very similar to that of the neurotransmitter serotonin in the brain. The only difference between them is the position of a hydroxyl group. It may be because these plant substances have a similar structure that they are able to intervene in the action of our brain hormones.

OMNI: You have said that you see a broader future for LSD in the context of meditation centers. Won't there be the same potential for misuse that existed in the sixties?

HOFMANN: I don't think so. The leader of a responsible meditation center should serve as something like a psychiatrist and know the people with him well enough to decide who should and should not use LSD — who is ready to use it as a pharmacological catalyst.

OMNI: Do you think there's a realistic possibility that Western governments will ever sanction this kind of LSD use?

HOFMANN: Yes, but not in the near future. It's more important that it become more readily available for psychiatry, where its use should never have been stopped. But official Western medical schools are relying more and more on meditation as a means of treatment. Eventually LSD can be used as an aid to meditation, not just for the ill but for healthy people as well.

OMNI: You also mention that LSD might be used for the terminally ill — to soften their experience of oncoming death.

HOFMANN: Yes. In certain American clinics it has already been used for terminal cancer patients who are suffering extreme pain and no longer responding to conventional medication. The reason LSD can alleviate or even abolish pain may be that patients under its influence are psychologically so dissociated from their bodies that their physical pain no longer penetrates their consciousness. There are many case histories telling of patients who, once freed from acute pain, gained meaningful insights about life and death and their fate — and died peacefully.

OMNI: Huxley took a massive dose of LSD when he was dying. Would you use it if you saw your life ending?

HOFMANN: I don't know. Maybe I will be very happy without LSD when I am dying. Maybe if I were suffering as horribly as Huxley was from cancer, I would. It's a situation I can't foresee.

OMNI: You yourself haven't used LSD since 1972. Do you anticipate doing it again?

HOFMANN: Maybe some time, but there's no pressing need. I have a wonderful life now with my seven grandchildren and my home in the Jura Mountains. And I still get a lot of visitors, young people from the United States and around Europe, who come to speak about their problems, about God and nature and our world situation. I like these young people and receive them whenever possible. We get into long discussions . . . I'm still a kind of guru.

Altered States
John Lilly

The highest intelligence on the planet probably exists in a sperm whale, who has a ten-thousand-gram brain, six times larger than ours.

The rugged bleached Malibu canyons, twisting roads, dusty scrub oaks, and desert sagebrush above the Pacific Coast Highway speak a supernal language. It is a landscape of the spirit more than of the body, and Dr. John C. Lilly, dolphin magus and scientist-turned-seeker, seems at home here — where the spectacular surf down at Zuma Beach is a mere rim of white foam on the edge of the world. If life imitates art, Dr. Lilly should live on just such a mountaintop.

It hadn't been easy to find him. When Judith Hooper asked scientist acquaintances about Lilly's whereabouts, most of them said something like "Do you mean, what dimension?" Someone thought he worked with dolphins at Marine World, in Redwood City, just south of San Francisco — and, it turns out, he does. But when Hooper phoned there, she talked to a succession of secretaries who had never heard of Dr. Lilly. She finally left a message with "Charlie," a gate guard who sometimes "sees him go in and out." No luck. When at last she called his house in Malibu, Lilly answered the telephone himself and gave her road directions that were accurate to the tenth of a mile.

Lilly's autobiography The Scientist *(1978) begins with the creation of the universe out of cosmic dust, but his own human chronicle started in St. Paul, Minnesota, in 1915. A scholarship prodigy at the California Institute of Technology, Lilly graduated with a degree in biology and physics in 1938 and went on to earn his M.D. from the University of Pennsylvania. Though he became a qualified psychoan-*

Photograph: Christopher Springman

*alyst, his first love was brain "hardware." His mastery of neurophys-
iology, neuroanatomy, biophysics, electronics, and computer theory
gave him something of the technical ingenuity of the genie in* The
Arabian Nights. *From 1953 to 1958 he held two posts — one at the
National Institute of Mental Health (NIMH) and one at the National
Institute of Neurological Diseases and Blindness — each part of the
National Institutes of Health (NIH) in Bethesda, Maryland. In his
early years at NIH he invented a technique that allowed scientists for
the first time to take brain-wave recordings from the cortex of unanesthetized animals. He also mapped the brain's pleasure and pain
systems by direct electrical stimulation of its core regions. And in
1954, tackling the classic puzzle of what would happen to the brain
if it were deprived of all external stimulation, he built the world's first
isolation tank.*

*Floating in his dark, silent, saltwater void — the original version
of which required his wearing a skindiver's mask — Lilly discovered
that sensory deprivation did* not *put the brain to sleep, as many
scientists had supposed. Furthermore, tanking led him far afield from
the doctrine that the mind is fully contained within the physical
brain. The tank, he declared, was a "black hole in psychophysical
space, a psychological free fall," which could induce unusual sensations: reverie states, waking dreams, even a kind of out-of-the-body
travel. (Today, of course, isolation tanks are so much a part of the
culture that even straitlaced businessmen routinely spend their lunch
hours — and upwards of $20 per hour — relaxing in health-spa
tranquillity tanks based on Lilly's original design.)*

*More and more enamored of the deep, womblike peace he experi-
enced in the tank, Lilly began to wonder what it would be like to be
buoyant all the time. Whales, dolphins, and porpoises sprang to mind,
and the rest, of course, is history. By 1961, Lilly had resigned from
the NIH to found and direct the Communications Research Institute,
in the U.S. Virgin Islands and Miami, Florida, for the purpose of
studying these big-brained, sea-dwelling mammals. Convinced that
dolphins are not only smarter but more "humane" than* Homo sapiens,
*and that they communicate in a sophisticated sonar language —
popularized, rather inaccurately, by the baby-talking dolphins of the
film* Day of the Dolphin *— Lilly began a lifelong quest to "talk" to
the Cetacea. Today he uses a "two-faced" computer called JANUS,*

named after the two-faced Roman god, to work out a human-dolphin language.

While Lilly was experimenting with otherworldly states in the isolation tank, the halcyon days of hallucinogenic research were underway at the NIMH. Lilly, however, did not try LSD until the early 1960s. Once he did, it became his high mass. Mixing LSD and isolation tanking for the first time in 1964, he entered what he described as "profound altered states" — transiting interstellar realms, conversing with supernatural beings, giving birth to himself, and, like Pascal, exploring infinities macroscopic and microscopic. "I traveled among cells, watched their functioning . . . and realized that within myself was a grand assemblage of living organisms, all of which added up to me," he later wrote of his illuminations, in The Center of the Cyclone (1972). "I traveled through my brain, watching the neurons and their activities . . . . I moved into smaller and smaller dimensions, down to the quantum levels, and watched the play of the atoms in their own vast universes, their wide empty spaces, and the fantastic forces involved in each of the distant nuclei with their orbital clouds of force field electrons . . . . It was really frightening to see the tunneling effects and the other phenomena of the quantum level taking place."

By all accounts, Lilly has probably taken more psychedelic substances — notably LSD and "vitamin K," the superhallucinogen he prefers not to identify — than anyone else in the consciousness business. Since the scientific establishment usually looks askance at experiments with hallucinogens, Lilly today reports his findings in popular books instead of in neurophysiology papers. He makes the scene at such New Age watering holes as Esalen, in California, and Oscar Ichazo's Arica training place, in Chile. He hasn't received a government grant since 1968. When asked about him, mainstream scientists tend to shake their heads sadly, as if recalling someone recently deceased.

"The trouble with Lilly is that he is in love with death," said one neuroscientist friend of his. "But God, is he brilliant!" Yes, he is brilliant, and yes, he does seem to have flirted quite flagrantly with death. Though LSD- or K-related accidents have almost killed him on at least three occasions, Lilly still keeps going back to the void, once tripping on K, he told Omni, for a hundred solid days and nights. It *is also true that he has always returned to Earth, however constraining its boundaries, and that his wife, Toni, has had a good deal to do with that.*

The moment Hooper arrived at his house, having driven her car over zigzagging mountain roads, Lilly announced, "We have one rule in this house. No one can take drugs of any kind and drive back down that road." Five minutes later, he seemed to be offering her acid and K.

He taped her with a matchbook-size Japanese recorder while she taped him. As the interview proceeded, Hooper watched various expressions play across his chiseled-granite face — unexpected sweetness whenever he spoke of Toni or of dolphins. (When talking about a dolphin, Lilly always used the pronoun "he," never "it.") Sometimes his language was full-bodied and poetic, sometimes a private blend of computerspeak and Esalenese, filled with phrases like "Earth Coincidence Control Office," "metaprogrammings," and "belief system interlocks." At one point in their conversation, Hooper felt that her own questions were echoing stupidly in her head, and that Lilly seemed bored, on the verge of walking off abruptly into a zero-g universe of his own. Possibly to get rid of her for a while, he escorted her to his samadhi isolation tank.

In this warm, sticky sea of isolation, where such luminaries as Nobel physicist Richard Feynman, anthropologist Gregory Bateson, psychologist Charles Tart, and est czar Werner Erhard have floated and had visions, Hooper tried to sort out her dissonant emotions. Her visions were disconnected, rudimentary; she recalls: "I was a swamp plant trailing its leaves on the water, a fetus, a dolphin, a whirring brain in an inert shell. An hour and a half later (one loses track of time), I emerged and tried to continue the interview. The problem was, in my state of tranquillity, I had lost interest in asking reporterlike questions, and, besides, Lilly was retreating more and more into some remote, glacial interstellar space behind his eyes. From another room a manic laugh track from what sounded like an old 'I Love Lucy' show floated out.

"Some time later Toni Lilly suddenly walked in, smiling and carrying bags of groceries. Her husband jumped up to help her unload the car, and I took my cue to depart back down the mountain. Only later, at home in the Los Angeles lowlands, did I notice that I was altered

— that for twenty-four hours after isolation-tanking, reality looked and felt quite different."

Four weeks later, Hooper telephoned Lilly, and they talked again. The following interview is the result of their afternoon together in his Malibu home and of their subsequent telephone conversation.

OMNI: You're probably best known as "Dr. John Lilly, the dolphin man." What is the aim of your current dolphin research?

LILLY: At Marine World, we're working with computers to develop a human-dolphin code, analogous to the Morse code used in telegraphy. The project is called JANUS — for Joint Analog Numerical Understanding System. Like the Roman god Janus, it has two "faces" — a dolphin side and a human side.

A human-dolphin language must contend with the fact that dolphins communicate at frequencies ten times above the human range. While our speech falls between three hundred and three thousand hertz, or cycles per second, dolphins talk to one another underwater at frequencies from three thousand to thirty thousand hertz. If you go into a pool with a dolphin and he starts whistling, you'll hear what sounds like very high-pitched squeaks. So the problem is to bring their frequency down into our sound window and ours up into theirs.

We're using a computer system to transmit sounds underwater to the dolphins. A computer generates electrical energy oscillating at particular frequencies, which can vary, and we use a transducer to convert the electrical waveforms into acoustical energy. You *could* translate the waveforms into any kind of sound you like: human speech, dolphinlike clicks, whatever.

OMNI: Do you type something out on the computer keyboard and have it transmitted to the dolphins as sound in their frequency range? And do they communicate back to the computer?

LILLY: Yes, but we actually use two computers. People type into the keyboard of an Apple II, which transmits sounds to the dolphins while displaying visual information on an underwater screen. Then there is another computer, made by Digital Equipment Corporation, which listens to the dolphins. A hydrophone, or underwater microphone, picks up any sounds the dolphins make, feeds them into a frequency analyzer, and then into the computer. That computer in turn analyzes the sound for linguistic meaning.

On the human side it's rather ponderous, because we have to

punch keys and see letters on a screen. People have tried to make dolphins punch keys, but I don't think dolphins should have to punch keys. They don't have these little fingers that we have. So we'd prefer to develop a sonic code as the basis of a dolphin-computer language. If a group of dolphins can work with a computer that shows them visual images of what they just said — names of objects and so forth — and if we can sit behind the computer terminal, I think we can eventually communicate.

OMNI: How long will it take to break through the interspecies communication barrier?

LILLY: About five years. I think it may take about a year for the dolphins to learn the code, and then, in about five years, we'll have a human-dolphin dictionary. However, we need some very expensive equipment to deal with dolphins' underwater sonar. Since dolphins "see" with sound in three dimensions — in stereo — you have to make your words "stereophonic words." Can you imagine what that would be like?

Many researchers besides me believe that "acoustic pictures" are the basis of a complex dolphin language. The dolphin maps his surroundings with reflected sound waves: he emits clicks, and the echoes tell him the distance of an object, its size, its material composition, and so forth. That's hard for us to understand, though people born blind can navigate with sonar techniques, too.

OMNI: You've said that dolphins also use "sonar beams" to look at the internal state of one another's body or that of a human being, and that they can even gauge another's emotional state that way. How does that work?

LILLY: They have a very high-frequency sonar that they can use to inspect something and look at its internal structure. Say you're immersed in water and a sound wave hits your body. If there's any gas in your body, it reflects back an incredible amount of sound. To the dolphin, it would appear as a bright spot in the acoustic picture.

OMNI: Can we ever really tune in to the dolphin's "stereophonic" world view, or is it perhaps too alien to ours?

LILLY: I want to. I just did a very primitive experiment — a Saturday afternoon–type experiment — at Marine World. I was float-ing in an isolation tank and had an underwater loudspeaker close to my head and an air microphone just above me. Both were connected through an amplifier to the dolphin tank so that they could hear me and I could hear them. I started playing with sound — whistling and clicking and making other noises that dolphins like. Suddenly I felt as if a lightning bolt had hit me on the head. We have all this on tape, and it's just incredible. It was a dolphin whistle that went *sssshhhheeeeeeoooo* in a falling frequency from about nine thousand to three thousand hertz, in my hearing range. It started at the top of my head, expanding as the frequency stopped, and showing me the inside of my skull, and went right down through my body. The dolphin gave me a three-dimensional feeling of the inside of my skull, describing my body by a single sound!

I want to know what the dolphin experiences. For me, it's totally exciting, and I want to go back and repeat the experiment in stereo, instead of with a single loudspeaker. Since I'm not equipped like a dolphin, I've got to use an isolation tank, electronics, and all this nonsense to pretend I'm a dolphin.

OMNI: Human language isn't merely descriptive; it has also evolved abstractions — symbolic units to stand for things that aren't physically real, that have no material composition. You've written that dolphins probably have "ancient vocal histories that their young must learn." Do you believe their language is a symbolic system?

LILLY: Sure. If it weren't, they wouldn't exist. They have to know different kinds of fish and coral, the distinction between edible and inedible — that sort of thing. I suggest you don a dolphin suit and join them. It's an incredible experience to hang out with them.

OMNI: You've pointed out that the bottle-nosed dolphin's brain is 40 percent larger than ours, and the orca [killer whale] has a brain four times larger. These big-brained dolphins and whales also have a larger association cortex, uncommitted to basic sensorimotor processing and therefore available for thinking. If cetaceans are smarter than we, why do we humans assume we're the crown of creation?

LILLY: Because we can't talk to anyone else. The highest intelligence on the planet probably exists in a sperm whale, who has a ten-thousand-gram brain, six times larger than ours. I'm convinced that intelligence is a function of absolute brain size. Some years ago I solved the brain weight–body weight problem, demonstrating that a large brain cannot exist in a small body; it needs a massive body to protect it. A brain is very fragile, and if it is rotated very fast —

by a blow to the jaw, for instance — it tears loose from its moorings and kills itself by intracranial bleeding. So, too, as a brain gets larger, the head surrounding it must increase to prevent dangerous rotation. Maybe the human brain can evolve further if we get control of our genetic code. But in what direction? That's the problem.

OMNI: What do you suppose porpoises, dolphins, and whales think of us?

LILLY: I don't know. That's one of the reasons why I want to communicate with them. They've tried to teach us their language, but they go too fast. So we'll invite them to match us for a while; then they can teach us to go faster. They can probably teach us a lot, if we're willing to learn.

OMNI: What has your long and intense acquaintance with cetaceans taught you about their character? What is their world like?

LILLY: It's mostly sonic, as I've said, since they live in the water twenty-four hours a day and can't see at night. They have no sense of smell, but a very discriminating taste sense. And, of course, they're buoyant, as you are in an isolation tank. One day while I was floating in the tank at NIMH, I thought, "Gee, wouldn't it be great to do this twenty-four hours a day!" When I mentioned it to a friend, he said, "Well, try the dolphins." So that's how I started to work with dolphins.

Having voluntary respiration, needing to surface for air, dolphins are interdependent in ways in which we aren't; they have a group mind. If a dolphin passes out for any reason, his friends must wake him up. Otherwise he'll drown. So every dolphin is aware of where every other dolphin is, just in case he's needed. "Do unto others as you would have them do unto you" is one of their rules, and, unlike us, they follow it twenty-four hours a day. They're also more spiritual, since they have more time to meditate. Try the isolation tank and you'll see what it's like.

OMNI: Tell me the circumstances that led you to invent the first isolation tank.

LILLY: There was a problem in neurophysiology at the time: Is brain activity self-contained or not? One school of thought said the brain needed external stimulation or it would go to sleep — become unconscious — while the other school said, "No, there are automatic oscillators in the brain that keep it awake." So I decided to try a sensory-isolation experiment, building a tank to reduce external stimuli — auditory, visual, tactile, temperature — almost to nil. The tank is lightproof and soundproof. The water in the tank is kept at 93 to 94 degrees. So you can't tell where the water ends and your body begins, and it's neither hot nor cold. If the water were exactly body temperature, it couldn't absorb your body's heat loss, your body temperature would rise above 106 degrees, and you might die.

I discovered that the oscillator school of thought was right: the brain does not go unconscious in the absence of sensory input. I'd sleep in the tank if I hadn't had any sleep for a couple of nights, but more interesting things happen if you're awake. You can have waking dreams, study your dreams, and, with the help of LSD-25 or a chemical agent I call vitamin K, you can experience alternate realities. You're safe in the tank because you're not walking around and falling down, or mutating your perception of external "reality."

OMNI: At the time you invented the tank weren't you doing nuts-and-bolts brain research at the National Institute of Mental Health?

LILLY: Yes. I invented a technique called an electrocorticograph, or ECG, for implanting multiple electrode arrays onto the surface of the brain itself without injuring brain tissue as much as previous methods did. It was the first method for taking electrical recordings from the brains of unanesthetized animals — or even of humans. On a kind of television monitor, you could watch the brain waves moving across the cerebral cortex in two dimensions. Basically, you pound a short length of hypodermic needle tubing through the scalp, adjusting it to the depth of the bone so that the scalp closes over it. Then you can come back and put electrodes down through that little channel.

OMNI: Was this the same technique you used for your direct-electrical-stimulation experiments to map the brain's pain and pleasure systems?

LILLY: No, that requires putting electrodes *below* the cortex, into the brain's deep motivational systems. The electrodes were the same; we just pushed them in deeper. At McGill University, in Montreal, James Olds and Peter Milner had discovered the positive-reinforcing systems in rats' brains. [In these famous studies, conducted in the early fifties, rats learned to self-stimulate by activating electrodes in their brains' "pleasure centers."] And H. E. Rosvold, of Yale University, had uncovered the negative-reinforcing systems in cats. I was the man who mapped *both* sides, positive and negative, and I went to a higher animal, the macaque monkey.

When I did the experiments again in the dolphin, I found he could *inhibit* his angry, aggressive responses when I stimulated the negative systems. That was fascinating. With his large, eighteen-hundred-gram brain, he had enough cerebral cortex to veto messages from the lower centers. Humans can do that, too, as scientists like [Tulane University medical researcher] Robert Heath have shown. Once, when Heath was stimulating a patient's negative system, the patient said, "You stimulate that point again and I'll pull the electrodes out." The dolphin also vocalized and tried to tell us, in his language, to cut that stuff out. But the monkey, with a mere hundred-gram brain, just tore up his restraints and tried to bite anything that came near him.

OMNI: Then is intelligence a function of the ability to inhibit stimuli?

LILLY: Yes. You need a cerebral cortex of a critical size, with fine fiber connections running in both directions to the lower systems. That's where the middle self (I-me) *lives*, up in that cortex — not in the lower centers. The lower centers (our lower self) prod us from below, as it were, with love or hate or fear. The superself controls from somewhere "above the brain," in the spiritual domains.

OMNI: What structures are involved in the brain's pain and pleasure pathways?

LILLY: Well, the preoptic nucleus, a group of cells in the anterior hypothalamus at the base of our brain, is our survival center: the stimulation it responds to is very negative. If the temperature is too hot or too cold, this nucleus freaks out the rest of the brain. If there's too much sodium in the blood, it freaks out the brain. It's an area for total fear. Then, moving downward toward the spinal cord, you hit a part of the hypothalamus that stimulates extreme pain all over the body. If you move sideways in either direction in that area of the brain, however, stimulation becomes incredibly positive. You run into the sexual system, which, in males, controls erection, orgasm, and ejaculation — each in a separate place — while farther back, in a part of the brain called the mesencephalon, the three are integrated and fired off in sequence.

The brain has other pleasure systems, too — systems that stimulate nonsexual pleasure all over the body, and systems that set off emotional pleasure. That is a kind of continuous pleasure that doesn't peak — a *satori* of mind. *Satori* and *samadhi* [terms for enlightened bliss states, in Zen Buddhism and Hinduism, respectively] and the Christian states of grace seem to involve a constant influx of pleasure and no orgasmic climax — like tantric sex. Spiritual states use these brain systems in their service. Many philosophers, including Patanjali, the second-century B.C. author of the *Yoga Sutras,* have said that *jnana yoga* — the yoga of the mind — is the highest form of yoga. In this self-transcendence one can experience bliss while performing God's work; only recently have I achieved this for days at a time.

OMNI: In your book *The Scientist* you wrote, "If we can each experience at least the lower levels of *satori,* there is hope that we won't blow up the planet or otherwise eliminate life as we know it." Are altered states necessary to our survival?

LILLY: Yes, the experience of higher states of consciousness, or alternate realities — I don't like the term *altered states* — is the only way to escape our brains' destructive programming, fed to us as children by a disgruntled karmic history. Newborns are connected to the divine; war is the result of our programmed disconnection from divine sources.

I am writing a book about alternate realities called *From Here to Alternity: A Manual on Ways of Amusing God.* On vitamin K, I have experienced states in which I can contact the creators of the universe, as well as the *local* creative controllers — the Earth Coincidence Control Office, or ECCO. They're the guys who run the earth and who program us, though we're not aware of it. I asked them, "What's your major program?" They answered, "To make you guys evolve to the next levels, to teach you, to kick you in the pants when necessary."

Because our consensus reality programs us in certain destructive directions, we must experience other realities in order to know we have choices. That's what I call Alternity. On K, I can look across the border into other realities. I can open my eyes in this reality and dimly see the alternate reality, then close my eyes and the alternate reality picks up. On K, you can tune your internal eyes. They are

not what is called the "third eye," which is centrally located, but
are stereo, like the merging of our two eyes' images. Perhaps someday, if we learn about the type of radiation coming through those
eyes, we can simulate the experience with a hallucinatory movie
camera — an alternate reality movie camera.

OMNI: What's so special about vitamin K?

LILLY: It's a lot more fun than LSD or any of the other agents,
because it induces a short trip, and you can train yourself to the
state. Pretty soon you can take ten times as much and still walk
around and talk to people, in spite of the fact that reality is vibrating.
I can run my computer, ski, or do just about anything on K. I've
been on it as much as a hundred days straight. You don't really
sleep, you don't really dream, because you don't need to. And on
K, I can experience the quantum reality; I can see [University of
Texas physicist] John Wheeler's hyperspace from within.

OMNI: Can you explain what you mean by experiencing hyperspace from within?

LILLY: According to quantum mechanics, hyperspace would be a
region in which possible realities exist side by side, at once. The
hyperspace with which I've been working is one in which I can jump
from one universe to another — from this reality to an alternate
reality — while maintaining human structure, size, concepts, and
memories. My center of consciousness is here, and I can know
immediately what's going on anywhere in the universe. It's a domain
I now call Alternity, where all choices are possible.

OMNI: What first inspired you to use psychotropic drugs?

LILLY: I never use the word *drug*, because it leads into a legalistic
morass. The Food and Drug Administration has been putting out
bulletins lately about K, which is now listed as a possible "abused"
drug. Because "abuse" means literally "away from use," I prefer the
term *hyperuse*, or "too much use." So I don't want to call it by its
chemical name, and I think of it as a vitamin, anyway, because it
gives me spiritual energy. I've never proselytized, never advocated
wholesale use of psychedelics. They are not for everyone. When
Timothy Leary said, "Turn on, tune in, drop out," I did not agree
with him; my use was carefully controlled investigation, not "recre-
ational use."

There were a lot of LSD pushers around our LSD research at NIMH when I was there in the fifties, but I didn't take LSD then. After about ten years in the tank I decided there was something new to be learned. So I came out here to California, where a lady I knew who had access to pure Sandoz LSD-25 gave me the LSD for my first two trips. On my first trip, I went through all the usual stuff: seeing my face change in the mirror, tripping out to music. During the first two movements of Beethoven's Ninth Symphony, I was kneeling in heaven, worshiping God and his angels, just as I had in church when I was seven years old. On that trip I did everything I'd read in the psychedelic literature so as to save time and get out of the literature the next time. During my third trip, in the isolation tank in Saint Thomas in 1964, I left my body and went into infinite distances — dimensions that are inhuman. Some of this is described in *Center of the Cyclone*.

OMNI: The Ken Russell–Paddy Chayevsky film *Altered States* bears a remarkable resemblance to your life. What did you think of it?

LILLY: I think they did a good job. The hallucination scenes are much better than anything ever produced before. I understand that some of the crew, the actors, and the producers were trained on K. The tank scenes were fine — except that in reality there are no vertical tanks, only horizontal ones — and the film implied that use of the tank itself would cause those out-of-body trips, which it doesn't.

The scene in which the scientist becomes cosmic energy and his wife grabs him and brings him back to human form is straight out of my *Dyadic Cyclone* [1976]. Toni did that for me. As for the scientist's regression into an apelike being, the late Dr. Craig Enright, who started me on K, while taking a trip with me here by the isolation tank, suddenly "became" a chimp, jumping up and down and hollering for twenty-five minutes. Watching him, I was frightened. I asked him later, "Where the hell were you?" He said, "I became a prehominid, and I was in a tree. A leopard was trying to get me. So I was trying to scare him away." I said, "If you do that again, I'll kick you in the ass." He laughed.

OMNI: Can substances like K take one to lower, as well as to higher, states? Could one get "stuck" in a lower state, and is that a possible explanation for psychosis?

LILLY: You can get into lower states — rock consciousness, solid state consciousness, whatever. If people do get stuck there, we would never hear from them, would we? As for so-called psychosis, it's just an insistence on staying in altered states, in spite of everyone else. Psychotics hang around and play games with everyone around them; it can be rather cruel. Anyone who has worked with them knows there's a wise and healthy essence back there, and what you have to do is contact it. Of course everyone's different. Some schizophrenics feel pain; others pretend pain so that they'll be taken care of.

OMNI: Did Chayevsky interview you for either the book or the screenplay version of *Altered States*?

LILLY: No. The manuscript of *The Scientist* was in the hands of Bantam, the publishers. The head of Bantam called and said, "Paddy Chayevsky would like to read your manuscript. Will you give him your permission?" I said, "Only if he calls me and asks permission." He didn't call. But he probably read the manuscript.

OMNI: The UCLA psychologist and drug authority Ronald Siegel maintains that the chemical you call K can simulate the near-death experience, proving that the near-death experience is hallucination rather than a foretaste of things on the "other side." What is your view?

LILLY: Ron and I totally disagree, though I like him. He is theorizing on the side of the law. With his belief system — that these experiences are all wastebasket stuff — he apparently doesn't *know* alternate realities.

My experiences have convinced me that Eastern yoga philosophy is right: that there is a *purusha* or *atman* [soul] for each person — one for the planet, one for the galaxy, and so on. As the mathematician-philosopher Franklin Merrel-Wolff says in his book *The Philosophy of Consciousness Without an Object*, consciousness was first — before the void even. When consciousness got bored and turned in upon itself, creation began. He/she/it created time, space, energy, matter, male, female — the whole tableau. And he made it all so complicated that sneaky things may go on beyond its ken.

If you get into these spaces at all, you must *forget* about them when you come back. You must forget you're omnipotent and omniscient and take the game seriously so you'll engage in sex, have children, and participate in the whole human scenario. When you come back from a deep LSD trip or a K trip — or coma or psychosis

— there's always this extraterrestrial feeling. You have to read the directions in the glove compartment so that you can run the human vehicle once more. After I first took acid in the tank and traveled to distant dimensions, I cried when I came back and found myself trapped in a body. I didn't even know whose body it was at first. It was the sadness of re-entry. I felt squashed.

OMNI: Some of your critics have made much of the fact that intense experimentation with LSD and K has brought you to the brink of death at least three times. While giving yourself an antibiotic injection during your early days of LSD experimentation, you once used a hypodermic containing detergent foam residue, which sent you into a coma. Then, during a period of prolonged K use, you nearly drowned, and later you seriously injured yourself in a bicycle accident. Were these accidents quasi-suicides — collisions with your brain's "self-destruct programs"?

LILLY: The whole issue of suicide is a very complex program. I've never tried to commit suicide, though I've been close to death. The near-death accidents resulted from my taking something and acting in a certain way so that I ended up in great danger, and so I've hypothesized that the brain contains lethal programs — self-destruct programs — below the level of awareness, which LSD or K can release or strengthen. My accidents were near-death learning experiences. There's nothing like them. They train you faster than anything I know.

The year leading up to my bicycle accident in 1974, I spent in satori, or a state of grace. I was having a ball, mostly living in alternate realities and sometimes falling flat on my face. In *The Autobiography of Ramakrishna* [1836–1886, a famous Indian saint], there's a story about Ramakrishna getting ready to board a river steamer. Two of his disciples began to fight, and so Ramakrishna went into samadhi. Since he was out of his body, his disciples had to stop fighting and carry him aboard the steamer. Well, that was the sort of state I was in, and Toni was the disciple who had to "carry me around."

OMNI: In your reflections in *The Dyadic Cyclone*, you seem to consider the accident as a way of your paying for that year of bliss.

LILLY: It terminated that year. In our workshops we have a saying: "If you pass the cosmic speed limit, the cosmic cops will bust you." I got busted. I had taken forty-two milligrams of PCP [angel dust].

I'd been out there too long and hadn't paid enough attention to my planet-side trip; so the Earth Coincidence Control Office called me back by throwing a bike accident at me while I was on PCP. I appreciate what they did. They're not cruel; they're in a state of high indifference.

While my body was in the hospital and in a coma for five days and nights, I was in alternate universes, where the guides instructed me about various planetary catastrophes. I can't make up my mind whether that was an experience of genuine realities or just a projection of the damage to my body. In any case, I begged the guides to let me go back. I had to say, "I want to go back to Toni." At one point I clung to Toni for six solid hours so I could stay with her. It was very frightening. The guides told me, "You can stay here, in which case your body dies, or you can go back." I chose to go back to Toni, as I have chosen to go back every time.

OMNI: Toni has obviously been a crucial counterpoint to what you once described as the "stainless steel computer" part of yourself. In your recent books you've stressed the importance of what you call the "male-female dyad." Will you please explain this idea?

LILLY: That's the way the universe is constructed. Do you know about the Eleventh Commandment? It says, "Thou shalt not bore God, or he will destroy your universe." The first step in not boring God is to set up two opposing intellects, male and female, so that neither can tell what the other is thinking. If you totally fused with your mate, it might be a very dull trip.

I love female intelligences. Every single cell in your body has two X chromosomes. Every cell in my body has one X chromosome and a crippled X chromosome, an X chromosome with an arm missing, called a Y chromosome. You women are so well balanced with your two X's. You can be grounded and do the gardening and take care of the kids and give them nurture, but we males have got to go out and explore the universe, banging our heads together and shooting one another.

OMNI: Was it really necessary for you to have the near-death experiences you've recounted?

LILLY: It was for me. It was necessary to frighten the hell out of me, but many other people are just born right and don't have to struggle as I did. I had a Catholic background, a traumatic childhood — the whole business.

OMNI: What was it specifically about a Catholic background that you had to "unlearn"?

LILLY: The whole construct. I'd been taught by Irish Jesuits, who are very clever. They made up multiple layers of rationality for the whole Catholic structure. The nice thing about Catholicism, however, is that it teaches you what to believe. So when you throw it over, you know exactly what you're throwing over. You can say, "I *don't* believe in the Father Almighty," and continue right through the Apostles' Creed, the Confiteor, and the rest of it, tossing out one tenet at a time.

I believe in God, but not in the "Catholic God," who is vengeful. There's the whole business about guilt, "impure thoughts," going to hell if you don't do what the church commands. One way this was solved for me, intellectually if not emotionally, was by reading the "Grand Inquisitor" chapter of Dostoevsky's *The Brothers Karamazov,* in which Christ comes back to Earth. The Grand Inquisitor tells him, "When we saw those miracles in the street, we knew you were back. But this time we're not giving you any publicity. We're keeping you in this cell. *We* know how to run these people now." That just knocked the church right out of me, and by the time I was finished with Cal Tech, medical school, and psychoanalysis, that belief system was pretty well cleaned out of me.

OMNI: What about psychoanalysis as religion? Both use the confessional, an elaborate rational system for structuring the irrational, transference, and so on.

LILLY: Well, I didn't get into the religious aspects, as I was fortunate in having an analyst, Robert Waelder, who was free of the dogma. He had been trained by Anna Freud in Vienna, had a Ph.D. in physics, and was an analyst's analyst. I took psychoanalytic training under him for eight years, and he would go anywhere with me. Right off, practically in our first session, I told him I wanted to get a divorce from the first of my three wives, but that I thought I couldn't if I was in analysis. "Where did you learn that?" he asked. I said, "In the Freudian literature." He said, "Dr. Lilly, we are not here to analyze Freud, psychoanalytic literature, or other people's rules for your behavior. We are here to analyze *you.*"

OMNI: How is it that, trained for eight years in psychoanalysis, you decided to devote yourself to brain hardware instead?

LILLY: I'd already had enough neurophysiological training to know there were a lot of mysteries in the brain. As Waelder said, psychoanalytic theory accounts for about one tenth of 1 percent of what goes on in psychoanalysis. I had to go further than that to find something more satisfying, and I found it in the concept of metaprogramming the human biocomputer.

A human being is a biorobot with a biocomputer in it, the brain. But we are not that brain, and we are not that body. A soul essence inhabits us, and, under acid, under K, under anesthesia, you'll find that the essence isn't tied to brain activity at all. Brain activity can be virtually flat, and you can be conscious — off somewhere in another realm. You just can't communicate with people in consensus reality.

OMNI: In your experience, does the brain possess "trap doors" into the domain of the soul? For example, the neuroscientist Arnold Mandell, of the University of California at San Diego, has said that chemicals such as LSD can be "pharmacological bridges" to transcendence.

LILLY: I agree with Mandell. Acid — and, better, vitamin K — set up the chemical configuration of your brain so as to loosen the connection between the brain/body and the soul/essence. Then the essence can move into alternate realities. I call this phenomenon the "leaky-mind hypothesis," or the "escaping-self hypothesis." There are a lot of ideas about the soul's location in the body, of course. In Spanish, when you're scared out of your wits, you say your soul is in your mouth — you have *el alma en la boca*. But the junction between the biocomputer and the essence is *not* localized in the brain; it's throughout the body. If you get out of your body, you can assume a fake body, an astral body, which can walk through walls. Your essence is represented in every cell in your body.

OMNI: Orthodox scientists accuse you of unscientific practices, and some even suggest that your consciousness-altering experiments and near-death accidents have impaired your judgment. How would you reply to them?

LILLY: Well, I'd just throw my credentials at them, and I'd ask them to sit down and read my papers. Only narrow-minded people criticize me anyway; the broad-band people, who can move easily across boundaries and disciplines, love my work. Down in Mexico, for instance, people have been educated to respect the superscience of the next century that their *brujos* and *curanderos* [sorcerers or witches and healers] are capable of calling up. My son John Lilly, Jr., who has lived for sixteen years among the Huichol Indians, has a wonderful movie about these matters. Our orthodoxy, on the other hand, is very Germanic, very European: if you can't see it, touch it, or taste it, it doesn't exist.

I was brought up to divide science into theory and experiment, each guiding the other. The pure experimentalists who attack me lack good theory, but the theorists haven't done the experiments. There are really three departments to science: experiment, theory, and experience. Experience is the part that doesn't get into the scientific journals.

OMNI: How would you answer the charge that your self-experimentation is subjective, and therefore unverifiable?

LILLY: Subjectivity is nonsense. Neither subjectivity nor objectivity exists in nature. That's the contained-mind-in-the-brain belief of some psychiatrists and other scientists. The subject is an object is a subject. In a cybernetic system, you go around in a circle, and subject and object have no reality. The only way to isolate subject and object is to cut off the feedback and destroy the system. It's a false dichotomy — a word game.

OMNI: Do you believe that neuroscientists are on the verge of explaining the mind by mapping brain chemicals, and so forth?

LILLY: I haven't yet seen any breakthroughs that are worth talking about. Neurochemistry is interesting but not specific enough yet. I suspect we'll find there are a million different compounds operating in the nervous system — specific compounds for specific regions and specific neurons. The regeneration experiments of Roger Sperry, Cal Tech neuroscientist and Nobel laureate [in which he rotated a salamander's eye and the severed nerve fibers somehow reconstructed their original connections to the optic tectum in the brain, as if they "knew" where to go], show that there are chemotropic substances that are specific to each fiber. I don't read neuroscience journals anymore; I depend on my friends to tell me what's going on.

You know, Kurt Gödel's theorem, translated, says that a computer of a given size can model only a smaller computer; it cannot model itself. If it modeled a computer of its own size and complexity, the model would fill it entirely and it couldn't do anything. So I don't think we can understand our own brains fully.

OMNI: Is it an extension of Gödel's theorem that states that some propositions can be neither proved nor disproved within a logical system?

LILLY: It's the same thing. If you have a closed system, the closed system can't account for itself. A set of sets that contains itself is a set that cannot possibly replicate itself. We are biological computers, and what Gödel said is that you cannot conceive in full a computer the size of your own, for it would take up all the space you live in.

A sperm whale, with a brain six times the size of ours, could model a human and do a pretty good job of it. Since the model would take up only one sixth of his software brain, he could use the remaining five-sixths to manipulate the model, predict its actions, and so on. The trouble is that this big computer is caught in a body that man can kill. Maybe he wants to get out of that body.

OMNI: Could you elaborate on your concept of programming and metaprogramming the biocomputer?

LILLY: Have you seen the movie *Tron*? You must, because *Tron* is in us. In it, the computer grabs the character played by Jeff Bridges and takes him inside, making him a program in a computer. The Master Control Program revolts, takes over the computer, and defies the users. So the users send in Tron, which is a program to destroy the Master Control Progam that is preaching disbelief in the users. *Tron* shows you things that are very, very spiritual. You can think of yourself as a biocomputer, or an intelligent terminal, run by a cosmic computer in the Earth Coincidence Control Office. The biocomputer contains certain wired-in survival programs, dealing with eating, reproduction, and so on, that lower animals also possess. But when the biocomputer reaches a certain threshold of complexity, there are higher-level programs in the association cortex that permit such things as making models, learning to learn, choosing, and so forth. We have short-term choices, but God help you if you go against the Master Control Program. A terminal cannot understand itself, because it lacks sufficient space, but a replica of itself is in the cosmic computer, which can understand it. At the highest level, your true self (the "user" in *Tron*) is a cosmic game player, with access to an infinite computer — the ECCO computer. That is metaprogramming, self-metaprogramming.

OMNI: How does one contact God?

LILLY: In many cases, I didn't know whether I was taken on a trip by God or by one of his business officers in the outer galaxy. Guides at each level above ours pretend to be God as long as you believe them. When you finally get to know the guide, he says, "Well, God is really the next level up." God keeps retreating into infinity. I've thought that I was in the mind of God — seeing rotating universes, yin and yang, male and female — but perhaps God himself is beyond that. Have I told you about the Dust-bowl God?

OMNI: No. What is the Dust-bowl God?

LILLY: In my new book I have a theory called the Dust-bowl God. God got bored with this universe and the distribution of intelligence in it. So he made a dust bowl out beyond the galaxies. In this dust cloud, every particle is intelligent; on the atomic level, each particle is as intelligent as a human being. The dust particles made themselves into stars and planets and animals and humans, and everybody knew everybody; everything was totally aware of everything around it. Now the problem is, if every particle is equally intelligent, and greater assemblages are even more intelligent, what are the traffic rules for relations between, say, humans and elephants? It would be nice to see such a universe, wouldn't it — the Dust-bowl Universe?

OMNI: How would it differ from ours?

LILLY: Right. How would it?

Emergence
Roger Sperry

The mind can quickly scan not only the past, but also the projected future consequences of a choice. Its dynamics transcend the time and space of brain physiology.

"Science was wrong. Its interpretations of man and the world were demeaning and dehumanizing," declared the pioneering brain researcher Roger Sperry. "All physical reality, including the human psyche, was reduced to quantum mechanics. The richness, color, and beauty were all lost in mathematical concepts."

At sixty-nine, the man who shared the 1981 Nobel Prize in medicine and physiology for his famous split-brain studies has turned his attention to battling the materialist legacy of twentieth-century science. This latest assault on orthodoxy comes as no surprise, because Sperry, though shy and reserved, has never been afraid to challenge accepted doctrine. In his forty-year quest to understand the nature of human consciousness, he has overturned more than one cherished belief. Bearded, with bullet eyes capped by gracefully arched brows, Sperry may have been destined to play the part of scientific debunker. As one former colleague noted, Sperry is "constitutionally able to be interested only in critical issues."

Even as a graduate student at Oberlin College in Oberlin, Ohio, Sperry challenged his distinguished mentor, Paul Weiss, who propounded the view that neural connections were determined by experience rather than genetic mechanisms. To test his theory, the young scientist designed an intriguing experiment that involved rotating the eyes of a salamander by 180 degrees. If Weiss's theory that "function precedes form" was correct, the salamander would eventually adjust to seeing the world upside down and alter its behavior accordingly. But even after hundreds of training trials, Sperry's salamander continued to dart in the opposite direction of any lure placed in its tank. Moreover, when Sperry severed the nerve pathways to the eye, the

Photograph: Christopher Springman

tangled fibers somehow sorted themselves out, only to re-establish the same "upside-down" connections as before. Neural networks, Sperry concluded, organize themselves independently of the function they ultimately come to perform. Even today, his landmark study is touted by those who believe that basic behavioral patterns are heavily influenced by genetic factors.

The way that growing nerve fibers are guided to predetermined connections preoccupied Sperry for the next decade, and eventually led him to postulate that brain cells use "a kind of probing chemical-touch system." His theory — that the nervous system arranges itself according to a chemical code roughly analogous to the color code that governs the wiring of circuits in a telephone receiver — is now considered a keystone of developmental neurobiology.

But in the intellectual climate of the early forties, Sperry's concept of a "hard-wired" brain met with strong resistance. One major opponent of this viewpoint was the eminent neurophysiologist Karl Lashley, whom Sperry worked under at the Yerkes Laboratories of Primate Biology, then located in Florida. Lashley's arguments against the specificity of nerve connections stemmed in part from reports about a rare group of patients who had undergone radical brain surgery to stop intractable epilepsy. These people were treated by surgeons, who cut through the corpus callosum, the main nerve cable that connects the right and left cerebral hemispheres.

"At that time the corpus callosum was an enigma," recalled Sperry. "You could cut it out completely — two hundred million nerve fibers — and it didn't seem to cause any functional deficit that people noticed. This fit in with a commonly held notion that the brain is characterized by wholesale plasticity and comes out functioning fine, no matter how you cut or scramble its nerves."

A decade of animal studies soon dispelled many false ideas about the corpus callosum, including Lashley's assertion that it was little more than a mechanical prop to stop the hemispheres from sagging. Once the connection was broken, it was as if two minds resided in the one brain. Each half of the cerebrum was capable of learning, remembering, and feeling thoughts completely unknown to the other. To Sperry, the conclusion was inescapable: the neural isthmus must be vital for an integrated sense of awareness.

Still greater revelations followed. In 1954, Sperry was appointed

Hixon Professor of Psychobiology at the California Institute of Technology, a post he has held for the last twenty-nine years. Shortly afterward, he launched a series of now-classic studies of split-brain individuals, patients whose corpora callosa had been severed surgically. At first the test results appeared to support the popular contention that the right hemisphere was "mentally retarded" in comparison to the left hemisphere, which has long been recognized as the seat of linguistic abilities. Careful examination, however, altered the picture drastically. For example, a split-brain individual might categorically deny the existence of an object placed out of view in his left hand (visual information is transmitted from the left hand to the right half of the brain). But if that same subject is given a nonverbal mode of identifying the object, such as feeling with his left hand for its match in a collection of items, he will invariably make the correct choice, despite frequent protestations that he is merely guessing.

Clearly the right brain was neither dumb nor devoid of consciousness, as early authorities had insisted. It just lacked the words to inform investigators of its hidden talents. As Sperry's disciple Michael Gazzaniga recalled, "No one was prepared for the riveting experience of observing a split-brain patient generating integrated activities with the mute right hemisphere that the language-dominant left hemisphere was unable to describe or comprehend."

Interestingly, the left hemisphere often proved all too willing to comment on matters it knew nothing about. During one routine test of a female patient's ability to make visual discriminations, Sperry substituted for a slide of a household object a slide showing a nude woman. Using a special apparatus, called a tachistoscope, he was able to project the picture only to her right hemisphere. The arresting stimulus triggered a sudden change of expression, and her face reddened as she laughed nervously. "What's so funny?" Sperry asked. Forced to rationalize an embarrassed response to something it had not seen, her left hemisphere replied, "I don't know . . . nothing . . . oh, that funny machine!"

From this experiment and hundreds more like it, Sperry and his colleagues gained powerful insights into the dual nature of human consciousness. Today it is widely recognized that the left hemisphere is primarily verbal, mathematical, and logical. The right side is viewed as more intuitive and emotional, specializing in visual-spatial problem-

solving and other situations where a single impression or mental image is worth a thousand words.

For the most part, Sperry is glad that this distinction has entered the mainstream of public knowledge. In his Nobel lecture, he noted that split-brain studies have led to a better appreciation of nonverbal forms of intelligence and increased understanding of "the inherent individuality in the structure of human intellect." He also feels his research has helped to underscore the need for educational tests and policies "to selectively identify, accommodate, and serve the differentially specialized forms of individual intellectual potentials."

An intensely private man, who prefers the solace of nature to life in the limelight, Sperry conveniently vanished from sight at the time of the Nobel announcement. While his Pasadena office struggled to handle the deluge of calls and telegrams that poured in from well-wishers all over the world, he and his wife snorkeled along the beaches of Baja California, returning only after the hoopla had passed.

When not retreating to the wilderness, Sperry spends most of his quiet moments exploring the broader ramifications of his revised view of consciousness, applying his knowledge of individual awareness to global phenomena. He is, in effect, superimposing the bicameral mind on the collective consciousness of society, attempting to reconcile two schools of thought: the reductionist view of the scientific materialist, who adopts the left brain's strategy of chopping up reality into fragments; and the humanistic view of the philosopher, who favors the right brain's holistic perspective, incorporating emotions, ethics, and other complex values into the scheme of reality.

Just as the left hemisphere was once thought to dominate human consciousness, its cultural counterpart — reductionism — has been given too much weight in society, Sperry feels. Still the zealous debunker of his youth, he is quietly chipping away at this last great pillar of modern science. And when it finally topples, he intends to lay the foundations for a much more integrated world view of science, one that encompasses the concerns of the humanist and the reductionist under one intellectual umbrella. In his recently published book, Science and Moral Priority, *Sperry explains how these revisions could make science a partner with religion in the quest for an ultimate ethical and moral frame of reference. Changes in our social priorities, he believes, are a prime requisite for civilization's survival.*

*Sperry met Yvonne Baskin in his office in Cal Tech's Norman Church
Laboratory on several occasions during 1982 and 1983.*

OMNI: Aren't ethics and moral values pretty far afield for a brain
scientist?

SPERRY: In some ways, but actually they're a natural follow-up
to something I came upon in the mid-sixties, a modified concept of
the mind-brain relationship. It's common practice in science to follow
up on the most promising leads opened by any new discovery, and
these human-value implications seemed to be far and away the most
important.

OMNI: Granted human values are important, but don't they take
you way outside the bounds of science?

SPERRY: Well, my scientific colleagues sometimes think that I've
gone off the deep end or something, but I don't look at it that way.
I view it more as a shift to a new scientific area that's now developing.
You see, according to our new views of consciousness, ethical and
moral values become a very legitimate part of brain science. They're
no longer conceived of as reducible to brain physiology. Instead, we
now see that subjective values themselves exert powerful causal
influence in brain function and behavior. They're universal determinants in all human decision-making, and they're actually the most
powerful causal control forces now shaping world events. No other
causal system with which science now concerns itself — earthquakes,
chemical reactions, magnetic fields, you name it — is of more critical
importance in determining our future.

OMNI: Your research defined with new clarity the different but
complementary roles of the right and left sides of the brain. A lot of
follow-up work remains to be done on the way the two hemispheres
interact and how the dominance of right or left brain in an individual
correlates with sex, musical or math ability, creativity, occupational
preferences, right- or left-handedness, and so on. Doesn't this work
interest you anymore?

SPERRY: Yes, of course, it's all interesting and important science. But you always have to ask "What difference does it make?"
Or better, "What difference is it going to make ten years from now?"
You look around at all the looming threats of global disaster and the
declining quality of life, and wonder, "What difference will it make

if we succeed in improving educational policies a little, or neurological diagnoses, or our understanding of right-left differences, or details of hemispheric interaction?"

Then, by contrast, think what even a very slight shift of values would do in the delicate balance of opposing positions in the abortion controversy, for example, or in various environmental matters, or other global issues. We're talking here about hundreds of thousands of lives, pro or con, about the kind of world we and our grandchildren will live in — if they live at all — and the kinds of laws we're governed by. When you see your science having direct and compelling implications in these areas, it's hard to turn away and go back to more laboratory experiments, especially when you see in this new path the one humane means for getting us out of our current global straits.

OMNI: But doesn't science in its traditional role provide hope for concrete technical solutions to many of today's problems?

SPERRY: Technological answers by themselves, in the absence of population controls, just put us deeper and deeper in a self-feeding, vicious spiral of mounting population, pollution, energy and resource demands, and so on.

OMNI: And you think the best way to break these spirals is to change man's sense of values — to evolve a new global ethic or theology?

SPERRY: That's the most humane way. A nuclear holocaust, global famine, or some other worldwide catastrophe would do it, of course; so would letting things continue as they are. But the most painless and reasonable solution presently visible is to change the kinds of values and beliefs we live and govern by. Others agree with this. Lester Brown, of the Worldwatch Institute, came to the same conclusion in his latest book, *Building a Sustainable Society*. The National Council of Churches sponsored a meeting three years ago at which representatives from different faiths affirmed that what the world needs today is a new religion, a new theology that will promote the values of conservation, renewable energy, respect for the land, and the like.

Think what would happen if the values of conservation, population control, and so on were to be lifted above the level of just wisdom and experience to become matters of deep religious conviction. Imagine if people worldwide believed it to be deeply immoral, even sacrilegious, to pollute, overpopulate, or in any other way degrade the quality of the biosphere for future generations! This is where our changed views of brain and consciousness ultimately seem to lead. The main point is that our recently changed views in mind-brain science radically alter traditional beliefs about the nature of man and the world, about the relation of mind to matter, of science to values, about free will and moral responsibility.

OMNI: Aren't people worried at the thought of changing human values through science?

SPERRY: It's not a matter of altering values directly or experimentally. It's more a matter of bringing scientific knowledge to bear where values are already in conflict. We're still in the early phase of this. It wasn't too many years ago that values were generally considered to be off limits to science.

OMNI: Let's start at the beginning. What was the change in the concept of consciousness that first prompted you to endorse the merging of science and values?

SPERRY: It's the change involved in the so-called consciousness or mentalist revolution in psychology that took place during the seventies, a complete turnabout in the treatment of consciousness. Behaviorist principles, which had been dominant for over half a century, were overturned. Psychology suddenly began to treat such subjective events as mental images, inner thoughts, sensations, feelings, ideas, and so on as factors having a genuine causal role in brain function and behavior. The contents of introspection, the whole world of inner experience, suddenly became accepted as elements that could influence physical and chemical events in the brain instead of being treated as passive, noncausal aspects or even as nonexistent ones.

OMNI: What you're saying is that neuroscientists previously found it difficult to see how the sequence of brain events could ever be influenced by anything other than strictly material, physical, and chemical agents.

SPERRY: Exactly. That was the view accepted by psychologists as well, and the further neuroscience advanced, the more convincing their arguments seemed. It appeared that a complete account of brain function, and for that matter all of nature, could be given in purely material, physicochemical terms, without any need to refer to conscious, mental, or vital forces of any kind. Science claimed it had absolutely no use for consciousness, since it couldn't do anything in the brain and didn't change anything. There was just no need for consciousness in a causal explanation. The progress of brain science toward an ultimate physicochemical description of behavior seemed to leave less and less for anything like human dignity, moral choice, meaning, purpose, and such things that go hand in hand with human values. That's what I meant when I said science was demeaning and dehumanizing.

OMNI: What happened to cause the shift in psychology away from these established behaviorist views?

SPERRY: In part, the time was right. Many things came together that collectively outweighed the old arguments in favor of the new. Earlier views had been floating around that came close to the current revised concepts: Gestalt and humanistic views in psychology, concepts of phenomenology, systems theory, tacit knowing, emergence, holism, and so on. The question is, what happened to change all of this from the status of occasional scattered philosophy and minority science to its present status as the dominant doctrine?

I think it was largely a matter of demonstrating a logical flaw in our seemingly airtight reasoning, finding a new, different logic that fitted more widely and combined earlier threads into a new formula for mind-brain interaction. Mostly, perhaps, it was the introduction of some new ideas about causation applied to the chain of command in brain dynamics. When you talk about causes and cause control, science listens!

The key realization was that the higher levels in brain activity control the lower. The higher cerebral properties of mind and consciousness are in command. They call the plays, exerting downward control over the march of nerve-impulse traffic. Our new model, mentalism, puts the mind and mental properties to work and gives them a reason for being and for having evolved in a physical system. It also shows how it's possible for mind to be created out of matter in fetal growth.

OMNI: How do you define mentalism?

SPERRY: Mentalism is contrasted in psychology to behaviorism and materialism. It's a doctrine holding that mental events (as consciously experienced in the mind) determine and explain behavior. The mental qualities used to be conceived in nonphysical or supernatural terms, but we now view them as emergent properties of brain processes.

OMNI: Emergent properties?

SPERRY: *Emergent* is the same as *holistic*, the Greek word for whole. The properties of the whole are contrasted to those of its parts; it encompasses the old maxim that "the whole is greater than, and different from, the sum of the parts." As evolution progresses, combining the atomic building blocks into ever newer and more complex compounds and then compounding the compounds, new properties emerge at each step. So you start with the subatomic physical properties and work upward through chemistry, biology, psychology, sociology. In the brain, too, you have these nested hierarchies from subatomic levels upward, with emergent properties at each level and conscious properties at the top.

OMNI: How does your shift to this mentalist view fit in with the split-brain studies?

SPERRY: It was a matter of explaining the effects of split-brain surgery on conscious experience. We found that each disconnected hemisphere was capable of sustaining its own conscious awareness, each largely oblivious of experiences of the other. The separated hemispheres were able to carry on independently at a fairly high level. They could even perform mutually contradictory tasks at the same time, and each was able to exert its own control and select its own differential preferences.

For example, in a blindfold test for tactual sorting, both hands may search together through a scrambled pile of different-shaped beads. One hand would sort out spheres into an upper tray and cylinders into a lower, while the other hand would do just the reverse. In the process, each hemisphere would consciously and voluntarily make decisions opposite to those going on in the partner hemisphere. And neither disconnected hemisphere would seem to know what the other was doing. The vocal left hemisphere could report that it had no clue about the experience in the right hemisphere. Left and right domains of conscious awareness and volition seem to be almost as separate as if they were in two different heads.

Since each side of the surgically divided [or split] brain is able to sustain its own conscious volitional system in this manner, the question arises as to why, in the normal state, we don't perceive of ourselves as a pair of separate left and right persons instead of the single, apparently unified mind and self that we all feel we are.

OMNI: And the answer required a changed view of consciousness?

SPERRY: Not directly. I had earlier proposed that conscious meaning emerges because brain processes adjust to interact with perceived objects. For example, when we look at a house, the brain prepares for a functionally adaptive response with respect to the house — the approach, location, form, memories, associations, and so on.

In wrestling with the split-brain problem, I realized that this kind of interaction with objects requires that consciousness have a causal impact on brain activity. Consciousness can be viewed as a higher emergent entity that supersedes the sum of its right and left awareness.

OMNI: So the two hemispheres normally function together as an integrated whole, and the mind as a bilateral unit then arbitrates and integrates the activities within each hemisphere, making decisions that are carried out as physical or chemical events in either or both sides?

SPERRY: That's the idea, yes. Putting all this together with some notions about emergence and causation, I found I could see a way around the old behaviorist logic and the mind-brain paradox, a way finally to affirm the causal usefulness of consciousness without violating scientific principles.

OMNI: The "mind-brain paradox"?

SPERRY: The puzzling contradiction traditionally posed by subjective versus objective views. On the one hand, introspection gives the impression that consciousness is very important in determining our thinking and what we do. On the other hand, objective science told us that consciousness has absolutely no role in controlling brain activity or behavior. Each view seemed strong in its own right and irreconcilable with the other. Carl Rogers, the eminent psychologist, considered it a deep paradox with which we'd have to learn to live.

OMNI: What about free will, the idea that we seem to have the power to do whatever we choose at any instant, regardless of any laws of brain function?

SPERRY: This is opposed, of course, to the old reductionist scientific view that we are causally controlled and have to do everything exactly as we do it — that we could not have behaved other than we did at any time. This was one of the so-called Big Three, another of the great unresolved paradoxes of science.

OMNI: What are the Big Three?

SPERRY: Consciousness, free will, and values — three old thorns in the hide of science. Materialist science couldn't cope with any of them, even in principle. They're in direct conflict with the basic models. Science has had to renounce them — to deny their existence or to say that they're beyond science.

For most of us, of course, all three are among the most important things in life. When science proceeds to deny their importance, even their existence, or to say that they're beyond its domain, one has to wonder about science.

OMNI: Did science deny free will and call it just an illusion?

SPERRY: In principle, brain science always assumed it could show just what physical and chemical events in the brain led you to make every single decision you made. Psychiatry and all the behavioral sciences are based on this principle, that all our behaviors, even the slightest mannerisms and nervous twitches, are caused, and if one probes deeply enough into the past, into the subconscious or into brain physiology, one can find the causes and thereby explain and predict behavior.

OMNI: Is there any real proof of this determinism?

SPERRY: Proof seemed evident in experiments with posthypnotic suggestion, where a person would think he'd done something special of his own free will, but witnesses knew he or she had been instructed to do it under hypnosis and then told to forget having been hypnotized.

OMNI: But you believe our actions can be considered free despite this kind of causal control. How?

SPERRY: We have to recognize different degrees of freedom and also different types and levels of causation, including higher kinds of causal control involving mental and vital forces that materialist science has always rejected. Remember that the revised mind-brain model makes conscious mental events causal. It follows that the causal antecedents of any consciously willed act or decision are not just physiological but also mental. It's no longer a matter of the laws governing nerve-impulse traffic or inexorable physicochemical mechanisms. We deal instead with a sequence of conscious, or subconscious, mental processes that have their own higher laws and dynamics.

The higher-order mental processes move their neuronal details much the way a rolling wheel carries along its molecules, or the way different program images on a TV receiver determine the pattern of electron flow on the screen. Only, unlike a TV, the brain not only "receives" or "plays," but generates, creates its own mental programs.

OMNI: Are you reversing the usual scientific interpretation, saying neural events don't determine mental events?

SPERRY: Not at all. It's always a reciprocal relation with mutual interaction. But because of the long history of reductionist bias in science, we need actively to emphasize the kind of causal control exerted by the higher over the lower.

OMNI: So our actions are still caused and directed, but the causes are mental in the form of perceptions, insights, memories, ideas, reasons, and logic?

SPERRY: Yes, and also feelings, wants, needs, wishes, and values. We musn't forget the right brain. Remember also that the mind can quickly scan not only the past, but also the projected future consequences of a choice. Its dynamics transcend the time and space of brain physiology. When you put it all together on these revised terms, we come out doing what we please, what we decide we want to do. And this resolves the paradox.

OMNI: But actions are still caused, not free?

SPERRY: They're free to an extent. We're no longer subject to, or in the grip of, the laws of physics and chemistry as inanimate objects are. Nor do we have to obey the laws of physiology, as do our autonomic and reflex responses, our hormones and our heartbeat. In general, we are freed of the kind of mechanistic, materialist forces with which science used to saddle us. We are lifted above these into a higher realm with a different kind of control — a control unequaled in freedom anywhere else in the known universe. If you think about it, you wouldn't really want total freedom from all causation. It would be chaos.

OMNI: I've seen occasional statements that equate your views with animism or dualism [the belief that all life is produced by a spiritual force separate from matter]. I gather this is a misinterpretation?

SPERRY: Yes. We wholly reject anything supernatural, mystical, or occult in favor of the kind of reality validated by science — with the proviso, of course, that the kind of reality upheld by materialist science for more than a century has to be revised. Mentalism is strictly a one-world, this-world answer. I don't see any way for consciousness to emerge or be generated apart from a functioning brain. Everything indicates that the human mind and consciousness are inseparable attributes of an evolving, self-creating cerebral system.

Some people have used the new mentalist concepts to bolster mystical and supernatural beliefs, including those of parapsychology. Actually, under the new model, mental telepathy, psychokinesis, precognition, and other so-called psi phenomena become even less likely than before.

OMNI: In the past it's been a choice: the materialist descriptions of natural science on the one hand or various mystical or supernatural schemes of religion and philosophy on the other. If the new stance in science rejects both these traditional choices, where does it take us?

SPERRY: Well, it's just a different, middle-of-the-road alternative, a changed scientific interpretation. Among other things, it includes mental and vital forces that science has traditionally renounced. Not only does it include mind, the historic antithesis of matter, but it also puts mind over matter in the hierarchy of causal controls.

OMNI: You say these principles are general, that they extend beyond mind-brain questions and apply to all the sciences?

SPERRY: Yes. For example, in biology I've illustrated this recently in reference to the old discarded notion of "vitalism," the idea that life and living systems are characterized by special "vital" forces over and above those of physics and chemistry.

When the early biologists started hunting for these special living or vital properties, they of course failed to find anything. The longer, the harder, and deeper they looked, the more convincing it appeared that there are no such things. So it was concluded that all living things are nothing but physicochemical processes in different forms and degrees of complexity. The idea of vitalism had already become a subject of scorn and derision among nearly all biologists by the 1930s, and remains so to this day.

OMNI: Would you revive the old idea of vitalism?

SPERRY: In a modified form, yes, although my colleagues shudder at this because of the mystic connotations the word has. A new word would be better, but I'm not sure in this case we should revise the language just because a good word has mistakenly been given bad associations. We biologists had just been searching in the wrong places. You don't look for vital forces among atoms and molecules. You look instead among living things, among cells and animals responding to each other, reproducing, breathing, eating, running, flying, swimming, nest-building, and so on.

The special vital forces that distinguish living things from the nonliving are emergent, holistic properties, not properties of their physicochemical components. Nor can they be fully explained in mechanistic terms. This doesn't mean they're in any way supernatural or mystical. Those who conceived vital forces in supernatural terms were just as wrong as those who denied their existence.

OMNI: You believe these vital phenomena and these holistic properties of living things are as deserving of scientific recognition as the properties and laws of molecules or atoms?

SPERRY: Exactly. The emergent living forces should be accepted in their own right, in their own form, at their own level. When reductionist doctrine tried to tell us that there are no vital forces, just as it also had long taught that there are no mental forces, materialist science was simply wrong. Biological theory in this case was concentrating on the material or mass-energy components of living things, thinking these explained everything, and neglecting the role played by the nonmaterial space-time or pattern components.

In anything, living or nonliving, the spacing and timing of the material elements of which it is composed make all the difference in determining what a thing is.

OMNI: Can you give an illustration?

SPERRY: As a very simple example, take a population of molecules, say copper. You can shape this into a sphere, a pyramid, a long wire, a statue, whatever. All these very different things still reduce to the same material elements, the same identical population of copper molecules. Science has specific laws for the molecules, but no such laws for all the differential spacing and timing factors, the nonmaterial pattern or form factors that are crucial in determining what things are and what laws they obey. These nonmaterial space-time components tend to be thrown out and lost in the reduction process, as science aims toward ever more elementary levels of explanation.

Modern molecular biology is quite willing to accept the power of chemical or molecular forces, but when the entities in question are no longer molecules but living organisms, the reasoning suddenly undergoes a flip-flop change. The whole reductive materialist philosophy of twentieth-century science is based on this flip-flop error, a failure to credit the nonmaterial elements in reality. This is how science has misled itself and our culture into the excessive emphasis on materialism.

OMNI: But how would this concept of modified vitalism alter scientific thinking?

SPERRY: Among other things, it says that most of the atoms on our planet are primarily moved around not by atomic or subatomic laws and forces, as quantum physics would have it, but rather by the laws and forces of classical physics, of biology, geology, meteorology, even sociology, politics, and the like. For example, the molecules of higher living things are moved around mostly by the living, vital powers of the particular species in which they're embedded. They're flown through the air, galloped across the plains, swung through the jungle, propelled through the water, not by molecular forces or quantum mechanics but by the specific holistic vital and also mental properties — aims, wants, needs — possessed by the organisms in question. Once evolved, the higher laws and forces exert downward control over the lower.

OMNI: Do you see applications also in physical science?

SPERRY: Oh yes, all through. For example, in the relation of quantum mechanics to classical physics. When physicists found that classical Newtonian laws didn't work anymore for elementary particles, but that a new theory, quantum mechanics, did work, they accordingly abandoned support for the old Newtonian doctrines in favor of the new quantum theory. The new theory was taken to be a better and more accurate description of nature.

As we see it now, this was a mistake. There's just no way quantum

mechanics can replace classical mechanics for things larger than
molecules. Quantum theory can't handle the pattern factors that the
classical laws naturally incorporate. Neither is wrong; we need both.
But for different things.

OMNI: Popularized accounts of the "new physics" imply a less
mechanistic and nonmaterialist kind of reality, drawing similarities
with Eastern religions. Do you see parallels or common features with
mentalism?

SPERRY: Well, not really. In my thinking, it's not legitimate to
extrapolate from the nature of subatomic events to the world at large.
The emergent entities at higher levels contain, envelop, and control
the properties and expression of the elementary particles. So the
common world is better described in the framework of the old classical Newtonian physics, plus biology, geology, and the other sciences. The world is not all dancing energy just because the ultimate
building blocks seem to be of this nature.

OMNI: Aren't you coming back to the initial impressions a non-
scientist would get anyway?

SPERRY: Much of it seemed a matter of common sense until
science came along and began telling us otherwise. Ever since,
there's been a growing conflict between scientists and the rest of
society, felt most keenly in the humanities and those disciplines
concerned with moral values. Perhaps what I'm saying here, in effect,
is an admission: that the humanities and common sense were on the
right track all along and we in science were misled.

OMNI: Looking back, one sees that yours is not the first attempt
at a value system based on science. How does your proposal differ
from that of Karl Marx or the French biochemist Jacques Monod or
others?

SPERRY: I think they were misled, as most of the rest of us were.
They accepted science as if this meant embracing the philosophy of
materialism and the interpretations of human nature and society that
implies. Marxism upholds values and a world view that are radically
opposed to the ones that would emerge from a system based on
science as we now understand it. In Marxism, what counts in shaping
the world and human affairs are the actions man takes to fulfill his
material needs. But this overlooks the key principle of downward
causation. Under the mentalist view, the higher idealistic properties

that have evolved in man and society can supersede and control and take care of these more primitive needs.

The espousal of science by the Marxists, Monod, and many others, including today's secular humanists, has usually meant also the rejection of institutional religion. This, I think, is a mistake, especially with world conditions as they are. We need to raise our sights to higher values than those of self-interest, economic gain, politics, daily needs for personal subsistence — to higher, more long-term, more godlike priorities. This isn't something the human brain does naturally or easily. It helps to have the continual reminders, influences, and teachings of people and institutions professionally dedicated to cultivating these higher perspectives.

OMNI: But wouldn't a merger with science demand excessive restraints on religious doctrines?

SPERRY: In the past, perhaps, under the materialist philosophy. Past efforts have been very one-sided, asking, in effect, that religion mend its ways in order to conform with the facts of science, but with no similar request the other way around. On our present terms, however, it becomes a two-way compromise. Religion gives up dependence on mystical concepts, whereas science gives up much of its traditional materialist legacy.

OMNI: Most of the changes you've described relate to science. What about the changes religious doctrines might have to undergo in a union with science?

SPERRY: Well, this is something for the theologians. It's not simple. It means concepts of transcendent value, salvation, and the like have to be redefined and translated into a world view and reference frame consistent with science. It's like asking, in some respects, what form the teachings of Christ, Mohammed, Buddha, Confucius, and other founders might have taken if Copernicus, Darwin, Einstein, and all the rest had come before their time instead of later.

It's something that would take time to develop and volumes to describe, with separate books for each religious faith, sect, and denomination.

OMNI: If science is to be a greater force in religion, do you think a naturalistic and higher mentalist view of man's creator would leave us enough to believe in and revere?

SPERRY: Yes, but this gets into matters best left to theology. That's why we need a partnership.

OMNI: But would the scientific view leave something that theology could really hope to live with?

SPERRY: I think so. Remember that the scientific view includes, along with the human factors, also the cosmic and the subatomic and everything in between — the entire evolving web of all creation and the whole matrix of forces involved. No one has yet described anything that even remotely compares in vastness, complexity, diversity, and awesome beauty. It's certainly something to revere!

One can even look at it the other way around, as an overall gain for religion, just as when mankind gave up the belief that the sun was driven across the sky each day by Apollo. We now think of the concepts that eventually replaced that as an advance, not a loss.

OMNI: But can visualizing God in this way help people deal with personal emotions, like loneliness and despair, the way faith in a personal deity does?

SPERRY: It would depend. There's nothing wrong with personalizing a difficult concept if one realizes what one's doing and doesn't take it literally, especially where it doesn't harm others. I emphasize science because of its rigorous standards for validation. Also, science, like revelation, takes us beyond the bounds of ordinary experience. Science gives us deeper insights into the nature and meaning of things. It helps clear the mystery and show the way. It enables us to get a better and more intimate understanding of the forces that made, move, and control the universe and created man.

OMNI: You argue overall that if religious beliefs were brought into conformance with the revelations of science, it would lead to the kinds of social values and beliefs needed to correct a lot of adverse trends in today's world. How does that follow?

SPERRY: Well, the shift from an otherworldly to a this-world reference frame, for example, would logically mean that our planet should no longer be conceived of and treated as merely a way station to something beyond. Among other things, it would result in added respect and concern for the quality of this life and what we do to this world.

OMNI: Where do you stand on claims of religion based on revelation?

SPERRY: Revelations are fine. We use them in science and welcome them. Whenever you become intensely wrapped up in a problem over a long time, it can become part of you. It gets ingrained in the subconscious, so that sudden breakthrough answers seem sometimes almost as if they're coming from somewhere else. Of course, science throws away many of these revelations when they subsequently fail to hold up under experimental test. That's the crux, the double-check against outside reality.

Anybody who has studied the brain, its inputs, outputs, the way it works, and so on, doesn't trust these inner workings on their own without some kind of validation. The human brain can easily go wrong by itself. You can let your logical processing run loose inside and arrive at all kinds of rationalizations. That's just the nature of brains. They have a built-in logical processing system, and they pick up reasons for this and that, but they're not always airtight. You can come up with all kinds of wonderful, wishful-thinking conclusions, entirely novel concepts made up just of the brain's own runnings. But science gets around this by demanding that the brain process check and double-check with outside reality. That's the difference between science and other sources of belief.

OMNI: You have suggested that an ethic based in science might work for the United Nations and world government.

SPERRY: Yes. The point there is that much of the difficulty in getting agreement for world government is that peoples of differing faiths and cultures don't want to be governed by the values of opposing ideologies. Capitalist countries don't want to have to submit to Communist values, or vice versa, Christians to Muslim values, et cetera. There seems little chance in the foreseeable future for getting all the different countries to agree to give up their own beliefs in order to unite around the ethical and value principles of any existing ideology. One can imagine the possibility, however, that all countries might be willing, for purposes of international law, to compromise on a new, relatively neutral ethic founded in the truth and world view of science.

OMNI: Is it wise to try to plan and direct a shift in values? Values usually change under the pressure of practical reality, when conditions reach what you've called the "margins of intolerability."

SPERRY: Well, you can go this way, letting world conditions force the new values, but by the time this course takes effect, it'll be too late. Availability of basic resources per capita is already going down. The law of diminishing returns shows everywhere. Species are being eliminated in alarming numbers every year. The dignity and meaning of life for minority creatures around us is almost gone already. The longer you wait for deteriorating conditions to force a value change, the worse the residual quality of our biosphere.

I'd rather go for ideals. I don't like to think only about a "sustainable society" — how many masses the world could sustain in terms of agribusiness, fisheries, and remaining topsoil if we get all of our technology working right. I'd much rather think of what the ideal population would be to make the life experience the best, most beautiful, and wondrous overall.

OMNI: It seems that many scientists turn their attention to global and philosophical problems as they get older.

SPERRY: Most scientists as they get older and see the end approaching no longer have the patience to waste their time on the kinds of things they formerly thought they could do forever. You do raise your perspectives with age. I don't think this is something to ridicule, as many scientists are inclined to do in their younger years. It's something to foster and value — put up rather than down.

Besides, it's the young people today, thinking young people, who are most concerned about these questions. They're the ones who are most affected and are afraid that in five or ten years we're all going to be dead. When my generation grew up, this wasn't a concern. We had a future and hope and heroes. The great cities of the world were still great, and things and people weren't so expendable.

The human brain has tremendous powers to become adapted and habituated. Unless you're old enough to have directly experienced the ambience of earlier times, you don't have much basis for comparison and don't sense what's happened. But these days, adults of all ages ought to be concerned about global problems. It's just a matter of looking around.

OMNI: Does the rational, antimystical approach you advocate leave any room in life for realms of the irrational, for fantasy, or for profound mystery beyond the reach of science?

SPERRY: Oh, yes, definitely. We certainly don't think science covers everything or has all the answers, or dogmatically proclaims a final, absolute, or infallible truth. The more we learn, the more new mysteries we uncover. The argument says nothing against mysticism, fantasy, and the like in art or drama, for example, or in the private sphere or anywhere else where it doesn't influence the laws we're governed by. The concern is mainly with those social values and beliefs that directly or indirectly get written into constitutions, manifestos, and "laws of the land" — and perhaps future "laws of the planet." Everything considered, it would seem safer for our children's children if we don't continue to gamble the world's destiny on conflicting mystical answers anymore — or on outmoded materialist ideologies.

Programmed Man

Walden Revisited

B. F. Skinner

We can discover general processes at work in every individual,
and with those we can conduct experiments to improve our
knowledge and develop a technology of behavior.

*In one of his essays, Professor B. F. Skinner reprinted a cartoon
that shows one mouse exclaiming to another, "Boy, have I got that
guy up there fixed! Every time I press this bar, he gives me food!"
Who is controlled, and how? Is the experimenter, in his desire to verify
a theory or to win the acclaim of colleagues, really "freer" or more
autonomous than the mouse? Questions like these — questions that
concern the causes, conditions, and control of behavior — have been
Burrhus Frederic Skinner's absorbing study for fifty years. And his
answers have directly challenged our most cherished belief — that we
are essentially self-directing beings tenaciously grasping the reins of
our own destinies.*

*After a Pennsylvania boyhood marked by a wide-ranging curiosity,
and after completing his undergraduate studies, Skinner began his
career as a graduate instructor at Harvard, in 1931. At that time the
school of psychology known as behaviorism had been developing for
two decades along lines laid down by its founder, John B. Watson. It
is only stimuli and the resultant behavior, Watson had insisted, that
the psychologist can observe and measure; therefore, only stimuli and
behavior (rather than motives, drives, emotions, or other abstractions)
can be the foundations of a genuinely scientific psychology. The goals
of such a discipline would be the prediction and control of behavior.
No one since Watson has done more to develop techniques for achieving
those intriguing, if controversial, goals than B. F. Skinner.*

Photograph: Pat Hill

*He has been a researcher (the "Skinner box" for operant conditioning of animals, the first teaching machines, the "air crib" for efficient and healthful infant care are all his inventions); writer (*The Behavior of Organisms, Walden Two, Beyond Freedom and Dignity*); and teacher (at Harvard, the University of Minnesota, Indiana University, and finally Harvard again, where he has been Pierce Professor of Psychology since 1958). Although his experimental techniques and findings are widely accepted, his interpretation of them — and his advocacy of their application to social goals — has kept him at the center of controversy. Skinner, however, remains unflappable.*

Critics have charged that his theories of behavior deny all that is most important about human beings, and that his widely influential views could lead to a society of puppets continually manipulated by rewards and punishments, or "positive and negative reinforcements." But we are already *manipulated, Skinner had rejoined, by parents, institutions, economics, and such potent forces as advertising and the media. "The best defense I can see is to make all behavioral processes as familiar as possible. Let everyone know what can be used against him. When people are being pushed around, controlled by methods that are obvious to them, and when things become too aversive, they turn against the controller."*

That Skinner wants to see behavioral principles used to fulfill human potential has not spared him vehement opposition. "What people do about such a scientific picture of man," he said, "is call it wrong, demeaning, and dangerous, argue against it, and attack those who propose to defend it. They do so not out of wounded vanity but because the scientific formulation has destroyed accustomed reinforcers" — such as the reassuring but unprovable notion of free will. Although he is an accomplished and deliberately provocative controversialist, Skinner still feigns surprise at the violent responses that some people have to the utopian community depicted in Walden Two. *"I've often asked myself, what's eating these people? Apparently the main difficulty is that my 'good life' was planned by someone."*

The ideas of planning and control are so loaded that it is sometimes difficult to remember Skinner's first and lasting commitment: to attaining a scientific understanding of human behavior in accord with the evidence, rather than with what we might *like to believe. Largely owing to Skinner's influence, that understanding is growing steadily. The implications of our increasing knowledge of human behavior were explored by Professor Skinner and the British journalist Michael Hollingshead in 1979.*

OMNI: Can there ever be a genuine science of human behavior?

SKINNER: It all depends on how complete a science you mean. There are things the biochemists can't explain, and the astronomers know how difficult it is to make sense of the radiation coming in from the universe. Their fields are obviously much more advanced. But there is at least a "core science" of behavior.

I don't think for a moment that we'll ever be able to predict what an individual will do next, because that depends on his genetic make-up and personal history, and we can never know enough about that for detailed prediction. But we can discover general processes at work in every individual, and with those we can conduct experiments to improve our knowledge and develop a technology of behavior: better ways of teaching, of inducing people to work carefully and well and to enjoy what they're doing, of solving psychological problems, and so on.

OMNI: Perhaps the best-known tools of the behavioral technology you've envisioned are negative and positive reinforcement — punishment and reward. There seems to be a long-term tendency in your work to move toward the latter.

SKINNER: Yes. I don't like punishment. I don't like to be punished or to see others punished. One of the first tasks of a science of behavior should be to find substitutes for traditional punitive methods. Over the centuries we've successfully moved away from many of them, as in education and psychotherapy. Now it is being done in industry, too. Many people feel that a worker's wages are positive reinforcement, but they aren't, really. You don't work on Monday morning for the paycheck on Friday afternoon; you work to avoid being discharged and missing the paycheck. In other words, an industrial-wage system establishes a level of existence from which you can be cut off if you don't work.

Systems that involve positive reinforcement yield better results and remove the side effects of negative reinforcement that people try to escape: absenteeism, frequent job changes, and so forth.

OMNI: You've spoken of the possibility of a controlled environment for retarded people. Can you expand on that?

SKINNER: I think the goal there is to build a "prosthetic" environment. Eyeglasses, hearing aids, crutches, are prosthetic devices that enable people to function well despite deficiencies. Why can't a whole institution be a prosthetic environment, a world in which a retarded person can lead a reasonably dignified, happy life? It won't be the everyday world. It also won't be what most of today's institutions for the mentally retarded are like; these people are political footballs and don't have the money they need to live along these lines.

OMNI: In *Walden Two* you envisioned a "controlled" environment that would stimulate growth and happiness. Today there are several communities based on those ideas. [Twin Oaks is the most famous.] Did you imagine that this would happen?

SKINNER: I was guessing at what might be done. I wrote the book in 1945, before much work had been done in the field of behavior modification. There had been some work on the desensitization of fears, but the background of the work we have now just didn't exist.

I guessed wrong some of the time, but right, I think, a surprisingly large part of the time. I described a world of minimal consumption and minimal pollution and of maximal socializing and opportunity for creative behavior. It substitutes direct interaction for economic exchanges and police action. Instead of punishing your neighbor by going to the police, you censure with a frown. There are no contrived reinforcers: no one passes out tokens or candies. It's a world so designed that the behaviors needed to keep it going are automatically reinforced.

OMNI: A documentary film showing your visit to Twin Oaks, one of the communities based on Walden Two, raised the question of "defection." The film showed that people came for a short time but didn't stay on. In fact, only one of the founding members was still there after twelve years. Did they ask for advice on how to create a more stable community?

SKINNER: I don't believe they were asking me for advice, but I thought they paid attention when I made some suggestions — for example, about their scarcity of entertainment. There was almost no money in their budget to make life interesting. They had a fiddler for square dancing but very little equipment for recorded music. There was no television set, but they are now putting in a single color set with a video recorder so that a program can be put on a cassette and people can drop in at any time and play it. I suggested also that by adding a video camera they could record their own plays and other programs.

I don't think their high turnover is as much of an implicit criticism as you might suppose. People go to Twin Oaks, spend a year or two, and leave, but they leave in much better shape than when they arrived. It's a therapeutic experience for many people who learn how to get along well enough to adjust to the outside world, which is where they may eventually prefer to be.

OMNI: The idea of an extensively *planned* community worries many people, perhaps because they associate planning with despotism and associate "muddling through" with democracy.

SKINNER: There's nothing necessarily autocratic about planning. I don't see it as a problem, if I'm to judge from the communities that are modeled a bit on the pattern of Walden Two — not completely, of course; they're too small, for one thing, nor are the residents all good behaviorists. I understand that at East Wind, a similar community in Missouri, they tried for a few months, as an experiment, to get a consensus on every decision. If it works better, then you adopt that way; that's how things should be done. Twin Oaks has had groups who practiced meditation. At one point there was a strong anti–Walden Two group, and it was tolerated. No one suppressed it.

OMNI: But the question of control keeps arising, because the planned environment seems to presuppose a controller.

SKINNER: *Quis custodiet ipsos custodes?* I don't see why my answer to that isn't more easily understood. The control, you see, emerges in the evolution of cultural practices. I'm not talking about social Darwinism, the emergence of a culture that will "take over," but about successful practices within a culture. If you design a better way of teaching, who is to put it into effect? Those, obviously, who profit from good teaching. At present the educational establishment in America is so inert that no one is in control of anything except a tradition that squanders half the lives of millions of people.

The thing about a small community is that everyone is asking, "Will it work? Will it survive?" We don't ask those questions about, say, the American way of life, because we think it's going to survive long enough that we needn't worry. In a small community, when it appears that a practice increases the chance of survival, that practice is adopted. You don't need a controller: the demonstrated advance takes control through action that furthers the adoption of the practice.

If the survival of America were really threatened by a 20 percent illiteracy rate, or whatever it is today, then new ways of teaching reading and writing would be adopted quickly. But we're not worried enough. If you have a culture that takes the future into account, then you can take steps to prevent some totalitarian "controller" from wreaking destruction.

OMNI: The word *survive* has been very important in the recent transformation of China. The Chinese people were told the nation wouldn't survive unless they worked toward certain social goals.

SKINNER: Any revolution brings that into play almost immediately. Since 1917, the Soviet Union has never gotten over its fear of attack. The whole question is, what kind of conformity contributes to the survival of a culture, and what kind threatens it? After all, we want conformity in paying our taxes, obeying the law, respecting the rights and property of others, and so on.

OMNI: What about education? People resist the idea of teaching machines, which they think of as leading to too much conformity in the students.

SKINNER: I object to teaching everyone precisely the same thing, because diversity is essential. A system that doesn't recognize this threatens survival.

OMNI: You have said that we should teach things more important than geography, arithmetic — things such as ways of memorizing, clear thinking, three-dimensional thinking.

SKINNER: I don't think anyone has adequately analyzed the behavior we call thinking; certainly no one I know of is working on the most effective ways of teaching it. Trying to teach people to think would be a good way to discover what thinking really is.

OMNI: Are you describing the teaching of abilities rather than teaching facts?

SKINNER: I don't believe in "abilities." To say that an artist is creative because he possesses creativity is double-talk. If you look at what the creative artist *does* that is different from what others do, you might find out something that would suggest ways of producing more creative behavior.

Or take "curiosity." People don't look about them because they possess a trait or faculty of curiosity. They look about because looking about has been reinforced, because surprising things have turned up underneath objects and around corners. If you grow up in a world in which everything is visible, you go through life accepting whatever you see and never exploring.

OMNI: How do you distinguish between conditioned behavior and what the ethologist Konrad Lorenz calls imprints — genetic, neurologically determined behavior that seems to be inborn and is very powerful? Doesn't conditioned behavior require continued reinforcement?

SKINNER: It has been clearly shown by Neil Peterson, one of my students, that what is inherited in the case of imprinting is *not* a tendency to follow the mother or another imprinted figure, as Lorenz's gosling followed him; it is a *susceptibility to reinforcement by proximity.* Peterson showed that if, when a duckling pecks at a spot on the wall, you bring the imprinted object closer, the duckling will continue to peck. In nature, the behavior that brings an object closer is walking toward it. But Peterson went on to show that if you arrange things so that the object moves away when the duckling walks toward it and comes around in front when the duckling walks away, the duckling will walk away. So even that "innate" behavior depends on appropriate reinforcement.

There may well be redundant mechanisms, though. A colt struggles to its feet after being born and stays close to its mother, probably as a result of natural selection, although I daresay we could also get it to stamp its hoof to make its mother come close, as Peterson did with the duckling in another experiment.

OMNI: Do you apply your findings to motivate yourself?

SKINNER: Yes, quite definitely. Most of my professional life these days is verbal — I no longer have a laboratory — and I have carefully designed a world in which I can come up with as much verbal behavior that is strictly mine as possible. I could write books by commenting on or revising what others have said and written; I could get books out of books, but I don't. I get them out of my own research, my own books, and my own life.

OMNI: Can you extrapolate to others? Are there general principles by which we can learn to guide ourselves?

SKINNER: Oh, yes. Several books have recently been published in the field of self-management. You don't control yourself by using your will power, but by arranging a world in which behavior that is important to you actually occurs. You control your behavior precisely as you would that of someone else. I'm not saying that I do this perfectly or that anyone can. But, by noting the conditions under which we work well and by making every effort to maintain them, we can maximize the probability of the behavior that is important to us.

OMNI: Is writing conditioned by the reward of seeing it in print, or would you say it's force of habit?

SKINNER: "Force of habit" doesn't tell you anything. Of course it's important to get something published, but that's not the reinforcer when you're at your desk. The main thing is getting sentences to say what you have to say. And you punish yourself when you discover that a section is badly written and must be done over. The critical response after publication undoubtedly has some effect. But when, say, you're practicing on a trampoline, it's not the award at the Olympics that makes the difference. It's doing it right and not cracking your skull.

OMNI: Have you paid attention to such modification programs as est?

SKINNER: Yes. Three of my friends have been through it. Two of them wrote a report, saying that they felt that it had had favorable consequences for them. I suppose any rather violent episode in one's life could have favorable effects, but it can also be dangerous.

I'm not going to try to explain the Guyana tragedy, or to explain the almost equal tragedies of the Moonies and Scientologists. They're still alive — some part of them, at least — but it's a kind of behavioral death.

OMNI: People talk loosely about how others have been programmed and need to be deprogrammed. How do you feel about this question of reconditioning people?

SKINNER: In a way, all psychotherapy is reprogramming. You aren't curing a disorder; you're adding something to the history of the individual. If what you add is powerful enough, it will almost certainly lead to different behavior.

OMNI: One prospect for the design of environments arises in the current discussion of space habitats; that's an area where your work could have important applications. Have you talked with Gerard K. O'Neill or others working on that?

SKINNER: No, although I have thought about it. I think it's going to be a long time before space solves the problem of overpopulation here, but we are probably going to have space platforms for small populations, and their survival raises the question of design. If things turned sour, you'd be in real trouble. So you must think very carefully about how people are to interact. Wouldn't it be wonderful if we thought as seriously about a classroom, a factory, or a family? But our sense of the future is still too far away.

OMNI: Is that because awareness of a future is not a motivation in itself? People can be aware of the connection between smoking cigarettes and lung cancer, but it doesn't stop them from smoking.

SKINNER: It's the whole question of whether remote consequences can have any effect upon people. Obviously they can't, in a literal sense, because a future event does not affect anything. But some cultures have managed to give those who belong to them reasons for behaving now in ways that have a bearing on the future. Successful cultures give the best current reasons for behaving in ways that make a future possible.

OMNI: Do you see anything developing in current American attitudes or behavior that might threaten our future? Do you detect any promising signs?

SKINNER: If you think about threats to the human species, there are many areas in which the United States plays an important role. First of all, we have stockpiles of nuclear weapons and a general unwillingness to reduce them, and particularly to make sure that not one nuclear bomb falls into the wrong hands. Second, America consumes a disproportionate amount of resources. We are using up critical materials and energy at a very high rate, compared with the rate of consumption by, say, the people of India. This poses a threat to the whole world.

However, there are things in our favor: our technology is superior to most nations, and we are far ahead in the analysis of behavior. No other country comes near us in this field. Interest is spreading now, but the technology of behavior has been primarily an American achievement. If it proves to be the case that our only hope is to catch ourselves before it's too late and to apply scientific analysis to our problems, then perhaps we can be forgiven our carelessness in other areas.

Genetic Destiny
E. O. Wilson

Society increasingly has neglected the substructure of biology, to its own peril.

The publication of E. O. Wilson's Sociobiology *in 1975 was a landmark event in the history of biology. This enormous volume is a remarkable compendium of Wilson's observations on the relationship between biology and social behavior throughout the animal kingdom, covering everything from* Homo sapiens *to insects. (Wilson is by trade an entomologist; his specialty is ants; he calls them his "totem animal.")*

The message Sociobiology *carries is a startling one: that various kinds of social behavior are genetically programmed into many species, including our own, and that this programming is particularly true of the social behavior human beings label "altruism," which Wilson defines as "self-destructive behavior performed for the benefit of others."*

The elegant theoretical construct that underlies this assertion is the notion of kin selection. According to Darwin's theory of natural selection, the organism that possesses traits that help it to cope successfully with its environment is the one that survives and passes on its genes to its offspring. But the altruistic organism, as Wilson defines it, dies, usually leaving comparatively few offspring. This means, in Darwinian terms, that genes for altruism, if they exist, will be wiped out before they can be passed on. The kin-selection theory provides an explanation of this apparent paradox by pointing out that altruistic behavior protects those with whom one has genes in common — relatives or kin. Thus, such behavior is equivalent to saving pieces of oneself; and those pieces will continue to persist in the offspring of one's relatives, if not in one's own progeny.

Sociobiology *has also rekindled the century-old nature-nurture question: Which is more important in the making of human beings, heredity or environment? Wilson argues strongly on the side of nature, declaring that the sexes behave differently because of differences in the genes.*

Following the publication of Sociobiology *and* On Human Nature, *which appeared in 1979, critics charged that Wilson, an entomologist, did not really have the background to speak about human behavior. Responding to such attacks, Wilson commented that* On Human Nature *is "not a work of science, but a work about science and how far the natural sciences can penetrate into human behavior before they will be transformed into something new . . . . Its core is a speculative essay about the profound consequences that will follow as social theory at long last meets the natural sciences."*

Edward Osborn Wilson, an only child, was born in Birmingham, Alabama, in 1929, and was raised and educated in Alabama until he went to Harvard to work on his doctorate. He has been in Cambridge ever since and now holds the positions of Frank B. Baird, Jr., Professor of Science and curator of entomology at the Museum of Comparative Zoology. He is tall and rather thin, an enthusiastic and unabashed talker, and a dedicated jogger. The people he admires most are "the ones who have great goals they persevere toward over long periods of time in a controlled and fully rational way." In 1978 Dr. Wilson was interviewed for Omni *by Tabitha M. Powledge, a science writer with an expertise in genetics.*

OMNI: One of your conclusions in *On Human Nature* is that there are what you call "modest" differences between the sexes that are genetic; these become emphasized by culture in most places. You then go on to say that these innate differences between men and women could probably be canceled through careful training. Should they be?

WILSON: That's one of the questions I raise.

OMNI: Answer it.

WILSON: I'll leave the question open. I say there are three things we could do. We could decide to exaggerate the differences. But that would exacerbate the current circumstances. Domination and injustice would continue, and individual development would be stunted. The person who might want to move into roles not ordinarily associated with his or her sex would be deprived.

The second alternative would be to erase the differences. As the evidence appears to me, they are so slight they could be erased with only a little bit of tinkering. You could probably get statistical equivalence in roles, so that you would have approximately the same percentage of women doctors as men doctors or women senators as men senators or men nurses as women nurses, et cetera, and approximately the same amount of time being spent by each sex in the home in domestic chores and in raising children and so forth. The evidence seems to suggest that predispositions are modest enough that they could be erased without a great deal of difficulty, but it would require more knowledge than we have.

The third alternative would be laissez-faire, which essentially is what this society has been exploring: equal access, equal opportunity rigidly enforced, but then letting the chips fall where they may. However, if those genetic predispositions which appear to exist do in fact exist, then you probably would get, even with rigidly enforced equal access, some statistical difference in the outcome.

OMNI: One of the examples you cite is the second generation of the kibbutz.

WILSON: Yes. I started off feeling that the Israeli kibbutz was a good piece of evidence of the stubbornness of sex differences, but that has been compromised, in my opinion, by the presence of powerful influences from Jewish patriarchal ideology. However, the kibbutz is still very suggestive. It's interesting to see the regression of women toward more traditional roles even in a culture that explicitly calls for egalitarianism and equality. And the second generation of daughters has gone further than their mothers. They demand and receive a longer period of time each day with their children, time that is significantly entitled the "hour of love." Some of the most gifted have resisted recruitment into higher levels of commercial and political leadership.

Laissez-faire, on first thought, might seem to be the most congenial to personal liberty and development. But that's not necessarily true. With identical education for men and women and equal access to all

professions, men are more likely than not to continue to be dispro-
portionately represented in political life, business, and science.
Many would fail to participate fully in formative aspects of child-
rearing. The result might legitimately be viewed as restrictive on the
complete emotional development of individuals.

I should add that this last note entered into my thinking as a result
of a discussion with a feminist. It was pointed out to me that males,
especially in our society, tend to think of the professions as being
the summum bonum, that the purpose of everyone in society is to
move toward the professions, and that the entire women's liberation
movement consists of women demanding or getting access to the
professions. But it cuts the other way, too. The more balanced
feminists tend to see that the dichotomization of society according to
sex also prevents men from taking part in many activities and many
emotional involvements. I had to concede the point. I don't feel at
this stage that there is any basis for suggesting what should be done,
I'd only point out that there is a cost connected with each one of
these alternatives. I use the sex-role problem as the paradigm in this
book for discussing a new kind of calculus for social design that we
will have to begin to develop. The fact is that we do have to consider
the cost of certain moral standards or certain societal goals, as
opposed to others.

OMNI: Relate what you just said about sex roles to your discussion
of homosexuality, which, it seems to me, also has a lot of policy
implications.

WILSON: I'm arguing for a whole different view of homosexuals.

OMNI: You base it on an intriguing argument, describing what
you think sexual relationships are all about. Though your interest is
in genetics, you present the fascinating argument that it's not procreation that is the terribly important function of sexual relationships,
but rather —

WILSON: It's bonding. And once you appreciate that what sexual
behavior is all about is primarily bonding — the establishment of
particular kinds of human relationships that are needed for the
rearing of offspring, for the maintenance of human society, and not
for procreation alone — once you appreciate that, then you suddenly
get a completely new view. For one thing, it suddenly makes sense
why sex and sex relationships and sexual imagery pervade almost all
of our social existence. We —

OMNI: It's not just a creation of Madison Avenue?

WILSON: [Laugh] No. Certainly not. And I don't think it's just a creation of Western culture, either. Sex is pervasive and it's important in *all* cultures, though more in some than others, obviously. In cultures that have been sexually repressive and are going through sexual liberation, of course, it probably commands an abnormal amount of attention. But it's pervasive in most aspects of life in all cultures. In subtle and difficult ways sexuality has confounded psychologists; it's been the source of endlessly complicated psychoanalytic theory, such as why it pervades the relationship with one's father, or why sexual images can be transferred so easily to automobiles, and so on.

I think the general answer is that sexual behavior in human beings as primarily a bonding mechanism transcends even direct, heterosexual, man-wife relations. And we need to explore the possibility that homosexual bonding may be a biological mechanism. In presenting this rather radical hypothesis — I didn't want to defend it too strongly, because I don't think the evidence is overpowering — I did want to stress that the Judeo-Christian view, that sex exists for procreation, and the particular customs and particular attitudes toward sex that are embodied therein, is a view that is optimal for an expanding, rapidly growing population but inappropriate for stable, steady-state populations.

OMNI: But in your discussion of homosexuality, you tend to be much more prescriptive than you are in your discussions of sex roles.

WILSON: That's quite true. I felt the need to be more emphatic. Also, it may be that the strength of the predisposition is different.

OMNI: You mean that homosexual proclivities are somehow more genetic than sex roles?

WILSON: That may well be the case. It may be harder to erase homosexuality than to erase sex-role differences. We ought to consider things like the "hardness" of various predispositions when we add biological dimensions to social science. I believe the immediate benefit of the sociobiological approach is to put on a much firmer basis what is natural and what is not natural. Sociobiology, then, can aid us in making moral judgments and also in the process of evaluating cost.

Take the case of homosexuality. There is a lot of evidence to support my hypothesis, and, furthermore, it should be explored;

biology has not been explored properly in the case of homosexuality. The hypothesis should be explored, and if it turns out that the evidence favors it, then suddenly we would see that the benefits from suppressing homosexuality, from trying to cure homosexuals, from depriving them of their rights so that they cannot teach at school, the benefits would shrink enormously, and we would simultaneously see the cost expand. The results would be — and I believe should be — toleration, a completely different view of homosexuals, acceptance.

OMNI: Okay. Then that leads into what seems to me to be an interesting point, and certainly a source of some worry over sociobiology, and that is the use of genetic explanations to excuse some forms of behavior. Let's take aggression as an example. You argue fairly strongly for aggression's being innate. Why can't you use the same line of reasoning to argue for toleration of aggression as well as of homosexuality?

WILSON: If I am going to say what I am saying about homosexuals, why can't the same argument be used to save a war? But that is why I refuse to accept the naturalistic fallacy; that is, to say that what is natural is good. In the case of homosexuality, what I am saying is that you cannot condemn homosexuality on the grounds that it is biologically unnatural. I hope I demolish that argument. And then I say that we will have to recognize that there are some things that represent biological predispositions that are extremely difficult to eradicate. Some of them are absurd legacies of the hunter-gatherer society. It's just one of those crazy things we got stuck with, like hair on the backs of our hands, or the difficulty blue-eyed people have when they go to the tropics. There are certain things we've inherited that are inconvenient. Sex-role differentiation may well be one of those. Homosexuality may be one of those. The readiness to switch into violent aggressive behavior surely is one of those. And all I can suggest is the cost-benefit analysis made possible by sociobiology and other biological studies, and then an open discussion of what we want to do about it.

You know, aggression, even violent aggression by itself, is not necessarily an evil thing. All I'm saying is that with the present global situation, it clearly is to be proscribed, because it is harmful to everyone, including ourselves. We need to study it more and find ways of getting around it. This cost-benefit analysis I'm talking about, deciding what we want in societies — stabilization, rapid technological progress, whatever — has to do with things that are not going to be decided by reference to our crazy-quilt biological heritage.

OMNI: I find those three examples particularly interesting, because it seems to me the implications of what you're saying are quite different in each case. One is that as far as sex roles are concerned, we may want to choose a route that tends to eliminate the differences. As far as homosexuality is concerned, we may want to do the opposite; that is, grant homosexuals a lot more recognition than we have. And as for aggression, we may sometimes want to curb it and sometimes not, which seems to be the hardest possible sort of thing.

WILSON: I would say that on the earth as it is today, we would always want to curb violent aggression.

OMNI: But you and I would not have wanted to curb the United States' aggressive response to attack in 1941. You think it is possible to choose to suppress a behavior or not suppress it or to treat it variably, depending on the circumstances?

WILSON: Exactly. I think it depends on the circumstances that we really want society to move toward. All that sociobiology can do, in my opinion, is to tell us more about where we came from, what we've got, what our predispositions are, as an aid in the cost-benefit analysis that goes into any discussion of our future goals. That's what a large part of politics and social planning is all about: what our goals are, what we want to achieve beyond mere survival.

OMNI: You make some suggestions about channeling aggression. One of the suggestions you appear to be making is that sports, particularly organized sports — professional sports, I think, is the phrase you use — serve part of that function.

WILSON: There is a strong tendency to engage in competitive sports and to identify chauvinistically with them. You see nationalism at its worst in world soccer meets. Good, kindly Americans can develop a real hatred toward Cincinnati or Seattle at the height of the championship play-offs. It's so strong that we can identify with it and do it even though the team members are being traded back and forth and come from all over the country. It's interesting to listen to interviews with athletes who have just been traded into a local franchise. They may come from Texas or have played for UCLA, but now they're joining the Celtics, and what they say is predictable: "Boston's a lovely town. I feel a sense of community here." We have a predisposition to be xenophobic, to be chauvinistic, to identify with a familylike group that occupies a particular territory. This is all quite naked and open, and it's not harmful unless it exacerbates nationalistic feelings or racial or ethnic feelings, which can then become deadly. Another example is what I call biophilia. I am inclined to think of that as a very strong natural predisposition. That's the desire to be surrounded by other living things, like plants and pets. Pets are not just child surrogates, you know.

OMNI: No. I quite agree.

WILSON: And I think that all these things we've been talking about — sports, sexual bonding, biophilia, the things that occupy our existence and make us uniquely human — ultimately have a pragmatic basis. That's the whole point of my book: that human beings are unique. Their behavior is much more narrowly circumscribed than most people realize. But when you start comparing us with other kinds of animal societies, you realize we are really peculiar, and that these peculiarities are based to a large extent on early tendencies and inclinations. Those inclinations are not the simple-minded gene-to-behavior pattern that some people think I mean. That would be true in the case of an ant or a mosquito; but for us, they are the learning rules, the predispositions to learn one thing as opposed to another, to seek immediate and large rewards from doing one thing instead of the other. In other words, we are much more predisposed to learn to play soccer, or to watch soccer, than we are to, shall we say, cumulate prime numbers.

OMNI: Well, the emotional reward may be the immediate reason that we do something, but you're saying there's an underlying functional reason that gave rise to the emotion that promotes the behavior.

WILSON: And that doesn't come completely clear unless you consider that valuation in the genetic coinage, particularly in early human history. This is kind of a crazy thing, but it really is at the root of the absurdity of human existence.

OMNI: Let's not get too existential! But while we're on the subject, just as another example of this, one of the things that's provoked the most discussion and most controversy around *On Human Nature* is what you say about religion. You make a case for the genetic origins of religion, including why it has been maintained and what its future is.

WILSON: That's possibly the most original chapter in the book.

OMNI: I found it original and striking. It may end up overshadowing what you say about sex, as far as public discussion is concerned.

WILSON: I think you're right. There's a rule about dinner conversation — that you don't discuss sex or religion or, I might add, aggression.

OMNI: The biological origins of both sex and aggression are subjects that have now been discussed an awful lot in the last ten years or so, but a biological origin of religion really has not.

WILSON: I agree with you and think you've put your finger on something very important. I have tussled with people — critics and others — in endless reviews and seminars and so on on sex and aggression. I really think I understand virtually all the concerns that people have about these: the people who think that talking about aggression as a natural predisposition is dangerous or the ultrafeminists who think that talking about any difference in biological predisposition is sinful.

But in the case of religion there is a yawning pit. Religion's really the pivot of *all* that we do and *all* that we really fight about, particularly when you incorporate ideology into it, the propensity people have to identify with a particular ideology, with a world view that becomes absolute in their minds. In my view, such identification is tribalistic, so I have looked at it that way.

Religion has not been examined by biologists or sociobiologists or evolutionists at all carefully. One of the main reasons is that it's uniquely human. This is one area of behavior where you *can't* draw any principles from ants or baboons. But that doesn't lower the value of taking a more biological approach to religion. One can look through all the animal kingdom and plant kingdom and see case after case of unique structures or unique behavior patterns that have developed. They make sense only when you study the particular biology of that species.

Along with our productive, semantic language, I think religion is the unique human trait, sui generis. It has to be studied on its own terms, but it has to be looked at as a biological phenomenon, not just a cultural phenomenon nor as an aberration nor, as some would like to have it, the conduit for divine guidance to man.

So, with that proposition in mind, I then explored in that chapter an interesting hypothesis: that religion is essentially an extension of tribalism and of the need for human beings to be able to subordinate themselves, at least temporarily, to concerted, irrational, and even frenzied group activity.

This view has forerunners in some of the anthropological studies of religion, where the students of the subject, like [anthropologist] Anthony Wallace and even going back all the way to [Emile] Durkheim, have looked for functional explanations of religion; the group-activity hypothesis is *one* of the primary functions they see in it. There are also other explanations, such as the psychoanalytic one, which is, to me, just an intermediate-function explanation, like looking for why we eat in terms of metabolism and digestive enzymes. Sure, those are important, and I'm sure psychoanalytic explanations are important for understanding the full range of religious behavior, but we are interested in the ultimate understanding — where did it come from and why is it so powerful?

What the chapter attempts to do is to examine the main features of religious behavior, from magic to witchcraft to ritual to mythology, in light of the hypothesis that among our learning predispositions are almost certainly strong predispositions to xenophobia, to attention to charismatic leadership, to subordination, to group worship, to the ability to regard a covenant and a set of dogmas and rituals as beyond question. These may be unique human behavioral properties that have to be studied on their own, but they are genetic predispositions, nonetheless. I'm thinking of the ability to go through an epiphany toward religious conversion. Or the powerful tendency to identify with a religious group you think has the absolute truth, especially embodied by the utterances of a principal leader in it.

I think these capabilities can be related back to the behavior in prehistory of human beings who were required to develop a covenant, a social contract, such that they followed certain rules absolutely, even though many of the rules were arbitrary. They had the ability to subordinate themselves temporarily to the unity of the group they belonged to for the welfare of the tribe. And this, of course, contributed to their own ultimate genetic welfare.

In many cases you can see the evidence of benefits to the devotees, but even that isn't necessary, as long as the family, the genetic allies within the tribe, are being benefited in the long term through the devotion of the individual. That's kind of a stark, and perhaps to some people even an unpleasant, way of viewing religion. Yet I find it fascinating. To me, it explains an enormous amount about religious belief, the phenomenon of the true believer, the ease with which people use ideologies for tribalism and for self-seeking, and the capacity, the endless capacity human beings have for hypocrisy and self-deception when they give a religious reason for selfish or group-centered behavior.

OMNI: Assuming that's the reason for the origin of religious practices, do those reasons still apply? What's the future?

WILSON: I was just reading Anthony Wallace's book *Religion: An Anthropological View* last night. He addressed exactly the same question. In 1966, when it was written, he came up with that very unsatisfactory answer that others, going back to Auguste Comte, had come up with; namely, that we need a secularized religion: we have to recognize the power of religion, but we need to have ritual without God. That, to me, is very unsatisfactory. We need a real myth. The one I adopted is scientific materialism as a mythology and whatever we can make out of it. You must realize that most scientists think about the world about as much as bank clerks do. They get pleasure from working on neutrinos or polyglycosides, but as far as the rest of the world is concerned, they have very little knowledge and very little interest. Most scientists think of science as being a kind of purifying intellectual machinery that leads to honesty, to the withering away of ignorance and wrong ideas, including, provided they are of the atheistic persuasion, those of religion. They see the scientific method as a mechanism for getting at certain kinds of truth.

But the greatest scientists have always looked on scientific materialism as a kind of religion, as a mythology. They are impelled by a great desire to explore mystery, to celebrate mystery in the universe, to open it up, to read the stars, to find the deeper meaning. Many of them have found total philosophical satisfaction in this conception, particularly when it can be harnessed to humanism, to the viewing of the human species as central.

What I've done in this book is simply to make all this much more explicit. That is, I've said the religious impulse is a uniquely human impulse, but it is biological nonetheless. But the religious faith, in the hundred thousand forms it has taken, is almost always linked to imaginary scenarios and false mythology, false stories. It's a part of the predisposition to make *complete* stories about the universe and about the tribe. But they are almost always false; they are arguments of convenience to achieve another ultimate purpose. Science tends to wipe them out, one after the other. And the most dedicated and inspired of all scientists have been the people who are entertaining, explicitly or implicitly, a mythology of their own, a belief that the world is thus and so. There are unchanging laws, and scientists are exploring them.

The trick is to capture religious energies. This is where I think the natural sciences and the humanities will really come together at last. We can't abolish those energies. They are overpowering; they are magnificent; they are the source of many wondrous parts of our own culture; they can't be abolished. But they can be captured, and science itself can serve this function by adding new depth to subjects that have hitherto been the province of the humanities.

OMNI: One of the arguments you make in the book is that the Big Bang cosmology theory is really a lot more interesting and exciting than any biblical or other religious theory of the origin of the universe.

WILSON: There are a lot of those things. You know, the way a cell is put together is more intricate and wondrous than any preliterate or early religious conception of what life is all about. I felt that science should be addressing these more humanistic subjects directly — or shall we say, in order not to seem imperialistic, that humanistic scholars and social scientists should be utilizing the natural sciences more fully and efficiently to account for the phenomena they are most interested in.

OMNI: Yet you predict a long and happy future for traditional forms of religion.

WILSON: Not for theology, but for religion. I did that because I am not at all certain that the emotional rewards from scientific materialism would be sufficient for most people. I foresee many people maintaining, as an emotional refuge, belief in God and ties with formal religion because the final readout of Deism is something that scientific materialism cannot, at least as I see it, touch: the belief in the original, creative God.

OMNI: Even a Big Bang needs somebody to light the fire?

WILSON: You might go further than that. You might want to argue in the way of a more personal God who has actually set the clockwork going, with the whole thing developing toward an ultimate expression of some transcendental mind set or goal.

OMNI: For me the ritual is by far the most appealing part of religion. And ritual is something we just don't have any cultural substitutes for.

WILSON: I think those things will endure, even though there will be increasing uncertainty, in cold, rational moments, about the explicit claims that these rituals make about the nature of God and the nature of a particular church.

OMNI: At one point I think you argue that Marxism is likely to fail because its biological base was not explored — which presumably you would not argue vis-à-vis Roman Catholicism. Maybe you can make that distinction?

WILSON: Yes, I think that the secular ideologies, like Marxism, are more vulnerable than the traditional religions, because the traditional religions depend upon a transcendental explanation of human existence, whereas Marxism in particular, which is now the all-encompassing secular ideology, depends upon historicism and materialism and is meant to be a scientific explanation of human history.

OMNI: You say it's sociobiology without the biology.

WILSON: Yes; well, that's what I meant. I was trying to explain the way societies are and the way they are going in entirely materialist ways. But society increasingly has neglected the substructure of biology, to its own peril.

OMNI: One of the things that really struck me about your book was the extensive discussion about free will versus determinism.

WILSON: Three chapters, yes. I worked a lot on that. I didn't want to get into that philosophical discussion but was forced to because of the sort of criticism that has been mounted against sociobiology. Most people are prone to respond with gut feelings about it. They say, "Oh, sociobiology says we're programmed by instinct to do that and do this, but I know I'm not that way: I'm a human being with free choice." But, of course, that's a completely erroneous way of talking about it. People don't really understand what's being said. It takes a little bit of thinking and learning about genetics and what the evolutionary process is before you can really start applying the ideas of sociobiology systematically. I'm hoping that subjects like homosexuality and religion, and maybe altruism, which are the gut issues that people worry a lot about, will cause them to think more about the basic ideas.

OMNI: One thing growing out of your discussion of religion is your belief that ethics have to be biologized.

WILSON: Yes. I didn't want to go too far with that, because you start getting on very slippery ground, but I did want to discuss some primary values that I thought we might arrive at right now. My point in taking on what I call the cardinal values in the last chapter was to show, by taking perhaps the safest and hardest cases, that biological knowledge really will help us arrive at a firmly based moral code.

One of the values is diversity; that's one of the most controversial. If you take an elitist's or extreme eugenicist's point of view, what we should be doing is looking for the ideal human type. If the whole world could be made up of that type of person, then we'd be far more intelligent and far more moral, far better off. That would be the eugenicist's ideal.

What I am suggesting, however, is that modern biology seems pretty strongly to indicate that we ought to want to go, at least temporarily, in the *opposite* direction; that is, that we ought to want to preserve genetic diversity. The reason for that is that the very process of sexual reproduction tears down and rebuilds genotypes each generation. We are being torn apart and reassembled in such a terrific and unpredictable manner with each generation that it would be extremely dangerous to narrow the genetic basis for humanity as a whole. If we had some great world congress of politicians, scientists, philosophers, and so on, it is very likely that we would arrive at the position I am suggesting; namely that, for the time being, we would want to preserve genetic diversity and even cherish it until such time as we can come to a better understanding of human heredity. Then we might talk about eugenics, but that will not be within our generation.

OMNI: So what you're saying is that even diversity may not necessarily be anything like a permanent value; that ultimately our state of knowledge may be such that we might want to practice eugenics. It's exactly the sort of statement that leads your critics to charge that you're serving conservative, racist interests. When you imply that in the twenty-third century, or even in the twenty-eighth century, we may know enough genetics to practice eugenics, that's going to offend a lot of people.

WILSON: Yes. That's not saying that I believe we should, that our great-grand-to-the-eighth-power descendants should do that. I'm just stating what may well be a fact, which is that our knowledge may be sufficient then to make that choice. *We* won't make it, not in our lifetime. But it's there to be made. And I think it's worth saying, or worth extrapolating, just as a part of our understanding of what we are. If you refuse to think about it, then I think you are closing your mind to an important part of what the human species really is.

You know, that reaction does occur from the most extreme of the critics. And they make the same argument about recombinant DNA. That may be the reason they want to close off debate. Their ace card always seems to be that if we let people go ahead with their research, or we let them go ahead with a discussion of these subjects, then the next thing you know, they're going to be redesigning the human species, controlling humanity through genetics. That seems to be the real fear in the back of their minds.

They weren't really worried so much about monsters or runaway viruses, although they had that in mind, as they were about one more step toward genetic control of the human species. So one has to put them at ease by simply saying that we have to think these things through. We're not talking about anything that *could* be done for generations. And even then it will be done, I hope, by free choice, by an electorate, with careful thought and preparation. I closed my last chapter by saying I think it's very likely that there's something in our nature that will make us decide we'll never change, even though we're lumbering along on a jerry-built Pleistocene vehicle.

I think the scientists themselves need to be more explicit in addressing what they're doing to the effects it will have on human emotion. I don't know whether you noticed it, but I did try to tie those things together throughout the book. To the best of my ability, I made allusions to literature; I've used quotes from Yeats and Joyce and so forth. I was saying, in effect, that science now addresses human nature, and *that's* where the two cultures come together. Science and the humanities can enormously enrich each other.

Death Hormone

W. Donner Denckla

Throughout the history of endocrinology, hormones and vitamins are almost always defined as being good for us, and here I'm getting up and saying that this hormone may actually be part of a self-destruct program.

A distinctly youthful fifty, W. Donner Denckla has nevertheless been immersed in the study of aging for fourteen years. An endocrinologist and self-taught biochemist, he holds the unorthodox conviction that we age and die because we are programmed to do so by our evolutionary heritage. At specific times in our lives, he believes, our genes dictate the release of a hitherto-unknown pituitary hormone — or family of hormones — for the specific purpose of ensuring that our physiological deterioration will take place approximately on schedule. If Dr. Denckla's genetic-hormonal "clock-of-aging" theory proves to be valid — and his exciting experimental results with rats suggest that it well may be — then he may see the benefits of his research, in terms of increased, high-quality human longevity, come to pass in his own lifetime.

Denckla, a native of Philadelphia, got his first Harvard degree in history before switching to medicine. With his M.D. in hand, he opted for research rather than private practice. After a brief stay at Harvard, he continued his investigations at the National Institutes of Health, the Roche Institute of Molecular Biology, the National Institute of Alcoholism and Alcohol Abuse, and finally at his present berth, George Washington University. At the Roche Institute, Denckla, through his work on thyroid hormones, became fascinated with the aging process. He developed a theory that aging as we have known it is not inevitable; that we can perhaps do something about it. If highly developed or-

Photograph: Anthony Wolff

ganisms like ourselves have built-in clocks that record aging, Denckla posits, then researchers can learn how such clocks work and how to adjust them for our own ends.

Denckla's work has only slowly begun to gain recognition among his scientific peers. "But that is not surprising," he said, "since what I'm really doing is introducing a new paradigm, a new way of thinking about an old problem. Scientists are by nature skeptical, and they should be. But once I have in hand the purified hormone (assuming I am successful), and especially its antidote, my colleagues in the aging field will cheerfully, as scientists have repeatedly done throughout medical history, accept the proof and simply revise their own views accordingly. If I fail — well, then . . ." he trailed off with a shrug.

Denckla is an avid reader of science fiction and an enthusiastic sailor (his favorite spot is Woods Hole, Massachusetts) and gardener. He designs furniture and has also designed many of his own instruments and some new laboratory technologies — on which he holds a number of patents. He is the father of three children, whose mother, Martha Denckla, is a well-known pediatric neurologist.

This interview was conducted in 1981 at Denckla's home in Washington, D.C., and at Woods Hole by Albert Rosenfeld, former science editor of Life *and the* Saturday Review *and the author of* Prolongevity.

OMNI: You have a novel approach to aging research. Can you describe it?

DENCKLA: Perhaps the best way to begin is to go back to the way I discovered it, or, I should say, fell into it, because at that time I had no particular interest in aging.

OMNI: Were you working with hormones?

DENCKLA: Yes, specifically with thyroid hormone. We do have some tests that measure thyroid levels in the blood, but when I first started in this field a dozen or so years ago, we didn't have a really good test for the biological effectiveness of thyroid hormones. So I developed a modification of an old test, which could detect how well the hormone worked by measuring how much oxygen the body consumed; the more effective the hormones, the faster oxygen is metabolized. While trying to develop this biological test — and I happened to be working with rats — I noticed a change with the rats' advancing age. It was already known that thyroid blood levels remain constant in rats, as in humans, through most of the middle years of their lives. But a careful measurement of their oxygen consumption indicated that the biological *effectiveness* of the thyroid hormone decreased with age.

OMNI: In other words, the blood level of thyroid — the availability of the hormone — stayed the same. And with plenty of thyroid in circulation, a rat's tissues and organs simply couldn't use it effectively as the animal grew older. Is that correct?

DENCKLA: Exactly. This struck me as bizarre. The thyroid level was just fine, but the animal couldn't make use of it. It raised some fairly tough questions, and it has taken me a long time to come up with some answers that begin to satisfy me. The dropoff in apparent sensitivity to thyroid hormone began to occur at puberty, was most dramatic during that time, and then gradually decreased throughout the animal's life span. It looked suspiciously like some sort of maturational or developmental, hence genetic, program that was somehow *designed* to decrease the body's ability to respond to thyroid hormone.

OMNI: Why is thyroid hormone so important, anyway?

DENCKLA: Well, it's one of the two or three principal hormones that seem to get involved in all of the body's major systems. It has some unique functions of its own, to be sure, but it is also one of those special hormones described as "permissive." That is, it allows other hormones to do their own thing. Thyroid also permits growth hormone and cortisone to work, for example. Moreover, no one can be fertile without thyroid hormone; ovaries do not respond properly to the normal cycles that females go through. Males, too, become partly infertile without thyroid. The muscles weaken, coordination falls off, a whole variety of systems seem to go awry.

OMNI: Thyroid appears to have an overall regulatory function, then?

DENCKLA: Well, not really regulatory. It essentially makes almost every tissue in the body work better and more normally, either because it acts on that tissue or because it helps other hormones or substances to work properly. It is the body's metabolic rate-controlling hormone. There are only two or three like it: insulin is one, cortisone is another. Consequently, the removal of it, or an excess of it, affects nearly every tissue in the body. A low-thyroid state is extremely unpleasant. People don't die from it, but many are reported to wish they were dead. They may sleep fourteen hours a day. They're barely able to move around. They're mentally sluggish, too.

OMNI: If what happens in rats also happens in people, would you expect that, as thyroid effectiveness diminishes over the years, there would be an accompanying decline in function in the whole organism?

DENCKLA: That certainly is true, and the decline appears to be programmed. In the rat this decline is highly precise; it comes on at exactly twenty-one days — the very first day of puberty. We of course wanted to figure out what system of the body controlled this decline. We suspected the pituitary because it is the so-called master gland, maintaining a lot of the body's day-to-day activities. More than that, the pituitary is the orchestrator of all those hormones that control growth and sexual maturity. Simply put, it is the gland responsible for extrauterine development. All phases of it. People without pituitaries become dwarfs. They have no sexual or reproductive capacity whatsoever. They grow to about the size of a six- or seven-year-old and then just stop. Functionally, they are idiots.

A total, instantaneous wipe-out of the pituitary in the adult results in death, usually within twenty-four hours.

OMNI: Then how could you manage to show that the pituitary is responsible for the decreased thyroid effectiveness with age?

DENCKLA: We removed the rat's pituitary and replaced some of the good hormones that the pituitary makes and, lo and behold, we found there was no decrease in most of the thyroid-dependent systems that we studied throughout the animal's life span.

OMNI: I take it that you removed the whole pituitary from your experimental rats, then gave them thyroid and other essential hormones so that there would be no disastrous consequences.

DENCKLA: Well, all we could afford to provide for a long period of time was two other essential hormones — both of them adrenal steroids — including the rat version of cortisone. But when we gave back only these and thyroid hormone in young animals that lacked their pituitaries, we found very little loss in the thyroid-dependent systems. It seemed quite obvious that we were in the presence of a new pituitary function, one that has not been previously described — a function that blocks thyroid progressively and increasingly.

OMNI: At this point were you thinking in terms of aging at all?

DENCKLA: No. We were working with young rats just entering puberty. The work was frustrating, too. If I gave an intact six-week-old rat dose X of thyroid hormone, I got a certain response. If I gave the same dose to an intact eight-week-old rat, I got a lower response. In fact, I got lower responses as the animal got older, and it drove me crazy. I said, well, you know, you can't do comparisons between animals of different ages. It made no sense. During puberty there was a 55 to 60 percent fall in apparent thyroid sensitivity in the tissues.

OMNI: And did the decline go on from there?

DENCKLA: It sure did. We plotted an age curve and found that through the life span of the animal on this particular assay [measurement of presence of activity], the juvenile retained roughly three times as much responsiveness to thyroid hormone as, say, a twenty-four-month-old rat. Now when you start finding a threefold change in sensitivity to a major hormone like the thyroid, which does an awful lot of good things for us, your suspicion is very strong that this isn't terribly healthy for mammals. Over the last ten years we and others have been studying other systems that have been known to decline with age in human beings.

We have known that both the immune system and the cardiovascular system decline in humans as well as rats. In most mammals studied, in fact, there's a pattern of decline in function, usually starting, interestingly enough, shortly after or during puberty. So we said, aha! Is it possible that a certain percentage of these major bodily functions that decline with advancing age are thyroid dependent and that the loss of response to thyroid hormone might account for some or all of the decline? So we started. By now we have found almost two dozen systems that appear to be thyroid-dependent, that do decline with age, and that can be shown *not* to have any age-associated decline for the lifetime of the rat — which means two years, roughly — if you take out the pituitary! Even if you remove it when the animal is already, say, a year of age, which would be equivalent to a thirty-five-year-old human, the function reverses back to a very young level of competence.

OMNI: What's the latest age for the safe removal of the animal's pituitary?

DENCKLA: Twelve to eighteen months. The operative fatality rate is too high if we wait beyond that. It is a highly traumatic procedure.

OMNI: What kinds of functions have you been able to restore?

DENCKLA: Well, as one example, the ability of the aorta to relax, or dilate. The aorta is the main blood vessel in both man and rats. It loses the ability to relax in response to certain of the body's substances. In the rat this loss is pretty far along by the age of three months, and by six months it's completely gone. We operated on a rat nine months of age. And for more than a year after the operation, even when the rat was twenty-four months old, we had — in this rat with no pituitary — the return of this function to 90 percent of what would have been normal for a four-week-old rat in the early days of puberty. This is only one of many such examples.

OMNI: Did all this suggest to you that the pituitary must be releasing another hormone that keeps the thyroid from doing what it's supposed to do?

DENCKLA: Yes. The simplest, most straightforward explanation was that we had run across a new pituitary hormone.

OMNI: Is this the hormone that people have been referring to as the death hormone or the aging hormone?

DENCKLA: Yes, but I avoid those designations.

OMNI: What do you call it?

DENCKLA: I call it DECO, because it is a neutral, totally operational definition. It is the acronym for "decreasing oxygen consumption" hormone, since that's how I discovered it. I think it's too early to call it a death hormone. One thing that it's not too early to say, however, is that DECO is certainly antiphysiological in the mature animal. The only evidence we have that it may be a death hormone comes from comparing the life span of animals without their pituitaries with the life span of normal animals.

OMNI: Have you already done this?

DENCKLA: Yes. In a preliminary study we compared the life spans of 125 intact rats with those of 95 rats whose pituitaries we had taken out. At thirty-four months of age, only two of the intact animals were still alive. That's about 99 percent mortality.

OMNI: If twenty-four months represent seventy years of human age, what would thirty-four months represent?

DENCKLA: Well, pushing ninety-five. Only 1 percent of humans would be left at that age. Let's look at the animals without pituitaries at that age. We had twenty of these handicapped creatures still alive out of the ninety-five we started with. In other words, there was a tenfold increase in the number of survivors among animals without pituitaries. So I think we're entitled to say that something in the pituitary is not beneficial, and *that* something has never been identified before.

OMNI: Besides that, you've been able to restore "juvenile competence," as you call it in your papers; that is, to revive abilities the rats had when they were much younger, in a number of systems. You mentioned relaxation of the aorta as one. What were some others?

DENCKLA: First, let me set the scene a little better. For most of our latest experiments we worked with rats from twelve to fourteen months of age. And most of this work has been with females. The female rat at this age is menopausal, hence an oldish rat as judged by fertility, equivalent at the very least to a woman in her forties. What we do is replace a few hormones, as I mentioned earlier. And then we study whatever function it is that needs to be studied. Among the ones we studied that were of general interest are maximum aerobic capacity, which declines in man and rat with age and is generally considered to be an index of overall cardiovascular competence. We have been able to restore that function in an animal whose chronological age was twenty-four months. Its capacity then was the same as that of a three-month-old rat — actually, slightly younger than that. So we suspect that the cardiovascular system can be normalized.

OMNI: What about the immune system?

DENCKLA: Ah, I was coming to that. Immune function declines in men, mice, dogs, almost any species studied, in varying degrees. The immune system comprises a variety of different cells and cell functions. I tend to think of the immune system as our whole defense system, anything that fights off a foreign invader, whether it's a bacterium, a virus, grafted cells, or even a cancer, which represents a kind of foreign presence in a sense. Anyway, we studied the two major branches of the immune system — using criteria that ranged from antibody reaction to graft rejection — and we found that by removing the pituitary, we could at least partially restore age-associated losses in both. A major loss has been found in most mammals to be in the T-dependent branch — the white blood cells known as T-lymphocytes. We were able to restore between 80 and 90 percent of function in these systems.

OMNI: You seem to be concentrating much of your effort on the cardiovascular and the immune systems. Why?

DENCKLA: Well, it's very simple. When you go to medical school, you get hit by massive textbooks describing all these awful diseases that people die of. But as you stand back and look at these diseases, you see that we really do not die from the failure of every cell in the body. We die primarily of three major diseases, and these diseases are involved with an inadequate supply of blood to tissues. This means heart attacks, strokes, and the consequences of hypertension. Our kidneys, for instance, get hell when we have high blood pressure. That's why we studied the ability of blood vessels to dilate. Diseases in which the blood supply to a tissue — primarily the brain, kidney, or heart — is interrupted account for slightly more than half of all deaths in the modern Western world.

And adult cancer is the largest remaining problem. It's my opinion, from reading the literature and talking to a lot of people who are far better versed than I, that in cancer there is some kind of failure in the immune system — the defense against "not-quite-self" tissue.

OMNI: Yes, cancer specialists do increasingly suspect that a failure of the immune system is involved.

DENCKLA: We picked the T-cell-dependent functions, because those seem to be especially important in fighting cancer. We picked the graft-rejection system as a model for the ability to fight cancer. With these two systems — the immune and the cardiovascular — we felt we could account for a significant portion of the changes attendant on age that promote the diseases that kill approximately four out of five of us.

OMNI: Are you saying that if these two major systems are dependent on thyroid hormones in one way or another, then a single substance could drastically affect both systems, the failure of which kills most of us?

DENCKLA: Well, that's what we think. But we don't know what percentage of the deterioration is due to thyroid blockage. All we know is that we can restore an awful lot of the apparent normal function of these systems by taking out the pituitary and giving back thyroid. The immune system is an incredibly complex one. Some of its functions are *not* restored by our method, even if we give back both thyroid and growth hormone. The pituitary does contain many beneficial substances. Removing the pituitary is a very preliminary way of demonstrating the presence of a bad hormone.

OMNI: But meanwhile you're using this technique of removing the pituitary only because you don't have the hormone in hand, right? But if you had a supply of DECO, could you use just that for finer manipulations?

DENCKLA: Right. We don't have the pure hormone yet. What we've got now is a crude preparation of DECO, contaminated by some other pituitary hormones. [It takes a hundred ground-up cow pituitaries to get enough extract for testing thirty rats.] But even that preparation does — in the three systems we've studied in juveniles — do exactly what we predicted would happen in the aging rats.

In one series of experiments we picked a couple of unusual enzymes. One of them, malic enzyme, normally declines with age, and it is thyroid-dependent. The other one, histidase, actually increases with age. Now, when we gave the rats the crude extract, presumably containing DECO, we found that the malic enzyme did go down and the histidase did go up. If both had declined, we would suspect some general suppression of protein production. But the fact that we made one go up and the other down, within ten days of injection, rules this out.

OMNI: So an injection of this crude DECO extract mimicked what happens with aging.

DENCKLA: Yes. And the oxygen consumption of the whole animal also went down. So we now have three different indices — two enzymes and a whole-body oxygen consumption — that can mimic the effects of age in juveniles within a few days. And these animals actually "aged" roughly twice as fast as they normally would have.

OMNI: Now, let's go back a step. You talked about all of this beginning at puberty in a programmed fashion. Do these aging effects, then, seem to be part of the normal genetic program built into the animal?

DENCKLA: Yes, I think so, and I think there's a terribly good reason for it. I asked myself the question a number of years ago: What earthly good would a hormone be that blocked the thyroid, since the thyroid is obviously so important for so many functions? And the tentative answer is very clear. It may be wrong, but it's very clear. Young animals have a very large surface area compared with their very small body mass. They dissipate heat very quickly. Yet they have a constant rectal temperature throughout life.

All mammals have to maintain a rectal temperature roughly between 96 degrees and 105 degrees. You've got to be a real powerhouse when you're a young animal, to keep up with your heat losses. And this function is thyroid-dependent; thyroid controls the rate at which you can burn oxygen.

An animal is going to grow enormously from the time he leaves his mother's womb until he's full-grown — anywhere from one to three orders of magnitude. When that happens, there is an incredible increase in body mass, along with an enormous relative loss of ability to dissipate heat. So my hypothesis is that DECO was originally a hormone designed to turn the thermostat down in order not to be burning at full bore, using up all this energy just to keep the rectal temperature up. DECO slows the thyroid down and allows all those extra calories to go into growth while ensuring that you won't cook inside your own skin. According to our preliminary studies, if you had the metabolic rate as a fully grown adult that you had when you were a two- or three-year-old, you would have a rectal temperature of roughly 115 degrees, which means your brain would be cooked.

OMNI: How were you able to study this?

DENCKLA: Well, we took adult animals four or five months old and injected them with an excess of thyroid to raise their oxygen consumption to the level that it should be if they had been, say, one month old. When we got close to the juvenile level, all the animals died. One could say that this simply represents a toxic level of thyroid, affecting the heart, liver, kidneys, and what-not, but our data argue against it.

OMNI: If DECO is the mechanism for pathologically aging the organism, do you believe that this has come about by accident, or that the aging program itself is genetically programmed by design?

DENCKLA: Well, since Darwin, we're not allowed to use the term *design*. That's a no-no.

OMNI: An evolutionary program perhaps?

DENCKLA: Yes. It's my opinion — and in this case I think I'm virtually alone — that in many situations an evolutionary change in program is the only way to adapt to changes in the environment, such as a big temperature change in the Ice Age, such as the incredible rate at which bacteria can mutate and produce new and virulent forms of bacteria, such as the way plants sometimes die out. Pity the poor koala bear, for instance, if the eucalyptus tree ever vanishes, because that's the only source of food it has. If the eucalyptus tree was under attack by an insect and the koala's only food source vanished, the koala would have to evolve very rapidly the ability to eat another kind of food — or die out.

Let us suppose the only way to adapt is by selecting those members of the species that have a better way of surviving, in the case of the diminishing eucalyptus tree supply. The koala bears that can learn to eat grass or lettuce or turnips or asparagus or whatever will be selected for survival. Let's now put it into a more realistic situation. Suppose the whole eucalyptus forest is about to vanish — because of a certain insect, say, or a change in temperature — in a hundred years, and you have a thousand koala bears, and their reproductive capacity is such that they live fifty years. If their forest is going to vanish in a hundred, it's almost inconceivable that they can adapt biologically to so rapid a change, relative to their total numbers. There's no turnover time. They'll die out. If they produce a new generation every five years, however, that same a hundred years now gives them twenty generations to select those few koala bears in each generation that can tolerate eating more and more plants that are not eucalyptus. So by the end of the hundred years, when the eucalyptus forest has vanished, a few survivors will be there, and they'll be able to make it.

OMNI: Is the difference between the turnover of generations the difference between species death and survival?

DENCKLA: In a rapidly changing, hostile environment, yes. Those animals that have survived tend to have short life spans in the wild. Moreover, they have predictable life spans — mice, koala bears, orangutans, humans, all of them. This is obviously a genetic program, because each species has a specific life span that is as characteristic for that species as its coloration, its size, its heart rate, and many other parameters.

Suppose there's a change in the environment. There's obviously an advantage in having a fairly high turnover rate when an environment is changing rapidly. The greater the turnover rate per century, the greater the chance of survival by brute evolutionary force. An animal that is turning over ten or twenty times faster per century than his competitors is obviously going to have twenty times as many opportunities for natural experiments. He is going to become cleverer, faster, tougher, bigger, whatever is necessary. He is going to dominate totally those animals with a long life span.

OMNI: To the individual who's dying in five years and who wants to live longer, that may be small compensation. The evolutionary program, you might say, is nature's game rather than the individual's game.

DENCKLA: True enough. It is clear that in natural selection, once the individual has procreated and allowed its progeny to reach maturity, as far as evolution is concerned he can be dispensed with.

OMNI: Well, at some times in history, the average life expectancy has been — what — twenty, twenty-five years? Are you saying it would be better for the species if that continued to be so?

DENCKLA: Any living thing — a rat, a dog, a chicken, even a eucalyptus tree — has only one way of adapting. It must develop randomly, yet successfully, to counter a changing environment. Its rate of adaptation has to exceed the rate at which potentially lethal elements are introduced into the environment. The rate of adaptation is controlled by the number of genes, the number of recessive genes, the number of individuals breeding, the number of times that they breed, per century. It's the number of turnovers that matter.

OMNI: In the case of human beings, whether we as individuals die at the age of twenty-five or at seventy-five, our built-in genetic program doesn't change, does it?

DENCKLA: It doesn't change our ability *as animals in the prelanguage state* — and that's very important — because the largest amount of information that an animal without language can pass on to another animal is contained in the DNA. The total information kit for survival, up until the invention of language, depended on DNA transmission.

OMNI: Do you mean we can now interfere with nature's game?

DENCKLA: Maybe so. With the invention of language, we began to get real information about the world around us: "That is a poisonous mushroom." "Now is the time to plant." "That water is unfit to drink." These words and observations could now carry information outside of the genetic material to help us survive. As a consequence, we have developed through language, and later through the scientific method, a very large amount of extragenetic information that we can use to make successful adaptations to a changing environment. We developed penicillin. Some bacteria developed means of resisting penicillin. We then turned around and developed methyl penicillin, which these bacteria are now still sensitive to. We did not have to kill off half the humans to select only those humans who had high natural tolerance for this new microbe. We're the first animal that's ever made successful adaptations to life-threatening situations within a life span or a generation.

OMNI: So we are able to change some of the evolutionary rules as we begin to understand them. Is it fair to say then that your tentative theory, or part of it, is that we do have within us an evolutionary, genetic aging program to ensure the turnover of generations, to ensure that we age and die — and that the mechanism for this is DECO?

DENCKLA: Right. Well, not quite. I'd say that all animals and plants have mechanisms to ensure some reasonable degree of turnover. Plants are a special case. I won't say much about them. A single tree may be five hundred years old, but there's no cell in that tree that's more than five years old. A tree is really a colony of organisms that happen to occupy the same locus, but each year there are new leaves, and these new leaves are the actual descendants of other leaves. In other words, they're changing genetically. The leaves on the north side of an old oak tree do not have the same shape as the leaves on the south side.

OMNI: Then the leaves are the true individuals?

DENCKLA: That's too complicated. Let's go quickly back to animals. It's my considered opinion that there has been a high evolutionary advantage to some kind of programmed death in animals. Now I want to say two things very carefully. We know the mechanism of death in certain animals. For example, the Pacific salmon apparently dies of a massive hypersecretion of cortisone, which is directed by the pituitary. There is absolutely no evidence that this occurs in man. The mechanism by which the genetically programmed death is brought about may be very different when you jump across big differences in species. Because of the great evolutionary advantage in rapid turnover already discussed, many means have developed for many different animals to ensure the death of the individual so that the species can have a high adaptive coefficient per century. DECO seems to be limited to mammals. Dogs, horses, and the average barnyard animals all seem to die of the same patterns of disease that we die of. The textbook of veterinary pathology reads like a human medical textbook. The warm-blooded animals that we're more closely related to die in a pattern similar to ours. The water bug and the salmon clearly do not.

OMNI: Then if there exists a genetic clock of aging, is it in the pituitary?

DENCKLA: Well, the pituitary is probably the most logical place for it. The high index of suspicion for it is based on the work done by me and others who have found beneficial effects from the removal of the pituitary. We have actually increased the number of survivors at the maximum life span of the rat. But a high index of suspicion is a long way from proof.

OMNI: But in addition to a high number of survivors, you've been able to restore quite a number of functions that normally decline with aging — that have already declined with aging — and bring them back to what would be normal for younger animals. Isn't that true?

DENCKLA: Yes. We have been able to restore them, and I don't know of any other method in the history of gerontology that has done this. We've been able not only to restore them to juvenile levels, but to hold them, apparently indefinitely, at those levels. We see no aging changes!

OMNI: Suppose that all the things for which you now have a high index of suspicion, as you phrase it, turn out to be so and, further, that you now have in hand the purified hormone. By the way, would you care to make an estimate about how long you think it might be before that will come to pass?

DENCKLA: We have, right now, a usable purified hormone, in the sense that, though it's contaminated, we can demonstrate it does what we predict it should be able to do, judging from our experiments on rats without pituitaries. We have that in hand right now. So we can already start some of these studies. The hormone is about a thousandfold purified at the moment. To get it to the point where it is totally uncontaminated by any other hormone of the pituitary — where you can get a structural analysis and things like that — really depends on several things. With a great deal of luck, we could do it in a few months. We might have a structural analysis within one year.

But there's another big problem I'd like to mention. Unfortunately, this hormone, like so many of the pituitary hormones, seems to be highly associated with enzymes like those in your intestine that digest protein; thus, the hormone is very rapidly decomposed. That may make our isolation very difficult, and hence more time-consuming.

OMNI: Even so, suppose you had it in hand right now. You would have the means then, presumably, to accelerate aging. But wouldn't you then need an antidote? Or a means of stopping the pituitary from continuing to release it? What would be the next steps if you wanted to combat the ravages of aging?

DENCKLA: Well, it's very simple. We could use two or three basic approaches. We estimate the molecular weight of this hormone to be roughly two hundred amino acids, roughly the same as the other major pituitary hormones. Now we could possibly identify the active site. Most hormones have extra strings of amino acids that are there for God knows what reason. Only a fraction of the molecule is really necessary for biological activity. So one strategy we could employ is the lock-and-key method that's so often used between hormones and the cells they interact with. Let's say this is the key that turns the lock. We could develop some other key that would jam the lock of the cell to prevent the hormone from functioning. This would be very tricky. It is possible we could do it for a short time, but because of the lengthy sequence of amino acids required, the body might develop antibodies to it. The immune system, over the years, might begin to attack it as a foreign substance. You can develop antibodies even to insulin in five or ten years.

OMNI: How can you get around such a tough problem?

DENCKLA: The best approach, I think, would be the following. All pituitary hormones so far known are regulated by the brain through a little structure, right above the pituitary, called the hypothalamus. The hypothalamus sends out chemical messengers that are very small, containing perhaps three, four, or five amino acids, to the pituitary. These "releasing factors" direct the formation of specific pituitary hormones: growth hormone, prolactin, or the gonadal hormones. We hope that DECO will not be different from the other major pituitary hormones, that it will be under the direction of the hypothalamus by means of one of these little specific chemical messengers. Since these are almost too small to make antibodies against, if we could find a blocker against the releasing hormone for DECO, we would have a relatively safe and specific compound that could be taken orally or by injection, just like any other medication on the market.

OMNI: Is it true that the hypothalamus sometimes sends chemical messengers not only to release hormones but also to inhibit their release?

DENCKLA: That's true.

OMNI: Then there could be a natural inhibitor of DECO?

DENCKLA: That's quite possible. If we could find a natural inhibitor, that would be just super. In either case, I think the most sensible solution, even if ultimately the most difficult one, would be to try to prevent the pituitary from making so much DECO, instead of trying to block DECO once it's out in the circulation, which, though possible in the short term, is not a long-term solution.

OMNI: The evidence so far seems to uphold your theory. Yet your work does not seem so far to have attracted the enthusiasm of other longevity researchers, or induced them to drop their approaches to aging. Why?

DENCKLA: Well, it's a very new idea. So I'm the new kid on the block who has to prove himself. My colleagues are withholding judgment until I isolate DECO, and I think that's a reasonable skepticism. After all, I am making a claim for a really extraordinary new hormone. It's the first hormone that does two things: it's an inhibitor of other hormones, and it may be very seriously antiphysiological. Throughout the history of endocrinology, hormones and vitamins are almost always defined as being good for us, and here I'm getting up and saying that this hormone may actually be part of a self-destruct program. It may account for only 10 percent of pathological aging, or 5 percent, but, given our evidence in the rat, it certainly accounts for a finite percentage of the pathological aging process, whether it's 5, 20, 50. Who knows? We don't know yet.

OMNI: But it could be the major part of it.

DENCKLA: It could even be 75 percent. But, understandably, if someone even breathes of the existence of something like that, it's a little bit like being against Mom and apple pie. People find it a little hard to believe, and I don't blame them. In summary, DECO is a very radical new hormone, and I think that most people really want to see more evidence of its existence. There's another, much more complicated reason that we can go into, if you want.

OMNI: Sure, why not?

DENCKLA: Well, it's simply that this is a very different approach to pathological aging. My colleagues in aging have many other theories. This is a new and different theory. It's not twenty or thirty years old, like some of the other theories, and so obviously there will be resistance to it.

OMNI: Are you saying that the history of science demonstrates that every radical approach is resisted and that it would be foolish not to expect resistance?

DENCKLA: Exactly. Let's put it this way. If I simply said that I found a better explanation for one of the already-familiar theories of aging, and could extend it and show that it was true, people would accept it more readily. But most of the modern theories of aging may be supplanted by this one.

OMNI: If it turns out to be right.

DENCKLA: Yes, if it turns out to be right. There is a strong possibility that this is the dominant way that we pathologically age. Now, that doesn't leave the poor guy who's spent twenty or thirty years working on, say, collagen as the key to aging much room to maneuver. He may simply be studying a DECO-dependent system. I'm not saying that he is, but it's a possibility, and to expect that he would greet me with open arms would be absurd.

In the same vein, in medicine, the medical people are hardly going to be wildly enthusiastic, because their approach is to fight each disease as it comes up. They're not looking at the fact that all diseases that occur after puberty increase logarithmically.

OMNI: Is it possible that all the deteriorative diseases are an expression of the aging process?

DENCKLA: In my opinion, and my model suggests it. The current medical model says the primary problems are heart disease, cancer, and stroke. Today this is true. Tomorrow that can't be true, if we're really going to make a dent in the pathological aging that produces these ailments. If we can get at the process that causes the logarithmic increase in cancer with each year of life, if we can block the aging process itself, these diseases would be severely curtailed. That's the desired goal. We're a long way from there.

OMNI: So any piece of research that is outside the mainstream of current research, especially one as sweeping as this, is going to require more proof to convince people than would otherwise be the case.

DENCKLA: That's right. We're putting the emphasis in this case on an entirely different system of pathology. Why is it that a ten-year-old child has the highest probability of living that he will ever have the rest of his life? You are at your healthiest from ten to eleven years of age, just before puberty.

OMNI: Would you say, then, that this line of research with DECO holds out some real promise for doing something about human aging? And if so, what is that something it might do?

DENCKLA: Well, I'd say it holds out the promise of considerably slowing down pathological aging. What I'm hoping it will do, judging by my rats, is let us live healthier, longer lives. What we will then die of, I don't know. We've done preliminary autopsies on the rats, and they're extraordinarily good-looking at autopsy; it's very hard for me to determine the cause of death in many cases. But the point is that if all these experiments hold, we can, minimally, hope to live healthier and more vigorous lives throughout most of our life span. The characteristic feebleness that we see with old age will disappear. I also think we'd have to be prolonging the life span somewhat.

OMNI: Would there then be a greater number of people living beyond a hundred, let's say?

DENCKLA: There is certainly that possibility.

OMNI: Or would it be a case of people living out their normal life span, if it turns out to be, say, a hundred, a hundred and ten — whatever it is — and then, like the wonderful one-hoss shay, just going all at once?

DENCKLA: Both are possible. Let's put it this way. If we can do the same in humans as we can in rats, we can say it will be the one-hoss shay type of thing. We will live to a vigorous, healthy old age and die rather abruptly. In fact, that's one of the characteristics of these animals. They die very abruptly, within hours. And we're not sure why. We have actually started an experiment with an animal at nine o'clock in the morning, two and a half years old, and found him dead at noon. That's very unusual, because animals that old — a rat or a man — normally kind of waste away. They don't die suddenly. You can tell that they're sick, and they're kind of dragging their tails around. To have a vigorous, healthy animal at nine o'clock be dead at noon is pretty bizarre. We may do better in people, though, who will after all still possess an intact pituitary. I would say we probably have a better than even chance of prolonging the life span somewhat.

OMNI: Incidentally, I've heard that some human beings do actually have their pituitaries removed. In those cases, do they stop aging? Do they live longer? Do they rejuvenate in some way?

DENCKLA: No. That's a very good question. There are right now, alive in this country, probably several thousand people without their pituitaries.

OMNI: What would be a reason for removing the pituitary?

DENCKLA: There are very few reasons for removing the pituitary, except very severe illness. The mildest reason for removing the pituitary — unless it was an accident — would be the presence of a benign tumor. Most pituitary removals are done because of malignancy, the presence of which already indicates that the patient is unable to handle cancer, or in some cases of very advanced diabetes, in order to prevent blindness. When you remove a human being's pituitary, the patient is almost terminal to begin with. There's very poor follow-up. So I have no data with which to answer your question. But my guess is that these already-sick people are not going to do well without their pituitaries.

Patients without pituitaries — even if well replaced with hormones — do not live like rats in a cage under ideal conditions, or as close to ideal as we can make them. They live in a high-stress environment. They're getting exposed to bacteria the rat never gets exposed to. They're getting exposed to all their family problems. Clinicians who have had experience with these patients will confirm that people without their pituitaries do not do well.

OMNI: So it's certainly not a procedure you would ever recommend to combat aging.

DENCKLA: In no way.

OMNI: Most science-fiction writers, when they write about people living to great ages, talk about very expensive kinds of procedures, where a few old people — hidden off in some Swiss sanatorium — rob the organs of young people. The implication is that only the rich and elite would reap the benefits. Now, in your scenario with DECO, or an inhibitor of DECO, would that be the case? Would it be easily available to the general population like any other medication or, like a heart transplant, available only to the very few?

DENCKLA: It would definitely be available. To give you an example, to show that this is a really feasible thing, right now in both Denmark and the United States oral contraceptives are being developed that are based on synthetic blockers of the releasing factors that are necessary for normal ovulation. This is exactly the approach we would hope for. And to make these compounds available nationally, you're talking probably pennies a day per individual. You wouldn't need very much.

OMNI: Would it be in the form of a pill or a capsule?

DENCKLA: Probably a pill. It would be quite inexpensive. You're talking about a small protein chain of three or four amino acids, under ideal conditions. God knows what problems we will run into. But, with luck, our DECO blocker could be almost as cheap as aspirin.

High-Tech Prophecies

Artificial Intelligence
John McCarthy

People ask, "Well, what will happen when we have robots?"
And there is a very good historical parallel. Namely, what did
the rich do when they had lots of servants?

John McCarthy, the fifty-five-year-old director of Stanford University's Artificial Intelligence Laboratory, is, in a sense, the father of all close relations between humans and computers. It was McCarthy who, while organizing the first conference on the subject at Dartmouth in the summer of 1956, invented the term "artificial intelligence" to describe the then-emerging field. McCarthy also has the distinction of having founded two of the world's three great laboratories of artificial intelligence: the MIT laboratory, in 1957, with Marvin Minsky; and the Stanford laboratory, in 1963. (The third is part of Carnegie-Mellon University.)

While at MIT, McCarthy also invented a kind of computer time-sharing, called interactive computing, in which a central computer was connected to multiple terminals — the first practical one-to-one relation between a computer and its many users, each of whom could feel he had the machine all to himself. In 1958, he created the computer language LISP (List Processing Language) — the successor to the mathematical language of FORTRAN — in which most "intelligent" computer programs have been written. He also founded a subbranch of mathematics called "the semantics of computation," and solved its first significant problems, such as how to test certain classes of complicated computer programs to see whether they were correct, and how to "crunch down," or simplify, the number of steps involved in certain computer operations.

Photograph: Chuck O'Rear

Today, McCarthy is interested in developing programs to give machines common sense. To illustrate the problem, he offers the statement "Birds can fly." It is clear that his statement is usually true — but not in all circumstances. The ostrich and the penguin can't fly. Dead birds can't fly. Birds held down by their feet can't fly. These exceptions seem obvious to humans, but in a computer that has been given "Birds can fly" as a statement of fact, such exceptions can wreak havoc.

To deal with the dilemma, McCarthy is trying to create a new form of logic that can tolerate ambiguity. In mathematical logic it is easy to make the statement "A boat can cross a river," he explains. In the real world this may be true, but boats may also leak or be missing oars. In logic these conditions may be accounted for by simply tacking them on to the first statement: "and there must be no leak and there must be oars." But there are bound to be additional unanticipated disasters awaiting boaters. McCarthy's solution is to say "The boat may be used as a vehicle for crossing a body of water, unless something prevents it." In ordinary mathematical logic, this would not suffice, because every exception must be laid out, item by item. But McCarthy's approach provides a way of going ahead with incomplete information. If, for example, the computer hits the phrase "unless something prevents it," and finds nothing entered beneath that phrase — no leaks, no lost oars — it will continue on. If, on the other hand, it encounters "leak in the boat," it will turn down a new path, dealing with leaks, water, and repair.

McCarthy admits that this is probably not how the human brain works, "but this is AI," he says, "so we don't care if it is psychologically real."

A rather shy man, McCarthy possesses an extraordinary ability to concentrate on a single idea — to step wholly into it. "A large part of his creativity," said one colleague, "comes from his ability to focus on one thing. The hazard of that is, everything else gets screwed up."

Born to an Irish Catholic father and a Lithuanian Jewish mother, McCarthy was raised, along with his younger brother, Patrick, by parents who abandoned their respective religions to embrace atheism and Marxism. Thrown out of Cal Tech for refusing to attend physical education classes, McCarthy was among the last young Americans drafted into World War II. After the war he returned to Cal Tech to earn his bachelor's degree, then went on to earn his Ph.D. at Princeton. In 1956 he was offered his first teaching position, in the mathematics department at Dartmouth. In 1957 he moved to MIT, and in 1962 accepted an offer to head his own department at Stanford.

A widower and father of two daughters (his second wife, Vera, died in a climbing accident during the 1980 all-women ascent of Annapurna), McCarthy is a bit awkward socially, sometimes ignoring the usual conventions. But though he may appear absent-minded and distant, his interior life seems to be one continuous stream of ideas — not only in the fields of mathematics and computing, but also in politics, literature, music, and plumbing. An avid reader of science fiction, he is also the author of a number of stories that, thus far, remain unpublished.

When his home thermostats malfunctioned some years ago, causing the temperature in some rooms of his house to climb above 80 degrees F, McCarthy was inspired to write a philosophical treatise — available to anyone who cares to call it up on Stanford's computerized "memo system" — on the subject of whether it is proper to say that thermostats "believe" and can have "mistaken beliefs." He once had to struggle with moving a piano up a flight of stairs. Soon afterward, he was deep into the problem of transporting heavy objects over difficult and uneven terrain. His solution: a cleverly designed, six-legged mechanism that could carry a piano up and down stairs.

In conversation, McCarthy tends to leap from mundane questions to fantastical proposals, calculations, and other oddities. Indeed, his attention does not remain on factual, earthly matters for more than a few minutes before he is again taking off to consider another fanciful possibility.

This interview was conducted in 1983 by Philip J. Hilts, science correspondent for the Washington Post and author of Scientific Temperaments: Three Lives in Contemporary Science (which includes a profile of McCarthy). The conversation began with a discussion of the robot.

OMNI: What's the chief problem to overcome in developing intelligent robots?

MCCARTHY: I don't know. It always seems to me we ought to make faster progress in robotics than we do. When I started on robotics in 1965 or so, we stated in our first proposal that we would get a robot to assemble a Heathkit [a build-it-yourself electronics set]. It's still not entirely clear to me why that proved impossible.

OMNI: You actually got a kit and tried it?

MCCARTHY: No. The robot arms were never flexible enough to do the mechanical motions, nor did we have programs to control them. The old-fashioned Heathkits involved threading, bending, cutting, and soldering wires. It required considerable dexterity and sophistication to know where and how much force to apply; I don't think we were even close to it.

OMNI: Are we getting closer now?

MCCARTHY: No. I think everyone's working on the easier problems. In my view what everyone wants eventually is not only a robot that will take its place in the assembly line, but a "universal manufacturing machine." This would be more like one robot that could make a whole TV set, a whole camera, or a whole car. The robot might have several arms and a collection of tools. But it would be interesting if you could sell the thing, if you could go to your neighborhood assembly shop and say, "Well, I'd like that TV from the catalogue, but with this additional feature." The TV would be made by one machine. So you could retain the low cost of mass production, but still maintain individuality and custom design, as if it were handmade. What I would like is to extend with these automated means the power of an individual so that one man could build a house or car for himself.

OMNI: How would you do that?

MCCARTHY: Well, rent a gang of robots, as it were. As it is now, whenever you see a construction site, none of the cranes and bulldozers bears the name of the company that's doing the construction. They bear the name of the company from which the equipment is rented. So first you'd design the house or car and the design would go through a lot of computer testing; you'd simulate the construction before you began and the computer would tell you exactly what equipment to rent. You'd rent the robot equipment, and it would build the house or car.

Let's not imagine this is something the average person would do without the robots. The Rockefeller Foundation had a slogan around 1910, largely forgotten now, which was "Make the peaks higher." It meant, take the best existing research institutions and make them still better — the direct opposite of equality. And from the point of view of increasing what a particular individual could do versus what everybody could do, one would also like to make the peaks higher. And what can be done by one person, or a small group of people, has increased as technology has advanced. I believe robotics can advance that a lot more.

OMNI: I hear many inventors complaining that they have no way of approaching corporations — that they'd like to do something but they can't. I guess being able to rent robots would help.

MCCARTHY: Yes, right. But, of course, half of the inventors are crackpots. As for the other half — even the guys who aren't crackpots — 90 percent of their inventions aren't going to make it.

I had an experience trying to market an idea. In fact, I'm still convinced the idea is practical.

OMNI: Can you tell me what it is?

MCCARTHY: I suppose so. Since I can't make money out of it, I've recently been trying to give it away. It's a computer mail terminal. You could buy this thing from a department store, and then you could type on it: "Mail this message to so-and-so." It would be connected to the telephone system, and one computer would call up another terminal and deliver the message. It would be the *only* system permitting any home computer anywhere in the world to send messages to any other home computer anywhere in the world. It seems to me that inventing the thing itself was easy enough, but to persuade some company to make it was harder. My partner and I had a lot of contacts and interviews with sufficient numbers of prominent companies, so we didn't have any problems getting attention. Nevertheless, not one of them decided it was something it wanted to produce. I think, though, that there's a good chance IBM will develop one. At least, I tried to give them the idea.

OMNI: What do you think will ultimately be made possible through robotics, and what forms do you think robotics will eventually take?

MCCARTHY: It seems to me that what can be done and what will be done don't exactly coincide. There's an enormous variety of things that can eventually be done. The extreme example would be machines built along the lines of the science fiction robots.

OMNI: Humanlike things that walk around?

MCCARTHY: Yeah.

OMNI: Is that practical? I mean, is there any use for something like that?

MCCARTHY: In some sense science fiction's portrayal of robots involves a kind of sociological imagination. During the twenties and thirties, robots were depicted in films and stories as an enemy tribe that attempted to conquer the world, and our hero wiped them out. By the fifties, robots had become an oppressed minority and our hero sympathized with them. But those ideas had little to do with human needs. They had to do with literary needs. Now, Isaac Asimov, who is the most popular writer to write about robots, has formulated these laws of robotics in which he almost intentionally confuses natural laws — laws of motion — with legislated laws. He implies that his legislated laws — that a robot should not harm a human being, for example — are in some sense natural laws of robotics. And then he writes these sorts of Talmudic stories in which the robots argue about whether something is or is not permissible according to the law. Well, that, of course, is also literary.

Now, what shall we want? One thing that seems reasonably clear to me is that making robots of human size and shape is the least likely. Rather more practical would be a robot that is much smaller or much bigger than a human and could do things humans cannot do because of their size or shape. It would seem to me the first winners would be robots that were quite different from a human. There is, however, one advantage to robots of human shape and size: they could use facilities designed for humans.

One of my ideas along these lines that is ultimately possible — and I've been thinking about it for many years — is the automatic delivery system. I would like to be able to turn to my computer terminal, type into it that I want a half-gallon of milk or a new gadget, and, twenty minutes later, have the milk or gadget appear automatically.

OMNI: By what system?

MCCARTHY: The first system one thinks of as a child is, of course, little trains that run along in tunnels under the streets, and so forth. What's wrong with that idea as it stands? Well, the little trains are expensive and not very fast. They can't carry very big objects, and they require an expensive redesign of the whole city. My current scheme is as follows. There's a nineteenth-century version and a twentieth-century version, or eco-version. The nineteenth-century version involves cables strung on poles, like the cables at ski resorts. The carriers are two-armed robots, except that they've got one arm like a gibbon and they can hang on to the cable with one arm. They can switch cables by grabbing on to another one.

OMNI: And these things somehow carry the objects being moved, and then swing like monkeys across these cables?

MCCARTHY: Right. Now, the other thing that they can do is climb the outside of a building on handholds that have been built into the building. They deliver things to a box, maybe the size and shape of an air conditioner, which is built into an outside wall. And after a while you hear these clanking noises, and what you've ordered appears in this box.

Now, in the eco-version, which is much more expensive, these things are in tunnels under the streets, so you don't have them clanking around overhead. But the idea that they would either come down from their poles or come out from underground and climb outside the building strikes me as essential in order to make them compatible with present buildings.

OMNI: We could have a little tube running up the side of the building.

MCCARTHY: Yes, but remember, not everybody would subscribe to the service at first. Not many of us are of the generation that remembers the installation of electricity. Just consider what an enormous amount of work that was. You look at old buildings and say, "How did they ever install electricity in that house?" They had to tear up bits of the walls to run the wires through. The other possibility — or the other extreme possibility — is a walking robot that, after it comes down from the cables or up from underground, simply walks over and knocks on your door. In some sense that would be more flexible. Something could be delivered to someone who was not a subscriber to the service.

What I envision, actually, with regard to robots, are some fairly major social changes that would bring about a return to the Victorian

Age, in a certain respect. If you had a robot to work twenty-four hours a day, you would think of more and more things for it to do. This would bring about an elaboration in standards of decoration, style, and service. For example, what you would regard as an acceptably set dinner table would correspond to the standards of the fanciest restaurant or to the old-fashioned, nineteenth-century standards of somebody who was very rich. In other words, standards would conform to what we imagined to be those of the British aristocracy, because they had servants. People ask, "Well, what will happen when we have robots?" And there is a very good historical parallel. Namely, what did the rich do when they had lots of servants?

OMNI: How many years must we wait?

MCCARTHY: I don't know. It's not a development question. It requires some fundamental conceptual advances on the order of the discovery of DNA's structure. Maybe once these advances are made, progress will be straightforward.

OMNI: Would robot intelligence and human intelligence be alike? Humans are motivated by anger, jealousy, ambition, sensitivity. And in literature robots are portrayed as possessing these same motivations.

MCCARTHY: I don't think it would be to our advantage to make robots whose moods are affected by their chemical state. In fact, it would be a greater chore to simulate the chemical state. And it would probably also be a mistake to make robots in which subgoals would interfere with the main goals. For example, according to Freudian theory we develop our ideas of morality in order to please our parents. But then eventually we pursue these concepts even in opposition to our parents. The general human instinct to assert independence would require some effort to build into robots. It doesn't seem to our advantage to make that effort.

OMNI: What about the possible disruption — the unemployment that could be caused by robots?

MCCARTHY: Well, there are two questions that have to be answered. One has to do with superrobots. In other words what will happen when we have robots that are as intelligent as people, which is a long way off. The other has to do with simple automation, which is similar to the advances in productivity that have already occurred.

The United States and other countries have gone through various economic cycles of unemployment and full employment. These countries have also gone through various periods of rapid or slow technological development. No one has ever attempted to correlate these things. But I think what would be observed is that there is no correlation — that periods of high unemployment are not especially correlated with periods of rapid technological advance. In fact, on the average, more advanced countries have somewhat lower unemployment than do the less technologically advanced countries. We have unemployment, but Mexico has vastly higher unemployment.

To take the extreme example, the average productivity of a worker in the United States has increased five times since, I don't know, 1920 or something like that. So you would expect that four fifths of the population would be out of work.

OMNI: But obviously when automation comes in, people *are* out of work temporarily, and then go to something else.

MCCARTHY: That's right. Now there is an economic malfunction that causes unemployment — that causes this interaction between unemployment and inflation and so forth. But it seems to me that this malfunction has little, if anything, to do with technology. What seems clear is that nobody has any real idea about how to deal with unemployment.

OMNI: That's taking automation up to only a certain level. But if we go up to the next level and have smart robots, I imagine there would be a fairly major shift in people's ways of life.

MCCARTHY: There was a soap opera of the thirties in which a girl from the hills of Kentucky married an English lord. The question was "Can a young girl from poverty-stricken Kentucky adjust to life among the English aristocracy with dozens of servants and so forth?" And the answer was that she might have a real hard time adjusting — sometimes it takes all of ten minutes. So it seems to me that what we would have to adjust to is being rich. It could take all of ten minutes.

OMNI: What about the psychological benefits of being rich? If *everyone* had servants . . .

MCCARTHY: I don't think that's really important. If you read nineteenth-century literature, you don't find any indication of people taking pleasure in their position relative to their servants. As far as they were concerned, servants were part of the machinery. It doesn't seem to me that you will lose a very large part of the psychological benefits of being rich merely because other people are rich. As the saying goes, "Anybody who is anybody . . ."

OMNI: That raises another question: How do we deal with machines? People who work with home computers have a funny way of talking about them. "It likes," and that sort of thing.

MCCARTHY: In my view verbs like "believes," "knows" or "doesn't know," "can do," "can't do," "understands" or "doesn't understand" are appropriately used with many present computer programs. And such language will become increasingly appropriate.

OMNI: There's a certain amount of humor involved when people use personal terms to refer to machines.

MCCARTHY: Yes, there's also a lot of purely metaphoric use of these phrases, even in relation to old machinery, that is not really appropriate. That is pure projection. Of course, with regard to computers, that projection takes place. But there's also the appropriate use, and eventually the pure projection and the appropriate use will be inextricably entwined.

OMNI: Do you think as we move toward more automation that we are going through a period of Luddism [the Luddites were early nineteenth-century English workingmen who destroyed new textile machinery for fear that it would put them out of work] — revolt against the coming of robots? It seemed as if we were doing that for a while in the sixties. But that seems to have subsided now.

MCCARTHY: It seems to me that the cause of those incidents had nothing to do with computers. It was a social phenomenon of some kind that we don't clearly understand. If the cause was the computers, the cause didn't go away. The impact of computers on daily life was much more profound during the seventies than it was during the sixties.

OMNI: What about the predictions of millions of people suddenly being out of work because of automation?

MCCARTHY: That's by no means a prediction. That's merely a speculation as to what could cause Luddism on a substantial scale, and I don't think people would be quite so dumb as to do it. It seems to me that if we are all to be rich, there has to be a lot more progress in automating office work. More than half the U.S. population now works in services of one kind or another, and we won't be rich unless we succeed in automating those services.

Let me repeat a story someone told me about his vision of the future. A clerk in Company A hears a beep. She turns to her terminal and reads on the screen, "We need 5000 pencils. Order them from Company B." So she turns from her terminal to her typewriter, types out a purchase order, and sends it to Company B, where another clerk reads the order, turns to her terminal, and types in "Send 5000 pencils to Company A." The person who related the story told it, as far as I could tell, with a totally straight face. But what do we need those two clerks for? Why don't those two computers talk to each other? Interorganizational communication by computers is something that's hardly started.

OMNI: We're getting to the point where we have terminals that do communicate with each other. Of course, they don't communicate much.

MCCARTHY: My main complaint about technology has been the slowness with which it is developing. My impression is that the rate of technological innovation, so far as it affects daily life, has been slower, say, between 1940 and 1980 than it was between 1880 and 1920. So people who complain about technological change going faster and faster are simply wrong. A lot of the complaints are in a sense complaints that technology is advancing too slowly, that the individual doesn't see nearly enough improvement in his own lifetime.

Some important improvements are not appreciated. You don't spend five minutes a day thanking technological improvements in sanitation and housing for the fact that you and your children don't have TB. The normal attitude is to take health for granted until you don't have it anymore, and then you complain. The same is true probably of wealth, insofar as technology has really contributed to your getting a higher salary than you would earn otherwise. But you don't see the contribution that some specific invention has made to your increased salary.

It's interesting to look at what inventions could have been introduced thirty or fifty years before they actually were — the missed opportunities where the technology was available to build them. And there are a fair number of them.

OMNI: Name one.

MCCARTHY: Well, I have a white-disc, push-button combination lock on my front door. I can open it much faster than I could a key lock, especially in the dark. Mechanically, it's no more complicated than a key lock. It could have been invented a hundred years ago.

Another is the pulse-jet engine. Are you familiar with it? Its only application was the German V-1 rocket during World War II. It is a very simple engine. Gasoline is squirted in, and the jet explodes out the back end. The momentum as it goes up creates a vacuum that sucks air in the front, so the thing goes *phutt-phutt-phutt-phutt*. There is nothing in the technology of that engine that would have prevented its being built in 1890, and it's vastly simpler than a piston engine.

OMNI: You and Marvin Minsky propose different solutions to the question of artificial intelligence and common sense. Can you give me a brief description of the two different points of view?

MCCARTHY: I and some others are optimistic about the use of logic to express what a computer can know about the world. And Minsky is skeptical — one could say more than skeptical — about whether that will work.

But actually that's not quite the whole story, because in addition to his skepticism about what won't work, Minsky has positive ideas about what will work.

OMNI: Can you describe his ideas in simple terms?

MCCARTHY: Maybe he can! I can't. I can mention an idea of his that I'm skeptical about. This is the notion that in any particular situation, there is a dominant "frame." Minsky has pursued this idea. The restaurant frame, for example.

OMNI: Meaning that when you walk into a restaurant, you enter a context in which you speak, act, and understand things in a certain way that would make no sense if you were, say, in a skating rink?

MCCARTHY: Right. Put that way, it's almost a truism. But Minsky also suggests that a single dominant frame has "subframes" — other related concepts or bits of information. This notion can be contrasted with the notion that information from a variety of sources interacts to define the situation.

Here you are, interviewing me. That is a frame. One could put some slots into that. But if we actually tried following the details of the conversation, would the frame concept allow for that? It works fairly well at the top level. You have a collection of questions that you want to discuss, so at that level it works quite nicely. This interview with me is, in that respect, very similar to the interview we did for your book [*Scientific Temperaments*]. Or from my point of view, being interviewed by you is similar to being interviewed by someone else. But if you're not bored by this particular interview, that must be because it is, in some important way, different from the others. And that isn't quite caught by the frame.

Now, Roger Shank, of Yale University, who writes a lot of computer programs, seems to be finding that in order to make things work he needs "packets" of information, no one of which is dominant, that interact with one another. And given my point of view, I say, "Ah, yes, Shank is moving in the direction of logic."

OMNI: In other words, Minsky suggests that artificial intelligence should be based on associated processes, like those which seem to function in the human brain. You would like to rely on logic that is similar to, but more sophisticated than, that found in the computers of today.

MCCARTHY: Basically, yes. Those of us who like logic think we can modify it to accommodate the problems of the real world. That something of the kind was required has been known for a long time. Ideas on how to do it formally and still preserve the formal character of logic were first being developed from the middle to the late seventies.

OMNI: So the idea is that, regardless of what actually functions inside the brain, these things can be done logically in computers? Do they *have* to be done logically?

MCCARTHY: No, they don't have to. You can design a computer program that will make logical mistakes. For instance, some of the Expert Systems lack common sense. The example I usually give is MYCIN, which is a Stanford system that gives advice on bacterial diseases. It has no concept of events occurring in time. It has no concept of "patient," "doctor," "hospital," "life," or "death." It does have concepts of the names of diseases, names of symptoms, names of tests that may be performed, and so on. And it converses in a sort of English. But if you were to say to it, "I had a patient yesterday with these symptoms, and I took your advice and he died. What shall I do today?" it would just say "input ungrammatical." It wouldn't have understood about the patient dying. It doesn't need that information for its purposes. But in spite of all that, it's quite useful. To some extent it's a kind of animated reference book.

OMNI: That's a very good term for it, because it eliminates the notion of common sense, which most people automatically assume is there when they see a machine making a diagnosis.

MCCARTHY: MYCIN is a particularly limited system. The interesting thing — similar to what I was saying about robotics — is that people are discovering how to get around the unsolved problems and make systems that are useful, even though these systems can't do some of the things that are ultimately fundamental to intelligence.

Still, I take a more basic research–oriented point of view. These people make their very ad hoc useful systems, and that's fine. But I think the fundamental advances in artificial intelligence will be made by people looking at the fundamental problems. Now, for some reason, artificial intelligence is the subject of a great deal of impatience. When it had existed only for five years, people were saying, "Yeah, yeah, you've been unsuccessful." But when we compare it with, say, genetics, in which just about a hundred years passed from the time of Mendel to the cracking of the genetic code . . . Now, there may have been periods when people thought they would be able to create life in a test tube by 1910 or something like that, but we don't remember that today.

OMNI: Why do you suppose there is this unwarranted excitement and anticipation?

MCCARTHY: Well, there's always been unwarranted anticipation in science on the part of some people. I think some of the expressions of disappointment are disingenuous — people taking the fact that it hasn't succeeded so far as evidence that it won't succeed at all. On the other hand there has been some overoptimism within the field. Partly that's because if you see only certain problems, you can imagine a plan for overcoming those problems. But if there are more problems that you *haven't* seen, you will be disappointed.

OMNI: Decades ago, long before the enactment of the Privacy Act of 1974, you advocated a bill of rights, published in the September 1966 issue of *Scientific American*, to protect citizens from the abuse of information collection made possible by computers. You advocated national data banks as very important social tools, but wanted to ensure that their contents would not be misused.

MCCARTHY: I made a proposal for dealing with the misuse of information: that a person had a right to know what information about him was in the data banks; that he could sue for invasion of privacy; that he could challenge information in the file; and so on. I don't know whether my article had anything to do with it, but in many places these ideas have been incorporated into laws and the thing has been elaborated upon considerably. Now I'm beginning to think my 1966 proposals were a mistake.

OMNI: Why?

MCCARTHY: To some extent they pandered to superstition — the superstition that people can and will harm you on the basis of trivial information. For example, Princeton University is worrying about whether my privacy would be violated if they released a photograph of me to *Psychology Today.* It's a little bit like some primitive superstition that if you have a person's nail clippings and a few locks of hair you can cast a spell on him, or that if you know someone's true name you can harm him.

OMNI: Well, there's a point in there somewhere, isn't there? Your brother, Patrick, was thrown out of the army for admitting to being a communist, and then later in the seventies he was dismissed from a post office job for refusing to sign a loyalty oath. I think that your family's history and experience would lead you to fear the misuse of data banks and information.

MCCARTHY: But I think that the legitimate protection against misuse of information is at the level of action. In other words, the post office shouldn't have been allowed to fire my brother.

OMNI: But they still should be allowed to have access to various kinds of information about people?

MCCARTHY: What goes into data banks should be a matter of judgment, but I've become convinced that there should be no restrictions on the storage and exchange of information. In order to cut off these reverberation violations of privacy, rules should be enforced at the level of action and not at the level of information storage.

OMNI: So, for example, the FBI may have a long file on you, but unless they use it to harass, arrest, or convict you, then nothing happens?

MCCARTHY: That's my current view of it. The cost of looking at information and deciding what is valid and so forth is enormous. Normally it's done only when something is really important.

Nuclear Demons, Nuclear Dreams
Hans Bethe

The MX is an abomination. President Reagan has called it the
Peacemaker. That's just like calling Robespierre a cure for
headaches.

*The sun has been shining for billions of years, but it took a Hans
Bethe (pronounced Bay-te) to figure out just how it works. His discovery, made in 1938, was the culmination of his work in the then-
dawning field of nuclear physics. For nearly twenty years a number
of very good physicists had been speculating on the kinds of nuclear
reactions that might take place deep within the interior of the sun and
other stars to provide the sunlight and starlight we receive. Bethe did
more than speculate; he approached the problem systematically. Picking and choosing adroitly among the possibilities, he put together two
sequences of nuclear reactions — the proton-proton cycle and the
carbon cycle — then showed that, under conditions to be expected in
the interior of the sun and other stars, these sequences would indeed
produce energy at the observed rates. For this, he was awarded the
Nobel Prize in physics in 1967.*

*Born in 1906, in Alsace-Lorraine, then part of Wilhelminian Ger-
many, Bethe was one of the generation of brilliant physicists who
flourished in Europe during the 1920s and early 1930s, when modern
atomic theory was being born. Adolf Hitler's rise to power, in the early
1930s, presaged the end of that scientific renaissance, and in 1935
Bethe immigrated to the United States, where Cornell University has
been his home base ever since.*

Like most of his colleagues, Bethe was taken aback by the discovery,

Photograph: David M. Kennedy

in 1939, of a new kind of nuclear reaction — the splitting of uranium. He knew from the outset that, with war looming, this discovery of fission could lead to the development of an atom bomb. By 1942, he was convinced that the bomb could be ready in time to be used during the war. He then joined the Manhattan Project and soon rose to direct the Division of Theoretical Physics at Los Alamos, New Mexico. For his work on the project he received the Presidential Medal of Merit from Harry S. Truman in 1946.

Bethe's exceptional understanding of physics, his background in government service, and his ability to address a broad range of scientific problems made him a natural leader in the world of postwar physics. He was one of the founders of the Big Bang theory of the origin of the universe. He also contributed to some of the earliest studies on power-producing nuclear reactors and, in 1949, wrote the first paper on the safety of fast-breeder reactors. Along with many of the other senior leaders of the Manhattan Project, he was disturbed by the implications of his work. This concern led him into the world of public policy. During the 1950s Bethe served as a member of the President's Science Advisory Committee, which dealt with nuclear safety issues at the highest government levels.

In recent years, Bethe has not hesitated to plunge full tilt into debates over nuclear power. In a controversial article published in Scientific American in 1976, Bethe asserted that during the next quarter-century nuclear energy will be the only alternative to fossil fuels. "The general public is not well enough informed about science and technology and our role in our society," he wrote. "This allows any number of nuts to dispense misinformation couched in noble rhetoric." Taking his lead from antinuclear activists, he went on to marshal dozens of his fellow scientists as signers of a pronuclear petition arguing that objections to nuclear power should be outweighed by the benefits it would provide.

Today Bethe continues to be a vigorous nuclear advocate who looks ahead to the presumed success of fusion power — the earliest studies of which drew directly from his encyclopedic writings on nuclear reactions. At the same time, he is fiercely opposed to nuclear weapons, speaking out for disarmament every chance he gets.

What does Bethe see as the future of the world's energy supplies, of nuclear power, of fusion, and of physics? To find out, T. A. Heppenheimer, author of The Man-Made Sun, *a study of fusion, interviewed*

Bethe in 1982 at the California Institute of Technology, in Pasadena, where he was a visiting professor. In 1983, I met with Bethe in his large, utilitarian office at Cornell, where we discussed the early days of physics and nuclear arms. A synthesis of the two talks follows.

OMNI: Dr. Bethe, you were born in Germany, and it was in Germany during the twenties and thirties that you became a physicist. You must have seen German science change drastically under the Nazis. Can you describe some of that?

BETHE: The Nazis were antiscientific. Everything was done by feeling rather than by reason. In addition, many of the leading scientists were Jews, or half-Jews subject to anti-Semitic laws. So Germany lost maybe half of the good young scientists because of that, and then made sure the others were stifled, held down. The best German theoretical physicist, Werner Heisenberg, was held in disgrace for a long time; he wasn't considered enough of a Nazi, and he was severely attacked. Young German students were told that the great thing was fighting for the fatherland, not studying science. Consequently, Germany is missing a generation of scientists. In the postwar era, it took quite a long time for German science to recover. And it has not yet reached its previous eminence, except in one respect. They have a fabulous high-energy laboratory in Hamburg, which is simply excellent. The scientists working there come from all over Europe, from the United States, and Germany too.

OMNI: How was it that you came to leave Germany?

BETHE: Well, I'm half-Jewish, which meant that by early in April of 1933 I could no longer hold any position at any German university. I could have worked in an industrial laboratory, but I wanted to do pure science. So the decision was clear: I left. And I am very happy that I left as early as I did.

OMNI: You were involved with nuclear fission literally from the beginning. You were at Cornell in 1939 when Niels Bohr arrived on the S.S. *Drottningholm* with the news that Otto Hahn and Fritz Strassmann of Germany had discovered how to split (or fission) a heavy atom into two lighter ones, releasing energy in the process. How did you hear the news?

BETHE: I learned about it, I think, from people around me who were talking about it. I had one physicist colleague at Cornell, Georg Placzek, who was terribly interested and began working on this immediately. Then I learned more about it at a little meeting of some theoretical physicists in Washington. This was in March of 1939, and the whole subject of the fission of uranium was discussed there. Generally, our sessions were open to the press, but in this case we closed the meeting.

[Enrico] Fermi and [Leo] Szilard both outlined the possibilities of a nuclear weapon based on the creation of a nuclear chain reaction. [In a nuclear chain reaction, a heavy atom like uranium splits into two lighter atoms and one or more neutrons, subatomic particles with zero charge. Each neutron is capable of splitting another uranium atom, which then releases neutrons of its own. When enough uranium is present, the reaction becomes self-sustaining, going faster and faster, until an explosion occurs.] It was not at all clear that all this could be done. But these people at least saw the possibility.

OMNI: When you first heard these presentations, how did you respond?

BETHE: I thought it was largely speculation, that it would take lots of experimentation before it would become a real possibility. I was interested in this, at the time, because of the impending war. But I thought it was unlikely that nuclear fission would lead to a weapon that could be useful in the war, and therefore I didn't want anything to do with it. Instead, I concerned myself with such matters as projectiles penetrating armor plate and with underwater pressure waves from explosions. Most important was radar. That was what I worked on in the early years of the war.

OMNI: Then you did not associate yourself with the group that included Fermi, Szilard, and Einstein?

BETHE: Not Einstein.

OMNI: Well, Einstein signed the letter to President Roosevelt in August 1939, warning the president that the Germans might be working on an atomic bomb.

BETHE: Definitely. He signed the letter, but he never, never worked on the bomb or on the Manhattan Project.

OMNI: So you were not associated with the early group of physicists who, in 1939, sought to bring the potentials of nuclear weaponry to the attention of the highest levels of the United States government.

BETHE: That's correct. Nor was I associated with the group that tried to find out whether it was a real possibility.

OMNI: And yet shortly afterward, beginning in 1943, you headed the theoretical physics group at Los Alamos . . .

BETHE: That I did, yes. I joined the project in the summer of 1942, when it was shown to me, in a secret briefing, that Fermi's chain reaction, which he'd set up under the stands in a squash court in Chicago, was almost certain to operate. I'd doubted we could get enough material to make a bomb, because neutrons generally cannot fission [or split] ordinary uranium, but only uranium-235, a lighter and very rare form of the element. But Fermi was able to slow the neutrons down by embedding the uranium in a pile of graphite. Once they are slowed, more of them get caught in uranium-235 than in the much more abundant uranium-238. I saw that the project had developed quite well and that there was a good chance we could probably have the material for an atomic bomb during the war. And I did want to influence the outcome of the war — I was afraid, like most other people, that the Germans would build the bomb first.

OMNI: How did you get into that position in Los Alamos?

BETHE: I was a well-known nuclear theorist. Apart from Robert Oppenheimer, who was the leader of the project, and Eugene Wigner, who was busy at Chicago, I was probably the most knowledgeable person in nuclear physics.

OMNI: Have you seen the TV series "Oppenheimer"? How do you feel about its portrayal of your colleagues and of yourself?

BETHE: I watched it regularly. On the whole it reflected the spirit of Los Alamos very well and presented very good characterizations of my colleagues. As for Oppenheimer himself, it was very good, except that I don't believe — in the second episode — Oppenheimer tried quite so hard to persuade General Leslie Groves to make him director of the project. And I never lost my temper in Oppie's office while complaining about Edward Teller. And there are other mistakes. Some things are more dramatized than others; for instance, in episode five, the incident of Groves and Oppenheimer taking George Kistiakowsky to task [over a failed simulation of the bomb detonation]. That wasn't correct. But these are not really major criticisms.

OMNI: Once ensconced in your position at Los Alamos, what were some of the major technical problems you faced in developing the bomb, and how did you solve them?

BETHE: Well, the problem at Los Alamos was to get the bomb

assembled. One problem was that, when we started, there was no appreciable amount of material available on which to do experiments. So, much of our time was spent trying to calculate, theoretically, how such a weapon would work, beginning with the amount and density of material [the critical mass] we'd need to start an explosion. That would tell us how much fissionable material the large facilities, such as those at Oak Ridge and Hanford, would have to produce. Second, we wanted to figure out how much energy could come out from such a device and what it would do in less than one-millionth of a second.

OMNI: Solving these problems would have required a great deal of computation. There were no electronic computers in those days. What did you do?

BETHE: To begin with, we had adding machines that you turned with a crank — we had cranking machines by the dozens, and a number of people who operated these hand calculators. But we also had electromechanical computers — the old IBM machines. They combined electric sensing — reading data off punch cards — with mechanical computation. They were quite good. They could add, subtract, multiply, and divide at fairly good speed. A major multiplication might take them a second. And there were very high-class physicists and mathematicians engaged in writing the programs. One of them was Richard Feynman, at Cal Tech. There were three very knowledgeable people helping him, as well as others less trained. They kept the machines in running order. One of my friends said at a later time, "These are my card-carrying Ph.D.s."

OMNI: Despite all the expertise, you had a major upset midway through the project. Can you talk about it?

BETHE: In addition to a uranium bomb, we were also building a plutonium bomb. It turned out that plutonium gave off neutrons spontaneously, threatening to predetonate the bomb slowly, creating a fizzle rather than a bang. That was quite a surprise: it showed that we could not assemble a plutonium weapon by the so-called gun method, in which the explosion occurred when two halves of a spherical bomb were shot together. We had to find a faster way to detonate the bomb, and we finally did. We took a quantity of plutonium, somewhat below critical mass, and surrounded it with powerful explosives. When we detonated the explosives, they compressed the plutonium, greatly increasing its density until it reached critical mass.

OMNI: The first test bomb was exploded at the Alamogordo, New Mexico, test site on July 16, 1945. Did you have any moral question about your work at that point?

BETHE: Not at that point. The real moral dilemma came not after the successful test, but after the bomb [a uranium bomb] was dropped on Hiroshima and we got the first photographs of the destruction. We had tried to calculate the damage, but the actual devastation was a lot worse, and seeing it in pictures means a lot more than just having the figures before you. Many of us at Los Alamos soon came to believe that we had to prevent nuclear weapons from ever being used again.

OMNI: What did you do toward that end?

BETHE: I gave a lot of talks around the country, and I collaborated with Fred Seitz on an article in a book called *One World or None*. Our article said that a determined country could surely repeat our performance and build an atom bomb within five years, but we were wrong by one year. It took the Russians four years. In fact, one of my friends recently talked to a Russian who said that Stalin ordered physicists to build the bomb in 1943, in the middle of very serious fighting. This, of course, we were not aware of in 1945, but it gave them a two-year start beyond what we knew. And the Russians wanted to have their own weapon.

We did not name the Russians in our article — that would not have been proper to do at that time. But we certainly had the Russians in mind, and our article was in complete contrast to the statements of the higher-ups, who told Congress it would take the Russians twenty years to build the bomb. Our contention was simply that the secret could not be kept. We were suggesting that it would do the United States no harm to join an international agency dedicated to arms control.

OMNI: Despite your efforts, nuclear weapons have proliferated to nightmarish proportions. Those in today's nuclear freeze movement even suggest we're in imminent danger of blowing ourselves up. What do you think about that, and how do you feel about the nuclear freeze movement?

BETHE: I feel good about the nuclear freeze movement. I don't believe that we are in imminent danger of blowing ourselves up, but I do feel that the confrontational stance of the Reagan government has been destructive. They have taken a very hard point of view, always emphasizing the differences between the United States and the Soviet Union instead of emphasizing the common goal of getting nuclear weapons under control. In my opinion, their antagonistic approach has made it more likely that someday there will be a conflict. And if there is an armed conflict, then it may very well lead to the use of nuclear weapons.

Those in Ronald Reagan's administration are really very radical — they call themselves conservatives, but I don't think they are. They have decided to pursue nuclear arms superiority at a huge cost. The freeze movement is simply the natural reaction to such radical nationalism, and I think the movement has worked miracles. Seven of eight initiatives in favor of the freeze won in [1982] state elections, including California, which is the biggest state of the union. And this show of support has modified government policy, though not enough. One well-meaning senator, Claiborne Pell of Rhode Island, recently told me, "Just keep at it. We in the Senate cannot act without knowing that the American people are behind us."

OMNI: Those in the nuclear freeze movement have specifically suggested that the superpowers sit down and negotiate a verifiable freeze on the testing, production, and further deployment of nuclear warheads, missiles, and other delivery systems. What do you think of this proposal?

BETHE: I think the freeze is a very good idea as a first step, giving us time to negotiate. But any viable arms control negotiation takes a long, long time. The SALT [Strategic Arms Limitation Treaty] II treaty, which was very carefully negotiated, took nearly seven years. And at that time, the United States government was entirely behind the negotiator, which is not true now. So a simple, unnegotiated freeze without any complicated verification procedures would be a very good thing. A negotiated freeze with special verification procedures, on the other hand, is not a good idea. It would divert our negotiators from the real problem of reducing armaments way below the present level.

OMNI: What do you think about President Reagan's contention that the Russians will overpower us if we don't keep manufacturing arms at an ever-quickening pace?

BETHE: That is nonsense. The best way to prevent the Russians from getting ahead of us is to ratify the SALT II treaty, which Reagan has refused to do. Our government complains that the Russians have gathered great momentum; that is, that they have built many new weapons in the last five or ten years. Maybe so, but in my opinion, that's best controlled by putting a ceiling on the weapons they can produce. In fact, if we ratified SALT II, the Russians would immediately need to destroy some two hundred missiles.

OMNI: But President Reagan claims the Soviets are far ahead of us in producing countersilo weapons that can wipe out our land-based, intercontinental ballistic missiles [ICBMs]. If we don't produce more ICBMs and countersilo weapons of our own in a hurry, he contends, the Soviets may be able to wipe out much of our nuclear arsenal in a first strike. In fact, he says that by the mid-1980s this "window of vulnerability" will have opened wide enough to give the Soviets a clear advantage in any nuclear war. Are you suggesting that this so-called window of vulnerability doesn't really exist?

BETHE: That's right. All land-based missiles, whether they belong to us or to the Russians, are vulnerable. But only a quarter of our warheads are actually on land-based missiles, whereas the Russians have three quarters of theirs on land-based missiles. Therefore, the Russians are more vulnerable than we are. Furthermore, if the Russians were foolish enough to attack our land-based missiles, we could still retaliate with the main part of our force: airplane bombers, which have little vulnerability because they can take off if there's an alert, and submarine-based missiles, which are not vulnerable at all. These are never mentioned when the government talks about our alleged weakness.

OMNI: Yet the current administration is pushing Congress to fund the MX missile complex, a fourteen-mile-long site that would protect highly accurate ICBMs under a powerful vault of steel and concrete. The President claims an all-out Soviet attack, capable of devastating 90 percent of present-day Minuteman ICBMs, could destroy only 20 percent of the MXs. Even if you don't believe in the window of vulnerability, do you see the MX as having any value?

BETHE: The MX is an abomination. President Reagan has called it the Peacemaker. That's just like calling Robespierre a cure for headaches, and I think that comparison is generous. First of all, my friends say the MX will be very vulnerable, and they give good arguments. As long as its viability is in doubt, we should not build it. Second, I dislike the concept of building more vulnerable missiles to attack the enemy's missiles. Our best security comes from invulnerable weapons. The Russians won't attack our Minutemen, because they know perfectly well that we would shoot back with our submarine-based missiles and our bombers.

OMNI: What do you think about the contention that we can survive a nuclear war?

BETHE: I think it is nonsense. The idea is that we could keep a small-scale, tactical nuclear war at controllable levels. But nearly every military expert will tell you that this is impossible. If we are about to lose at one level, our general in the field would be likely to escalate the conflict to the next level. If the Russians are then about to lose on the next level, they will escalate to a higher level still. And before anybody knows it, a full-scale nuclear war will be raging, full force.

OMNI: Can't anything be done to avoid this doomsday scenario once the bombs start flying?

BETHE: The most important thing is to use the so-called hot line to the Soviet Union. If messages can go across, we might be able to negotiate a settlement or offer to stop the fighting. Senator Henry Jackson of Washington suggested we expand the hot line that exists today: instead of having just one line running from president to premier, we should have additional hookups between generals, senators, and the like. Such communication is especially important in case of an accident. Suppose there is that mad lieutenant in some bunker out in Wyoming who launches one of the Minutemen? We want to be sure we can tell the Russians that this was an accident, and that we are willing to compensate them for it. It is terribly important that the two superpowers do not react wildly.

OMNI: Do you think it's possible that a nuclear war could start as the result of a computer error?

BETHE: It could, especially if those in charge decided to shoot on warning. We have very elaborate early-warning systems aboard satellites that look down on the Soviet Union. Basically, these systems monitor the infrared emitted when missiles are shot outside the atmosphere. Of course, such radiation is released all the time, whenever there's a satellite launching, but those are previously announced, we know about them, and so we don't worry about them. Instead, we look for any sign of twenty to a hundred unexpected launchings in, let's say, one minute. The computers that detect such signals are probably fairly accurate, and infrared radiation cannot be easily falsified. But still, the computer transmission may be in error, informing us of hundreds of launches from known nuclear silos in the Soviet Union — even if not a single launch has actually occurred.

We've already had false alarms as a result of computer errors in our Distant Early Warning system, a radar network that scans northern Canada for approaching Russian airplanes. That system has mistaken the rising moon and even a flock of geese for a plane. Radar, of course, is a wonderful device, but the signals can be confusing.

OMNI: Could a computer error ever launch a missile for real?

BETHE: Computer errors in launches are very, very unlikely, and if such an error were to occur, it would presumably launch a single missile. It's like the mad lieutenant.

OMNI: One hot line call could ease the situation?

BETHE: Yes, the side in error would apologize.

OMNI: In any event, you said that computer errors of any sort would lead to war only if leaders attacked on warning. Is that the policy?

BETHE: It is not, and that is very important. It is a terrible doctrine. But some people have proposed it both in this country and the Soviet Union.

OMNI: Let's say a war does start. Would ordinary civilians be able to protect themselves with the fallout shelters and evacuation plans prescribed by the civil defense program?

BETHE: No. That program is almost totally useless. According to the administration, the program was first suggested, in part, because the Russians have such a program. From my best information, this just isn't so. An important part of any civil defense program would be a drill in evacuating people from a city. If that were ever to happen, we would see it from our satellites. We can see a single person in the open space in Russia — a single person! If there were a hundred thousand people streaming out of some city, we would surely notice that, even if they went on foot. And nothing like that has ever occurred.

But whether the Russians have a program or not, there is a wonderful argument against civil defense: it will not be on time. You can envisage two possibilities. In one, there might be a sudden attack out of the blue. In that case, civil defense is useless, especially against the primary effects of nuclear weapons. In the other possibility, some conventional war may have started in Europe, and I think the chance of that is very, very small. But suppose it occurs and then escalates into a nuclear war. Reagan's proposal is that we might take the precaution of evacuating people from the big American cities to the countryside. In fact, we in Ithaca [site of Cornell] and Tompkins County have been designated as one of the evacuation areas. Our County Council has given exactly the right answer. It has said, "No way. We cannot house these people, and we certainly cannot feed them." There's a further point: if all these people could be evacuated in time, and then sustained in a town like ours, then nothing would be produced in the city. All the manufacturing would be laid still, costing daily about half the gross national product of the country. Under such circumstances, we wouldn't be able to sustain ourselves for any length of time.

One thing that does make sense, though, is teaching people to find protection from fallout in case they haven't been bombed directly. If you want to avoid fallout, going into your basement does make some sense, and going into the basement of a skyscraper makes even more sense. Suppose we're faced with that scenario the Reagan government is so fond of — the Russians attacking our Minutemen. Now, there are few people living near the Minutemen silos, but fallout would extend five hundred miles downwind and would be tremendous. Therefore all the people, and there are a great many of them, in areas five hundred miles downwind should at least know how to protect themselves from fallout. But a major shelter program, as some people have suggested, isn't warranted.

OMNI: Dr. Bethe, in all fairness, the present government has proposed an arms control plan of its own. Would you care to comment?

BETHE: Our government's plan, the so-called START [Strategic Arms Reduction Talks] proposal, is, unfortunately, impossible for the Russians to accept. Reagan's first suggestion, that each side cut the number of nuclear delivery systems more or less in half, is a good idea. But that's only the first part of the proposal. The government has gone further, arguing that only half the warheads of each side be situated on land. That would mean a terrible sacrifice by the Russians, who have naturally stored most of their missiles throughout their vast land mass. They have much less access to the sea than we, so their decision was only logical.

Reagan has also suggested that we not count bombers when equalizing arms, but since we have great superiority in bombers, the Russians cannot accept that either. Nor will they tolerate the suggestion that we inspect each other's nuclear installations on the ground. They have always been very much opposed to any intrusion into their country. Everything is secret there, and military information, of course, is even more secret.

Finally, there is the matter of armaments in Europe. We have been very much troubled by the Russian SS-20, a fairly big, mobile missile threatening all of Western Europe. To counter that, we've begun to install the so-called Pershing II, a group of European-based missiles threatening Russia. That, I think, is a very bad move on our part.

OMNI: Many Europeans are upset at the thought of those missiles within their borders. They feel they'd be more vulnerable than ever to attack.

BETHE: Absolutely. That's the point. That's why we'd be much better off if we based our counterforce aboard submarines stationed off Europe. In fact, the Russians have said they'd cut the number of SS-20s in half if we didn't deploy the Pershing. The proposal is one that I think we should seriously discuss.

OMNI: It seems as if our government's proposals have been built to fail, as if that's really what's desired.

BETHE: I am afraid you may well be right. But we must keep discussion alive, because eventually the government will change.

OMNI: This is all rather depressing. Perhaps we should go back in time to discuss a more positive aspect of the nuclear age. You received a Nobel Prize in 1967 for your work on the nuclear reactions that power the sun and stars. How well has that work held up during the intervening decades?

BETHE: Very well. There are two reactions that power the stars, both of which are propelled by hydrogen. As the reactions proceed, hydrogen gets used up. The sun is now five billion years old, about halfway through its hydrogen life, which is quite satisfactory. But some stars about the size of the sun have come to the end of the hydrogen in their central region. They still have lots of hydrogen outside, but when they come to the end of this central hydrogen, their cores collapse, becoming about five times hotter than they were before. And, paradoxically, the star as a whole expands. That makes it a giant.

Now, one of the most striking proofs of the general idea of nuclear energy production in the stars is the existence of red giants. The details of how a red giant develops — increasing its luminosity, getting cooler and bigger, then shrinking again as the center gets hot enough for helium to react, then expanding again — work out beautifully, in accordance with the general ideas of nuclear reactions.

OMNI: Tell me about these fundamental nuclear reactions.

BETHE: The proton-proton cycle and the carbon cycle both generate energy as protons, or hydrogen nuclei, join to form helium nuclei. In the first type of cycle, the proton-proton cycle, two hydrogen nuclei simply combine directly to form a single helium nucleus. In the second cycle, the carbon cycle, protons collect around the nucleus of a carbon molecule until, finally, a helium nucleus splits off, leaving the original carbon alone once again. And both of these reactions, both of these cycles, produce enormous amounts of energy.

OMNI: You played a major role in developing the understanding of both cycles.

BETHE: Yes, that's true. The proton-proton reaction was really discovered in 1938 in Germany by Carl von Weizsäcker, who has not received enough credit for this discovery and who has received too much credit for discovering the carbon cycle, which is interesting. Nobody mentions him with regard to the proton-proton reaction, and that really was his discovery and his alone.

OMNI: Then what was your discovery?

BETHE: Charles L. Critchfield and I calculated the actual rate at which the proton-proton reaction occurs. Weizsäcker didn't do that. And I was convinced, after that, that this was the reaction. But that didn't fit the big and brilliant stars like Sirius. So, in an attempt to find an explanation for those, I found the carbon cycle. Weizsäcker discovered it at about the same time, but my theory was a lot more complete.

OMNI: You are one of the few people to win a Nobel for work in astrophysics. Why is that so?

BETHE: Well, the Nobel statutes were written in such a way as to make astronomers ineligible. I was the first exception, probably because I was also a pure physicist. The citation first mentions my work on nuclear reactions, and second, my study of the nuclear reactions responsible for the energy in stars.

OMNI: How did you learn of your selection in 1967, and what was your reaction?

BETHE: Because there is no prize for astronomy, I didn't expect it at all. One morning, at six o'clock, I was awakened by a telephone call. Usually a telephone call at that time means a wrong number, so I just let it ring, for about, oh, two minutes. Then I lifted the receiver, and it turned out to be a man from the Swedish TV network, who said, "Well, I am instructed to tell you that you have won the Nobel Prize for physics." Then he read me the citation. He had hardly hung up the receiver when there was another phone call. One after another, all the radio stations around the country called to interview me. By that time I was awake. It happened that my brother-in-law was in the house and in bed, and he decided that war had probably broken out and I was being called from Washington to be told what to do!

OMNI: Did the work that earned you the Nobel also lead to research on controlled nuclear fusion?

BETHE: Certainly. But when I published my work on nuclear reactions in *Reviews of Modern Physics* back in 1936 and 1937, I never thought that engineers and physicists would pick up on it and start thinking about fusion reactions as a new energy source.

OMNI: President Reagan's science adviser, George Keyworth, stated not long ago, "There is no doubt in my mind that fusion will work and will be the ultimate power source in the future." Would you care to comment?

BETHE: I am also optimistic about fusion. At this moment I am not sure that fusion will be used to generate commercial electric power. You want a plant that generates electricity to operate continuously. Yet for the first two decades or so, fusion-power plants may well have frequent interruptions — frequent downtimes. This would be a general feature of any complicated new plant, and a fusion plant will be far more complicated than an ordinary nuclear power plant — a fission plant.

On the other hand, I am very optimistic about the so-called fusion breeder concept. In that technology, neutrons escaping from the initial fusion reaction would combine with uranium-238, an essentially inert material, converting it into highly reactive plutonium. Likewise, the neutrons could combine with thorium, converting it into reactive uranium-233. The plutonium and uranium-233 could then be used to fuel fission reactors [the nuclear reactors in use today]. I do believe that, by the second half of the twenty-first century, this will probably be our most important source of energy.

OMNI: So the fusion breeder would act as an energy multiplier?

BETHE: That's exactly it. The fusion devices that are currently being worked on include the tokamak and the mirror machine. The tokamak is shaped like a torus [doughnut-shaped], and the mirror is a tube with magnets at each end. [Both produce energy much as the sun does. Gas within is heated until it moves violently. The protons and neutrons that make up the gas are then forced to collide, combining to form helium and releasing energy in the process. In the case of a fusion breeder, the moving neutrons would collide with uranium-238 or thorium, producing fissionable plutonium or uranium-233.]

OMNI: The tokamak dominates current fusion research. Do you see more promise, over the long term, in the mirror machines?

BETHE: The tokamak certainly is way ahead of everything else. It has a very convoluted geometry, and so it is quite difficult to operate and maintain and is particularly difficult to use in connection with a breeder. The mirror machine is less advanced. But if it succeeds, I think it is likely that the mirror machine will be a better machine than the tokamak. In any event, either machine is likely to put out only as much energy as it takes to run it — maybe a little more. So using it to produce fuel for a fission reactor would be your best bet.

OMNI: A few years ago William Metz, a staff writer for *Science*, wrote that such a fission-fusion-combined breeder would actually have all the complications of both a fission system and a fusion system and that this would necessarily be an exceptionally difficult way to go. How do you respond to that criticism?

BETHE: I think it is totally wrong. The first idea, it is true, was to surround the fusion device with a blanket of thorium or uranium-238 and make energy in that blanket. This I regard as a bum idea. It combines all the difficulties of both worlds. I want to separate the fission and the fusion completely by operating the fusion breeder off-line from the power plants. And I want the fusion device to make only material that is fissionable and that can then be used in a state-of-the-art fission reactor.

OMNI: You are talking about fusion as a source of cheap neutrons, which would be used to breed cheap plutonium. How do you prevent the plutonium from being used to make nuclear bombs?

BETHE: My idea is that these fusion breeder plants would be very heavily guarded and would be built in special locations. They would not be run by the utilities, which is an important point, but by the government, and the product would then be sold to utilities. The reason that all this is possible is that one such fusion breeder would supply enough fuel for ten to twenty ordinary fission reactors.

Moreover, I would prefer to produce uranium-233 rather than plutonium. None of the high-grade material would ever leave the site. It would be a military site, if you want. It would be subject to that level of security.

OMNI: So by a combination of clever physics and military-type security you would expect to safeguard these materials to prevent their misuse? In other words, have your cake and eat it, too?

BETHE: Exactly. Besides, we have tons of weapons-grade material — in the form of weapons. These are far more convenient for a terrorist to steal than just the material, and we have continued to safeguard them successfully.

OMNI: In 1974, using a Canadian-supplied reactor, India built a bomb — something India was not supposed to be able to do. Would these safeguards be sufficient to prevent anything like that from ever happening again?

BETHE: What happened in India probably will occur again. It is very difficult to prevent completely any accumulation of fissionable material for illicit purposes — that is, for making bombs. All we can hope to do is keep the amounts of material that are so diverted very small so that they don't make very much difference in the world picture.

OMNI: In other countries, such as France, Japan, perhaps the United Kingdom, certainly the Soviet Union, nuclear power is being developed rapidly. Here at home, though, that development is being held back. Why should this be?

BETHE: The reason is economics and the availability of material. We have coal, lots of coal, and it is cheap. The price of coal is still less than $40 a ton here in the United States. In Germany, it's $120 per ton. The Germans and the British like to use their own coal, but there is very little of it, and it is tremendously expensive. For those two countries, the cost of making electricity from coal imported from the United States is about the same as the cost of making it from fission.

OMNI: Isn't it true that South Africa, which has abundant and particularly cheap coal, is building nuclear power plants?

BETHE: I am afraid I have to attribute nefarious intentions to the South Africans. I believe that they are very much interested in nuclear weapons, not only in nuclear power. So that country's a special case.

OMNI: We actually have two classes of nuclear reactors in common use in this country. Far less well known than the power plants with their cooling towers, which one sees on the nightly news, are the nuclear plants used in naval submarines and other vessels. How would you compare the safety and performance record of the naval reactors with the civilian ones?

BETHE: We do know that no submarine ever blew up because the reactor malfunctioned. I think we know that there has not been a meltdown accident in a submarine — probably not even a partial one. The submarine reactors have extremely good quality control, in every detail. And the navy is willing to pay very high prices for these reactors. In my opinion, quality control — excellent quality control — should also apply to the civilian reactors. And I feel that this could be improved. The regulatory climate should shift in the direction of improving quality control.

OMNI: Do you believe that, for the sake of quality control, the navy pays relatively more per installed kilowatt than civilian plants do?

BETHE: I am sure they pay much, much more than civilians.

OMNI: So then, in order to meet economic criteria, civilian plants must necessarily pay somewhat less attention to quality control than the navy does.

BETHE: Probably somewhat less, that's true. But civilian power plants have one great advantage. They are big. Because they are big, the cost per kilowatt will automatically be less, even with the same amount of quality control. The typical naval reactor is maybe fifty megawatts and the typical civilian reactor is a thousand.

Now, I have high hopes for INPO — the Institute for Nuclear Power Operation — an organization created by the nuclear industry after the Three Mile Island accident. One of its several functions is to supervise the building of nuclear reactors. Another is to look after the safe operation of nuclear power plants. And I think that's an extremely important point. Some utilities are very good, and some are not so good. INPO is trying to raise the quality of operation by giving information to all the individual utilities, and also by having its own people go around to see whether the operations are completely up to standard. So in a way they constitute a second Nuclear Regulatory Commission.

OMNI: In Germany the Atomgesetz — the Atom Law — requires that safety take precedence over all other considerations, even economic considerations, and that no effort be spared in order to ensure that safety has been pushed to the limit. If we adopted such a law in this country, would that influence the choice between light-water versus far safer gas-cooled reactors?

BETHE: I think it probably would. I think it's a stupid law. It could greatly force up, even double, the cost of our energy. And that could begin to be intolerable.

OMNI: You obviously have a rather different view of reactor safety from that of many other influential people. Why do you feel as you do?

BETHE: Because I consider safety to be a matter of numbers. I consider everything to be a matter of numbers. The question is, what are you likely to buy with further increases in safety? At current safety levels in our nuclear industry, I anticipate an average of two fatalities per year. A major accident, which has not happened, might occur once in a thousand years. I define a major accident as one in which large amounts of radioactivity are vented on the public. In such an accident the estimate — and I think it a very sensible and good estimate — is that a thousand people would die from delayed cancers. Of course, it's not certain at all that anybody would die from delayed cancers. But going by present assumptions, that's a thousand deaths every thousand years. That's one a year.

I add to this the possibility that such a major accident could occasionally be coupled with very bad wind and rain conditions, which would increase the number of fatalities, because some of the radioactivity might fall out very close to a populated area. This is all in the Rasmussen Report [a 1975 study on nuclear safety]. For that reason I double the rate. That's two per year.

OMNI: For how many reactors is that?

BETHE: For a hundred reactors, for a thousand years.

OMNI: So if we had a thousand reactors, we could expect twenty deaths per year, on the average.

BETHE: Twenty fatalities per year. Compare this with the statistics on drunken driving. Half of all our traffic deaths are due to drunken driving. We could reduce the number of deaths caused by auto accidents by twenty thousand per year if we were absolutely rigorous in preventing drunk driving. But in our society we tolerate this; we don't lift the licenses of drunk drivers or put them in jail.

OMNI: What would you say then about the attitudes of antinuclear activists who cite the safety issue?

BETHE: I think they are confused. There was an article in the February 1982 issue of *Scientific American* that ranked a long list of risks that cause fatalities, ranging from smoking, alcohol, and automobiles at the top to power mowers and high school football at the bottom. And nuclear power ranked just above high school football and a little below commercial aviation, which, as we all know, is very safe. And the author has still overestimated the danger of nuclear power, probably by a factor of ten.

That article also contained a list ranking the perceived risks as reported by a poll of college students and of members of one chapter of the League of Women Voters. And nuclear power was right at the top — more dangerous than handguns, more dangerous than autos or smoking. Now the League of Women Voters are well-meaning people, and on many political issues they are extremely sound. But in their estimate of the dangers of nuclear power, they are just totally off the mark. They are not extremists in any way; they are simply confused.

OMNI: Do you think public opinion will change in this respect?

BETHE: Yes, I think so. And then the nuclear industry will be able to move ahead.

OMNI: If that happens, we may wind up with a great deal of electric power — even a surplus of electricity. Some people have proposed that surplus electricity could be used to produce hydrogen as a replacement for natural gas and perhaps even for automotive gasoline.

BETHE: Certainly natural gas will be the first thing to be replaced. I am rather optimistic that our natural gas will last a considerable time — much longer than oil, certainly much longer than domestic oil. But ultimately it'll have to be replaced. Hydrogen certainly is a very sensible replacement. The question is one of safety. People assure me that hydrogen can be transported and used as safely as natural gas. I don't know how well founded this assurance is. It may be entirely right, and in that case we will get to the hydrogen economy some time.

OMNI: You hold out more hope for nuclear than for fossil fuels. Could you comment on synthetic fuels?

BETHE: There are two energy problems. One is getting enough total energy, which we can obtain from nuclear power or coal, and the other is getting enough liquid fuels. We cannot drive our automobiles with electricity — at least, not very well. We cannot run our airplanes with electricity, and I think that will remain true for a long, long time. We need liquid fuels for that. And I strongly believe that oil will run out, in spite of the current glut. So I think we are going to need synthetic fuels.

OMNI: One final question, Dr. Bethe. What kind of work in astrophysics do you think would suffice to win another Nobel Prize?

BETHE: Perhaps if someone could more definitely prove theories about the formation of galaxies and stars and about cosmology; that might do it. But for me, I think one is enough.

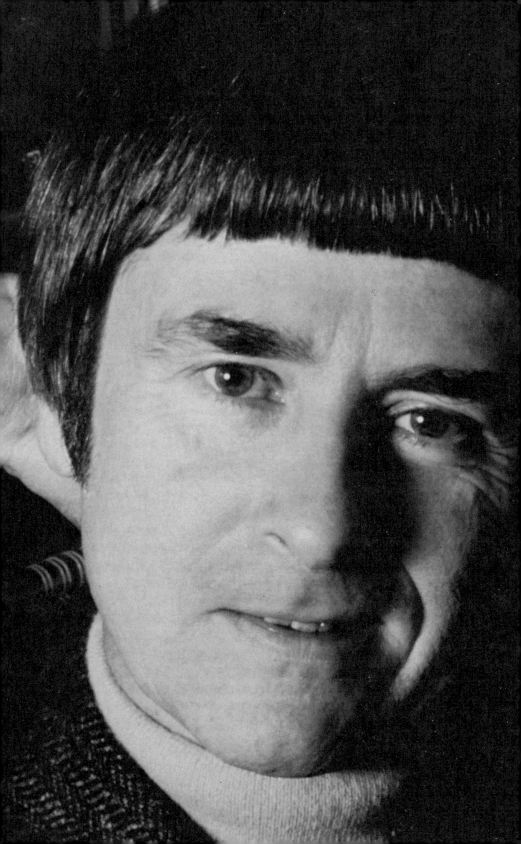

Cosmic Colonies
Gerard K. O'Neill

Every star around us is a favorable target for human migration.
You don't have to wait for just those stars that happen to have
earthlike planets; they may be very few and far between.

*Ever since Christopher Columbus made the rounds of potential royal
backers, the exploration of new worlds has required as much persuasive
salesmanship as it has intrepid navigation. Few men in that tradition
have been as articulate as Professor Gerard K. O'Neill, a high-energy
physicist who has become a prominent advocate of human colonies in
space.*

*In both scientific and popular articles, in lectures and on television,
and in his successful books* The High Frontier *and* 2081, *O'Neill has
argued that the unlimited energy and materials of space could make
possible a new and attractive life for millions of people. In his view,
the established practice of launching costly chemical rockets should be
replaced as soon as possible by permanent habitation and large-scale
manufacturing in space. What's more, while his predecessors advocated
metal-walled, compartmentalized "space stations," O'Neill envisions
colonies that resemble the earth, with soil, greenery, even blue sky,
sunshine, and clouds.*

*The concept behind O'Neill's space colonies — that there's more
potential energy in high orbit than on earth — is elegantly simple, a
characteristic that has become the hallmark of his brilliant career. His
first contribution to science came in 1956, when, as a twenty-nine-
year-old physics instructor at Princeton, he worked on a new proton
accelerator, a machine that made accelerating protons collide, permitting physicists to study the quirks of subatomic particles. Until that*

time, it was felt that particles had to accelerate and collide within the same chamber, a prerequisite that resulted in all sorts of design difficulties and expense. O'Neill's "simple" solution? To have subatomic particles accelerate in one machine and collide in another. Though his skeptical colleagues challenged his ideas, O'Neill went on to design a "storage ring" that could store accelerated particles awaiting collision. Today, most subatomic particle accelerators are based on O'Neill's storage ring concept.

"Perhaps it was the experience of that previous transition from incredulity to acceptance," O'Neill said, "that encouraged me to continue working on space communities, another 'crazy' idea that carried the same sort of logic. In both instances, the numbers came out right."

O'Neill's "numbers" convinced him, in 1969, to hold an exploratory seminar on space colonies for a few of his students. He waited five more years before finally finding a forum in print. But O'Neill does not regret the lag. "It gave people a chance to think about the possibilities," he said, "and to make their own assessments. People would raise questions and I'd go off and think about them and find solutions, and that was very worthwhile. The ideas kept evolving all along, but there's nothing I regret or would like to retract."

In 1974, following that small conference in Princeton, space colonization began to attract national attention. Since then, O'Neill has divided his time between teaching and working for his vision of the future. At home, he and his wife, Tasha, direct the nonprofit Space Studies Institute, dedicated to research on habitation and manufacturing in space. And today, O'Neill also spends much of his time working on Geostar, a satellite system that would allow millions of people to communicate "from anywhere to anywhere with pagers no larger than a pocket calculator."

"The system would be especially valuable," said O'Neill, "in terms of aiding the victims of a crime. If someone who subscribed to Geostar was attacked, he or she could simply push a button; within half a second, a police car would know the identity of the victim, as well as the exact location of the crime."

When O'Neill isn't designing space colonies or raising money for Geostar, he finds time to relax — by flying a light plane to workshops, lecture dates, and Washington, D.C.

The pace clearly agrees with him. At fifty-six, he looks a dozen years younger, and he discusses space colonization and industrialization with as much enthusiasm and animation as if the idea had just taken hold of him. While the rest of us may have to look to space for unlimited energy, Gerard O'Neill displays it here and now as he points the way. Professor O'Neill was interviewed by Monte Davis in 1979. I spoke with him on the telephone in 1982 and again in 1983. A synthesis of the three discussions follows.

OMNI: Why did you start advocating the colonization of space in the first place?

O'NEILL: My motives were largely humanistic. The Club of Rome concluded that as population continues to expand, we'll have to abandon the development of greater individual freedom and accept a much more regulated life with diminished options — not just for us, but for our children and their children and so on forever. I reacted to that with dismay and shock. It sounded like a hell of a world to leave to my kids.

OMNI: How would space colonies help us expand these freedoms and options once more?

O'NEILL: First of all, there would be fewer people living on Earth and an increasing fraction living in space, where there's unimaginable room. Those in space colonies would of course find the situation much more open and free. They'd be living in relatively small-scale structures, in habitats that would be community-size rather than nation-size. With a few thousand to perhaps fifty thousand people in each space colony, government could be as simple and intimate as a New England town meeting. Yet each colony could be quite self-sufficient, using pure solar energy to generate power for travel, agriculture, environmental control, and so on. Since the colony would be growing its own food, there would be no reason for it to tie into a large-scale governmental structure. As far as defense is concerned, colonies suspended in empty space could be widely dispersed. Here on Earth, no one can enlarge land area without crossing a border and going to war with a neighbor; a great deal of our warfare is essentially territorial. Look at everything that goes on in the Middle East and all that's happened in Southeast Asia. There were ideologies involved, of course, but behind a great deal of those conflicts were simply the aggrandizement of reaching out, crossing a border, and taking over more territory. In a space colony, on the other hand, there would be no need to run that risk. It would be easier simply to build additional colonies nearby. Space dwellers would have a lot less hassle in their lives than we do.

OMNI: Do you think that space colonies might affect even those people who decided to remain on Earth?

O'NEILL: Absolutely. The earth, of course, would eventually become far less crowded. Beyond that, important psychological effects would occur almost immediately. If you go back and consider, for example, Shakespeare's plays, you'll realize that they were being written at just the time when settlement of the New World was a very big issue. In Shakespeare's day, relatively few people had actually gone to the New World, but the opening up of that window of opportunity had already had an important effect on the lives, and literature, of the people in Europe. There were products coming back from the New World to the Old; there was always the possibility of people picking up stakes and moving. The very existence of the New World expanded options, enhanced freedoms, and even helped produce a man with the vision of Shakespeare.

Space colonies would clearly produce that spirit once again. Furthermore, we'll see a great deal of two-way travel to the space colonies. A lot of people who continue to make their homes on the earth will find a trip to the space colonies and back as economical as a long-distance trip in a jetliner. By 2050, some two hundred million people may be making annual trips out into space and back again. People will be going on business, on vacation, for all sorts of reasons. There are going to be people who will maintain two homes, one in space and one on the earth.

OMNI: It sounds a lot more tempting than owning a stretch of Riviera or a Swiss chalet.

O'NEILL: Yes, but the most important impact on Earth-dwellers might be a bit more subtle. The small-scale, self-sufficient communities in space will be very much heeded by people on Earth, encouraging them to dictate their own terms to central governments. Influenced by the freedom of space, they'll start demanding more local authority and relatively autonomous, decentralized communities. If their demands aren't met, they'll immigrate to space — and stop paying their earthly taxes. If you look back in history, you'll find that that sort of emulation, that sort of action by imitation, is very, very powerful. The French Revolution, for example, was largely set off by the American Revolution. And the revolutions that broke up all the old European monarchies were largely outgrowths of the one in France.

OMNI: Dr. O'Neill, what exactly would these utopian space habitats look like? Do you have a best guess?

O'NEILL: The design that's come out of all the engineering studies has been named Island One. It's a sphere most likely made of aluminum. It would be almost a mile in diameter, with two large regions of windows where sunlight would be reflected in; sunlight would be reflected [instead of direct] because you don't want to allow any straight-line paths through which cosmic rays could enter. In fact, the habitat would be completely shielded against cosmic rays with five or six feet of plain old dirt; in this case, moon dirt. The whole colony would rotate slowly to produce the earth's normal gravity for the people inside.

OMNI: I take it that people would live along walls lining the inside of the sphere. They would be pulled toward those walls by the force of the sphere's rotation. The walls would, in essence, serve as the ground.

O'NEILL: Yes, that's right, more or less. I should add that earthlike gravity would exist only at the equator. As you walked along the interior of the sphere toward the poles, the force of gravity would get weaker and weaker. Along the axis of rotation, which runs from pole to pole, there would be no gravity at all. Thus, most inhabitants would live along the equator. The old and infirm, who have trouble getting about, of course, might choose to live along higher or lower latitudes, with less gravity to impede their motion.

OMNI: You've suggested that these low- and zero-gravity regions would allow earthly inhabitants to pursue unusual types of sports.

O'NEILL: Well, in addition to all the usual Earth sports, which are played on a flat, two-dimensional surface, people could engage in athletics played on three-dimensional fields. The best candidate would be body contact sports, like soccer and football. I suspect that a lot of the games will probably use fewer players than the corresponding Earth sports because they'll just be so much more complex in their motion.

OMNI: In your book *The High Frontier*, you mention the sensual wonder of zero gravity, honeymoon hotels . . .

O'NEILL: You can expand on those at your leisure. I leave the details to the imagination.

OMNI: If you say so. I'll settle for a detailed description of the colony's interior.

O'NEILL: Okay. If you dwelled within, you'd feel as if you were living in a fairly steep valley, like the kind found throughout the mountainous regions of Italy. There would be terracing and there would be lots of lush greenery. The sun would seem to rise in the morning and set at night, an effect accomplished through a complex array of mirrors. Some homes may come with a spectacular design detail built into a living room wall: a window opening out onto the immensity of space. At least for the early colonies, the climate would be temperate.

OMNI: Like Carmel, California?

O'NEILL: Yes, that sort of thing.

OMNI: What would these inhabitants see when they looked up into the middle of the sphere?

O'NEILL: In the bigger colonies they may see a sky with clouds. That sort of effect would be created much the same way it is on Earth. Here, of course, clouds are created naturally, as a result of the instabilities of the atmosphere. The ground is continually heated, and it, in turn, heats air masses directly above it. When those air masses heat, they become lighter, and therefore they rise up past the cooler air around them. When the hot air gets cool enough, it condenses, and clouds are the result. To create clouds in a space colony, we can simulate the same atmospheric instabilities. That, however, may not be possible in the smallest, very first settlements.

OMNI: Would inhabitants of those colonies look up to see people and trees hanging upside down from the wall directly opposite them?

O'NEILL: Yes, they would, but, then again, you have to think about the question of scale. Even the smallest space colony would be about five hundred meters in diameter, and that means you'd have a third of a mile from your backyard to the backyard immediately above you. Recall, if you can, what it's like to fly a third of a mile above the ground in an airplane: you simply don't see details. You can tell a town is there, and, if you have good eyes, you may be able to see somebody riding a bicycle. But you can't see who it is.

OMNI: It's clear how we may create clouds and an earthlike day and night, but what about the rest of the space colony environment? Is our biological and ecological knowledge really up to creating the lush landscapes you envision?

O'NEILL: Some people feel, on philosophical grounds, that it would be good to create a closed environment that would maintain itself and be ecologically stable in all respects. Others say — quite rightly — that we're nowhere near achieving that on Earth, so how can we hope to do it in space? Well, that's not what we hope to achieve. Remember, there are botanical gardens all over the world where many different plant species thrive in a controlled environment — sometimes with desert and rain-forest plants just a few yards apart. You don't just turn it loose, you garden it . . . but it's not going to go by itself; it's not going to be a closed, inherently stable ecosystem any more than a botanical garden is. Artists' conceptions of space-habitat landscapes do not represent a natural climax forest, and they were never intended to.

OMNI: Now I'll turn the question around 180 degrees. You suggest that the environment in a space habitat could be as pleasant as that of an Italian hill town or, say, Carmel, California. But why settle for that? Shouldn't space habitats provide new ways of life, new ways of organizing social space? Obviously, one of the most important factors in advancing your ideas has been your demonstration that the habitats could be like Earth, but if you're building a world from scratch, shouldn't the sky be the limit?

O'NEILL: I felt I had to do an "existence proof" to show that it is *possible* to create an earthlike environment in space. I have no doubt that in the long run people born in space are going to do all sorts of new, strange, different things with the habitats they'll build.

I think it's fair to say that until I began looking into this question, everyone had assumed that life in space meant a very unearthlike situation. The Russian pioneer of space travel, Konstantin Tsiolkovsky, came closest to suggesting an earthlike environment with his greenhouses. His excellent designs, put forth seventy-five years ago, were basically tubular and very efficient. He had a lot of the essential ideas right: to go for unlimited, clean solar energy outside the planet's shadow; to make use of the resources from asteroids. Aside from him, almost everyone thought of space as a route from here to there. The destination was always assumed to be a planetary surface. But once you say that space itself can be the destination rather than just a corridor — that you can build large, earthlike environments in space — you get a radical change in viewpoint.

OMNI: That's true. The first settlers would probably be far more willing to give space a try if they knew their new home would resemble the earth. But how would we go about building these initial colonies in the first place?

O'NEILL: The materials for the first space colony would come from the surface of the moon. We'd get material from the moon to the vicinity of the colony by means of a Mass-Driver, a machine we're researching here at Princeton.

OMNI: What exactly *is* the Mass-Driver?

O'NEILL: Well, it's an electromagnetic catapult. Basically, electric current would be pulsed through coils of aluminum wire, generating a magnetic field. The magnetic field would then accelerate a small bucket packed with a sphere of lunar material about the size and weight of a baseball. The material would leave the bucket and accelerate through space toward its destination. The acceleration, in fact, would be quite high, up to about eighteen hundred gravities. That means you'd go from zero to about three hundred miles per hour in the first seven thousandths of a second.

OMNI: But if you're going to send material through space, why make the payload so small?

O'NEILL: It turns out that in the vacuum environment of the moon, there is no particular restriction as to how big or how small the payload should be. But when you go through the cost optimization for this machine, you see that it would be far more cost effective to send a large number of relatively small payloads than to send a few very big ones.

OMNI: So in other words, this Mass-Driver would just keep catapulting material . . .

O'NEILL: Like a machine gun.

OMNI: Like a machine gun, toward the exact spot in space where it would be used to build the colony.

O'NEILL: Not quite, actually. There is an intermediate stop. It turns out that it's easier to send material influenced by the gravitational pull of the earth and the moon to a particular location about forty thousand miles from the moon.

OMNI: I see. You'd have a space station up there to collect the material?

O'NEILL: Yeah, actually just a very simple collector, consisting of a cylindrical tube open at one end.

OMNI: And from that point it would be relatively inexpensive to bring the material to the site of the space colony?

O'NEILL: Yes, very simple, because at that point you're already in high orbit, and you don't have to apply any high thrust to move things from one place to another. All the hard work has been done by the Mass-Driver.

OMNI: Once this lunar dirt arrives at the site of the intended colony, though, how would it be converted into the metals and minerals needed to build the sphere?

O'NEILL: The lunar soil would arrive at a processing plant that would turn it into pure elements: oxygen, silicon, aluminum, iron, magnesium, titanium, calcium, and various other substances. The Space Studies Institute gave a grant of $100,000 to Rockwell International to do the chemistry of the separation of lunar soil into pure elements. And that research has now been completed, with very good results. They've just written their final report, and it indicates that they now know all of the chemical reactions required. With that information in hand, we can now go on to the next step of building a very preliminary model of a pilot plant.

OMNI: What sort of Earth-based effort would be required to send up the first processing plant and Mass-Driver?

O'NEILL: That's a question we've addressed in a series of workshops funded by NASA and our own Space Studies Institute. We concluded that a set-up to process lunar materials into pure elements could be built on a scale small enough to fit in the present shuttle payload bay. A plant that size could process two thousand tons a year, and it could operate unattended for long periods. We found that the only components subject to wearing out would be containers for the higher-temperature chemical reactions — and those could be replaced from spares by standard hand-and-arm industrial robots in fixed mountings. Our overall conclusion was that you could make the jump to a minimum production level with less than twenty shuttle launches. To reach that first level, only a few people would be needed, mainly for installation and occasional maintenance.

OMNI: It's hard to imagine so few people building a chemical-processing plant or Mass-Driver.

O'NEILL: The essential notion is that nearly everything is assembled and tested on Earth before it's taken up in units sized to the shuttle's cargo bay.

OMNI: What about cost?

O'NEILL: For the first step? Well, as I said, there's no denying it's a big step; I can't imagine doing it for less than billions of dollars. Quite possibly, though, we could do it for under ten billion, which puts it on the scale of something like the Alaskan pipeline. That's not out of reach for an industrial consortium or even for a large group of individuals that gets contributions from all over the world.

OMNI: To get that kind of commitment from individuals, you'd need a program very different from Apollo — not that it wasn't exciting to see human beings on the moon, but the astronauts were so few and so specially prepared that it was hard to identify with them.

O'NEILL: Yes, many people have concluded that it's a pity the Apollo program didn't develop more logically. It was highly visible and goal-oriented but essentially one-shot. What was there to do for an encore? If we had had space manufacturing and habitation in mind from the start, we'd have gone about it very differently — and space colonization could well be happening now, because it would have a continuing direction and purpose.

OMNI: Yet, a lot of people argue against your proposals, saying that space colonization is a "technological fix," a cop-out that evades dealing with our problems on Earth.

O'NEILL: You make the solution of any problem more difficult when you constrain the range of answers you're willing to consider. By opening up the option tree, you find new possibilities, such as moving fuel-burning industries off the earth into space, where they can run on clean solar energy. Certainly over the last few years we've recoiled from high-technology plans, indeed from any large-scale initiatives that might have profound consequences, because we've felt very acutely the sense of original sin that grew out of the Vietnam War. But that war was politically motivated, not technologically motivated.

OMNI: Yet those opposed to your ideas say they're defending the taxpayers' money against wild-eyed dreamers. They'd rather concentrate on immediate goals with immediate payoffs.

O'NEILL: Experience has shown that when the payoff is near-term, private industry can do a better job than government. But government does have a unique role that it should be filling, and that's to support research toward the development of whole new industries that are going to give millions of new jobs in ten or twenty years. Private companies can't fill that role, because it's beyond their time horizon. The Japanese understand that difference, and that's one of the main reasons they're clobbering us economically.

If the country is in economic difficulties, we ought to be, above all, concerned with how to make more money — to create new wealth and productivity. Before you have any money either to save or to redistribute, you've got to go out and make it. My own feeling is that if there's a dollar that's not desperately needed to keep people from starving, we should be spending it in a way that will earn back ten more dollars. Then we'll have seven dollars to spend on improving the human condition, three for this or that, and still have our original dollar.

OMNI: Then you think that space manufacturing and habitation can be productive on a far larger scale than the spin-offs we received in the 1960s?

O'NEILL: Much more so. We have a high standard of living and high labor costs, and in an increasingly technological world we have only a few years in any new field before others begin selling our innovations back to us at prices we can't match. That's happened with home electronics and a lot of other things, and it may happen soon with computers. Space offers a peaceful new development in which we could play a leading role. What else do we have to offset what some economists predict will be a hundred-billion-dollar trade deficit by 1985?

OMNI: What kinds of payoff do you foresee? It's not likely to be worthwhile to ship either raw materials or finished products down from the colonies.

O'NEILL: One recent study by the Aerospace Corporation concluded that over a number of years there will be good reasons to have several tens of thousands of tons of satellites in high orbit. We'll need at least that to do a thorough job of solving problems right here, to do remote sensing and monitoring of the Landsat type, to improve communications, air-traffic control — all the gathering and transmission of the information that is clearly going to become an even more important part of our lives than it is already.

OMNI: You obviously believe these first space colonies would actually make a profit through the construction and maintenance of satellites.

O'NEILL: Oh, yes. Without a profit such colonies wouldn't get built. The biggest potential payoff would be in the construction of solar power satellites [satellites that would collect energy from the sun and beam it back to Earth in the form of microwaves]. Now, each solar power satellite would weigh about 100,000 tons, so they're big. However, the electric power output of each such satellite would be equivalent to the output of about ten nuclear power plants. Thus, each solar power satellite would be valued at more than $10 billion. An initial investment of $10 billion would be required to build the facilities to produce these satellites. But since a space colony could probably build one satellite each year, the annual profit, after the first year, would be about $10 billion.

OMNI: Can you describe the people who would live and work in these first colonies?

O'NEILL: The early colonies would hold anywhere from ten thousand to fifty thousand occupants. A pretty large fraction of the people there would be rather sophisticated repair experts: they would be able to fix complex electrical and mechanical robotic machinery; they would be able to fix the processing plants; and they would have a lot of knowledge about fairly sophisticated process chemistry.

There would also be a fair number of children in the early space colonies. After all, the whole point of building residential communities in space would be to accommodate people whose tours of duty are so long that they would take their families with them.

OMNI: Would there be many scientists?

O'NEILL: I'd love to say that lots of them would move to the colonies. But I'm afraid that not many scientists will be able to justify the trip in the early days. Those who could certainly benefit a great deal, of course, would be observational astronomers studying deep space. In fact, there would probably be big telescopes near the early colonies for deep space observation.

OMNI: But wouldn't scientists in the colonies have a much better chance of finding evidence of extraterrestrial intelligence than their colleagues on Earth? After all, there would be no atmosphere to obscure their view of the cosmos.

O'NEILL: Well, if you wanted to set up a big radio receiving array to search for radio signals from another civilization, it would certainly be much more effective to do so near a space colony. After all, if scientists ever *did* find a signal, the first thing they'd try to do would be to lock on to it, and check it continuously over a long period of time. But if their radio receiver was located on the surface of the earth, then the antenna, along with the planet itself, would rotate away from the signal every twenty-four hours. A radio receiver in space, on the other hand, could keep track of the signal constantly.

OMNI: Back to more practical matters: How would the inhabitants of the space colony collect energy for themselves?

O'NEILL: Simply by having collector mirrors attached to the outside of the colony itself. The sunlight in space is about one and a half kilowatts per square meter, and it's there all the time. So it means that a colony with a relatively modest-size mirror could collect enormous quantities of power.

OMNI: What about growing food?

O'NEILL: The question of agriculture in high orbit has already been addressed by the Russians. They've kept people in enclosed environments for six months or so, growing wheat, making bread. It's worked out well, and they've even done some experiments in space. It's likely that agricultural modules at the colonies would be based, in part, on that initial research. Essentially, I envision agricultural cylinders attached to, but separate from, the main sphere. Since plants grow best with less air, these cylinders would have a low density of oxygen. They would be kept hot and moist for most crops, and day length would be controlled with aluminum foil shades that could shut out the sunlight. To reach these agricultural cylinders — or to reach industrial cylinders that would also be separated from the main colony — inhabitants would just walk from their homes at the equator up to the poles. There they would enter a large tunnel, or access corridor, leading to the agricultural and industrial areas. The tunnel would also lead to docking ports for ships entering or leaving the colony.

OMNI: That brings up another question: How would people travel from one space colony to another? With conventional, shuttlelike ships?

O'NEILL: Oh, no. The best vehicle would be one that doesn't require an on-board engine, or even an on-board crew. It would just have to hold an atmosphere and some comfortable seating. Basically, the craft would be attached to a cable powered by an electric motor. It would be slowly accelerated in a precomputed direction up to a traveling speed of one or two thousand miles per hour. Then it would drift in free flight through the vacuum of space until it came to the next colony, where it would simply hook up to another cable and slowly come to a halt. This sort of trip might take about an hour, depositing the travelers in a colony that might have a totally different culture, language, and climate than their own.

OMNI: Sounds like a good cheap vacation for the wanderlusting colonist. But won't some colonies be located more than a thousand miles apart? I thought you envisioned such habitats throughout the cosmos.

O'NEILL: If you were to come back in a hundred years, you'd see space colonies all over the solar system. In my book *2081*, I located one of them many light hours out from the sun, considerably beyond the planet Pluto. It was possible for that colony to have an earthlike environment and an earthlike amount of sunshine because of large collecting mirrors. You could even locate space colonies around just about any star. In fact, every star around us is a favorable target for human migration. You don't have to wait for just those stars that happen to have earthlike planets; they may be very few and far between. One day an Island One sphere, adapted with technology beyond the limits of present-day science, may set off for another part of the Milky Way. Generations of inhabitants would live their lives in transit, but eventually the colony would reach that distant star. By my reckoning, a space habitat could last for several billion years — plenty of time to reach its destination.

OMNI: At that distant date, how would space colonies obtain all the things needed for survival?

O'NEILL: The colonies would have the whole mix of industries here on Earth, because at that point the major markets would be other space colonies, rather than the earth itself. That's a natural evolution, one that occurs in every colonial movement. You start out supplying things for the mother country, but in the long run, a colony builds up to the point where its major trade is with itself.

OMNI: Wouldn't those colonies located out past Pluto or in a distant solar system become dangerously isolated from the rest of humanity?

O'NEILL: It's a question of what you consider "dangerous." They certainly wouldn't be exchanging goods with other groups. However, I think that being a great distance from someone like the Ayatollah Khomeini would be a big improvement. Colonists would become very independent; they'll undergo a lot of cultural evolution, generate enormous cultural diversity. By the time we have colonies around a number of different stars, there obviously are going to be different historical trends in these various areas. The habitats will, of course, continue to receive information from the earth, but it would be after a time delay of several years. They would also send information, presumably of a scientific and literary nature, but, again, that information would reach the earth only after a time lag of several years. There would be a great deal of communication, but the farther you got away from the earth, the more out-of-date the information would be. Some of those newer stellar centers may even become centers at the forefront of human civilization and knowledge.

OMNI: Those colonists might be more advanced than people living on or near Earth?

O'NEILL: Sure, that's again been a tradition in human history. When a bunch of interesting people break out and settle in a new area, they tend to be inventive, they tend to push forward and do things *before* the people they leave back home. That could very well happen again.

OMNI: Your ideas are now embraced by many of your colleagues, and the people at NASA as well. But when you introduced this fantastical vision in 1969, it was, understandably, met with a great deal of skepticism. Can you describe the struggle you went through to get to the point of acceptance you're at today?

O'NEILL: The basic problem was my realization that building and living in space colonies was technologically within our grasp. Therefore, I didn't want my ideas to be in any way tainted by science fiction. I could have published the space colony concept in fictional form — that would have been very easy to do at any time. But the whole point was to get it out as a reviewed article in a scientific journal, and that's what took all the struggle. That didn't happen until 1974, when my first space colony article was published in *Physics Today.*

OMNI: When you talk to congressmen and others who influence public planning and spending, how do you appeal to them? Are they more interested in economic prospects or in beating the Russians, or do they share your excitement and belief that this is a challenge we must rise to?

O'NEILL: I really don't tailor my statements to the audience, although I underline some things here and there. I find that elected representatives tend to have quite a good sense of their constituents' underlying feelings and desires — not surprisingly, since they do get elected! And many of them sense a national feeling of frustration, a feeling that the country isn't moving anywhere or is even falling back. We have for so long been a nation identified with new ideas, new technology, new social experiments, and now we seem to be losing that position. Where do we go from here? These representatives look at a new possibility like the colonization or industrialization of space, and they wonder: Is America going to be a part of this revolution or sit back and watch other countries take the initiative?

I think that the movement in space is going to happen, whether it's done by Americans or not. That substantial numbers of people will eventually make space their routine environment is inevitable, if we don't blow ourselves up first; the imperatives pointing that way are so basic and so consistent with previous human history.

OMNI: Some people are uncomfortable with the idea that life in space would mean life with a demanding, interdependent technology around them at all times.

O'NEILL: Getting those first colonies built would be demanding, yes. But when you go a little further and ask what life would be like in a space habitat, I think it turns out to be in many respects a *less* demanding technology than we have at present. You don't need internal combustion engines; you don't need big power grids; you don't need elaborate communications networks, because within the habitat it's all line-of-sight; you don't need high-strength materials. Take a terrestrial problem, the manufacture of fertilizer for agriculture. With a six-inch pipe at the focus of a solar mirror, you can combine nitrogen and oxygen to get the high-energy precursors of fertilizer in any quantity you need. That's a lot simpler and cleaner than burning fossil fuels to make chemical fertilizers, the way we do now.

OMNI: Don't you need sophisticated recycling, especially of water?

O'NEILL: If you have a reasonably tight pressure vessel, you shouldn't lose any of it, and you'd have plenty of energy to distill it. We have serious problems recycling on Earth, because we keep losing bits of what we're recycling and it gets dispersed in very low concentrations throughout the environment; in a space habitat, keeping track would be a lot easier. Overall, day-to-day life in a space habitat wouldn't require much technology above the level of some of the better agriculture you find around the world today — agriculture that's not even necessarily carried on by literate people.

OMNI: It's taken a lot of work, but you've at least started the ball rolling toward a national constituency for space colonization. Would it be fair to say that private groups could make that initial effort in case no massive government support is forthcoming?

O'NEILL: Well, it's certainly interesting to ask: Can it be made small enough to be nongovernmental? People are now appreciating in all sorts of detailed ways that the smaller you can make the first step, the better off you are. That idea ran through the workshops I described earlier. For example, we aren't locked into the plans for a Mass-Driver on the moon. You can draw up a very stripped-down scenario involving only chemical rockets, say, by setting up the lunar processing plant chiefly to extract oxygen, which is 40 percent of the unselected Apollo samples, and which constitutes 85 percent of the total mass of rocket propellant. An automated fifteen-ton unit would yield something like four hundred tons of liquid per year, which is enough for an awful lot of rocket flights bringing materials up into orbit.

OMNI: The Apollo lunar module wouldn't make a very effective cargo carrier, though. Aren't some new vehicles going to be needed?

O'NEILL: Yes, we'd probably need three new but conventional

vehicles: an interorbit freight-transfer vehicle, an interorbit passenger carrier, and a vehicle that could soft-land and take off from the lunar surface. None of them requires a big, new engine. They're in the class of the Apollo service and propulsion module, completely within the limits of what we've been designing for the past fifteen years. But we still have to build them.

OMNI: Any other projects on the horizon, Dr. O'Neill?

O'NEILL: Right now I'm working on Geostar, a satellite communications system that could be used by private individuals for a moderate price. It's very practical and not "blue sky" at all. The network we're planning would be based on a system of supercomputers on the ground and satellites in orbit. Four satellites would be used for coverage of the Americas, and ten for the rest of the world. The satellites I'm talking about would be in the same weight class as those RCA has been making for the last ten years. And there would be inexpensive transceivers of about the same size as a pocket calculator, which individual people could buy from places like Radio Shack. What subscribing to the system would give you is the capability to communicate, with short telegraphic messages of thirty-six characters or so, from any place to any other place in the world, and at the same time have your position measured down to a precision of a few feet.

I have two daughters in their twenties, and they're interested in the security issue. If they were walking alone on the street and were threatened by an attacker, they could push a button on the transceiver. Within half a second, the satellite would have located the nearest police car and informed the patrolman of the exact location and identity of the victim. Within another half a second, a subscriber would get a message saying that help is on the way. I've been working on this invention for a number of years, and last year [1982] the U.S. Patent Office granted my claims.

OMNI: Would we all be hooked up?

O'NEILL: The system could handle many millions of subscribers. We've already formed the Geostar Corporation to set up the system. The response and the backing seem to be tremendous. There's just a lot of work to be done.

Cosmos Unwinding

Universal Mind
Brian Josephson

As a scientist, I became interested only in seeking fundamentally new insights into the nature of reality. Unfortunately, conventional physics didn't offer much opportunity to achieve this sort of breakthrough. So I became interested in Eastern mystical teachings.

Brian Josephson was only thirty-three years old when he won the Nobel Prize in 1973. His award-winning work on superconductivity, carried out when he was still a graduate student, in the early sixties, marked him as the ultimate science prodigy, a man whose career in physics knew no bounds.

Yet today Josephson has left mainstream physics far behind. He describes his current research interests as "higher states of consciousness and the paranormal, intelligence, and language." His primary goal: to develop a theory that synthesizes the work of Western theorists like Jean Piaget with that of the Maharishi Mahesh Yogi. (Josephson began to practice transcendental meditation in 1970, and in 1979 he started the more advanced TM-Sidhi program, which is said to develop the student's paranormal powers. He now meditates a couple of hours each day.)

Josephson is a small, wiry Welshman. Born in Cardiff, he earned his doctorate at Cambridge University in 1964, two years after publishing his breakthrough paper. His manner is shy and retiring, a striking contrast to both his awesome scientific accomplishments and his unconventional taste for the paranormal.

Now forty-four, Josephson maintains that he is "not doing anything different from what scientists have done in the past." He is just using an extra instrument, the "meditative experience," to gain new ideas

Photograph: Robert Dowling

about the structure of reality, which he will then attempt to test in more orthodox ways.

If Josephson is open to subjects that some of his colleagues find odd, it may be because his early research confronted him with the unexpected, even the bizarre. He had been studying superconductors — materials that, when chilled to at least −422°F, lose resistance, allowing electric current to pass through at ultrahigh speed. He tried to calculate what would happen to the electricity if it ran into a barrier, or junction, in this case a layer of insulating oxide separating two adjacent superconductors. Common sense implied that the current would be stopped cold, just as a speeding car is stopped by a tree or brick wall. But his equations told a different story: electrons would tunnel right through the barrier, impenetrable though it seemed. Josephson's calculations predicted another oddity as well: the direction and speed of these electrons would be powerfully affected by subtle shifts in magnetic field.

Josephson's fantastical discovery has momentous implications for technology. Already, the junctions are being used to measure minute changes in magnetic fields, allowing scientists to detect anomalies of the human heart, subtleties of the brain, and far-infrared radiation from distant galaxies. More important, these superconducting junctions can serve as superfast computer switches, with magnetic controls steering electronic signals from one circuit to another. Such computers would function twenty times faster than the fastest computers in use today, says Josephson. And because superconducting devices require so little energy, a few million switches would consume only a few watts. Thus, they could be packed together as tightly as fabrication technology allows, leading to more computing power in a smaller space than ever before.

Though Josephson junction switches are not yet in use, Bell Laboratories is studying the technology, and IBM reportedly has spent $100 million to develop a computer based on it.

Psychologist and science writer John Gliedman interviewed Josephson in 1982 in the physicist's cluttered office at Cambridge University's Cavendish Laboratory. Their conversation ranged from the lapidary world of physical theory to the intangible realm of psychic phenomena. The story of Josephson's work and personal metamorphosis continued into the night as the two picked their way across footpaths and fields made icy by England's worst blizzard since 1948. I took up the trail in Cambridge, Massachusetts, long after the snow had melted, in 1983. This time the discussion took place in a large old house bought by Josephson's sister-in-law and her husband. Because the furniture had not yet arrived, we sat on beach chairs in a bay-windowed room full of boxes. Josephson's red-haired daughter, Miranda, four years old, played on pillows nearby. A synthesis of the two interviews follows.

OMNI: Professor Josephson, what exactly is superconductivity?

JOSEPHSON: As you cool a metal or other material, its electrical resistance falls toward a lower limit. However, in many pure metals and metallic compounds all electrical resistance abruptly vanishes at a critical transition temperature. This is never higher than minus 422 degrees Fahrenheit and often is much lower. Once a conductor enters the superconducting state, it will sustain a current indefinitely.

OMNI: How does your own work in superconductivity fit into this picture?

JOSEPHSON: I tried to calculate what would happen if you connected two superconductors with a very thin layer of insulating oxide. According to quantum mechanics [the theory that explains the behavior of subatomic particles], only a small number of electrons should have penetrated through. But to my great surprise, my equations predicted that an *appreciable* current would flow between the two metals, even when there was no voltage difference between them. This, in a sense, is comparable to an automobile going over a hill even if it doesn't have the fuel to propel it. In other words, it's a weird effect of the sort never seen in the world we're *used* to perceiving.

OMNI: Let's see if I can put it another way. At room temperature, an electrical current flows only where there is a voltage difference, just as water flows through a garden hose connecting two swimming pools only if one pool is higher than the other. Is that correct?

JOSEPHSON: Yes. The big surprise was that there could be an appreciable current flow even when the two swimming pools were level with each other — when there was no voltage difference between the superconductors. This was my basic discovery. Previously it had been thought that any such effect would be extremely small.

OMNI: Were you able to confirm your equation's unexpected prediction quickly?

JOSEPHSON: No. I tried to look for these supercurrents, as we now call them, and I failed. Later, other experiments were successful in demonstrating the supercurrent.

OMNI: Why was the discovery so important?

JOSEPHSON: Well, the equations also predicted that electrons flowing across the insulation, or the Josephson junction, would be exquisitely sensitive to magnetic fields, and the experiments confirmed that. This has turned out to have practical applications, such as measuring the magnetic field of the heart. Josephson junctions also allow one to detect very weak electromagnetic signals in the infrared frequencies, which are not easy to handle with other kinds of equipment.

OMNI: Many scientists believe that it will soon be possible to build high-speed computers based on the Josephson junction. Can you explain how they will work?

JOSEPHSON: They will use a magnetic field to control the current flow across the junctions. An increasing and decreasing magnetic field can switch a current on or off extremely quickly, on the order of a hundred billionths of a second. A computer using Josephson junction switches may be twenty times faster than one using the best competing technology. Another advantage is that very little heat is generated by a Josephson junction switch. This allows you to pack computer components more closely without producing enough heat to impair the computer's reliability. A computer based on Josephson junction switches could be as powerful as the most sophisticated present IBM model, yet fit into a cube six inches on a side.

OMNI: You won the Nobel Prize for your work in superconductivity at the age of thirty-three. How did that feel?

JOSEPHSON: Well, I'd won a number of awards already in my lifetime, but it was obviously a more significant one. I suppose I had the Nobel in the back of my mind, especially with all the applications for my work. It wasn't really unexpected.

OMNI: You just took it in stride?

JOSEPHSON: I suppose so, but one *is* rather overwhelmed by all the attention. And I haven't yet recovered from the increase in my mail. I thought that after about six months I would deal with the backlog, but the backlog is still with me.

OMNI: What has happened in superconductivity research since your breakthrough in the early sixties?

JOSEPHSON: I don't think there have been any very major developments since then.

OMNI: You yourself have left superconductivity research far behind. Why?

JOSEPHSON: When I was doing my work in superconductivity, I regarded it as highly important. Afterward, I started seeing things from a wider viewpoint, and I realized that many of my initial discoveries were not as important as I had thought, but I did not immediately have anything to replace my former interests. Then, when I was a senior research fellow at Trinity College in the late sixties, I talked a lot with another fellow of the college who had changed his views radically on a visit to the States. He kept trying to persuade the other members of the college that they had a limited perspective on reality. I was about the only person who took him at all seriously.

Then, some time later, I interacted with another fellow of Trinity, Dr. George Owen, who is now in Toronto. His side interest is in psychic phenomena, and I talked with him as well. He opened me up to the possibility that there may be a range of phenomena that were more or less rejected by conventional scientists.

OMNI: How did you reconcile such ideas with your background in hard, classical physics?

JOSEPHSON: Well, I was aware of Bell's theorem, postulated by the theoretical physicist John Bell in 1965. To me, it's one of the most important advances in recent physics. The theorem is related to a paper written by Einstein, Podolsky, and Rosen in 1935. The argument given in this paper appeared to show that if quantum mechanics were correct, then you could split two connected particles, sending each one traveling in opposite directions, and *still* influence one of the particles by disturbing the other, *even* if the partner had been flung miles away. In essence, the particles would be communicating instantly, faster than the speed of light.

Einstein, of course, believed this was impossible. But John Bell and, later, Henry Stapp used the well-accepted equations of quantum mechanics to show that such "superluminal" communication is just what one might expect. The theorem raises the possibility that one part of the universe may have knowledge of another part — some kind of contact at a distance under certain conditions.

OMNI: Some popular writers have claimed that the link between

Bell's separated systems may be typical of most processes in the universe. In other words, when a polar bear jumps into Arctic water, in some weird way it may cause a train wreck in the south of France.

JOSEPHSON: If the two systems have been together in the past, there's going to be some correlation between their subsequent behavior when they are physically separated. The main questions are how much correlation there is and whether random collisions with other particles make them negligible in most cases.

I certainly wouldn't expect the polar bear's leap to cause a wreck in southern France, although one couldn't rule it out.

OMNI: Are you saying that psychics may somehow be able to gain knowledge about what is going on elsewhere in the universe by making use of this effect?

JOSEPHSON: Yes. But we still don't have a precise model to explore this question.

OMNI: Bell's theorem seems similar to the equations that helped you develop the Josephson junction: both predict effects that blatantly defy everyday Newtonian physics. This departure from accepted reality in your work must have had a powerful effect on you.

JOSEPHSON: Absolutely. As a scientist, I became interested only in seeking fundamentally new insights into the nature of reality. Unfortunately, conventional physics didn't offer much opportunity to achieve this sort of breakthrough. So I became interested in Eastern mystical teachings.

OMNI: How did that happen?

JOSEPHSON: In 1971, shortly after I met George Owen, I spent some time at Cornell University in Ithaca, New York. I was listening to the radio when I heard an announcement for a lecture on transcendental meditation. I went and found that the lecturer's statements about reality were very consistent with my own beliefs. So I took the course, and learned the TM technique. I've been doing the meditation most of the time since then, and in 1979 I learned the more advanced TM-Sidhi technique.

OMNI: Have you changed as a result?

JOSEPHSON: I think that meditation has improved me in various ways. I used to make all decisions on the basis of rational arguments. Now I am much freer about things. I had some good experiences with meditation from the very start. It was as if, instead of being immersed in a kind of mental fog — immersed in my thoughts — I suddenly became aware of the outside world. I also think that I've become more spontaneous in relationships with other people — again, through not rationally deciding what I should say. Getting beyond the intellect is quite important in that sort of thing.

OMNI: I assume that the philosophy of TM as developed by Maharishi Mahesh Yogi influenced your scientific research. Can you explain how?

JOSEPHSON: In the TM course itself, naturally, you're given only the simplest description of the Maharishi's philosophy. Basically, you're learning how to meditate. But a couple of years after my stay in Ithaca, I started talking with some one visiting my lab. We were both interested in the question of how the brain works, and he told me about the Maharishi's theory, which is called the Science of Creative Intelligence.

OMNI: Can you summarize that?

JOSEPHSON: It's impossible to give a good feel for the theory in just a few sentences. The best one can do is to say that it's a kind of epistemology, or science of knowledge, with a strong biological orientation. Its emphasis is the idea that under favorable conditions living systems are always moving in the direction of a kind of ideal.

There is considerable similarity between the Science of Creative Intelligence and the ideas of the Swiss psychologist Jean Piaget. [Piaget said that specific cognitive abilities, or thought processes, develop as children advance in age. With each stage of development, the range of cognitive ability will increase.] But Piaget's work didn't embody the idea of evolution being directed toward a final goal, nor did Piaget discuss in any deep sense the role of consciousness.

OMNI: The Maharishi's theory as you've just described it seems too general to be of much use.

JOSEPHSON: That's the criticism leveled at the Maharishi by scientists. Our group in the Cavendish Laboratory has for some time been trying to reformulate his ideas in a more concrete and useful form.

OMNI: How?

JOSEPHSON: By examining the vague statements and trying to understand what they really mean. Then one's ideas can be tested by seeing to what extent they provide a convincing account of phenomena such as intelligence.

OMNI: The Maharishi talks about a "field of pure creative intelligence" that exists outside of us altogether. What are your views on that?

JOSEPHSON: That's a line of inquiry with which I haven't got very far as yet. My views are close to those of the physicist David Bohm, who infers from quantum mechanics the existence of an "implicate order." [Bohm's concept is that our brains construct *concrete* reality by interpreting a code from another time and space. If we could unravel the code, he says, we could glimpse true reality. He refers to this true reality as the implicate order.] I feel the implicate order might correspond to the Maharishi's field of pure intelligence. Bohm is concerned mainly with the physical aspects of this implicate order, while I'm more interested in the intelligence aspect.

OMNI: Can you give me an illustration?

JOSEPHSON: In one scenario, you might picture some kind of universal structure that has thoughts, makes plans, and then causes those plans to be executed. This universal intelligence would have three levels: first, the intelligence itself; second, the thought processes; and third, the concrete reality — the things the intelligence actually creates and perceives.

OMNI: Do you mean tangible products and artifacts like those created by human intelligence — this house, for instance?

JOSEPHSON: This house and everything else seen at the classical level — rocks and plants and so on.

OMNI: What's the process? How would this creation take place?

JOSEPHSON: I think the answer lies in quantum mechanics. According to quantum theory, it's impossible to predict the characteristics of a subatomic particle before it's measured — the particle exists merely as a wave of energy, as potential. But the likelihood of its acquiring each one of many possible characteristics is predicted with astounding accuracy by an equation called the wave function.

The wave function was derived through experimental observation — but nobody really knows why it works. Quantum theory becomes less puzzling if you say that there's some intelligence operating at a very basic level. You might say that the wide-ranging possibilities described by the wave function are really thoughts generated by the intelligence. The intelligence is simply imagining a variety of possible worlds, and when it actually chooses one of those possibilities, that becomes tangible reality. All the other potentialities simply collapse. That would explain where the wave function comes from — it simply describes the way this universal intelligence works.

OMNI: Does this universal intelligence connect up with our own? Are we part of it?

JOSEPHSON: Yes. I think that our thought processes are oddly dependent on it, and not entirely localized in our brains. For instance, say you have a problem, and you solve it only after inspiration comes to you. That inspiration may be the universal intelligence communicating with your brain.

OMNI: What you're saying is that we can perceive more than we might expect if we relied on our fve senses alone. For instance, people who have had extraordinary ii.sight may have been spoonfed by this greater, cosmic intelligence.

JOSEPHSON: Yes, that's about it. Ideally, you ought to learn how to interact with this cosmic mind. Some people may experience that interaction through meditation, using their skill to observe on a sort of universal scale. It's probably the same sort of channel that's used in remote viewing — the ability that some people seem to have to describe physical settings that they have never directly observed. It's as if you can see inwardly things that you cannot see directly. In my case I see only luminous clouds of various kinds and things like that — nothing very spectacular. And of course you can say that these are merely hallucinations on my part.

OMNI: But what do you think they may be?

JOSEPHSON: Well, there may be a paranormal component to the sense of sight, one that doesn't depend upon light converging on the eye.

Here is where I think that a study of mystical tradition comes in. The mystics talk of an astral plane. And what one perceives fits in with movement on this plane.

OMNI: Do you believe in the existence of an astral plane?

JOSEPHSON: Well, the experiences I have had are consistent with it, yes.

OMNI: Does the intelligence operating from this astral plane merely provide us with information, or does it actually control us?

JOSEPHSON: It's just one of the controlling factors. We also have our individual thoughts and plans. Of course, you may become emotionally disturbed if you wander too far from what's been specified. In addition, according to some views, there is a still higher level that can be identified with God.

OMNI: How does your concept of intelligence change our view of evolution, particularly the evolution of *Homo sapiens?*

JOSEPHSON: Everything that has evolved existed previously, in some kind of thought form. There's a tendency for these thoughts to become reality.

OMNI: Where did this intelligence come from? Was it always there? And how does it coincide with the theory of the origin of the universe?

JOSEPHSON: I think this intelligence has probably always existed in some kind of equilibrium state. It formed the universe and the laws of nature, just as it directed the evolution of intelligent species. The creation of the universe is really only evolution at a different level.

OMNI: What do you think would happen if all of humanity suddenly tuned into this universal intelligence?

JOSEPHSON: The Western world as a whole currently has a faulty, immature, incomplete view of the way we are — a materialistic orientation. This materialistic approach puts man at the top. But if we can show that that's not true, we'll start to shift people's perspectives.

OMNI: What you're talking about is a paradigm shift much like the one precipitated by Copernicus when he showed that the earth wasn't the center of the universe.

JOSEPHSON: Yes, but I have a better example. When people landed on the moon, everyone was saying how seeing the earth from outside would change our view of man. Some claimed it would stop the worst features of human behavior. Well, that didn't happen. There's no particular reason that it should have happened, since the moon itself doesn't really affect us. But if we expand in an inward direction and see that we're part of a spiritual universe, well, that would be much more likely to alter perspectives: in essence, people would realize that they were being watched.

In a way, it's like the difference in behavior between children by themselves and children who know there's an adult present. If you know that there's an external agency that can affect you and send some feedback, you might change your actions and start taking long-range, global consequences into account. The trouble, of course, is persuading people to accept facts that lie outside the ordinary reality.

OMNI: Are you doing any concrete experiments that may persuade people by proving your theories correct?

JOSEPHSON: Well, if you're working from general concepts, as I am, then you have to make things specific. At the moment I'm considering how the individual human intelligence might operate. I'm using a computer to simulate a simple motor skill — learning to hit a collection of targets, a task that is roughly equivalent to reaching out for the controls of a car. The idea is that intelligence is determined by a set of principles, and the computer is programmed to simulate a simplified form of these principles. In this case, I've drawn from the Science of Creative Intelligence to postulate that the learning process itself is directed toward a specific goal, perhaps by some higher force. It's a bit like embryology — the genes, not mere trial and error, determine the end product. Very simply, the algorithms of my computer program allow the system to evolve rapidly from its initial state to the state in which it has mastered the target-hitting skills. The computer can accomplish its target-hitting task with relative ease, because I've programmed it with a series of processes, each one taking the machine one step closer to its ultimate goal.

OMNI: Any other concrete projects?

JOSEPHSON: I'm also working on human language acquisition, trying to fit the problem of how children learn to speak into a conceptual framework that has both Eastern and Western roots. My work draws heavily upon the theory of language-learning outlined by Maharishi Mahesh Yogi, as well as conventional theorists, such as Mitchell Marcus and S. D. Dik.

OMNI: Can you be a bit more specific?

JOSEPHSON: I believe that children have innate mechanisms that permit them to learn how to speak and understand language. Most of my work consists of describing these mechanisms and showing how they make language-learning possible. However, instead of postulating anything like the existence of a built-in grammar, along Noam Chomsky's lines, I believe that the child constructs his model of language from experience. No part of his language model is innate. It is the set of language-acquisition mechanisms that is innate.

Suppose a child is exposed to a particular syntactic construction. According to my theory, he will be changed in a very specific way by that utterance, and in the future he will be sensitized to any influences that are roughly the same.

OMNI: You sound a bit like a behaviorist.

JOSEPHSON: Only up to a point. The way a person reacts to hearing language is partly innate. Children are programmed to explore certain kinds of interpretive possibilities and to ignore others.

OMNI: Can you identify the set of possibilities that the child investigates and the other possibilities that the child is programmed to ignore?

JOSEPHSON: I don't see language-learning so much as an investigation. I see it as a channel that the child is tuned into. In other words, the brain is essentially a receiver with innate systems that are sensitive to grammar, others that are sensitive to meaning, and so on. I'm actively studying the properties of these programmed systems.

OMNI: Has meditation helped you to develop your psycholinguistic theory?

JOSEPHSON: I think it has enabled me to use intuition effectively to a much higher degree than I used to be able to. I think one wouldn't get too far sorting things out in psycholinguistics by rationally running through the possibilities. It's much more a matter of intuiting how things are and then thinking through to see whether the intuition fits the facts.

OMNI: If you rely to such a great degree on intuitive information gleaned through meditation, don't you ever worry that you're learning only how to project new and fascinating images on the mind's inner screen?

JOSEPHSON: One has to put one's ideas to the test in the usual way. But my point is that as you develop along the usual lines in science and in life, you add more and more beliefs to your picture of the world's structure. This process restricts your ability to appreciate the richness of reality, because each time you take seriously a new belief, you exclude its converse from consideration. The higher state of consciousness achieved through meditation is supposed to be added to the everyday state. You don't lose your ability to reason logically. One has the knowledge that's been acquired as an adult, but also the ability to get beyond the constraints of this knowledge in case there's something better out there.

OMNI: How do you protect yourself against self-delusion? Suppose that during meditation a voice instructs you to paste up a portrait of Hitler in your office and organize a group of Brown Shirts in England. Would you act upon this vision because it meets all the subjective criteria for a powerful mystical experience?

JOSEPHSON: One occasionally does have powerful experiences in meditation, and well, one is advised not to take them too seriously, not to act upon an idea just because it occurred to one in meditation.

OMNI: But in that case aren't you applying the rationalist filter to these experiences?

JOSEPHSON: I have nothing against being rational.

OMNI: How can you escape the blinders of science if you do that?

JOSEPHSON: If one does one's meditation properly, one gradually removes those beliefs while remaining a rational being.

OMNI: Would you call yourself a mystic?

JOSEPHSON: At most, half a mystic. I see myself as following along the standard scientific tradition. I am just enlarging the scope of things and trying to construct more comprehensive theories. My approach is that of the scientist who reasons about phenomena and hopes to be able to give acceptable intellectual pictures of them. I always try to find concrete explanations of things. The world is full of mysterious entities.

OMNI: Do you believe in God?

JOSEPHSON: As I said, that highest level of intelligent being — the universal intelligence — probably corresponds to God.

OMNI: What about an afterlife?

JOSEPHSON: Many Eastern mystical traditions describe life and death as just being two different states. In meditation, one may cross the boundary and experience some of these afterlife states, though that's only speculation. For example, if one were in a meditative state where one's body didn't exist, that might be a precursor of what it's like to be dead.

OMNI: How do you defend yourself against your scientific critics?

JOSEPHSON: One tries to educate them as best one can.

OMNI: What about private reactions to your ideas?

JOSEPHSON: Well, some people are quite interested, but probably the majority are not very conscious of the issues involved. Discussions with people who don't share my openness toward the paranormal and Eastern mystical ideas don't get far. So the question about how I deal with their objections doesn't really arise.

OMNI: Have you found yourself ostracized because of your heretical views?

JOSEPHSON: Not particularly, no. I just get on with the job of trying to prove that my views are correct.

OMNI: A number of other physicists are trying to integrate Western science with Eastern mystical traditions. How do you assess their efforts?

JOSEPHSON: I think a lot of the people trying to join Eastern and Western perspectives have a good qualitative picture of how things are. But no one has the mathematics to make this picture quantitative. And I think it's basically a mathematical problem. Someone has to find the right mathematics to fit the situation.

OMNI: Are you actively working on a mathematical solution to this problem?

JOSEPHSON: No, not actively. It's a thing I would like to be able to make some progress in, but I don't devote much time to it.

OMNI: Just waiting for the moment of clarity?

JOSEPHSON: Yes, and I think these powerful meditation techniques make such breakthroughs more likely. But not many intellectual people meditate. So there's a split between people who do science and people who practice meditation techniques to raise their consciousness.

OMNI: Are you at all troubled by the ethical issues raised by the social consequences of your conventional and unconventional research?

JOSEPHSON: I'm fortunate in that these questions have never intruded to a noticeable extent in my own research.

OMNI: Take the worst possible case, the strong likelihood that supercomputers using Josephson junctions may be involved in World War III. How do you feel about that possibility?

JOSEPHSON: Well, my work seems more likely to have defensive applications. Defense against incoming missiles, for example, would seem to be the main kind of military application. My not having made my discovery would have had virtually no effect on the arms race.

OMNI: What is the scientist's moral responsibility toward his discoveries and inventions? Does he have any special responsibilities to prevent their misuse by society?

JOSEPHSON: I don't think the fact that a person happens to originate something new has any great bearing on whether he should try to prevent its misuse. I am against the misuse of all scientific research, not just my own. Of course if something you helped to develop had harmful social consequences, you might well have stronger guilt feelings. But I don't know whether the fact that you are the creator of a new idea gives you much influence over the way society uses it.

I can't quite see what effect it would have if I were to tell IBM that it should stop developing high-speed Josephson junction computers because these machines might be used by the military. I'm more concerned with expanding public acceptance of higher states of consciousness, which may help to produce a more peaceful world. But I do think that scientists are often irresponsible. Most scientists have little sense of values and therefore they don't choose projects very wisely, but only on the basis of self-advancement. A lot of research is trivial when seen in any global context. This goes back to a basic point about values. Perhaps one can change people's values so that they will see that a certain kind of behavior is suitable and socially harmful actions are not suitable.

OMNI: How does one go about changing values?

JOSEPHSON: By increasing understanding. Values are based upon putting a given action into a wider context. If you can see more consequences of an action, then you'll be able to come to better judgments.

OMNI: How would you seek to reduce the danger of nuclear war?

JOSEPHSON: Well, the intellect doesn't solve all these problems. It isn't just a matter of better understanding. There are forces that lie beyond the intellect.

Wizard of Time
Ilya Prigogine

Einstein wanted to travel away from the turmoil, from the wars.
He wanted to find some kind of safe harbor in eternity. For him
science was an introduction to a timeless reality behind the
illusion of becoming. My own attitude is very different, because
to some extent I want to feel the evolution of things. I don't
believe in transcending, but in being embedded in a reality that
is temporal.

---

*On a wall in the office of the physical chemist Ilya Prigogine at
the University of Texas is an Albert Einstein quotation, blown up to
poster size. "For us believing physicists," it reads, "the distinction
between past, present, and future is only an illusion, however
persistent." The poster is one of the few personal effects in a room of
austere, university-provided furniture (Prigogine is in Austin only three
months each year), and its presence is symbolic. To Prigogine, time
is the forgotten dimension; his lifelong efforts have been directed
toward better understanding its role in the universe. In recent physics,
time has emerged as a central theme in several major areas of inquiry,
from the instability of elementary particles to the problem of irreversible
processes in both living and inanimate systems. Prigogine's contributions have come mostly in irreversibility, or, as Prigogine calls it, "the
arrow of time."*

*In 1977, after skirting the edges of scientific acceptance for nearly
twenty years, he was awarded the Nobel Prize in chemistry, largely
for his theory of dissipative structures. "Prigogine has fundamentally
transformed and revised the science of irreversible thermodynamics,"
noted the Nobel Committee in making its announcement. "He has
given it new relevance and created theories to bridge the gap that
exists between the biological and social scientific fields of inquiry."*

Photograph: Malcolm Kirk

Ilya Prigogine's background may have been as tumultuous as his effect on the scientific community. Born in Moscow at the outbreak of the Russian Revolution, Prigogine and his family fled, first to Lithuania, then to Berlin, before settling in Belgium. Nevertheless, his parents tried desperately to raise their two sons with a sense of grace that war-torn Europe could not easily provide. His mother taught them music, and, according to her recollections, Ilya could read piano scores before he could read words. (He played Bach, Mozart, Schumann, and Debussy, and he dreamed of becoming a concert pianist.) And when he did learn to read books, he devoured the classics. Because of his early interest in history and philosophy he wondered why science paid so little attention to time. "The fact that in chemistry and physics, past and present could play the same role, I found a little strange," he remembers. "It was so much in contradiction to ordinary experience. Everyone knows that tomorrow is not the same as today. Yet chemists and physicists described a universe where present and past were identical, timeless, and reversible."

After completing his fourth year in chemistry at the Free University of Brussels, Prigogine decided to study thermodynamics (the study of the relationship of mechanical energy and heat), focusing on the special significance of time. He received his Ph.D. in 1941, and by 1946 he had already begun to formulate his concept of dissipative structures. This theory describes the workings of open systems; that is, systems in which there is an exchange of matter and energy with the outside environment. (A human being is an open system: an individual takes in food and oxygen from the outside for energy, and excretes waste, thereby achieving a remarkable, albeit temporary, order that is maintained, however, at the expense of the environment. A true closed system, on the other hand, is an ideal concept — as unattainable as a perpetual-motion machine. A terrarium or a space colony could be considered close approximations, but these, too, rely on external energy from the sun.)

Irreversibility is a key concept, Prigogine believes. Just as certain chemicals, when mixed together, can never "unmix" into their original molecular structures, the universe and what it contains are irreversible. "You cannot reverse the evolution of the universe," he has said, "even theoretically. And you cannot predict its future, except in terms of scenarios that depend on never-ending series of . . . crossroads in the chain of causality." Prigogine's definition of open dissipative structures encompasses human social behavior, chemical reactions, and ecosystems — things whose structures are maintained by continuous flows of energy permeating them. And energy flow, Prigogine observes, may become so complex that it causes fluctuations too great for the system to absorb, thus forcing it to reorganize. But each reorganization produces greater complexity and greater likelihood of random fluctuations. The result: more instability, more reorganization; in other words, a quickened creation of living matter into new structures. Evolution.

Among other things, Prigogine's theory vastly broadened the scope of the second law of thermodynamics, a hallmark of nineteenth-century physical science. The "terrible" second law depicts the universe as moving inexorably toward decay and disorder. The second law includes the concept of entropy, which assumes that in a closed system, disorder increases relentlessly until equilibrium (or random dispersal of particles) is reached. The idea of entropy was an outgrowth of the development of thermal engines; scientists noted that no machine ever yields as much work as the energy it consumes. Thus, whenever work is done, an amount of usable energy is irrevocably lost. Carried further, this ominous logic implies that all the matter and energy in the universe will ultimately degrade to a state of tepid, inert uniformity (equilibrium), or what is popularly called heat death.

Generally speaking, before Prigogine, the important advances made as a result of the second law concerned reversible processes in enclosed systems, such as the steam engine. Classical scientific inquiry confined itself to reversible processes, leaving outside its purview the more disquieting open or "nonequilibrium" systems. But rather than viewing nonequilibrium as a negative factor, Prigogine believed that it was actually a source of organization, order, and life. In effect, he went beyond the second law to describe nonequilibrium systems, such as the natural world, which is open and complex.

The impetus for his intuitive leap came from his observation of a phenomenon known as the Benard Instability. It occurs when a liquid is heated from below. As heating intensifies, the mixture suddenly begins to "self-organize," taking on a striking spatial structure sometimes resembling miniature stained-glass cathedral windows, with ovals of brilliant colors arranging themselves in kaleidoscopic patterns. The phenomenon intrigued scientists, because these patterns resembled living cells. This self-organization of matter represented to Prigogine a critical link between animate and inanimate matter. It could even provide a clue to the spontaneous eruption of life's beginnings.

Without proof, however, Prigogine's theory remained just that for nearly twenty years. Actual experimental evidence to substantiate it did not materialize until the late sixties. Then, chemical processes known as the Zhabotinsky Reactions (named after one of the Russian biophysicists who discovered them) confirmed Prigogine's theory. Just as he had predicted, the reactions, which require a continuous outside source of energy, are self-organizing, like animate matter itself. The concentrations of the various chemicals oscillate with clocklike precision, changing the solution from red to blue at regular intervals. The effect is what Prigogine calls "order out of chaos."

Since then Prigogine's output has continued unabated, as has his effect of stimulating new directions of scientific research. "As a person," lauded the usually restrained Chemical and Engineering News, *"Prigogine emerges as a figure whose work could create that long-sought bridge between the physical and social sciences."*

Already his theory has been widely adopted. The U.S. Department of Transportation used it to predict traffic-flow patterns. In biology the theory has proved useful in understanding a number of phenomena, including the glycolytic, or sugar, cycle, a metabolic process by which living cells extract energy from food.

Most important, perhaps, the theory offers a guardedly optimistic alternative to the pessimistic view of mankind's future — that winding down of nature toward a kind of heat death. Prigogine has emerged as a hero to those who hope to bridge the gap between the "two-cultures," sciences and the humanities, noted by C. P. Snow. One of Prigogine's recurrent themes, as he travels the international lecture circuit, is his rejection of Snow's explanation for the schism's existence.

"I think that as long as scientists had only naïve views of time, there was not much to communicate," he says. But now, Prigogine thinks society can begin to investigate cultural and social change in dialogue with science.

A short, sixty-year-old man, with a gracious manner and a sense of precision in thought and word, the "poet of thermodynamics" continues to direct the Solvay Institute, in Brussels, and teach at the University of Brussels, as well as at the Center for Studies in Statistical Mechanics, at the University of Texas. His book Order Out of Chaos *was published in the United States in 1983. It was in 1983, in Austin, that the Los Angeles–based journalist Robert B. Tucker interviewed Prigogine (with additional research supplied by former* Omni *European editor, Bernard Dixon).*

OMNI: The concept of time is central to your work. Was there a particular incident in your life that caused you to become interested in it?

PRIGOGINE: That's difficult to say. Perhaps my interest corresponds to impressions I received during my childhood. I was born in Russia in the year of the revolution. My family left Moscow, and I've always wondered whether this migratory part of my life left me with a vivid sensitivity to change. In any event, I was always deeply interested in humanities, where time plays a central role. Beyond that it is a question of inclination. Some people are interested in electronics; some in looking for archeological artifacts. I went on to study physics and chemistry. And I was astonished that the time element was missing.

OMNI: Can you recall a particular moment when you had a flash of insight into a specific problem you were working on?

PRIGOGINE: Well, I always remember with pleasure my first work on nonequilibrium thermodynamics, in 1946, when I realized that nonequilibrium might be a source of organization and order. I was very, very happy to have this idea, which has never left me. Perhaps in science, at some point, there is a close relationship between who you are and what you try to do. Science is a much less objective enterprise than is often assumed. It's true you need some tools. You need to write down your findings, and convince yourself and others. But the driving force for new ideas has to be a deep personal involvement in the problems you're working on.

OMNI: Are you an intuitive person?

PRIGOGINE: Oh, yes. For me mathematics is only a tool for writing down my ideas so that in the long run they can be communicated. I say "in the long run" because in my history all of the ideas I have proposed have been poorly accepted.

OMNI: What was the scientific climate like when you first began to study time?

PRIGOGINE: Well, quite naturally I was interested in the reaction of well-known scientists to this line of research. Their reaction was uniformly negative. It was 1946 or 1947 when one of the most famous scientists attending a lecture I gave stood up and asked, "Why is this young man devoting his interest to irreversible causes? Irreversible causes are just illusory. Time is just a parameter, so forget about it." I was so stunned by this reaction that I was unable to get up and respond. But I happen to be very stubborn, so I continued. Today the situation has changed quite a bit. Time has become an essential factor in elementary particles as well as cosmology.

OMNI: You were a nonconformist, a dissident. How did you muster up the conviction to go against the prevailing ideology?

PRIGOGINE: I would say, again, this probably corresponds to a deep psychological element that isn't easy to make explicit. The attitude of Einstein toward science, for example, was to go beyond the reality of the moment. He wanted to transcend time. But this was the classical view: time was an imperfection, and science, a way to get beyond this imperfection to eternity. Einstein wanted to travel away from the turmoil, from the wars. He wanted to find some kind of safe harbor in eternity. For him science was an introduction to a timeless reality behind the illusion of becoming.

My own attitude is very different, because to some extent I want to feel the evolution of things. I don't believe in transcending, but in being embedded in a reality that is temporal.

OMNI: You've said that recent studies you and other scientists have made in the area of irreversibility constitute a new dialogue with nature. How so?

PRIGOGINE: What was considered by classical physics to be the basic structure of the world is now appearing more as an exception, something almost artificial. And what was considered to be exceptional in the classical view is now becoming the central object, the most interesting part.

OMNI: What do you mean when you say the classical view?

PRIGOGINE: I mean a mechanical view of nature. This view held that the world is made up of unchanging substances — atoms, molecules, or elementary particles. It also held that the only type of change is through locomotion, such as the rotation of planets — that there's no qualitative change. The classical view gave rise to the idea of the world as an automaton.

OMNI: What assumptions of the classical view have now been debunked?

PRIGOGINE: Mostly those relating to the basic conviction that at some level the world is simple and is governed by universal time-independent laws. This now appears to be an excessive idealization. It's as gross as reducing a building to a pile of bricks. Out of those same bricks you could build a factory, a palace, or a cathedral. But only on the level of the building as a whole do we perceive it as a creature of time, as a product of culture. I believe, though, that this analogy isn't quite on target. In nature there seems to be nobody around to put the bricks together to make a cathedral or a palace. And everywhere, we're faced with complexity and time. So the existence of these two distinct levels — one of bricks ignoring time and the other of the building as a whole in which time appears — is a metaphor that cannot be transposed to nature.

OMNI: What you're really saying is that the world is much more complex than science wanted to admit, are you not?

PRIGOGINE: Yes, I believe that's correct. You see, in the classical view, we had already essentially discovered the great laws. In my view, we have yet to discover them. If you had asked physicists a few years ago what they understood of nature and what they didn't understand, the answer would have been predictable. They would have said, "We don't understand elementary particles; we don't understand cosmology. What we do understand reasonably well is the range between the microscopic world and the world of cosmology."

But now a growing minority, to which I belong, would be quite hesitant about making such a claim. We have discovered new properties of matter. And with all the progress in dissipative structures and irreversibility, we begin to see that the matter around us is much more interesting than we thought. There may be black holes in the middle of the galaxy. That's interesting but very, very far away. I don't deny the strong interest in elementary particles and cosmology, but if biological matter has different aspects that we have not yet understood, this makes science much more exciting. After all, it's the stuff we're made of.

OMNI: Since it was first described, the second law of thermo-
dynamies has been considered profoundly important to our understanding of nature. What have you done to change our idea of that
law?

PRIGOGINE: The second law of thermodynamics always had a
dual character. On the one hand, it introduced a kind of arrow of
time. In isolated systems, entropy, or disorder, is always increasing.
It introduced the idea of thermodynamic equilibrium [complete ran-
domness]: the state corresponding to maximum entropy. Our work
has shifted the emphasis from equilibrium to nonequilibrium —
irreversible processes.

Of course, in its original form the second law recognized the
existence of irreversible processes but gave them only a negative
role. The idea, you remember, came into prominence around the
time of the Industrial Revolution. Many people thought of irreversible
processes as destructive because of friction or rapid propagation of
heat or whatever.

According to the second law, entropy is increasing. And classical
physics was concerned with the point where all irreversible processes
have already played their role. Such systems are in equilibrium:
chemical reactions have stopped; heat conduction has stopped. Our
contribution has been to argue against the idea that equilibrium states
are the most important or interesting. On the contrary, it is nonequilibrium that is essential to the understanding of our world and
universe.

Within the framework of the second law, irreversible processes
can have a constructive, positive role, rather than a destructive one.
They give rise to dissipative structures [in which order is maintained
by a constant infusion of energy]. Now, looking at biology, social
behavior, ecology, and economics, we begin to have a meeting point
between the various concepts of evolution.

OMNI: Aren't there aspects of your theory that defy the laws of
thermodynamics?

PRIGOGINE: No. On the contrary, they show only that the meaning of the laws near equilibrium and far from equilibrium are different. Near equilibrium you always go to the most banal, the most
uniform state. The general idea of classical physics is that we progress toward the running down of the universe. What we see here on
Earth, on the other hand, is just the opposite of that. Instead of going

to heat death, we see successive diversification. And so, in spite of the fact that the second law is probably satisfied in the universe as a whole, we are not going toward equilibrium, basically because we receive a constant infusion of energy from the stars, the galaxy, and so on. This energy ultimately originated in the Big Bang or whatever.

OMNI: The concept of bifurcation is key to the theory of dissipative structures. [A simple example of bifurcation is seen in an audience's response at the end of a concert: a few people start clapping, and suddenly everyone begins to clap in a seemingly spontaneous outpouring. This changes the nature of the concert hall and the audience, and gives feedback to the performer.] How are you using the word?

PRIGOGINE: Bifurcation is the appearance of new states of matter at critical points. Before that critical point is reached you have a chaotic structure. But once that point has been reached you have order. The Zhabotinsky Reactions are an example of it. They show the possibility of chemical communication between molecules over long distances and long periods of time. That is a property everybody always accepted in living systems, but in nonliving systems it was quite unexpected. Through such experiments in dissipative structures we see that matter is much more integrated than we thought. The gap between life and nonlife is smaller than we used to believe. Before, we thought that life was the great exception, the contradiction of the laws of physics. Now we see that complexity can spontaneously arise in inanimate matter if it is far from equilibrium.

OMNI: How does bifurcation apply to life?

PRIGOGINE: The way structure appears is a tantalizing riddle. Of course, living organisms are historical — they carry genetic information from half a billion years of evolution. So the appearance of structure in biological systems is not easy to study, because you have to take into account what is heritage and what is assembled today. But it seems to me that bifurcation is the key phenomenon in shaping genetic and physical patterns, especially when you see the type of monster malformations produced after exposing living structures to x rays, for example. Here you have started with a very symmetrical system whose symmetry has been broken. How does this happen? In a sense, there are choices and the system can go in one direction or another. A good example is the formation of the body: the egg cell is basically spherical and symmetrical, but then goes into less and less symmetrical structures. Of all the problems in biology, the rule of bifurcation, the transition from one direction to another, is vitally important.

OMNI: You once used highway driving as an example of dissipative structures as applied somewhat loosely to social situations. How does that work?

PRIGOGINE: When you drive on the highway, you have your own program, your own speed. When other people drive at the same time, competition begins. This competition brings about a change in your driving. This is feedback. You can make a very simple theory, which I did twenty years ago, that incorporates the effects of your own wishes, the way other people wish to drive, and the competition between the various wishes. You come out with the kind of nonlinear equation that describes this evolution.

First you drive as you want to. Then you take into account the other drivers, but you still drive as you want to. Then you go beyond the critical concentration [of cars] and come into a new organization in which you force the other drivers to drive as you drive. Now, this is not necessarily beneficial. You are embedded in something that does not depend on you and in which you are a part. You contribute to it but can't escape.

OMNI: What are the characteristics of being embedded in something?

PRIGOGINE: Being embedded implies a mutual situation. You drive in a way that influences others, and other people influence you. You can no longer say that you have free will. You are part of a collectivity to which you contribute, even in a sense against your will. And data on highway driving show there actually is a transition to a different phase when the critical concentration is reached. Driving is a very good example of bifurcation. In effect, there's a phase change from a group of individuals driving to a coherent structure — the highway as a whole.

OMNI: Can you cite another example of feedback?

PRIGOGINE: The way in which music developed. Music evolved in each society according to the particular types of instruments people invented. Metal, wood, and string have the same physical properties everywhere. But the musical instruments that emerged affected the music that could be played, which in turn influenced the type of music that was composed, which altered the evolution of the instruments. So a symphony orchestra is one expression of what wood, string, and metal can do.

OMNI: What effect do you suppose your vision of nature will have on the philosophy of classical science?

PRIGOGINE: Well, the classical view of nature was passive. The world was thought to be an automaton; the universe, clockwork. Joseph Needham, the great British historian of Chinese science and civilization, often said that Western thought has oscillated between seeing the world as an automaton and seeing it as a theological construct in which God governs the universe. Actually, these two views are not so inconsistent. If the world is an automaton, it needs a God to govern it. An automaton is not self-governed. But this kind of concept presents us with a rather tragic choice: to accept scientific rationality and the alienation that is the consequence of this acceptance; or to go into philosophical speculations that are divorced from contact with science. I think such a choice is no longer necessary.

OMNI: Why is that?

PRIGOGINE: The classical view divided the universe between spiritual self and the physical, external world. Yet inside us we see time, activity; we experience change. This internal experience is in complete contrast with the view of the world as a timeless automaton. As we begin to discover the roots of time outside us, this duality tends to disappear. We see a convergence between the world outside and the world inside us. With the paradigm of self-organization we see a transition from disorder to order. In the field of psychological activity this is perhaps the main experience we have — every artistic or scientific creation implies a transition from disorder to order.

OMNI: What was the classical response to time-dependent processes?

PRIGOGINE: To try to avoid them. Because there was such a distrust of time, there was also a distrust of life, because all life is obviously time-oriented. Still, you will find many people saying that life is an accident — that life is not within the laws of physics.

Clearly, in the physical universe four types of phenomena occur. Structures appear, as with biological systems and social systems; and they disappear, as when you mix two liquids. There are also deterministic processes, like the motion of the earth around the sun, and nondeterministic processes. What has changed is the perception of the relative importance of these processes. We begin to see now that the deterministic processes can be seen only in isolated, artificial systems.

The natural world, on the other hand, is a world of irreversible processes, of self-organization. So I talk about a new dialogue with nature, because I think we are beginning to perceive nature on Earth in a way exactly opposite to the way we viewed it in classical physics. We no longer conceive of nature as a passive object. I can't stress enough that it is an active object in our lives. And we see now that life has much deeper roots than we once suspected.

OMNI: Why did you choose to call those systems that are embedded in a stream of activity dissipative structures?

PRIGOGINE: I wanted to bring together two concepts: the idea of structure, which generally is static; and dissipation, for which you need energy continually brought in and going out. This is the type of structure that may appear at some distance from equilibrium. Far from being in equilibrium, the world is multiple: we have ants, elephants, plants, and civilizations. New, highly specific solutions appear when you go far from equilibrium.

OMNI: Why do you suppose this emphasis on reversible processes existed for such a long time?

PRIGOGINE: Your question reminds me of a story about meteorites. We know they were observed long ago. And by the beginning of the nineteenth century there was a marvelous collection in the museum in Vienna. Then a new curator appeared who said that meteorites were obviously products of superstition. They did not exist, because there was no place for them in the Newtonian view of the planetary system. So he threw the entire collection away. Then the French Academy was asked to give its opinion about some meteorites found near Paris. It sent a deputation there and they came back with the message, "Meteorites do not exist; they are artifacts — probably old industrial debris." Then a little later still a real rain of meteorites smashed nearly all the windows of the academy. At this point its members could hardly help concluding that meteorites existed.

OMNI: And how would this analogy apply to the classical world view?

PRIGOGINE: Well, I think today we have begun to accept the idea that our physics is the result of our conscious activity. The classical idea was that when you studied physics, you looked at nature from the outside, as if you had the infinite wisdom that traditionally has been attributed to God.

OMNI: How important is human consciousness in determining the kind of world view we ultimately construct?

PRIGOGINE: Consciousness plays an essential role, because we construct reality through mathematical concepts. If our consciousness had a different structure, we probably could not use the same type of constructs that we do. That's not to say physics is subjective; there must be a relation between our physics and reality. However, the way in which we speak about this reality is something we create.

OMNI: Has our desire to understand reality led us to greater complexity?

PRIGOGINE: Max Born, one of the great founders of quantum mechanics, once wrote that he believed that ideas such as absolute certitude, absolute exactness, final truth, and so on are figments of the imagination and should not be admissible in any field of science. I agree with him most in his belief that this loosening of thinking was the greatest blessing modern science has given us. You see, to me this coexistence of unconscious and conscious activity — of opacity and transparency — will ultimately lead to a new cultural unity.

OMNI: Of what sort?

PRIGOGINE: Well, by rediscovering time as well as randomness in physics, we encounter many things that are of basic interest in other fields of human endeavor. All this leads to a common perspective. I think there is a common stream running through the development of physics in our century — be it relativity, quantum mechanics, or the second law of thermodynamics. In a variety of ways they all show that there are limits to our power to manipulate matter. In classical physics we thought we could send signals with infinite velocity and measure any physical quantity with arbitrary precision. Today we know both of these feats are impossible. For example, the velocity of signals is limited by the velocity of light. Measurement is limited by quantum mechanics, which says that the parameters of any one particle have a number of potential outcomes. [The very act

of measuring one parameter will physically alter other parameters.]
Our manipulation of matter is limited by the second law of thermodynamics. But these limitations don't mark the end of our knowledge
of nature. On the contrary, they are the starting points for some of
the most powerful theories humankind has ever constructed.

OMNI: In a commemorative lecture you gave several years ago
honoring Albert Einstein, you noted that he has become the Darwin
of physics. Darwin, you said, taught us that man is embedded in
biological evolution, and Einstein taught us that we are embedded
in an evolutionary universe. How would you characterize Einstein's
contribution?

PRIGOGINE: Einstein became the Darwin of physics against his
will. His view was of a static, nonevolving universe. And when people
showed that this static universe was unstable and had to be replaced
by an evolving universe, Einstein was astonished. I knew some of
the founders of the expanding-universe theory very well, among them
the Belgian physicist Lemaitre. Lemaitre told me that Einstein was
always saying, "Well, this Big Bang, this evolving universe, sounds
too much like Genesis. I'm not so happy about this. I think you take
my theory too seriously." But today we have all kinds of confirmation
of the existence of this large-scale evolution. However, let's be
careful, because we don't know whether this is the evolution of the
overall universe or just some galactic neighborhood in which we're
living.

OMNI: In the lecture on Einstein, you noted that his most striking
contribution was the idea that we are in an evolving universe, and
that therefore the laws of physics must have changed. What did you
mean?

PRIGOGINE: The fact that there is an evolving universe, which
started from very different conditions than now exist, completely
changes our idea about the laws of physics. When the universe
started, the conditions of matter were so different that present-day
laws have no meaning. You can't speak about laws of life when there
is no life. You cannot speak about laws of human behavior if there
are no human beings around. Therefore, the very idea of law itself
becomes an evolutionary concept to a certain extent.

OMNI: Do you see any relationship between the way society has
evolved in recent years and the way science is now considering new
pictures of nature?

PRIGOGINE: That's a very difficult question to answer. There is an internal history of science, corresponding to the evolution of theoretical views. There's also an influence of culture on physics as a whole. On the one hand, the discoveries of unstable particles and of the dissipative structures haven't much to do with societal problems. Yet they lead to a rethinking of the concept of a natural law. The whole notion of a law of nature was formulated by Descartes and Newton in the seventeenth century, a time of absolute monarchy. Nature had to follow, somewhat as the people had to follow, the edicts of the kingdom or the emperor. The idea of natural laws certainly has a sociological context.

I find our period remarkable precisely because some of the questions in social science and in natural science form a kind of confluence. We've seen two other periods in which such convergences occurred: the Greek classical period and the Renaissance. And during those periods you had people like Plato and Aristotle, and Descartes and Newton, who were philosopher-scientists.

OMNI: A number of social thinkers now cite your theory of dissipative structures to explain the transformation they see occurring in American society. What relevance does your theory have to social systems?

PRIGOGINE: What they are saying is that I emphasize self-organization, and therefore spontaneity and amplification. In large societies it becomes increasingly difficult to maintain the spontaneous activity of the members of that society. I'm not a social scientist. However, I think what we need in society is amplification, spontaneity, and fluctuation. And that is exactly what is missing in forms of society where one tries to categorize people, to pattern their activities into well-defined channels. Nature gives us a different model. Nature is trying experiments all the time; some of them are amplified, others are not. This spontaneity of nature is a model we must keep in mind.

The common denominator in these very different issues is the desire to avoid the mistake of classical physics, which believed we could control nature.

OMNI: How do your ideas apply to an open system such as climate?

PRIGOGINE: Well, not very long ago everybody was convinced that the history of climate was an external history. The sun was changing, for example; there may have been cosmic dust around and supposedly this would explain how the axis of the earth had changed. And these external events accounted for climatological changes.

But today we have quite a different picture. We ask whether climate is really stable. What will happen as a result of small fluctuations? Scientists now believe that climate is generally unstable. Even today we could have various climates evolve. For example, a difficult situation could develop if there was a series of cold winters in succession. The glaciers would come down, Earth would absorb less energy from the sun, and the planet would start to cool down. There would be a multiple effect, which could continue until the earth was completely covered by snow. With the same planet, the same chemicals, and the same flow of energy from the sun, various climates are possible.

OMNI: It sounds as if we are living under a permanent threat.

PRIGOGINE: Yes, but we are also living under what may become a promise, because once we have recognized the situation, we can hope to change things. I mean in the long run, not tomorrow. In a sense, we are following a bifurcation, one of several possible structures. There were times, say twenty thousand years ago, when we had humid and warm interludes between two glacial periods. During these times the earth was much more fertile than it is now. So the notion that the present climate completely determines the future is an oversimplified one. It is being replaced by a picture of multiple features that hinge upon fluctuations. That is, of course, a very threatening idea. But it's also an idea that brings hope, if there are no catastrophes that destroy us.

OMNI: What role does society play in fostering scientific creativity?

PRIGOGINE: It's very difficult to be creative in science and not be creative in more general terms. When you are living in an oppressive or repressive society, it's difficult to be creative in science. This is one of the reasons why, in spite of the great attention and money Soviet Russia is lavishing on science, creativity and new ideas there are relatively exceptional.

OMNI: You speak of the Soviet Union's scientific environment. What about the scientific contributions of other countries or continents. Asia, for example?

PRIGOGINE: It seems to me the recent evolution of science takes us away from the cultural context of the West, where modern science was founded. The idea of a self-organizing universe is close to the Chinese scientific tradition. The idea of a universe within us — with its important temporal component — converging with a universe outside us, is reminiscent of many traditions of Indian thought. I don't want to imply that modern science will justify Oriental wisdom, however, or vice versa, for that matter. But I do believe that the growth of science now makes it a planetary endeavor. An ever-increasing contribution will flourish from outside the Western world.

OMNI: What kind of scientific progress do you see over the next twenty years?

PRIGOGINE: The purpose of classical physics was to find some fundamental level of simplicity in terms of which our universe could be deciphered. I doubt if this level exists. Instead, we will have to deal with the complexity we have discovered. But this very complexity will lead to new disciplines, which will help us to transfer our knowledge from one domain to another. Perhaps the challenge of these coming years will be to master complexity.

OMNI: What are the religious implications of your research?

PRIGOGINE: I think that the duality that Needham described — between seeing the universe as an automaton or, on the other hand, as the picture of a guiding God who acts through us and has created both a dead universe and the human soul — is mistaken. I see us as nearer to a Taoist view, in which we are embedded in a universe that is not foreign to us.

OMNI: Your views sound similar to those of Teilhard de Chardin.

PRIGOGINE: Not really. Chardin described the world as if he were outside it. He was sure that every change, every new bifurcation, was going in the right direction — in the direction of increased spirituality. On the contrary, I am more impressed by the existence of multiple time horizons. A bifurcation can lead us to the best or to the worst. We are participating in an evolution whose outcome isn't clear to us. So I leave open the question of the meaning of being. I'm not even certain whether, put in these terms, a scientific answer is possible. Probably it has more to do with feelings or emotions. In any event, I believe it is more hopeful, more exhilarating, to be embedded in a living world than to be alone in a dead universe. And this is really what I try to express in my work.

Imagine . . .
Freeman Dyson

In five billion years or less, we've evolved from some sort of primordial slime into human beings. What will happen in another ten billion years? It's just utterly impossible to conceive of ourselves changing as drastically as that over and over again, but I think all you can say is that the material form that life would take on in that kind of time scale is completely open.

He sits perched in his chair like a bird about to swoop. Then his eyes soften, and he cracks a half-smile, which soon turns to a jubilant laugh. The laugh seems much too large for its compact owner, but not for the subject at hand: the fate of life in the universe.

"Either we all get fried," he explains, "or we all get frozen. If we all get fried, the universe collapses into a big black hole, temperature goes to infinity — it's all over, nothing you can do. But if the opposite happens, if the universe expands forever, life and intelligence could probably survive in the form of a black cloud. Such creatures would be made of dust grains charged and working on each other with electrical and magnetic forces. One can imagine enormously complex beings, more complex than what we see around us now."

For more than twenty years, Professor Freeman J. Dyson has been discussing mind-boggling prospects in just that enthusiastic, "one can imagine" way. It is his hobby, he says disarmingly; something that grew up alongside his career as one of the finest mathematical physicists of our time. To his colleagues at Princeton's Institute for Advanced Studies, Dyson is known for his writings on stars, high-energy beams, and subnuclear particles — contributions that have earned him the American Institute of Physics Dannie Heineman Prize and the Royal Society's Hughes Medal, among other honors.

Photograph: Jim Kalett

To a wider circle, though, he is known for the "Dyson shell," a vast structure that could be built by dismantling a Jupiter-size planet and using the raw material to create a hollow sphere around a star like the sun. People could live within the sphere, Dyson suggests, capturing every last bit of solar energy to sustain a vast civilization the likes of which we've never seen. He further suggests that the powerful gravitational field of a star might serve as a super-slingshot to accelerate interstellar voyagers, free of fuel costs . . . and that an army of self-reproducing automatons could mine the ice of Saturn's moons, melting them to make chilly, arid Mars a garden planet.

Freeman Dyson was born in Crowthorne, England, in 1923. He attended Winchester, where his father taught music, and entered Cambridge during World War II. An ardent Gandhian pacifist, Dyson managed to avoid a stint at the front. Instead, he spent two years as a civilian scientist with the Royal Air Force bomber command, where he investigated the losses on nighttime bombing missions of the fearfully overloaded Lancasters. Though Dyson and his colleagues found that heavy gun turrets and an especially small escape hatch had turned the Lancaster "into a death trap for the boys who flew it," they failed to convince the military to change the craft until the tail end of the war.

After two years with the bomber command, a disillusioned Dyson finished his B.A. in mathematics (his specialty was numbers theory). Then, in 1947, he left England for Cornell University. There, under the tutelage of theoretical and nuclear physicist Hans Bethe, Dyson began his study of subatomic particles and the universe at large. In 1953 he moved to the Institute for Advanced Studies, where he has worked ever since.

Dyson's speculative side was relatively tame, he says, until 1956, when he met the physicist and bomb designer Ted Taylor at a series of conferences convened by the General Atomic Company in San Diego. First the two spent time working together on the TRIGA (the letters stand for Training, Research, and Isotopes, General Atomics), a nuclear reactor that could produce radioactive isotopes for medical applications. Then, a couple of years later, they teamed up on Project Orion, a plan to propel ultralarge spacecraft (even the size of a city!) by detonating nuclear bombs behind a "pusher plate." The collaboration resulted in a close friendship between Dyson and Taylor, a man of extraordinary talent and imagination — and someone who enjoyed freewheeling speculation as much as Dyson himself.

Today, at sixty-one, Dyson is more audacious in his speculation than ever. Conversing with him leaves one slightly breathless. He jumps easily from details of a rocket that might be launched tomorrow to the outlook for the next ten billion years of evolution. After a while, one begins to sort out what he says by how he begins each sentence. "It's inevitable . . ." signifies his certainty about the next century or two; "It seems obvious . . ." enlarges the scope to the future of mankind on Earth; and "One should expect . . ." extends the reach anywhere from the Big Bang to the end of the cosmos.

In the last decade and a half, Dyson has been advising Gerard K. O'Neill on his plans for self-sufficient colonies in space. This interview, conducted by contributing editor Monte Davis for Omni's *maiden issue, began with that subject.*

OMNI: What do you think about the idea of colonizing space, proposed in the last few years by the Princeton physicist Gerard K. O'Neill?

DYSON: I think O'Neill saw what I and others did not see — that the public was ready to get excited about space again. It seemed after Apollo that people were turned off; they'd seen too many moon rocks. I thought it would be hopeless to get people interested in space colonies for twenty years or so. But O'Neill showed that you *could* get them interested, especially young people. It showed great courage and insight on his part.

OMNI: Is it because he's talking about colonization, rather than a there-and-back expedition like Apollo? Or because he's showing how the colonies could pay for themselves by building solar power satellites that would beam energy back to Earth?

DYSON: I doubt the economic aspect was that important. It came later, when O'Neill was trying to get the establishment — NASA and Congress — interested. He had to sell it on economics, but as far as the public is concerned, it isn't that.

OMNI: How do you explain O'Neill's success, in view of the current mistrust of "big technology," of big government projects, and so on?

DYSON: I don't really know. Perhaps I should say that, while I have the greatest respect and admiration for O'Neill, space colonization on that scale isn't entirely to my taste; the big colonies he envisions are a little too hygienic for me. I've done some historical research on the costs of the *Mayflower*'s voyage, and on the Mormons' emigration to Utah, and I think it's possible to go into space on a much smaller scale. A cost on the order of $40,000 per person would be the target to shoot for; in terms of real wages, that would make it comparable to the colonization of America. Unless it's brought down to that level, it's not really interesting to me, because otherwise it would be a luxury that only governments could afford.

OMNI: Where would your *Mayflower*-style colonists go?

DYSON: I'd put my money on the asteroids. Dandridge Cole and others suggested using a solar mirror to melt and hollow out an iron asteroid, and in O'Neill's book [*The High Frontier*] his homesteaders build their own shells from the minerals available out there. I wouldn't accept either of those as the most sensible course: I think you should settle on an asteroid which is not iron or nickel, but some kind of soil that you could grow things in.

OMNI: What do you mean by soil?

DYSON: Well, we have specimens of a meteoritic material called carbonaceous chondrite, which looks like soil — it's black, crumbly stuff containing a good deal of water; it has enough carbon, nitrogen, and oxygen so that there's some hope you could grow vegetables in it, and it's soft enough to dig without using dynamite.

OMNI: So you think it would be worth looking for an asteroid like that rather than trying to transform a raw stone or metal asteroid?

DYSON: Yes, if it's to be done on a pioneer basis, you'd jolly well better find a place where you can grow things right away. Otherwise, it's inevitably a much slower and more expensive job.

OMNI: Is the sunlight at that distance adequate to grow plants?

DYSON: I think so. Plants are very flexible in their requirements, you know, and they could be genetically altered, if it's needed. After all, a lot of things grow very well, even in England. . . .

OMNI: What about colonizing the moon?

DYSON: It's simply too close to home. Too easy for the tax man to find you. And choosing a place to go is not just a question of freight charges. There have always been minorities who valued their differences and their independence enough to make very great sacrifices, and it seems obvious to me that it's going to happen again.

OMNI: So you think we may not go in for the big O'Neill-type colonies after all?

DYSON: We may not, but others may. I was in Russia two years ago for a conference on telescopes, and all that anyone there wanted to hear about was O'Neill's ideas. They knew that he and I were both in Princeton, and assumed I could tell them everything about space colonies. The point is that in Russia they have very little of our current mistrust of technology on the grand scale. In fact, O'Neill's concept fits in very well with their ideas about our relationship to nature. Thousands of engineers working on a giant framework floating in space; that's a picture that excites them very much. I wouldn't be surprised if they choose that.

If they do, the historical analogy becomes very strong: the Russians play the role of the Spanish colonists in the New World, and people like me are more like the English, with smaller, scattered, decentralized colonies. Of course, it took the English much longer to get going, but when we did go, we did a better job.

OMNI: As for the "going" — how will that happen? In your Project Orion proposal, you suggested propelling huge spacecraft with energy supplied by detonating nuclear bombs. Looking back on it today, do you think that "bomb" propulsion should have been followed up?

DYSON: First, you have to remember that the background against which we're judging Orion has changed dramatically since the nuclear test ban treaty of 1963. At the time we were working on it, we calculated that launching Orion would add no more than 1 percent to the radiation from atmospheric tests. But that amount would be quite unacceptable under the current ground rules, and rightly so. In some sense, I do regret that we didn't try it — but history simply passed it by.

OMNI: What about using chemical rockets to put an Orion-type ship into orbit, then going from there on nuclear explosions?

DYSON: We did consider that in the later proposals. It would have been disappointing to sacrifice Orion's advantages for the first and most difficult stage . . . and in any case, although the radioactive debris using that approach would not have been nearly so great as that from a ground launch, much of it would still have made its way down into the atmosphere.

OMNI: Are there any current propulsion ideas as promising as Orion was in its time?

DYSON: There are several that I think are just as good, if not better. First, there's the ground-based laser system that physicist Arthur Kantrowitz has advocated. The ship would simply carry reaction mass — it could be water — and the lasers would follow it upward, delivering energy to vaporize the reaction mass. What's nice about the idea is that it would permit you to get into orbit with one stage, costing perhaps $10,000 for a ton of payload. The launching facility could be a "public highway" into space for the kind of small-scale colonization we were talking about; you'd make your reservation and show up with the equipment you'd need wherever you were going — perhaps not an individual or a single family, but certainly a small group.

OMNI: What would lasers putting out that kind of power do to the air as they passed? It sounds like there'd be a spectacular Star Wars beam-snapping, crackling, and so on.

DYSON: Actually, it wouldn't be like that at all. Remember, air is very transparent. There shouldn't be more than a 10 or 20 percent energy loss along the way, and it would be spread over quite a large volume of air. The idea isn't without problems, of course; the air would be heated slightly, which would cause it to expand, so it would tend to defocus the beam. But the biggest problems are in the design of the motor, the structure that receives the laser energy and converts it into heat as efficiently as possible. Unfortunately, no one has built even a prototype yet.

OMNI: Then you foresee no problem as far as the laser itself is concerned. Does that mean work on very high-powered lasers is progressing satisfactorily — for military applications, say?

DYSON: I couldn't say. But there's no reason to use a single giant laser. You could just as easily use a battery of smaller ones, each with a power level that's attainable today.

Another possibility is O'Neill's Mass-Driver, which would thrust a payload toward its destination in space. It shares the laser system's chief advantage: you needn't carry along your energy source.

The third idea, which would be for travel within the solar system, although hardly for launching anything, is our old friend the solar sail, a huge gossamer-thin sail made of aluminum-coated plastic film. [In principle you could steer a course by balancing the pressure of sunlight on the sail against the force of the sun's gravity, in the same way the skipper of an earthly sailboat balances the pressure of the wind in his sails against the pressure of the water on his keel.]

OMNI: Has anyone worked that idea out in detail?

DYSON: Not too long ago, NASA invited proposals for a mission to rendezvous with Halley's Comet in 1986, and several groups did studies. It's a terribly hard mission, and chemical rockets can't even begin to get near. It means getting into an orbit going the other way around the sun, a huge velocity change, so the only possibility of doing it at all is with some low-thrust, long-duration propulsion system. So a group of solar-sail enthusiasts at the NASA Jet Propulsion Laboratory did a summer study on the mission. They put together a very thorough and really promising proposal, with launch dates and everything. They were working with a Mr. McNeil, a private-enterprise type, who is the inventor of a solar sail he calls the Heliogyro, which is very clever from an engineering point of view and much easier to manage than just a big square piece of foil.

So they put this document together, and when it was finished they went to the JPL management and asked them to recommend to NASA that it be tried. The outcome was, and I quote: "The principal limitation preventing the sail from receiving a positive recommendation . . . was the high risk associated with asserting its near-term readiness in the face of absolutely no proof-of-concept tests."

OMNI: Hmmmm . . . Who else did they expect to test it?

DYSON: The problem is, of course, that they can't afford to fail. The rules of the game are that you don't take a chance, because if you fail, then probably your whole program gets wiped out.

OMNI: Would a change at the top, say in NASA, open it up to ideas like the solar sail or laser launching?

DYSON: I don't think the problem is with NASA, but with the whole political system by which government projects are funded. You can't afford to fail; it's as simple as that. Congress just doesn't provide money for things unless they're sure to work. Of course, the situation could change, but the change has to be primarily in Congress; I don't think any management at NASA could do anything very differently from what they're doing at the moment. The trouble is, the scientists aren't interested in new propulsion methods, either. They just want the good old reliable rockets; they want to get their stuff into orbit — and that's it. So scientists are not going to provide the kind of push that's needed.

OMNI: Well, then, how *do* you reach Congress?

DYSON: Perhaps you can't. That's the whole question. I'd like to explore and colonize space with private enterprise. There are people like Gary Hudson, who would like to go into business completely independent of NASA and put stuff into orbit commercially. He believes he can undersell NASA by a factor of ten. Maybe he's right; I wouldn't be surprised. It's just hard getting the customers. Well, as he says, he has lots of people lined up for his *second* launch.

OMNI: Is it fair to say that for you the most important aspect of space colonization is that it be cheap, flexible, and small scale?

DYSON: Yes, but I'm not altogether fanatical about it. One needs the big enterprises, too. There may be things that demand them, and I think it would be a great mistake to be too ideological and say "We must not do it because it's big," which some of my friends tend to do. I merely say that at the moment we're only doing the big expensive stuff, and that's stupid.

OMNI: Short of orbiting enough solar power satellites [which would send solar energy back to Earth] to fill all our needs, what do you see as possible answers to our current energy dilemmas? What about fusion?

DYSON: I would have to say that at the moment fusion doesn't look good. Even the best fusion reactor would use ten times as many neutrons to produce a kilowatt of electricity as a fission reactor. Of course, with fission you have a very different set of problems, and we may make the political decision to avoid those — but on technical and economic grounds alone, fission looks better. I'm very wary of any statement that something can't be done, though; somebody may come up with a new approach to fusion power tomorrow, and I could be totally wrong.

OMNI: And what about near-term uses of solar power?

DYSON: Right now I'm involved with a solar energy scheme that Ted Taylor is promoting; I'm just as excited about it as I was about our collaboration on Orion. Ted's a man I'll always be willing to follow. He's always years ahead of the rest of us, and he decided a few years ago that solar energy was the thing to work on. What we're aiming for is a trial here in Princeton of a system centered on a solar pond. [The idea is to dig a large pond enclosed by dikes and covered with transparent plastic air mattresses, so that the water is heated by sunlight and insulated against cool winds and evaporation.] The water would stay hot summer and winter, providing a hundred homes with energy for heating, cooling, and electricity. The cost? Perhaps half a million dollars.

It's a very earthbound, low-technology project — essentially village technology, something that the Indians, the Thais, the Nigerians, could put to use at once. The basic requirement is a lot of plumbing, and you can find plumbers anywhere. In fact, you may find better plumbers in the "underdeveloped" countries than here! And the only mass-produced component would be the heat engines, and those you can buy off the shelf right now, cheap and quite efficient.

I don't know if we can do it, but if we can, we'd turn the world upside down; it beats anything.

OMNI: How far along is the project?

DYSON: Oh, it's nowhere yet — just Ted's enthusiasm and a few pieces of paper. We've had negotiations with the Department of Energy, but it's just laughable — you can't even get to the people who matter with anything this small.

OMNI: Even you? Even Taylor?

DYSON: That's right. But the amusing thing is that it really doesn't matter whether we succeed or not, because there are hundreds of other little groups like us around the world. One or another is going to come up with the right idea, and it's no tragedy if ours fails. If it isn't solar ponds, it'll be something else along those lines. There are so many variables — it's like finding the best way to design a bicycle; lots of details that you only get right after a long time. The most difficult part will no doubt turn out to be figuring out how to dig the ponds cheaply, how to keep children from falling in, and so on.

This is a wild extrapolation, but I think it's worth saying. One of these solar pond systems takes just about the same amount of money and land, per capita, as a highway. If the United States were to derive all its energy from solar ponds, it would mean essentially making over again the same kind of investment we've made in our road system — 1 percent of the land area, and something like a thousand billion dollars.

OMNI: Presumably a cleaner investment.

DYSON: Not all that clean. I'm sure there'd be a lot of people who'd object to having these ponds around, and it'd involve many of the same problems as roads. But at least ponds won't stop you from walking from one place to another! Oh, there'd be problems. Sunlight is so abundant, though; if you can just think up any sensible scheme that will make use of it at 5 percent efficiency, you're in. That doesn't mean we should drop fission or the research into fusion, of course.

OMNI: As you know, a number of science fiction books and stories have made use of your speculations. Was there a reverse influence — did fiction influence you?

DYSON: Certainly. As a child I read through all the Jules Verne books I could find. I read Wells, and enjoyed him very much. I read very little else, actually, because I was a poor reader. But the one who set my style of thinking, certainly the most influential, was Olaf Stapledon, with his *Star Maker* and *Last and First Men.* I remember they were in Pelican paperbacks, nine pence each, and one day I sat in Paddington Station for two or three hours, reading *Star Maker.* It seemed to me perfectly obvious that that was the way to think about space and about the future — that kind of broad scope, that kind of scale.

OMNI: You must be aware that some of your colleagues take a jaundiced view of your ideas about giant trees growing on comets, taking Jupiter apart to build a Dyson shell [a hollow sphere that totally surrounds the sun and whose inhabitants would live on the inner surface], and so on. Does it bother you to know that they're out there, muttering about "Dyson's crazy ideas"?

DYSON: Not at all. Keep in mind, I'm also a perfectly respectable physicist, and the speculation is a hobby. It's become well known, but I've grown used to the idea that people very often become famous for accidental reasons. It's amusing to think that someday all my "serious" work will probably be a footnote in a textbook, when everybody remembers what I did on the side! Anyway, what do I have to lose? I have tenure here, and no one expects much from a theoretical physicist once he's past fifty anyway.

OMNI: In an article some years ago, you pointed out that chemical energy — the kind in our bodies and brains; the kind we've built a technological civilization on — is very small, even trivial, compared with the major forms of energy in the universe: gravitational, kinetic, nuclear, and so on. Yet here we are. Is there something about chemical energy to account for that?

DYSON: It is very, very special. The beauty of chemical energy is that it's so enormously flexible, and it can serve so many different purposes at once. It's a good way of storing energy, a good way of releasing it in a controlled fashion, a good way of transferring it from one point to another. I think that's why life makes use of it. There have been ideas, people trying to imagine creatures living inside neutron stars and various other unlikely places. Olaf Stapledon, of course, wrote about living stars —

OMNI: And there's Fred Hoyle's Black Cloud, an intelligent nebula of gas and dust —

DYSON: All these things may be possible, but we've absolutely no reason to believe them at the moment. What chemical energy has that the other forms don't is versatility, the huge variety of structures, the variety of types of chemical bond. It's a very many sided thing. But it's hard to know just what is responsible for its "specialness," because we've nothing else yet to compare it with.

OMNI: What's your immediate reaction to, say, Hoyle's Black Cloud? Does it seem unlikely?

DYSON: I think it's very plausible. In fact, I was thinking about just that in another connection, another of the things I've been working on as a hobby. What is the ultimate fate of living creatures in the universe? There seem to be two possibilities: either we all get fried or we all get frozen. If we all get fried, the universe collapses into a big black hole, temperature goes to infinity — it's all over, nothing you can do. But if the opposite happens, if the universe expands forever, life and intelligence could probably survive in the form of a black cloud. There would be no way for chemical life to survive.

OMNI: So we would be transformed into Hoyle's creature? How?

DYSON: It's . . . it's hard for us to grasp the time scale involved; it's unimaginably long. As a rule of thumb, it takes a million years to evolve a new species, ten million for a new genus, a hundred million for a class, a billion for a phylum . . . and that's about as far as your imagination can go. In five billion years or less, we've evolved from some sort of primordial slime into human beings. What will happen in another ten billion years? It's just utterly impossible to conceive of ourselves changing as drastically as that over and over again, but I think all you can say is that the material form that life would take on in that kind of time scale is completely open. To change from a human being to a black cloud may seem a big order, but it's the kind of change you'd expect anyway, over billions of years. There's all the time in the world for evolution before the sun runs out of fuel.

What I envisage as the structural unit of such a creature is simply dust grains, probably made of iron or some convenient stuff, charged and working on each other with electric and magnetic forces. One can imagine enormously complex structures built out of these things. What would correspond to a muscle or a nerve synapse? I haven't the faintest idea . . . it's an open-ended system, just as the organic fluids we're made of are. The electromagnetic forces would give you a means of tying it together, coordinating it. It could be just as complex, even more complex than what we see around us now.

OMNI: How can we manage to understand the universe at all? Do you agree with Carl Sagan, for example, that we find the mathematics of gravitation so simple and elegant because natural selection eliminated the apes who couldn't understand?

DYSON: Not at all. For apes to come out of the trees and change in the direction of being able to write down Maxwell's equations . . . I don't think you can explain that by natural selection at all. It's just a miracle.

OMNI: You have also written that "as we look out into the universe and identify the many accidents of physics and astronomy that have worked together to our benefit, it almost seems as if the universe must in some sense have known that we were coming." Is that a playful suggestion?

DYSON: It's not playful at all.

OMNI: Then we seem to be talking about sentiments that most people would consider religious. Are they religious for you?

DYSON: Oh, yes. It's always difficult to mix science and religion without making a fool of oneself. In fact, it's probably impossible, and one is probably very unwise even to try.

OMNI: Well, let's say that the pressure of this interview is forcing you out on a limb. As we all know, the dominant tendency in modern science has been to assert that we occupy no privileged place, that the universe does not care, that science and religion don't mix. Where do you fit into those ideas?

DYSON: The tendency you're talking about is a modern one, not

old. I think it became almost a dogma only with the fight for acceptance of Darwinism, Huxley versus Bishop Wilberforce, and so on.
Before the nineteenth century, scientists were not ashamed of being
religious, but since Darwin, it's been taboo. The biologists are still
fighting Wilberforce. If you look now, the view that everything is due
to chance and to little bits of molecular clockwork is mostly propounded by biologists, particularly people like Jacques Monod,
whereas the physicists have become far more skeptical about that. If
you actually look at the way modern physics is going, it's very far
from that. Yes, it's the biologists who've made it so hard to talk about
these things.

I was reading recently a magnificent book by Thomas Wright,
written about 1750, when these inhibitions didn't exist at all. Wright
was the discoverer of galaxies, you know. So I'd like to read from
that; it's easier to say these things by quoting others. He's talking
about how many inhabited worlds there are, and he writes:

> In this great celestial creation, the catastrophe of a world such as ours, or even
> the total dissolution of a system of worlds, may possibly be no more to the great
> Author of Nature than the most common accident in life with us. And in all
> probability such final and general doomsdays may be as frequent there as even
> birthdays or mortality with us upon the earth. This idea has something so cheerful
> in it that I own I can never look upon the stars without wondering that the whole
> world does not become astronomers, and that men, endowed with sense and reason,
> should neglect a science that they are naturally so much interested in, and so
> capable of enlarging the understanding, as next to a demonstration must convince
> them of their immortality, and reconcile them to all those little difficulties incident
> to human nature, without the least anxiety.

OMNI: That's the long view indeed, even at the Institute for
Advanced Studies. How much do you discuss your "hobby" with
your colleagues here?

DYSON: This place is a motel, and people change from year to
year. That's what I like about being here: a fresh crowd every year.
The number of permanent people is very small, so most of the time
I'm talking to visiting members. In the school of physics we are,
generally speaking, very serious; the young people are highly specialized and want to talk about their professional work, so the people
I talk to about speculative things are usually historians and sociol-
ogists and anthropologists and such people. One of the most fascinating was a Brandeis professor named Frank Manuel, who's inter-

ested in the concept of Utopia and its history, and how it has been transformed through the centuries. Actually, he was studying me as an example of the modern utopian, so we had long sessions in which I would talk about space colonies and so on, and he would say, Ah yes, that came out of such-and-such a German writer of the seventeenth century — whom I'd never heard of.

OMNI: Do you think that "a modern utopian" is a good description of you?

DYSON: Yes, in the sense of someone who imagines ideal societies. I certainly am.

OMNI: And the colonization of space will open up chances for new utopias and many different societies in the asteroids.

DYSON: Even many different kinds of humanity. I don't think humanity is going to be a single species much longer — maybe because of divergent evolution as we expand into space, and maybe sooner than that via genetic manipulation. Unless you enforce a total prohibition on genetic research — unless you effectively outlaw the study of biology — I think it's inevitable that people are going to want to make their children better than themselves, and the techniques to do that will be available in the next century.

I've recently been on a local committee formed to consider Princeton University's plans for recombinant DNA research. Our official responsibility was just to assess the potential danger from a laboratory accident that might release dangerous organisms, but I found that everyone on the committee was more concerned about the steps beyond that. They were concerned with "what are they going to do to *us?*" It surprised me, because I had thought that only I worried about these things. And I think their concern is much more realistic than some of the comforting reassurances about how far away human genetic engineering is. It's nearer than we imagine.

And beyond that, there's a continuing social strain that can only increase. It's a tension between the idea that all men are brothers and the idea that every individual or group should be free to do its own thing. You see it in racial problems, in national and ideological conflicts. Conceivably, if you give people the choice of being brothers or going out into space, that could provide the impetus for colonization. It's very striking, how often in the past a journey that looked like exile from one point of view has turned out to be an opportunity from another.